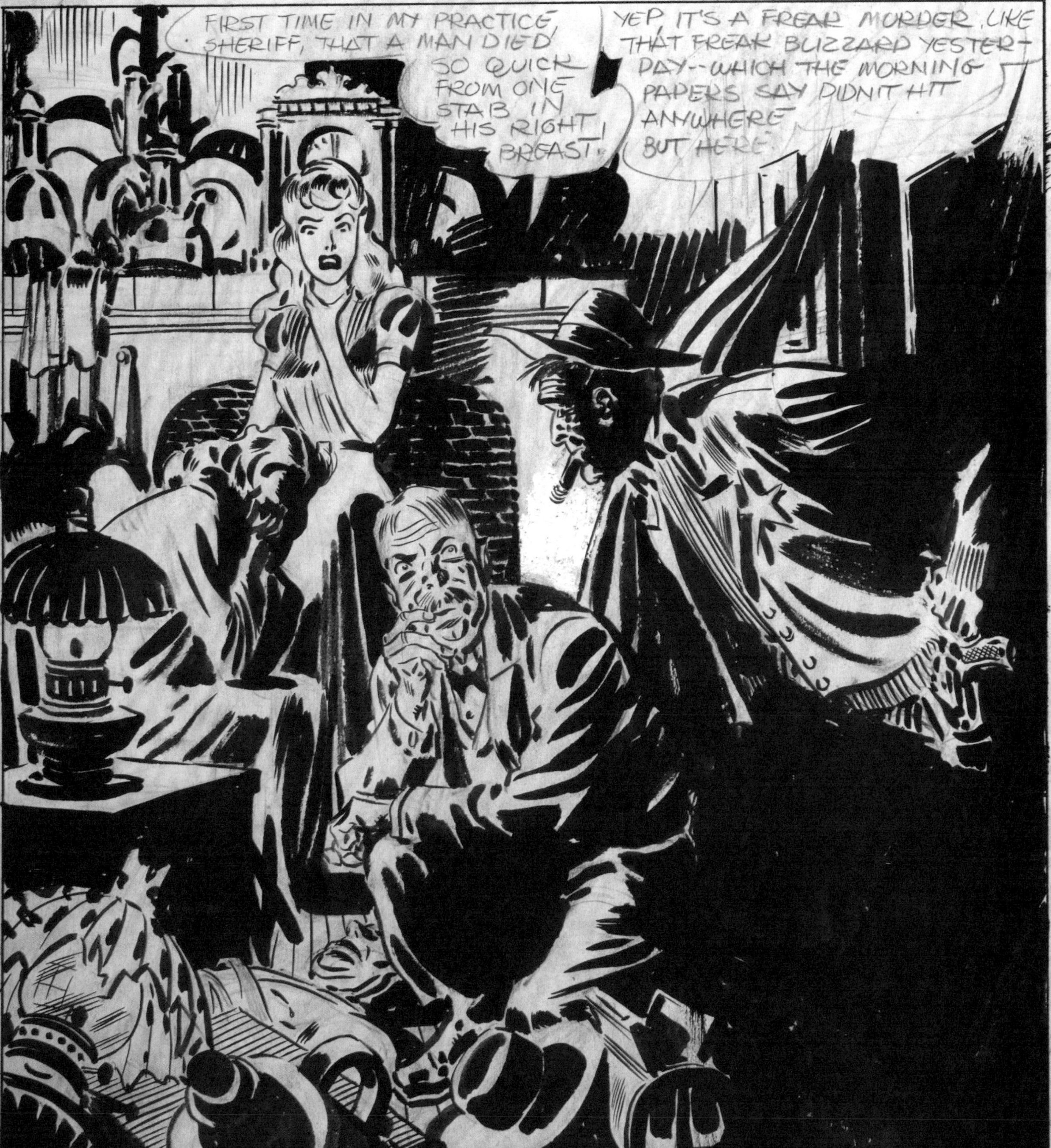
FIRST TIME IN MY PRACTICE, SHERIFF, THAT A MAN DIED SO QUICK FROM ONE STAB IN HIS RIGHT BREAST!
YEP, IT'S A FREAK MURDER, LIKE THAT FREAK BLIZZARD YESTER-DAY--WHICH THE MORNING PAPERS SAY DIDN'T HIT ANYWHERE BUT HERE

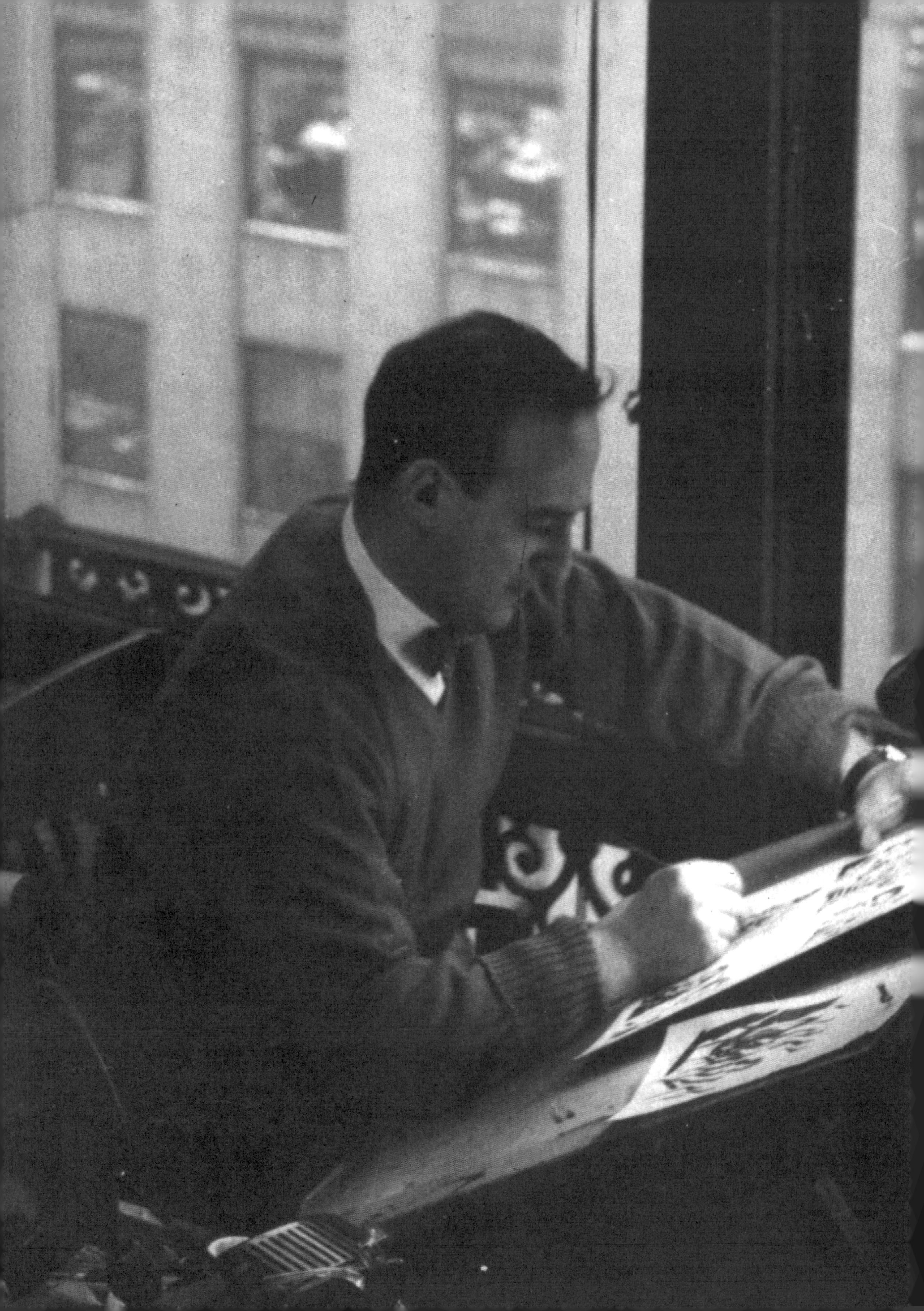

FROM SHADOW TO LIGHT

The Life and Art of Mort Meskin

STEVEN BROWER
with Peter and Philip Meskin

Fantagraphics Books

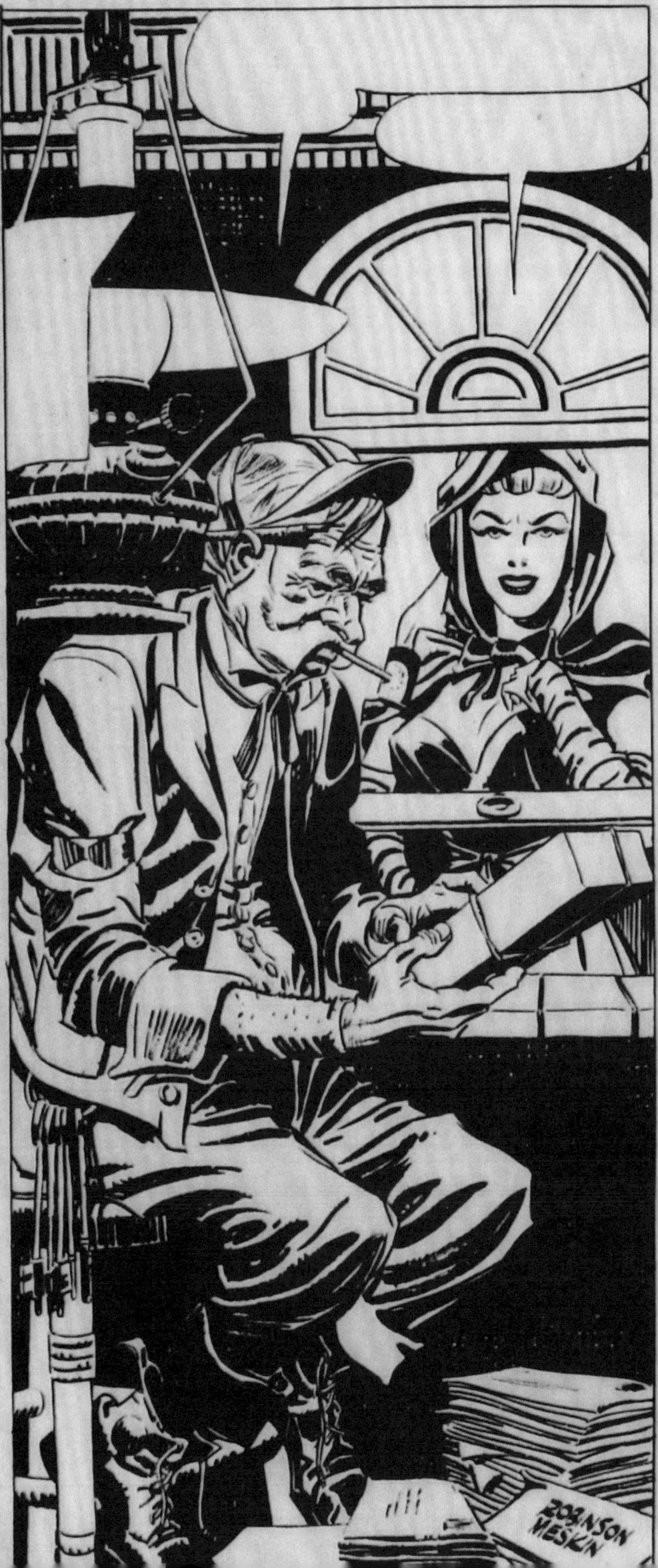
ROBINSON
MESKIN

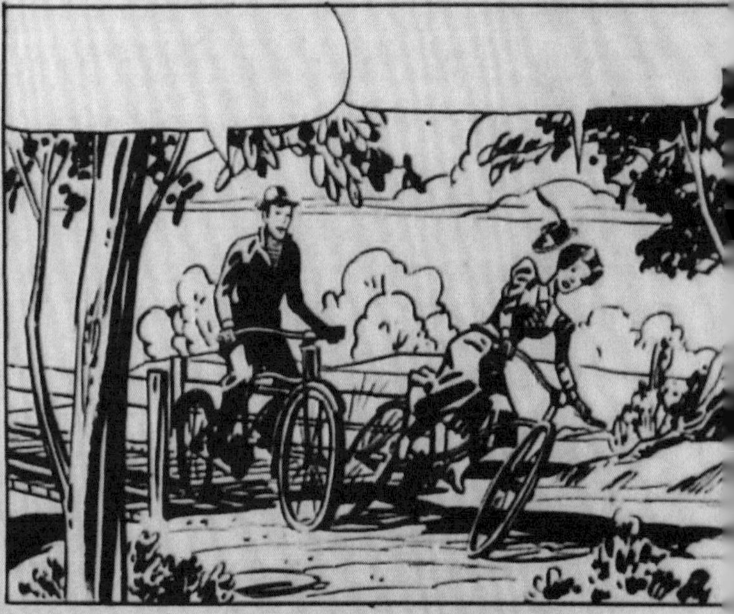

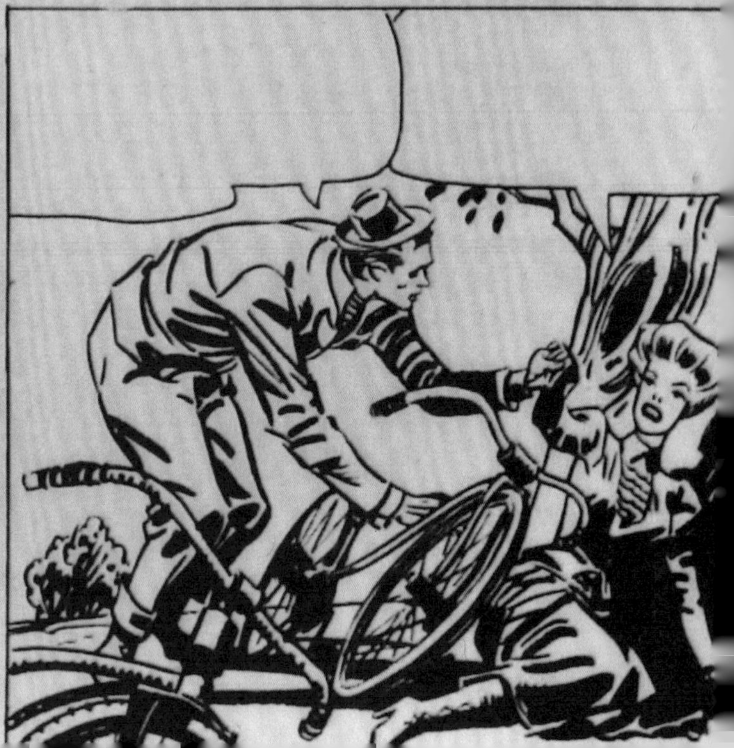

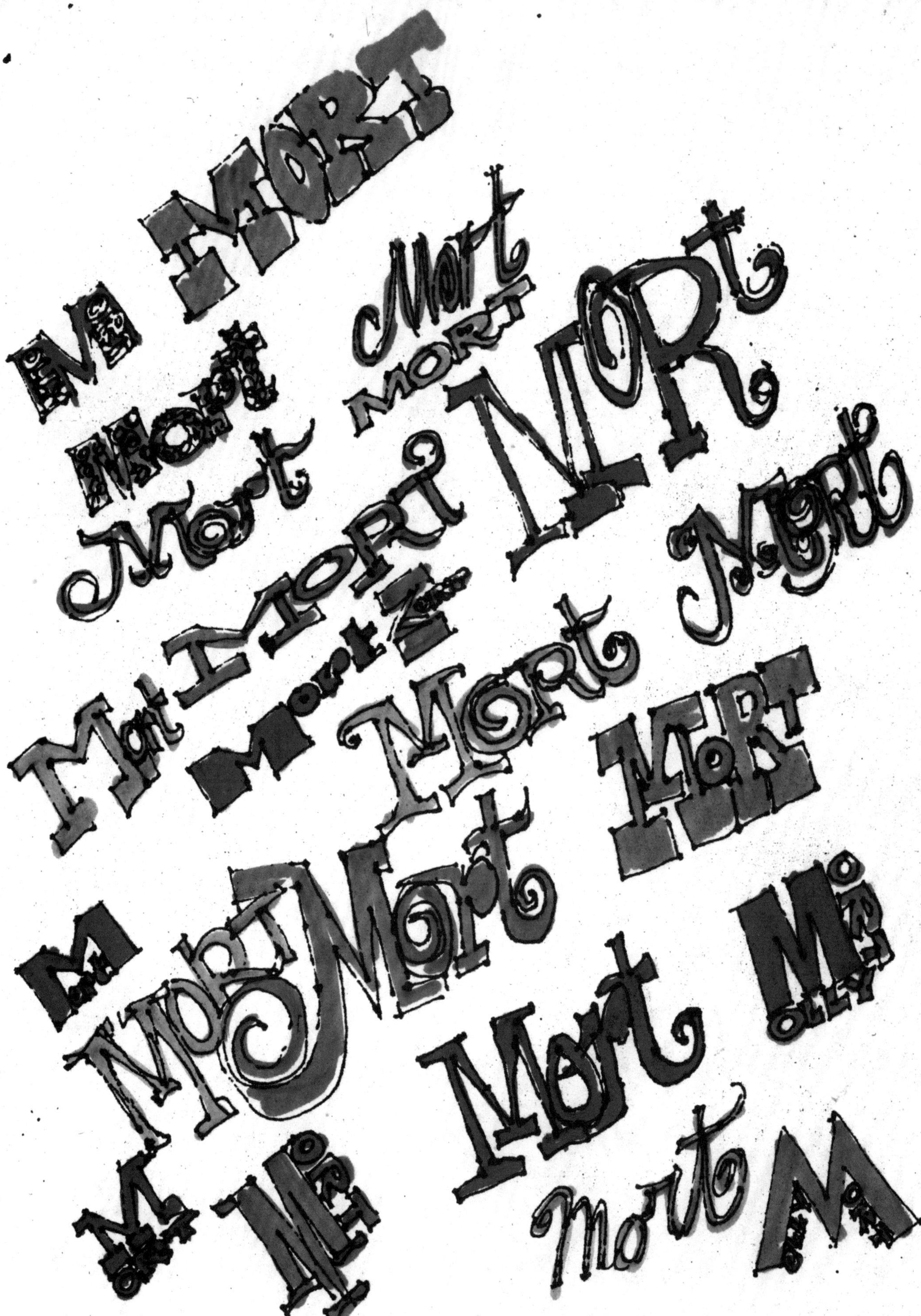
MORT
Mort
Mort
MORT
Mort
MORT
Mort
MORT
Mort
Mort
Mort
MORT
Mort
Mort
OLLY
Morte

I miss Mort Meskin. Mort was my mentor, colleague, partner, collaborator, confidant, and a lifetime friend from the day we met in 1940. It was at the MLJ publishing house, one of the smaller comics companies competing with the giants of the time: Detective and Timely. The meeting was serendipitous as I was only there to see another cartoonist whom I had just met shortly before: Bernie Klein, who'd recently come from my hometown, Trenton, New Jersey. Their art department was small, but filled with exceptional artists including Mort and Bernie, many of whom became close friends and collaborators: Charlie Biro and Irv Novick—both excellent artists—and prolific writer Bob Wood. Charlie and Bob became partners and editors of the hugely successful *Crime Does Not Pay* and other titles including *Daredevil Comics*, for which Bernie and I created features some years later.

I was impressed with their work, but especially with Mort's. I knew he was an exceptional creator from the first time I saw his art. One look at Mort's pencil pages and I could see his excellent draftsmanship. I immediately made arrangements to bring Bernie and Mort to my editor, Whitney Ellsworth. While Bernie was just beginning his career, I knew Whitney would see his potential. Mort was already an accomplished professional; in fact, he was the only one of us who seriously studied art—a graduate of the famous Pratt Institute. Whit immediately added Mort to the staff of DC, where he soon began two features, *The Vigilante* and *Johnny Quick*. At the same time he gave Bernie freelance assignments. We had an impressive group back then: my drawing board abutted Joe Shuster on one side, and Jack Kirby on the other, next to Fred Ray, Mort Meskin, and George Roussos.

As fate would have it, some years later, when Mort and I opened our own studio and became collaborators, we continued those titles for National (now DC) and took on two others: *The Black Terror* and *The Fighting Yank*, as well as special commissions from the Joe Simon and Jack Kirby studio.

Bernie and I immediately bonded and decided to share an apartment, which we did till Bernie was drafted and became a combat photographer. He was shot down several times over North Africa and then again during the invasion of Sicily. On January 1944 Bernie was killed during the amphibious landing at Anzio on the Italian mainland. I was devastated.

Bernie, Mort, and I were a close trio. When Bernie left to serve overseas, Mort and I shared the apartment on East 33rd Street. Though a quiet man and not given to histrionics, Mort was intense. He still had a trace of stutter from his youth. It's

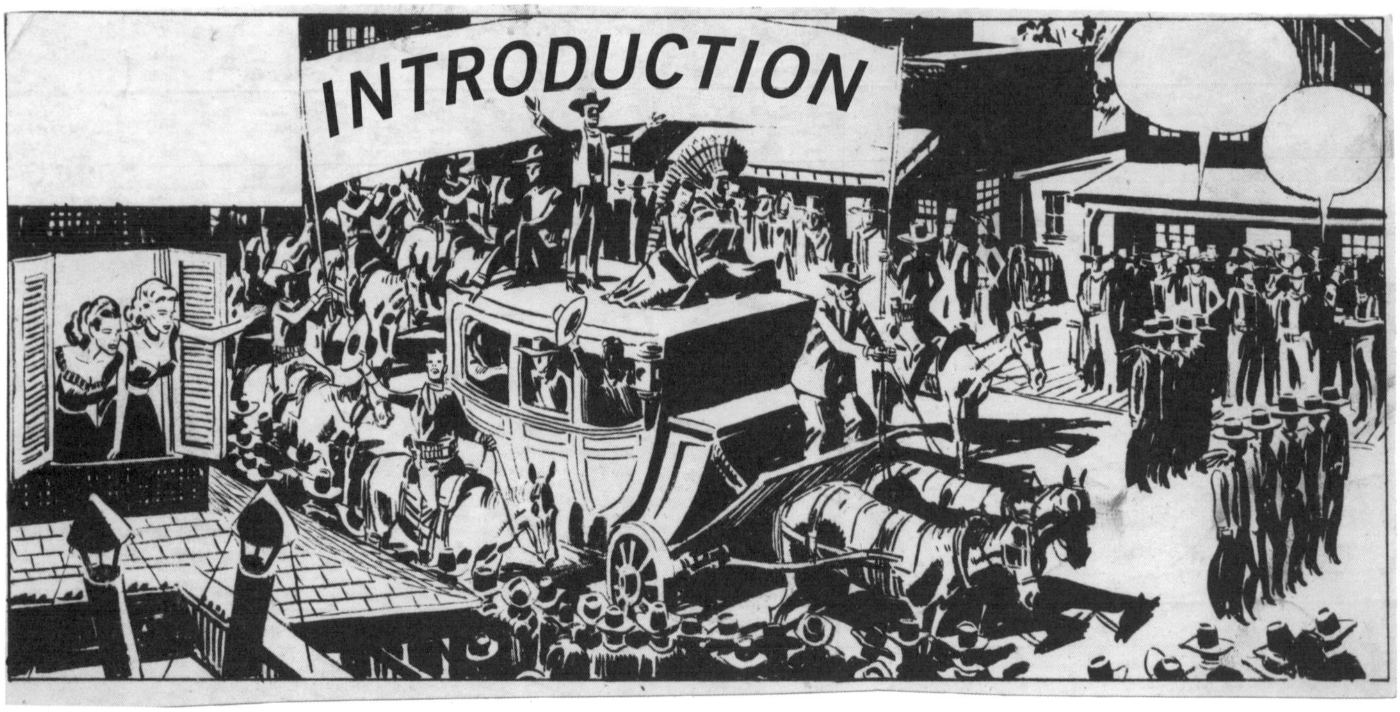
INTRODUCTION

hard to describe a close friendship as I had with Mort. He was certainly like a brother. We did everything together. We hunted down old movies, prowled the museums. We were both involved with the political issues of the day. In addition to art and the comics, the war was a regular topic of discussion. Mort loved to sing and one time bought an early recording machine. He had quite a good voice. Although we didn't belong to any union, we sang some of the popular union songs of the days with great gusto for our own amusement:

"There once was a union maid
who never was afraid
of goons and geeks
and the company finks…"

I'm sure our neighbors were convinced that some subversives lived in the second floor front apartment.

What did two young comic book artists do when they weren't at the drawing board where they usually were, sometimes for days on end? Sometimes we'd go bowling. Mort had a tricky curve ball that I could never master. We often went sketching around the neighborhood under the now torn-down Third Avenue elevated subway, casting its shadow on the frenetic street life. We'd browse the second-hand bookstores and have a beer on McDougal Street in Greenwich Village. Or we'd set up a bowl of flowers from the local florist and perhaps a few selected objects for an afternoon of watercolors, a medium that we both loved and a pleasant diversion from our usual black and white pen-and-ink drawings. Darts was a favorite pastime, as the pockmarked wall in our studio could attest, as well as with all the cartoonists and friends who dropped by. Mort may have won the vocals but I owned the dartboard.

Of course there was always time for girls and romance. We both loved to draw them and used the ability shamelessly to impress them. But we rarely double-dated. That was one assignment on which we didn't collaborate!

Mort had a superb command of composition and design. His figures were fluid and his gestures rang true. These costumed heroes like *Johnny Quick* were strong without the exaggerated and often invented musculature seen in many other characters of the genre. Mort was an innovator. For *Johnny Quick* he introduced the technique of depicting one figure in multiple actions to give the illusion of motion. Many years later I curated the first exhibition of American comic art at a major New York fine art gallery, the Graham Gallery. I included an original *Johnny Quick* cover of Mort's in the 1972 show and compared it in the catalog to Marcel Duchamp's painting "Nude Descending a Staircase."

Mort knew how to tell and pace a story. His pages flow from panel to panel and from page to page. In our studio during the time of our collaboration, we constantly altered our routine. When Mort did rough layouts of a story, I would tighten the pencils. One began to ink while the other started to lay out the next story. It kept things fresh. We'd experiment with different surfaces. Vellum, for example, gave a unique touch with the pen or brush. One time we tried lighting the entire story from above. On one fearless day we simply inked pages without any pencil at all. It got us to concentrate on the drawing for a day while we'd rather have been at a good movie followed by dinner and an animated discussion of the director's techniques.

Now you know some of the reasons why I miss Mort.

Jerry Robinson
New York, 2010

THE KID

The exodus had begun. They came from all over Eastern Europe: Russia, Romania, Hungary, Poland, Austria, Czechoslovakia; great was their need to escape. Under the Tzar and his ilk the pogroms had multiplied, making life unbearable. The shtetls emptied, and the wanderers went on the move again, heading west. Although some would stop along the way—Paris, London—most kept moving. Horace Greeley's advice was the shot heard 'round the world.

They paused at Ellis Island long enough to change their identities. Voices echoed across the vaulted ceiling as they crossed the threshold. Long tables took up most of the open space, officious-looking uniformed men on one side, starch in their collars, and on the other, the tattered and the torn—long faces, a lost look in their eyes, wondering exactly what they had gotten themselves into. Women with babushkas, men with black hats and yarmulkes, peyes, long black coats. Occupations were taken down as given names; other names were the result of on-the-spot shortening, or anglicization. Towns of origin were routinely listed as Vilna, which simply meant "village." These men, women, and children were the great unwashed, and they were handed a bar of soap to cleanse themselves. None of it mattered; they were trading an old life for a new. Now they were Americans.

Brothers Mort, age 4, and Nat, age 5, in Brooklyn, NY, 1920.

They poured onto the streets of lower Manhattan and spilled out over to Brooklyn and the Bronx. The children gazed out from their windows, searching for the streets of gold. Entire families would sleep in a single room, four, five, six, but the shared toilet down the hall reassured the children that they had indeed come to the promised land. Their fathers had secured jobs and sent for them. They shed their beards and went to work, often in the garment industry, making shmatas.

Amidst all this tumult Max Meskin made his way from Kiev to Brooklyn, and into the high end of the garment industry with his brother, as a furrier. Like most of his newly arrived generational peers, he abandoned both the old forms of dress and the traditions of his parents, substituting the new. He met Rose Stein, three years his junior. Unlike him, she was already an American, New York City born, her parents having made the trek earlier from Vienna, Austria. They were soon married and had two sons two years apart—Nathan in 1914 and Morton, born May 30, 1916—and a daughter, Muriel, six years after that.

Meskin Brothers,
Brooklyn, NY 1920.

As the next decade began, these émigrés continued their upwardly-mobile move to the sound of elevated trains and pushcarts in the streets of Brooklyn. At the age of six, Mort, as he was soon to be known, was also climbing—one day onto the icebox in the kitchen, striving, higher, higher, struggling to reach the top, when it toppled over, landing on his leg and trapping him. He was soon rescued, albeit with a broken leg and scar to remind him. But the deeper trauma was internalized in the form of a severe life-long stutter.

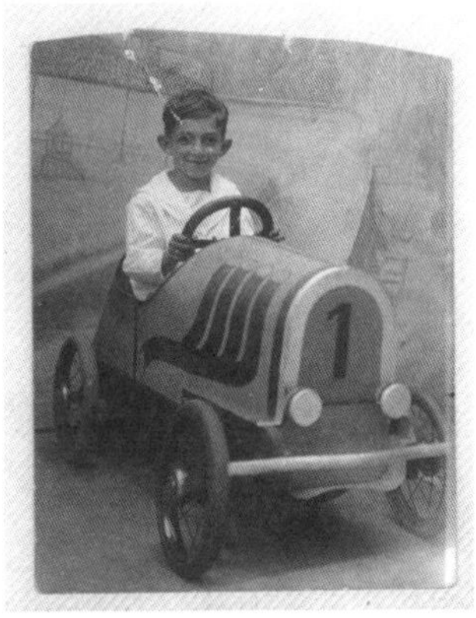

Mort, Coney Island, Brooklyn, NY, 1922.

Still, Mort did well in school, even though he did not like being a student. As a young boy he enjoyed going to Coney Island, spending time with his brother among the attractions and on the beach. He attended P.S. 189 and then Samuel J. Tilden High School, where he excelled at track and the gymnastic high-bar, as well as art. He became the art editor of his high school paper, *Tilden Topics*, and enjoyed a regular feature as a cartoonist, where he would comment on student life, sports, faculty/student relations, and assimilation into the Jazz Age society his generation

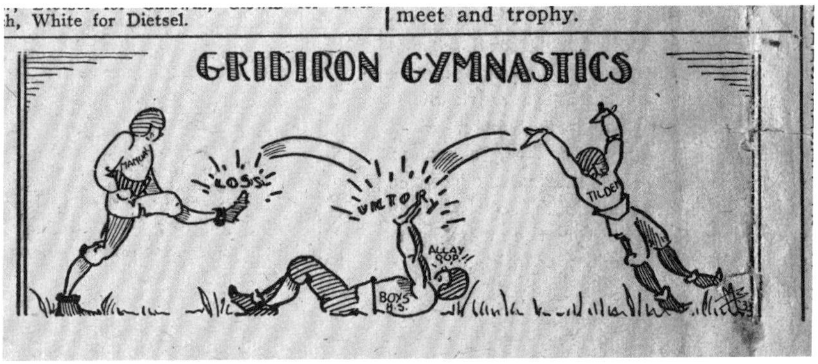
h, White for Dietsel.
meet and trophy.
GRIDIRON GYMNASTICS
LOSS
VICTORY
TILDEN
BOYS H.S.

This page and OVERLEAF: Meskin's cartoons were a regular feature of *Tilden Topics*, the school newspaper.

embraced. At home he read the pulps, affordable at a dime even during these Depression years, breathing in the artwork of Edd Cartier of *The Shadow* fame, of Herbert Morton Stoops in *Blue Book Magazine*, and of the popular illustrator Austin Briggs. In the newspaper there was *Scorchy Smith* by Noel Sickles, and later, *Terry and the Pirates* by Milton Caniff to learn from as well. Sickles in particular captivated Meskin, with his lithe figures, sketchy inking, and dramatic flashbulb lighting.

The pulps had appeared around the turn of the nineteenth century and combined serialized writing with often-lurid cover art. Pulps satisfied an urge for exaggeration: Athletes were stronger, heroes were nobler, and women were more luscious—with a dollop of sex to spice things up. These pages contained intrigues of crooked cops, clever criminals, sinister spies, creatures from space, and dangerous femmes fatales.

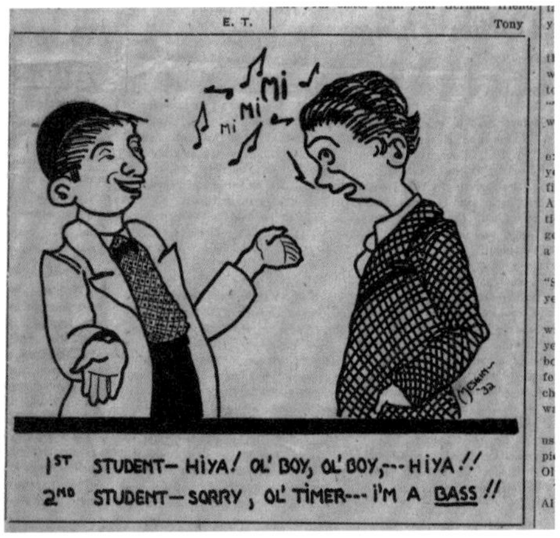
MI MI MI
1ST STUDENT– HIYA! OL' BOY, OL' BOY,--- HIYA!!
2ND STUDENT– SORRY, OL' TIMER--- I'M A BASS!!

is only a matter of days . .

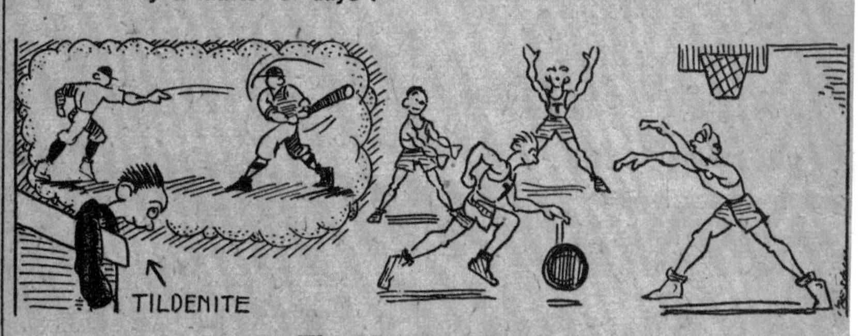
TILDENITE
The Merits of Baseball

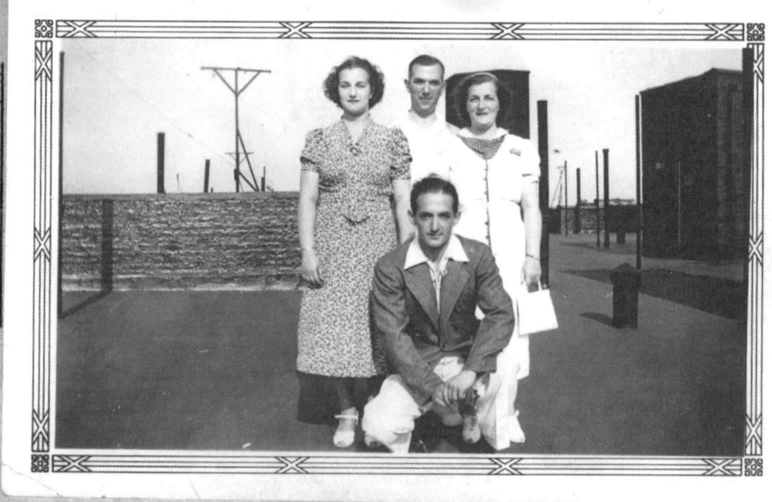

Mort (in front), sister Muriel, father Max and mother Rose on the rooftop of their apartment building at 318 Rochester Avenue, Brooklyn, NY.

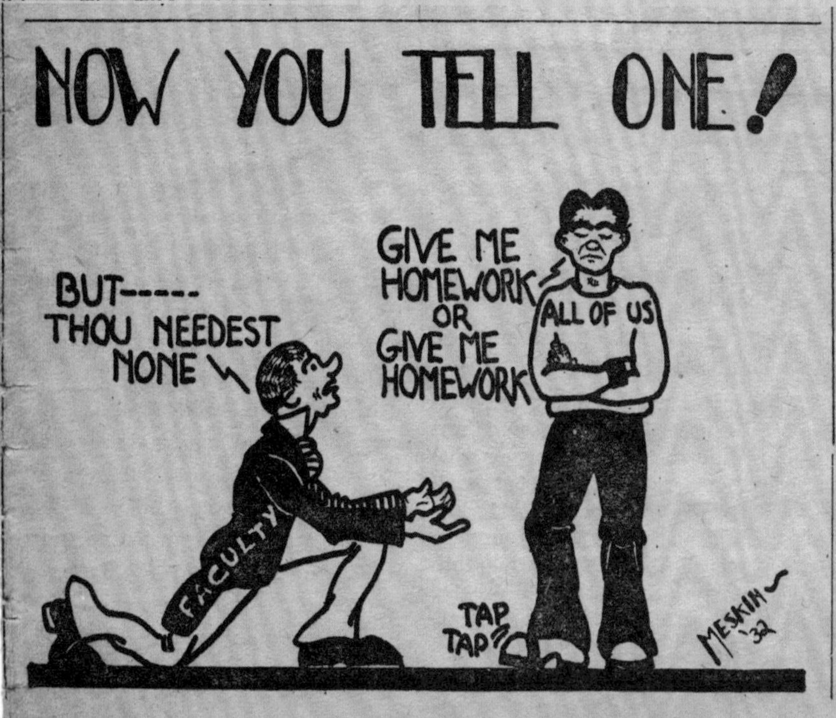
NOW YOU TELL ONE!
BUT----- THOU NEEDEST NONE
GIVE ME HOMEWORK OR GIVE ME HOMEWORK
ALL OF US
FACULTY
TAP TAP
MESKIN '32

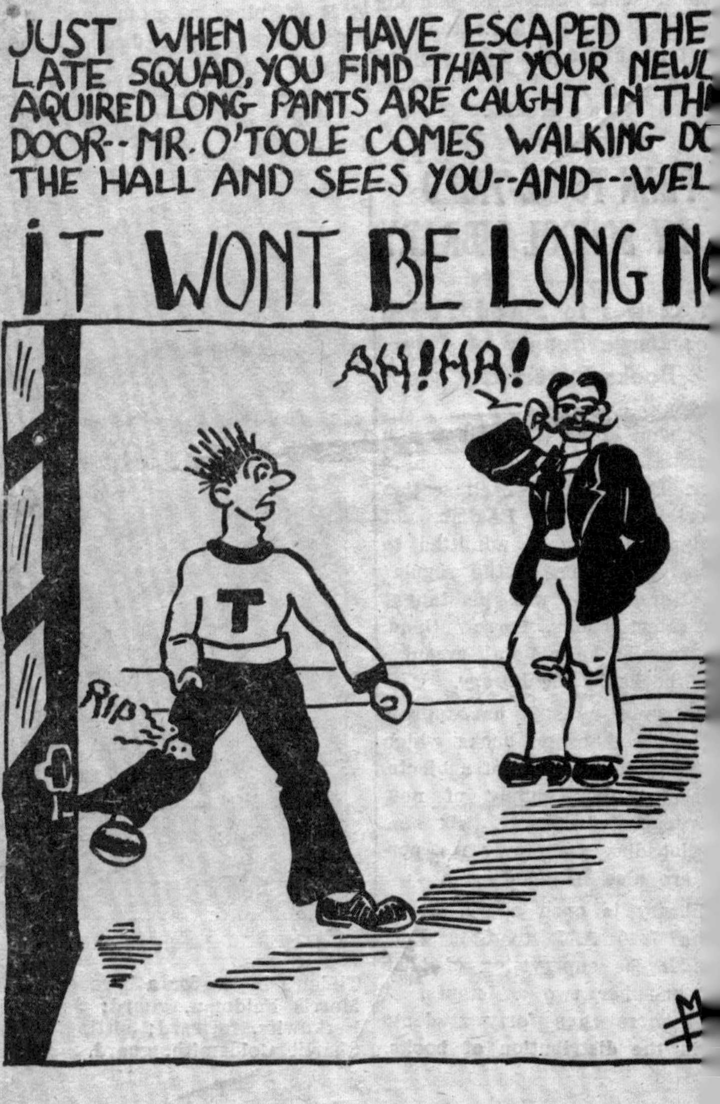
JUST WHEN YOU HAVE ESCAPED THE
LATE SQUAD, YOU FIND THAT YOUR NEWL
AQUIRED LONG PANTS ARE CAUGHT IN TH
DOOR--MR. O'TOOLE COMES WALKING DO
THE HALL AND SEES YOU--AND--WEL
IT WONT BE LONG N
AH!HA!
T
RIP

PROLOGUE

by Meskin

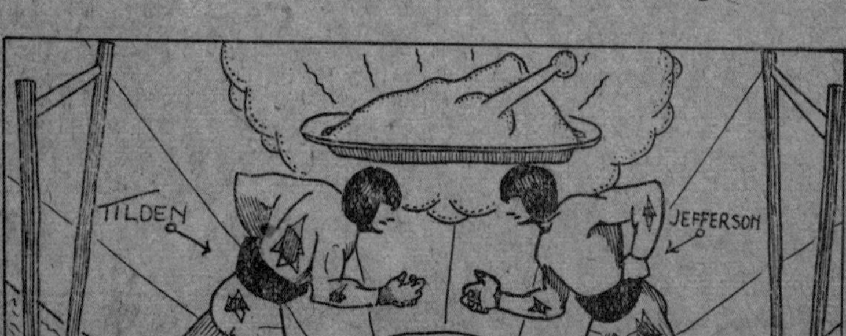
TILDEN
JEFFERSON

Tho'—A bit tattered and worn
As the new day espies them,
With hearts p'raps forlorn—
Still—One thing does guide them—

The thought of a Turk—
Big, luscious and brown,
Incites them to work,
For the winning touchdown

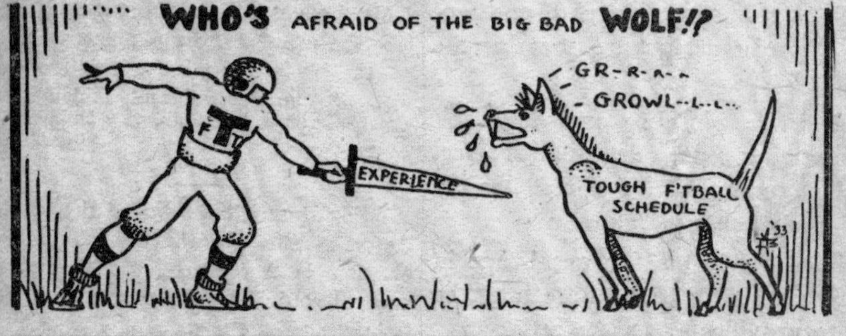
WHO'S AFRAID OF THE BIG BAD WOLF!?
GR-R-A-A
GROWL--L-L
FT
EXPERIENCE
TOUGH F'TBALL SCHEDULE
'33

At Tinton High School in Brooklyn Meskin combined two talents, gymnastists and art. He served as the art editor and cartoonist for the school newspaper and he competed on the track team; he also excelled at the high bar.

E. G. Becker
Guidance Counselor

ample defense for a prisoner on trial.
Victor Salzer—80A

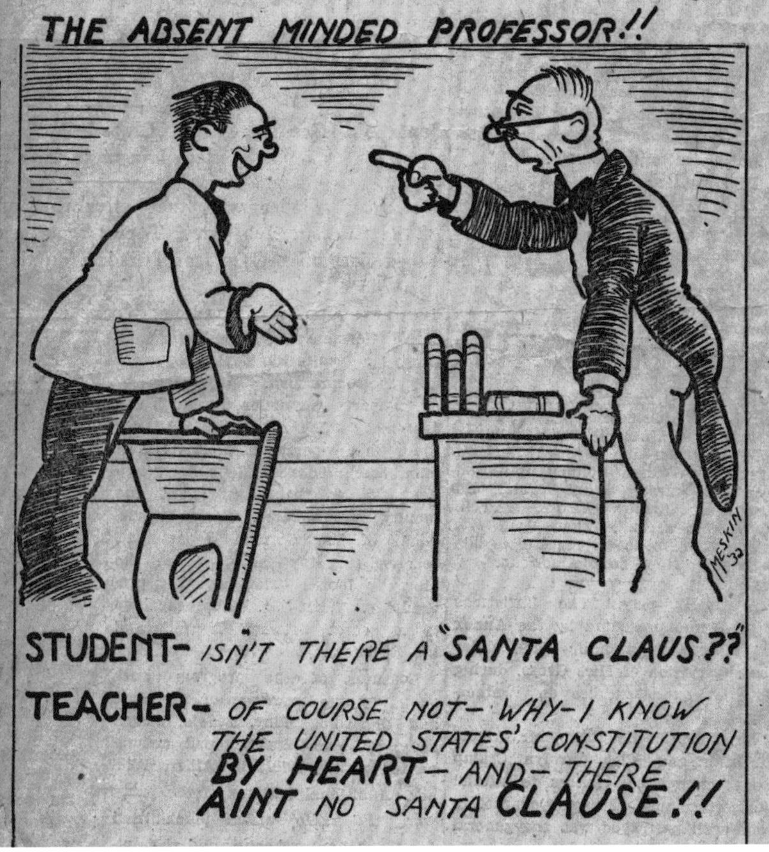
THE ABSENT MINDED PROFESSOR!!
MESKIN '32
STUDENT- ISN'T THERE A "SANTA CLAUS??"
TEACHER- OF COURSE NOT- WHY- I KNOW THE UNITED STATES' CONSTITUTION BY HEART- AND- THERE AINT NO SANTA CLAUSE!!

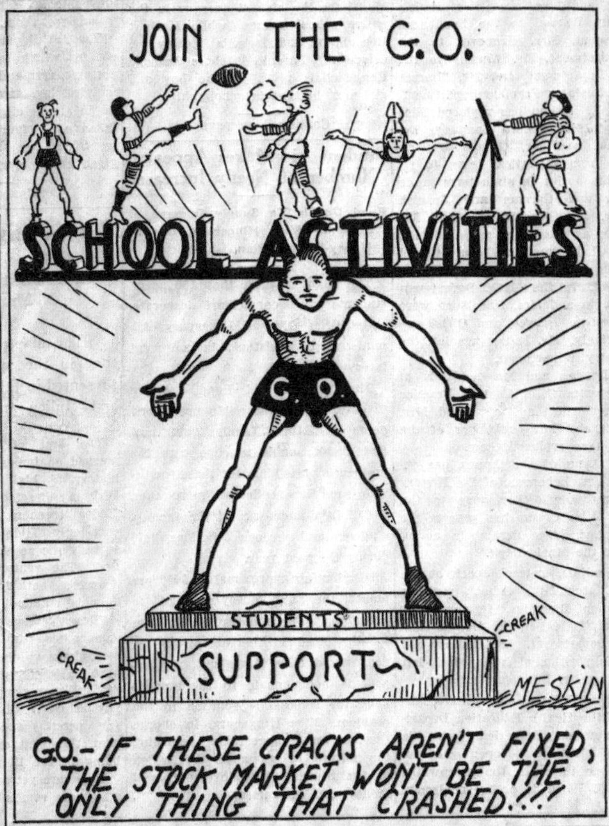
JOIN THE G.O.
SCHOOL ACTIVITIES
G.O
STUDENTS
SUPPORT
CREAK
CREAK
MESKIN
G.O.- IF THESE CRACKS AREN'T FIXED, THE STOCK MARKET WON'T BE THE ONLY THING THAT CRASHED!!!

MESKIN, MORTON
Commercial Artist
Art. Ed., *Tilden Topics;* Post. Cl.; Art. Cl.; Track Team; Major "T"; Co-Art. Ed. *Senior Yr. Book;* Cartoon Club.
An artist thou art to be.

"To a great guy"
I. Meyers

MEYERS, ISIDORE
B'klyn. College

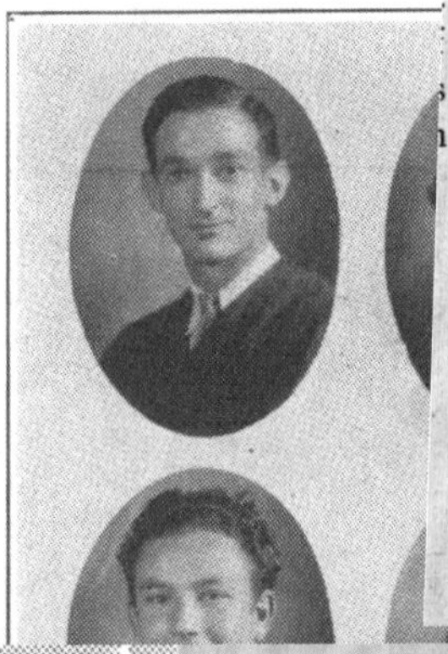

body and the team.

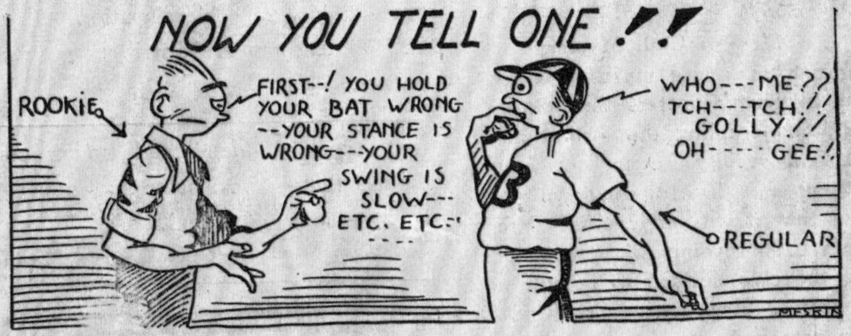
NOW YOU TELL ONE!!
ROOKIE
FIRST--! YOU HOLD YOUR BAT WRONG --YOUR STANCE IS WRONG---YOUR SWING IS SLOW--- ETC. ETC.----
WHO---ME?? TCH---TCH GOLLY!! OH-----GEE!!
REGULAR
MESKIN

Obituary—The Rifle Team

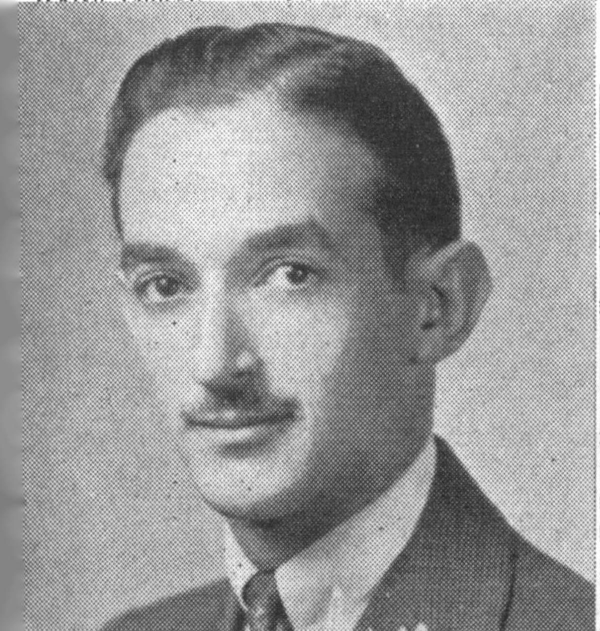
Mort Meskin

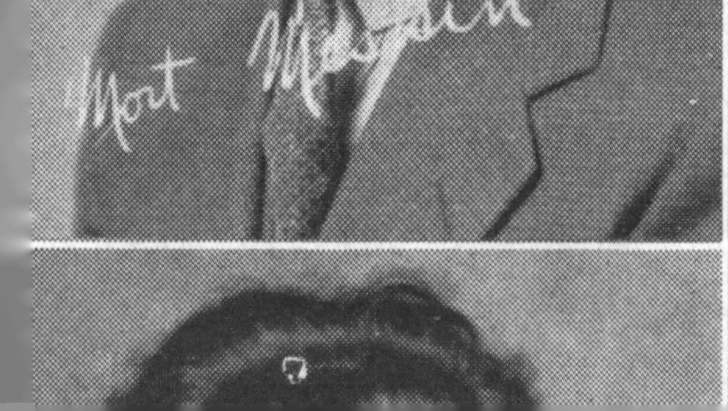

as no retakes of so unique a film are possible.

Regina C. Weiss,
Counselor, Guidance Dept.

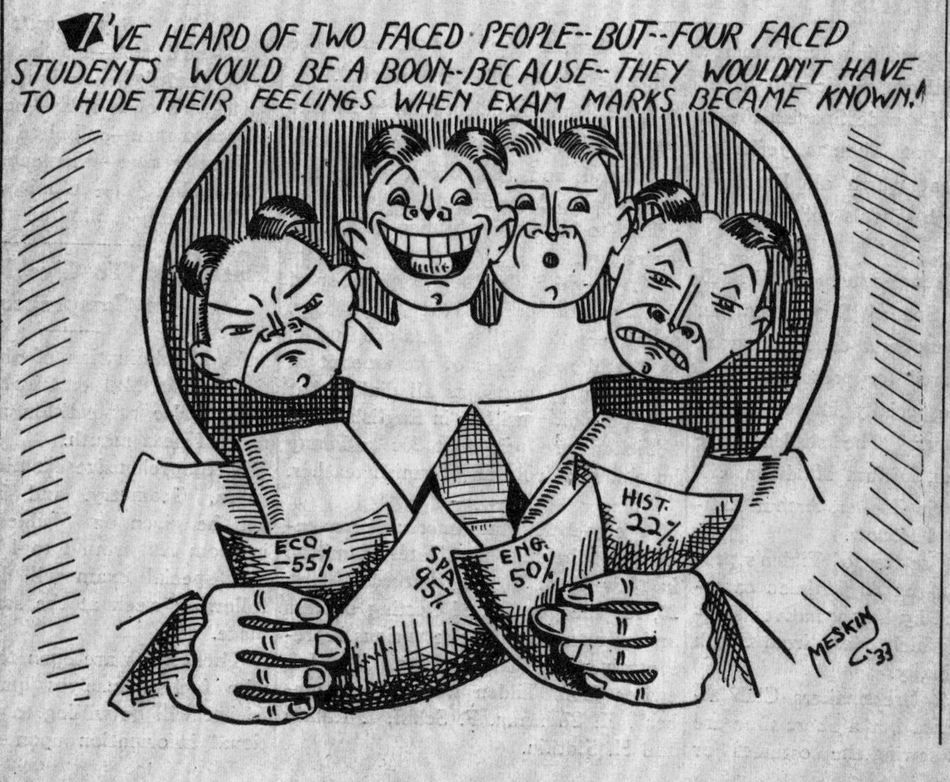
I'VE HEARD OF TWO FACED PEOPLE--BUT--FOUR FACED STUDENTS WOULD BE A BOON--BECAUSE--THEY WOULDN'T HAVE TO HIDE THEIR FEELINGS WHEN EXAM MARKS BECAME KNOWN!
ECO. -55%
SPA. 95%
ENG. 50%
HIST. 22%
MESKIN '33

THE GOLDEN MASTER

WELL, IF YOU CAN FLY AS WELL AS YOU COOK YOU'LL DO WELL ENOUGH! THAT WAS A GRAND DINNER!

— OH, THANKS, MR. SMITH! — I'LL GET YOU SOME MORE COFFEE!

CLOCKWISE: Early Meskin influences, men who loved shadow and light: Austin Briggs, Edd Cartier, Herbert Stoops, Noel Sickles. Their influence goes beyond chiaroscuro, and extends to compostion, line and facial features.

FROM COMIC STRIPS TO COMIC BOOKS

Back in 1895, the American comic strip had attained its definitive form in the *Hogan's Alley* (commonly known as *The Yellow Kid*) Sunday page. Drawn by Richard Felton Outcault for Joseph Pulitzer's *American Weekly* comic supplement to his *New York World*, *The Yellow Kid* became one of the paper's star attractions and was soon the subject of a battle between publishing rivals William Randolph Hearst and Pulitzer. Hearst, who had begun a series of raids on Pulitzer's staff the previous year, made a successful grab for Outcault. Pulitzer then bought Outcault back, but Hearst upped the ante once again. Pulitzer then hired George Luks to do a house version of *The Yellow Kid*, resulting in rival identical characters appearing in both Hearst and Pulitzer papers simultaneously. This battle between the publishers may have brought us the term "yellow journalism," a reference to the color of the Kid's nightshirt.

In January 1912 Hearst introduced the nation's first full daily comic page in *The Journal*, adding it to his other papers from coast to coast. Bud Fisher's *Mutt and Jeff*, Rudolph Dirks's *Katzenjammer Kids*, Winsor McCay's *Little Nemo* were among the earliest to be syndicated nationwide, soon joined by *Jiggs and Maggie* by George McManus.

Cartoonists were the superstars of their times, many enjoying lucrative contracts, touring the country, and giving chalk talks to a delighted public.

Milton Caniff was born in 1907 in Ohio. His rise to fame, indeed to the status of one of the best-known cartoonists of his time, began in 1934, when he was hired by the *New York Daily News* to produce a new comic strip, *Terry and the Pirates*. Initially, the strip told the tale of an American sailor and his adventures in China, where he battled the strip's eponymous pirates under the leadership of the sinister Dragon Lady. At the onset of the war Terry enlisted into the armed forces.

One of the innovations Caniff brought to the medium was the use of changing viewpoints from panel to panel, to arresting effect. This, and dramatic use of shadow and light combined with beautiful women, whom he fashioned after the movie stars of the day, influenced the way comics stories were told.

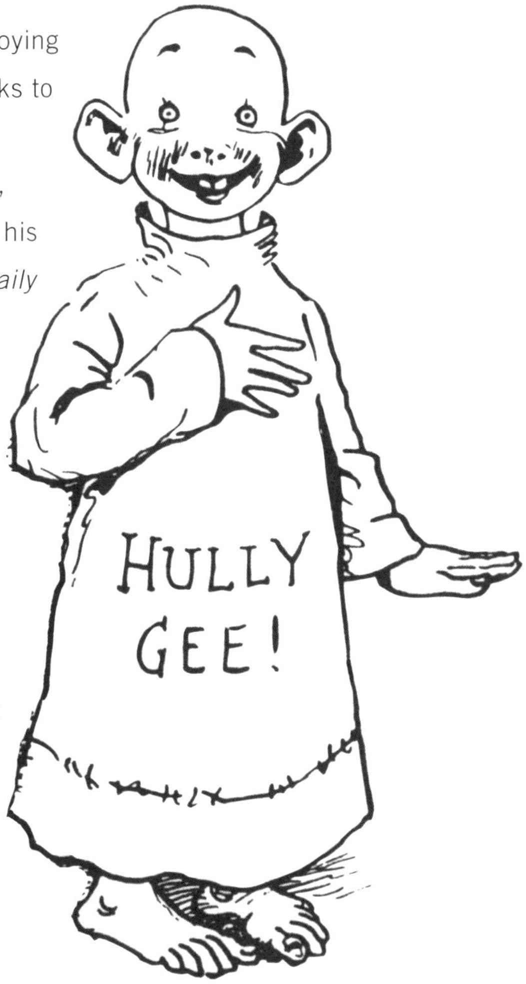
HULLY GEE!

Fellow Ohioan Noel Douglas Sickles, three years Caniff's junior, began his career as a political cartoonist for the *Ohio State Journal.* He met and shared a studio with Caniff, who was then working as a cartoonist for the *Columbus Dispatch.* Soon, both relocated to New York to work as staff artists for the Associated Press. Sickles inherited *Scorchy Smith*, an action/adventure strip loosely based on Charles Lindbergh, from ailing creator John Terry. Like Caniff, Sickles brought to the strip a cinematic sensibility and an impressionistic style of inking that he referred to as "chiaroscuro." Sickles, in turn, influenced the impressionable young Mort Meskin.

In 1934 a pulp writer from Portland, Oregon, Major Malcolm Wheeler-Nicholson, decided to enter publishing by recycling Sunday newspaper comic strips into a pulp magazine format, a format pioneered in *Famous Funnies* the previous year. Discovering that the existing strips had all been licensed, he commissioned new ones; the result was *New Fun* #1, composed of humor and adventure strips.

FUTURE
15¢—JULY FICTION
THE POISON REALM
by JOHN COLERIDGE
LIQUID HELL
AND OTHERS

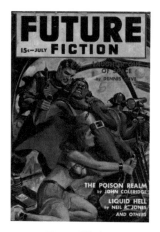

Future Fiction Magazine, July 1940.

It soon became apparent that unlike the single-page Sunday strips, "comic books," as they came to be called, required longer sequential storytelling. Two Jewish boys from Cleveland, Jerry Siegel and Joe Shuster, first-generation like the rest, sold their initial work to Wheeler-Nicholson: the adventure strip *Henri Duval.* Soon afterwards Wheeler-Nicholson was pushed out by his two partners, Harry Donenfeld and Jack Liebowitz, children of newly minted Americans themselves. After many tries, Siegel and Shuster sold a comic strip they had intended for newspapers, *Superman*, to what was now called National Magazines.

In 1938, Superman premiered in *Action Comics* #1, and the superhero was introduced into popular culture. It owed much to the movie serials and pulps of the day. Visually, the Superman stories were full of charm, but fairly straightforward in their storytelling techniques. It would not be until the following year with the birth of Batman, created by Bob Kane and Bill Finger, that German Expressionism would find its way into these pages. Steeped in shadow, The Bat-Man, as he was originally called, was the "dark knight," donning a vampire-like outfit complete with black cloak, to avenge the murder of his parents years earlier. The character was a direct descendant of Johnston McCulley's pulp hero Zorro, who had first appeared in 1919 in *All-Story Weekly.* Another prototype was The Shadow, who starred in his own magazine from 1931 to 1949. In addition, Batman's gallery of grotesque villains would soon rival that of Chester Gould's *Dick Tracy.* Still, Batman ultimately was a totally original creation, and one that was in sync with Depression-era angst.

The new form took off, demand rapidly grew, and the call went out to writers and artists. Studios were set up across Manhattan, designed in the manner of the garment shops: the creative act was broken down into piecemeal work, editors handing over scripts to artists to pencil, who handed it off to the letterer to add the text, who in turn handing it to an inker to outline the work, another to add backgrounds, yet another to spot the blacks. Victor Fox Studios, Harry A. Chesler, and Eisner-Iger soon employed dozens of young men, who, despite the low pay, were happy to be employed in these late Depression years.

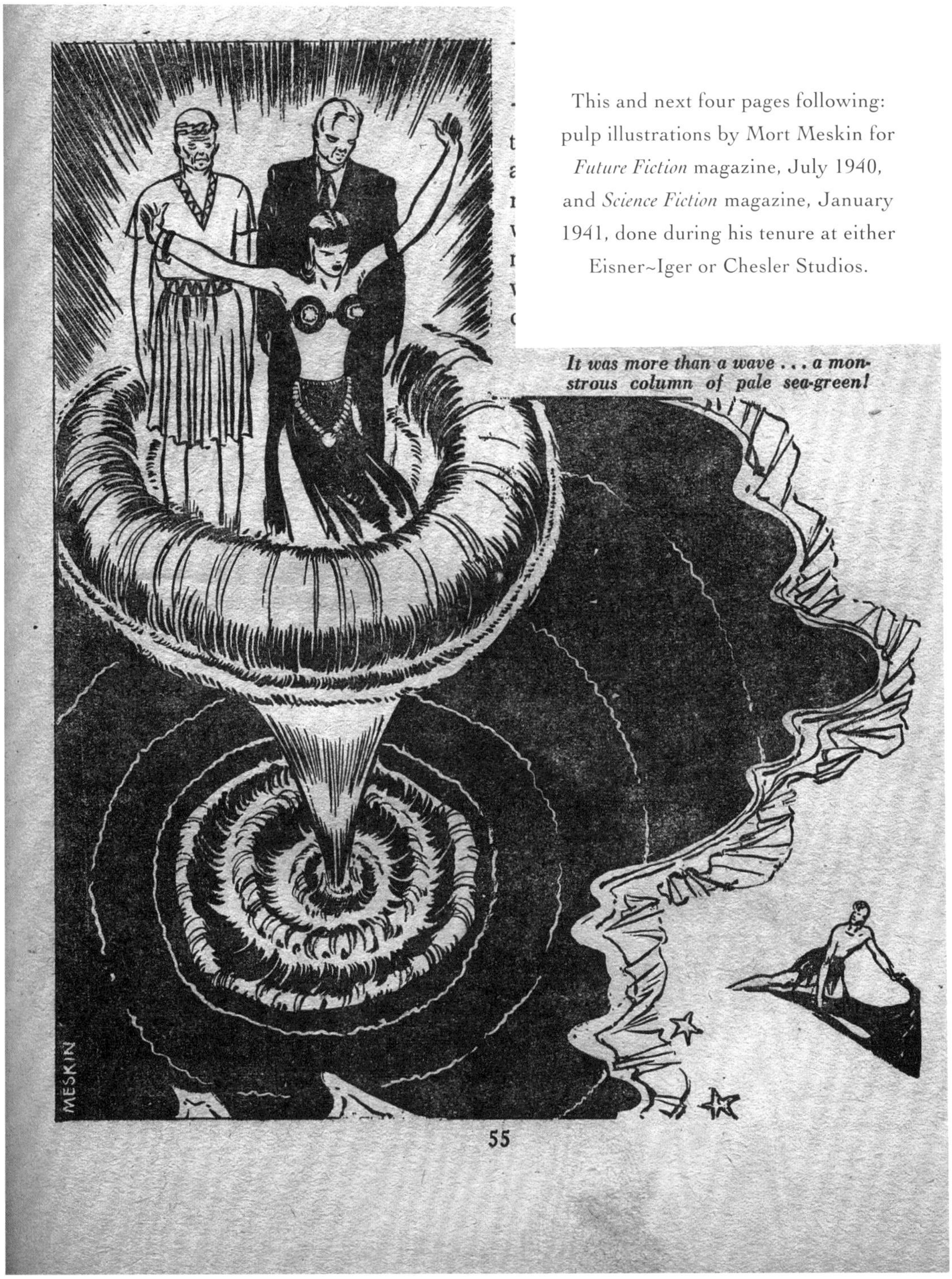
It was more than a wave . . . a monstrous column of pale sea-green!
MESKIN
55

This and next four pages following: pulp illustrations by Mort Meskin for *Future Fiction* magazine, July 1940, and *Science Fiction* magazine, January 1941, done during his tenure at either Eisner~Iger or Chesler Studios.

MASTERS of MADNESS

by BRAD BUCKNER

David Reeves was confronted with the greatest mystery ever to face a man from Earth—for here on Jupiter his first expedition discovers a city without life—and an unexplainable madness overtakes the minds of his companions! But an answer to it all comes in a cloud of alien death!

CHAPTER I

EXCITEDLY, David Reeves, commander of Earth's first colonizing expedition to Jupiter, clasped his hand over Ruth Manning's on the rail of the *Invincible*, leader of the fleet of spaceships that streamed out behind them in long, winding formation.

"Will you look at that, Ruth!" he said. "A city! There must be a civilization here on Jupiter similar to our own back on Earth!"

Together they looked down on the beautiful, well-planned metropolis ahead and below them. Its huge, domed structures and the bridged levels between them were built of some light yellow metal that gave off a dull gloss.

"The architecture is much like ours," Reeves went on with suppressed amazement. "And those flat areas on the larger buildings must be landing stages for planes. Yes, I can see a plane now in one of the

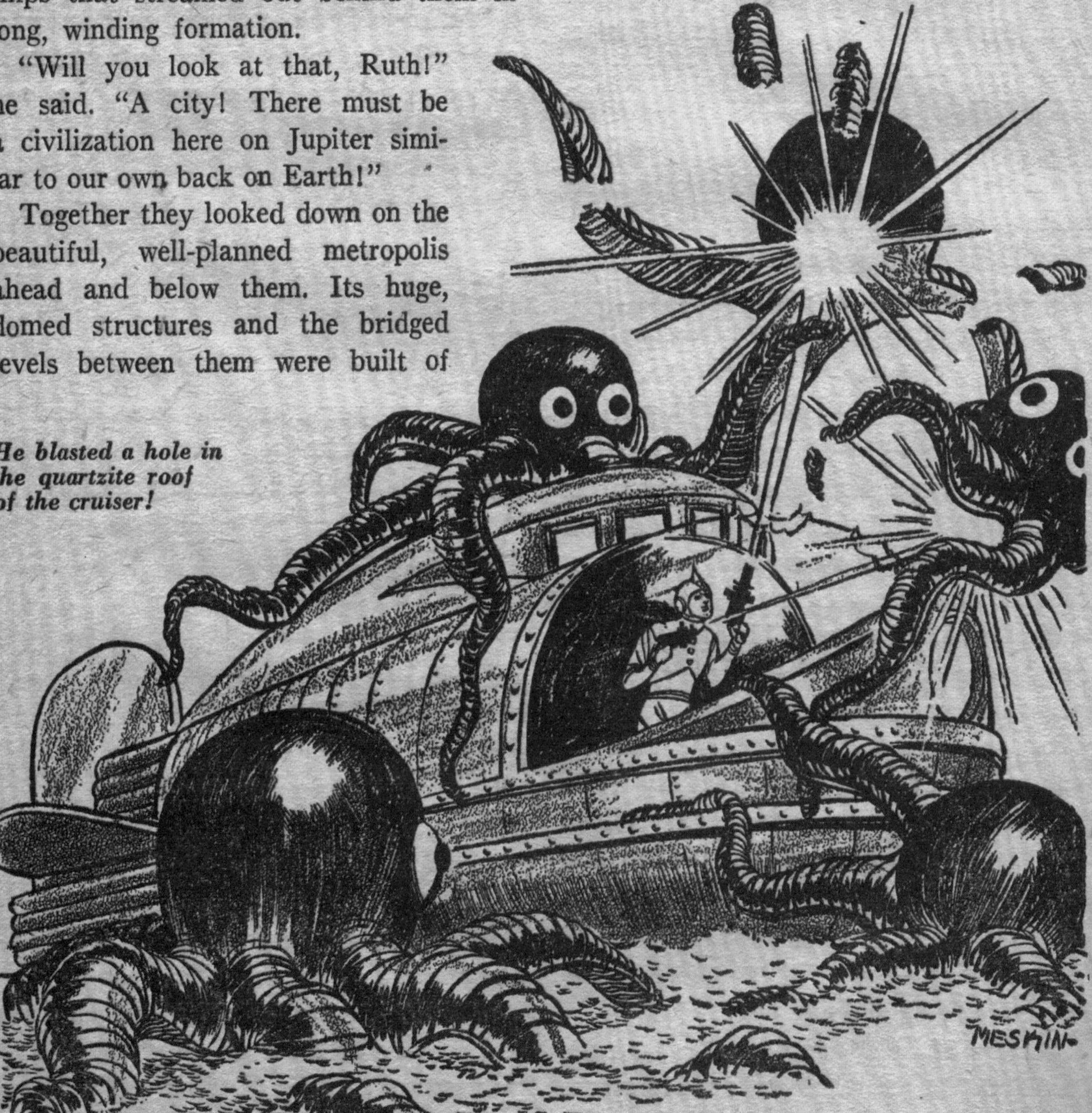
MESKIN

He blasted a hole in the quartzite roof of the cruiser!

Carson struck the gun aside before he could pull the trigger!

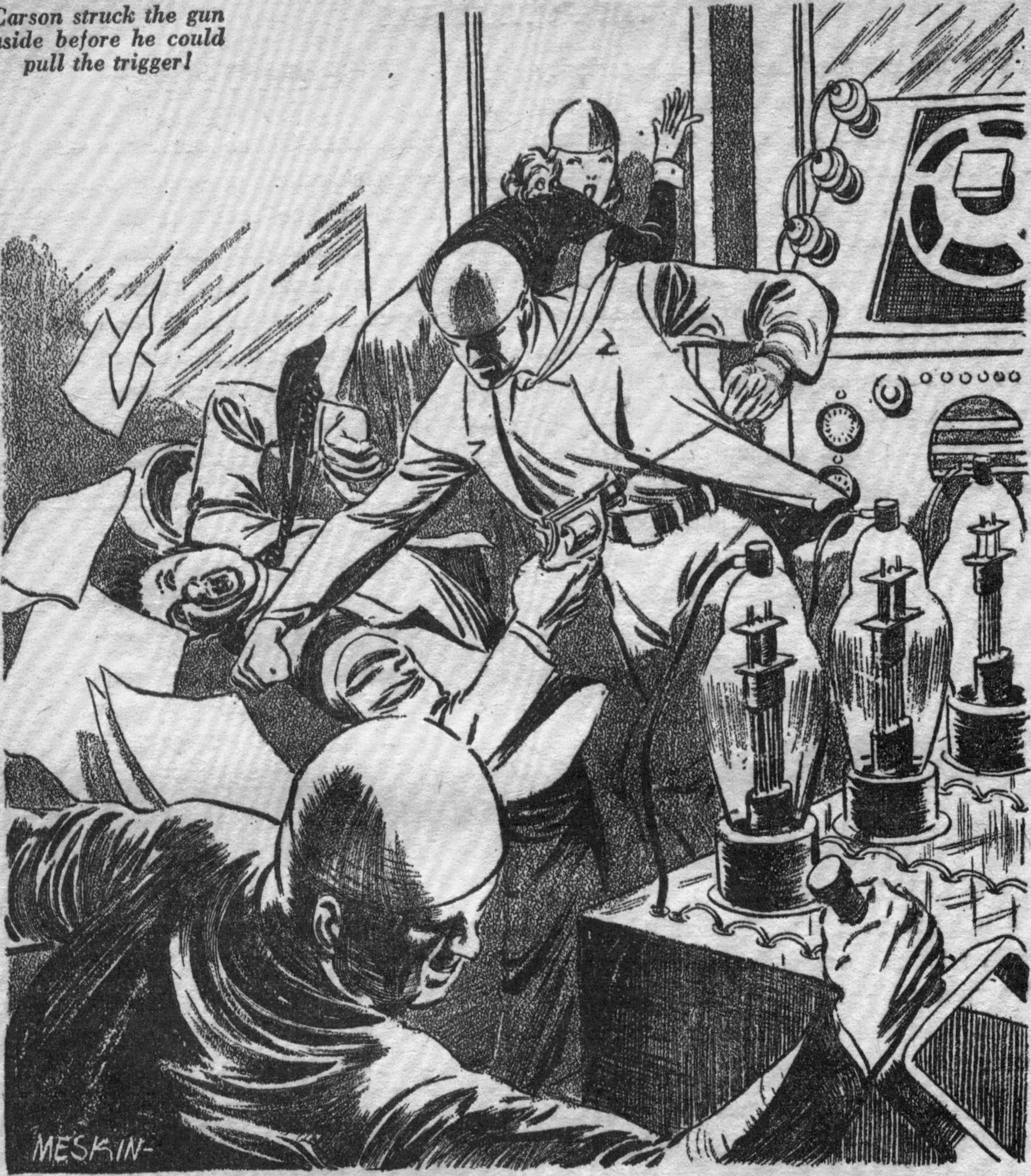
MESKIN-

HABITS VIA RADIO

by E. A. GROSSER

A miraculous accidental discovery broadcasts a very annoying phenomenon through the country—and complications arise when people find themselves forming useless and embarrassing habits! But Dan and Irene find this simple annoyance turned into genuine terror by a strange trick of fate!

DAN CARSON ran down the path toward the garage, feeling as though psychologist. The tall towers of KKOM, showing above the trees, marked the job

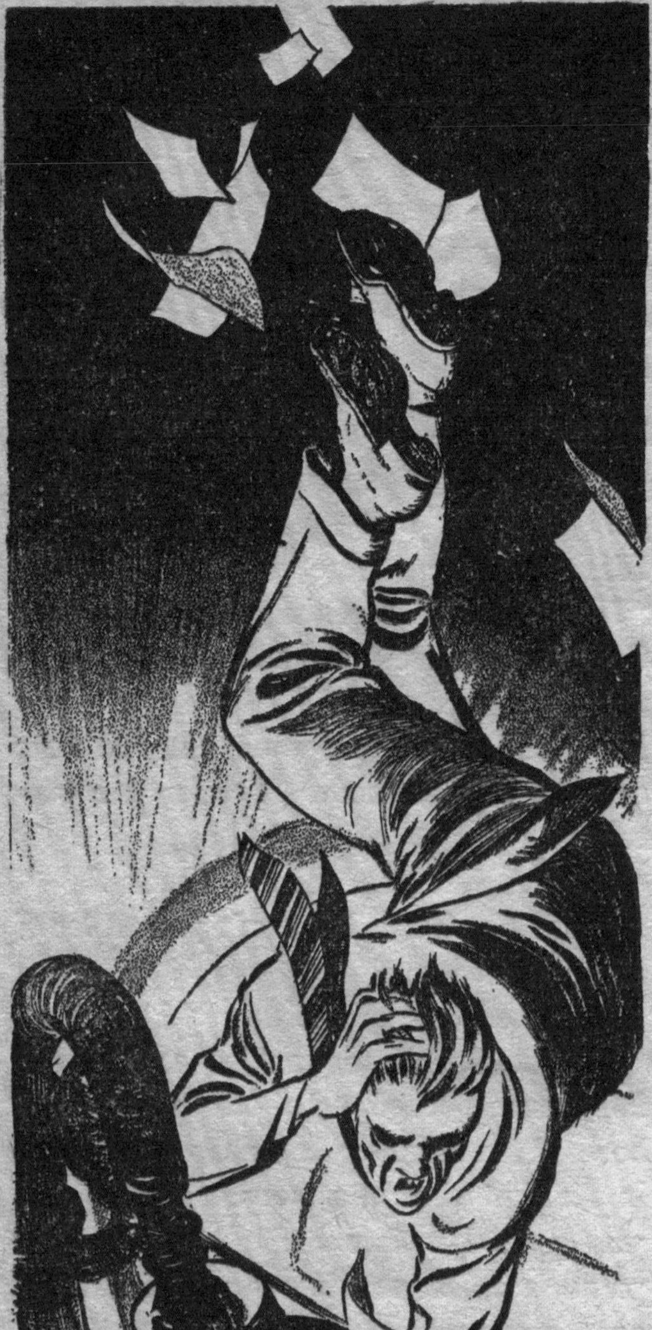

DESTINY MADE TO ORDER

by ED EARL REPP

If you discovered a new blessing that would save countless thousands from a life of horrible suffering, would you magnanimously donate your gift to Mankind? Joe Craven answered negatively—and the doom forecast by Dr. Tuttle's strange machine placed a heinous plan into his greedy mind!

CHAPTER I
THE FATE-SHIFTER

IT WAS a shame-faced, puzzled lot of reporters that shuffled uncomfortably inside Doctor Tuttle's office. Harry

Just before he struck, he could see the crowd scattering!

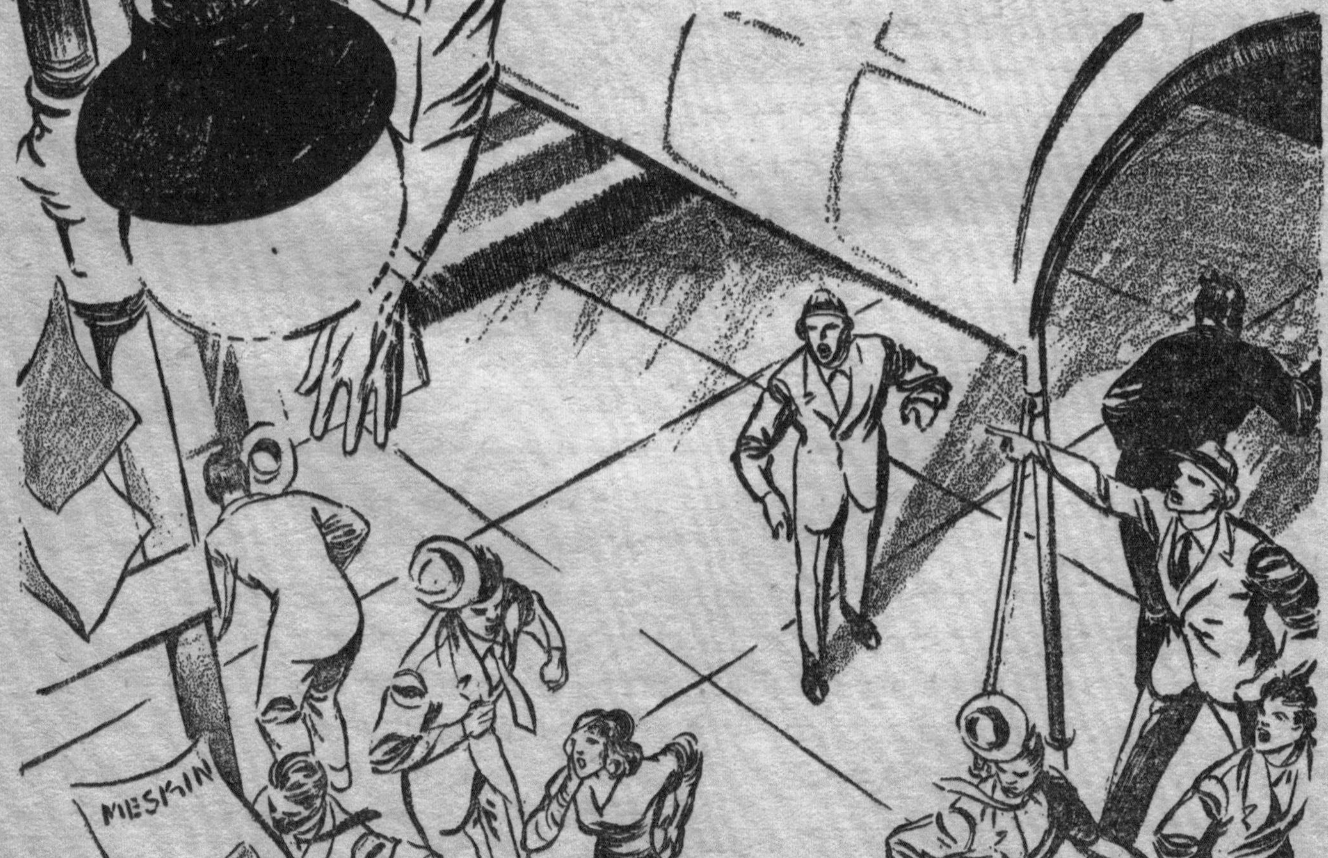
MESKIN

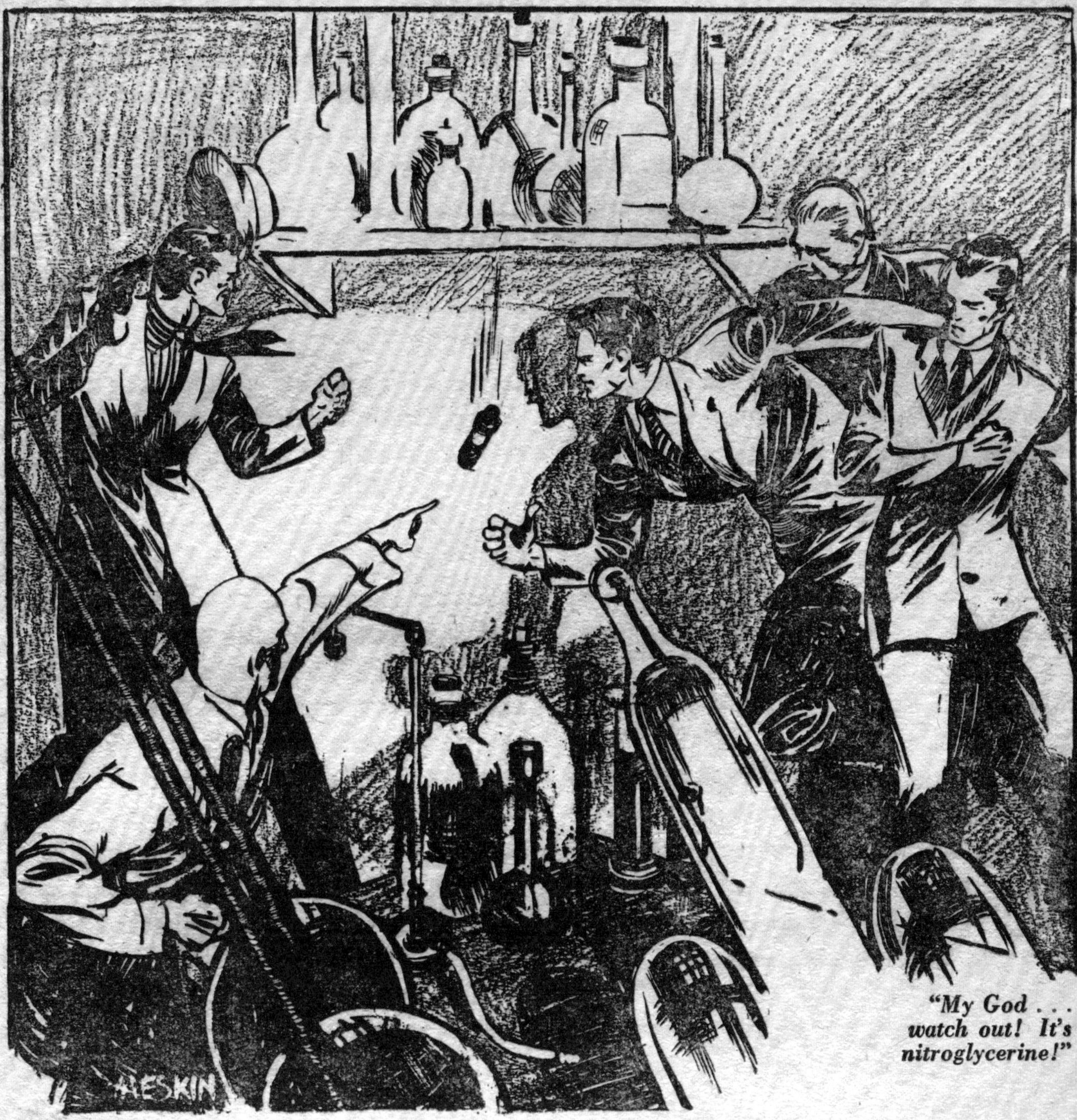
HESKIN

"My God . . . watch out! It's nitroglycerine!"

The Magnificent Possession

by ISAAC ASIMOV

Walter Sills labored for years as an unknown laboratory worker—but at fifty he makes his great discovery! Fame, riches are to be his fate—until interference looms up in the form of a few unlikeable characters — and Nature herself!

WALTER SILLS reflected now, as he had reflected often before, that life was hard and joyless. He surveyed his dingy chemical laboratory and grinned cynically—working in a dirty hole of a place, living on occasional ore analyses that barely paid for absolutely indispensable equipment, while others, not half his worth perhaps, were working for big industrial concerns and taking life easy.

He looked out the window at the Hudson River, ruddied in the flame of the dying sun, and wondered moodily whether these last experiments would finally bring

EISNER-IGER, CHESLER, AND MLJ

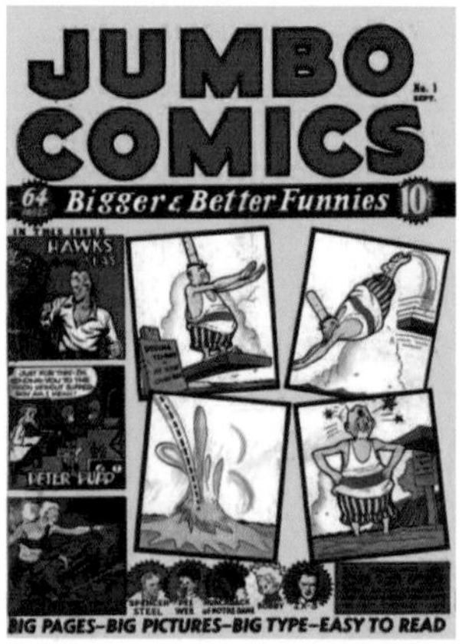
JUMBO COMICS
Bigger & Better Funnies
BIG PAGES-BIG PICTURES-BIG TYPE-EASY TO READ

Meskin had attended the Art Students League of New York in Manhattan and the Pratt Institute in Brooklyn, from which he graduated with a certificate in pictorial illustration in 1937. His love for anatomy, as well as the dramatic play of dark and light, made him a natural recruit for this new medium, and he soon found his way to the Eisner-Iger shop on 41st Street and Lexington Avenue, where he proved to be one of their fastest and most reliable artists.

Like Meskin, Will Eisner was the son of a furrier, one who grew up in the Bronx. He attended DeWitt Clinton High School along with Robert Kahn (who would soon change his name to Bob Kane) and Bill Finger, the co-creators of Batman. Others who worked for the shop at various times included Dick Briefer, Lou Fine, Kane, Bob Powell, Wallace Wood—and Jacob Kurtzberg, eventually to be known as Jack Kirby, who matched Meskin for speed and output. Originally freelance, the artists were put on salary so the shop could retain more control—although, as demand grew, artists were required to take work home as well.

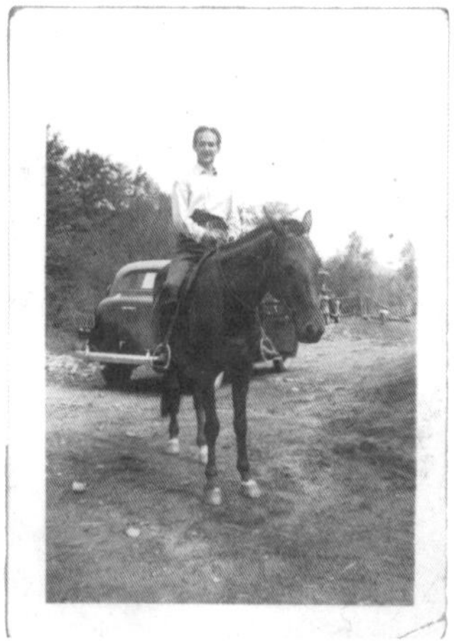

ABOVE: Meskin in the Catskill Mountains, New York, 1939. RIGHT: A Sheena page from *Jumbo Comics* #1. Meskin's myriad influences are apparent.

During his time at the Studio, Meskin was the first artist to draw the enduring character Sheena of the Jungle, which appeared in *Jumbo Comics* #1, published by Fiction House. A black-and-white tabloid (only the cover was in color) sized at 10 ½" x 14 ½", it premiered in September, 1938.

According to shop head Jerry Iger, "In addition to supplying comic strip material around the U.S., I had a business relationship with Editors Press Service. EPS represented American syndicated services overseas, and was interested in the features I was publishing. At that time, I was supplying strips for a magazine called *Wags*. This was a black-and-white tabloid that enjoyed a large European circulation, and was handled by EPS.

"Eduardo Cardenas, who was in charge of the EPS publication (and who later became the Foreign Editor for *Reader's Digest*), called me in to plan some new features for *Wags*. He mentioned the popularity of Tarzan, and asked me whether I could do a 'knock-off' for his magazine. I replied that my shop was known for its original material, and that I didn't like the idea of doing a male jungle hero. 'Why couldn't we have a jungle heroine?' I asked Eduardo. He replied that it sounded OK to him, but what would I call it? Thinking back—it's strange to remember all the random ideas that used to go into introducing new characters—for some reason, my mind wandered to early days in New York,

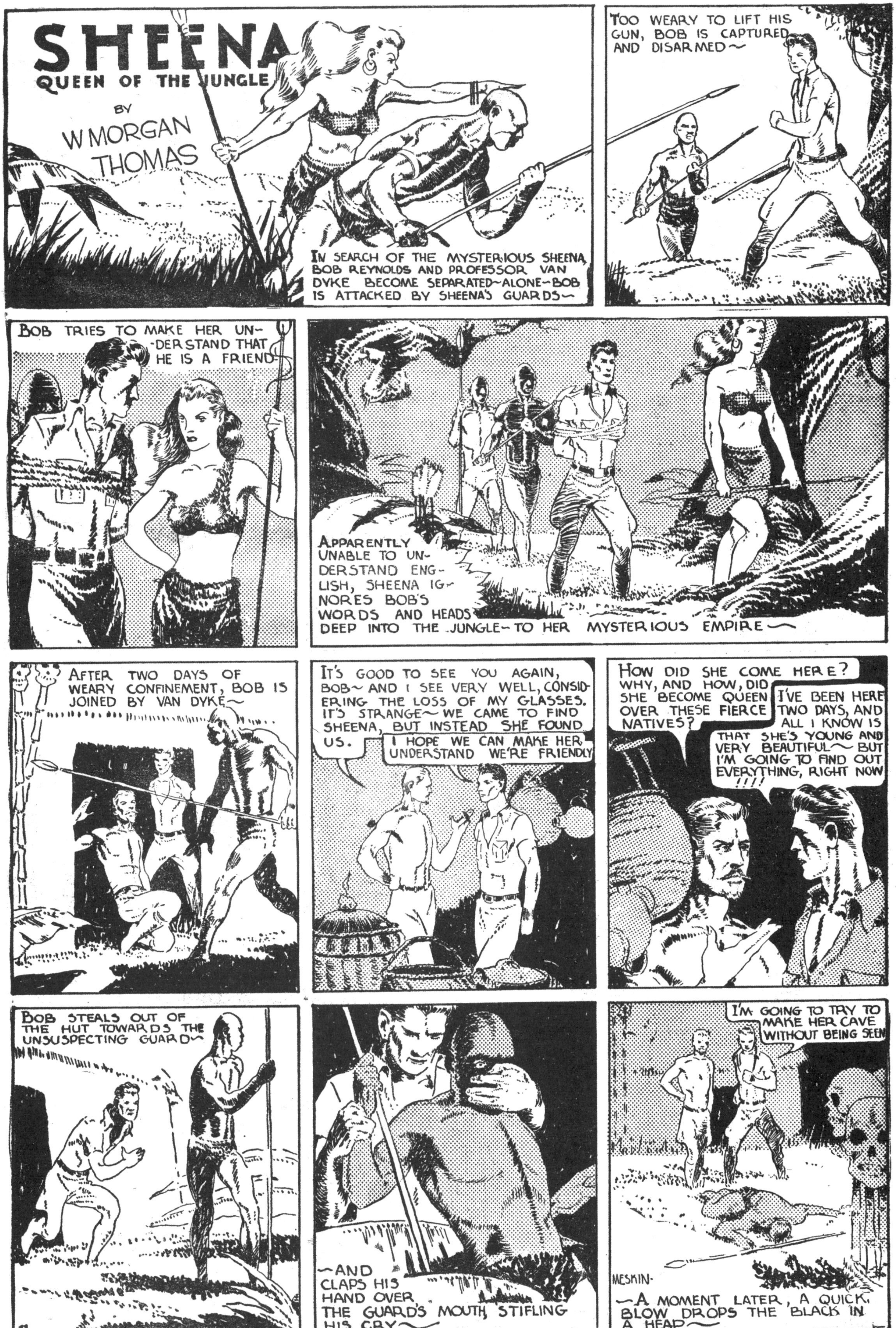
SHEENA
QUEEN OF THE JUNGLE
BY
W MORGAN THOMAS
IN SEARCH OF THE MYSTERIOUS SHEENA, BOB REYNOLDS AND PROFESSOR VAN DYKE BECOME SEPARATED~ALONE~BOB IS ATTACKED BY SHEENA'S GUARDS~
TOO WEARY TO LIFT HIS GUN, BOB IS CAPTURED AND DISARMED~
BOB TRIES TO MAKE HER UN-DERSTAND THAT HE IS A FRIEND~
APPARENTLY UNABLE TO UNDERSTAND ENGLISH, SHEENA IGNORES BOB'S WORDS AND HEADS DEEP INTO THE JUNGLE~TO HER MYSTERIOUS EMPIRE~
AFTER TWO DAYS OF WEARY CONFINEMENT, BOB IS JOINED BY VAN DYKE~
IT'S GOOD TO SEE YOU AGAIN, BOB~ AND I SEE VERY WELL, CONSIDERING THE LOSS OF MY GLASSES. IT'S STRANGE~ WE CAME TO FIND SHEENA, BUT INSTEAD SHE FOUND US.
I HOPE WE CAN MAKE HER UNDERSTAND WE'RE FRIENDLY
HOW DID SHE COME HERE? WHY, AND HOW, DID SHE BECOME QUEEN OVER THESE FIERCE NATIVES?
I'VE BEEN HERE TWO DAYS, AND ALL I KNOW IS THAT SHE'S YOUNG AND VERY BEAUTIFUL~ BUT I'M GOING TO FIND OUT EVERYTHING, RIGHT NOW!!!
BOB STEALS OUT OF THE HUT TOWARDS THE UNSUSPECTING GUARD~
~AND CLAPS HIS HAND OVER THE GUARD'S MOUTH, STIFLING HIS CRY~
I'M GOING TO TRY TO MAKE HER CAVE WITHOUT BEING SEEN
MESKIN
~A MOMENT LATER, A QUICK BLOW DROPS THE BLACK IN A HEAP~

when Jewish people were sometimes called 'Sheenies' as an insult, and I piped up, 'Why don't we call her "Sheena"?' Eduardo didn't ask how I thought that one up, and I didn't offer to tell him, but the name had a nice ring to it, and it stuck. Once we had agreed that the new character's name would be Sheena, Eduardo asked me to go back to my studio and bring him some sample drawings. I chose Mort Meskin to do the first drawings. Mort was one of the freelance artists I relied on. He mostly did illustrations, and this project offered him his first opportunity to sign his name to a published work."[1] While still in it formative stages, Meskin's work on *Sheena* already shows his storytelling ability and unique approach.

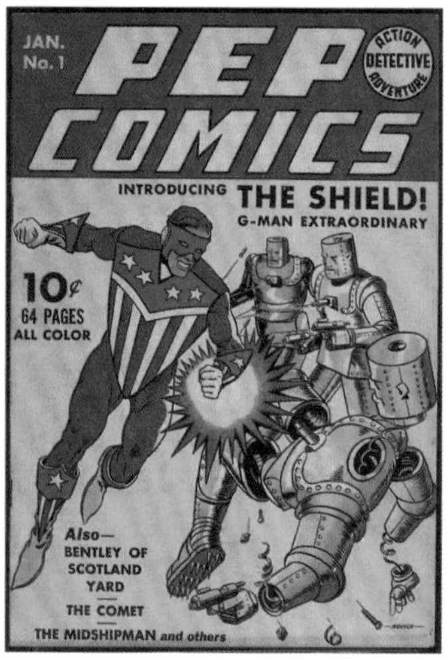
JAN.
No. 1
PEP COMICS
ACTION DETECTIVE ADVENTURE
INTRODUCING THE SHIELD!
G-MAN EXTRAORDINARY
10¢
64 PAGES
ALL COLOR
Also—
BENTLEY OF SCOTLAND YARD
THE COMET
THE MIDSHIPMAN and others

In late 1939, Meskin moved on to Chesler Studios on 28th Street and Fifth Avenue in Manhattan, where he worked on myriad titles such as *Dick Storm*, *Mr. Satan*, *The Press Guardian*, *The Shield*, and *Wizard*, as part of complete packages resold to emerging comic publishers such as Centaur, Fawcett, Quality, and MLJ, later to become Archie Comics. Artists were paid approximately $30 per week as salaried employees, good money at the time. The number of artists varied, between a half dozen and a dozen, sometimes more, and Meskin proved to be one of the most prolific.

ABOVE: *Pep Comics* #1, published by MLJ. BELOW: *Ty-Gor, Son of the Tiger*. RIGHT: *The Press Guardian*, in *Pep Comics*, art by Mort Meskin. OVERLEAF: *Captain Valor*; *Lee Sampson, Midshipman*, *Pep Comics*, art by Mort Meskin.

At Chesler, unlike at Eisner-Iger, the artists would often ink their own work, working from a script, and Meskin turned out to be an adept inker as well. His approach differed from the other artists, who would begin by sketching roughly in pencil. Instead, he would turn either the graphic or non-photo blue pencil sideways and cover the entire board with a tone. He would then take an eraser and begin to etch out shapes, exposing the white of the board. In this manner he would compose the entire page, rather than creating panel-by-panel breakdowns. Only then would he turn the pencil around and begin to draw each panel. Meskin's chiaroscuro approach was then accented with India ink. Conversely, he would occasionally begin directly with India ink, without penciling first.

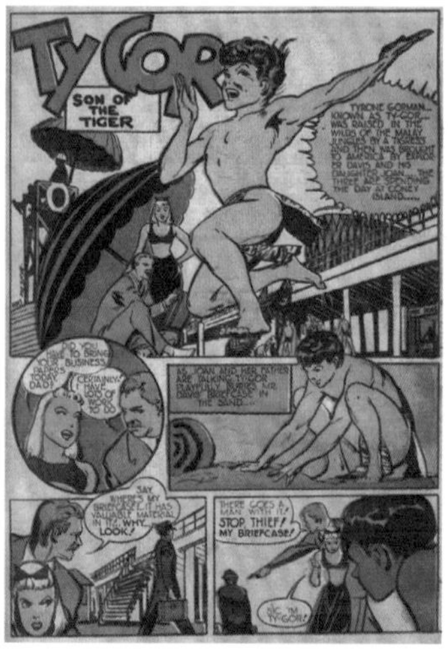
TY GOR
SON OF THE TIGER

Other artists who worked at Chesler included such notables as Charlie Biro, Jack and Otto Binder, Jack Cole, Creig Flessel, Tom Gill, Al Plastino, Mac Raboy, and Leonard Starr. The shop would produce whatever genre was demanded of them—adventure, funny-animal, humor, superhero, western—to generate a 64-page comic that sold for a dime.

Meskin, like many of the others, left Chesler to go work for MLJ.

THE PRESS GUARDIAN

EVEN THE PUBLISHER OF THE DAILY EXPRESS DOESN'T KNOW THAT HIS EFFETE SON, PERRY CHASE, SECRETLY IS THE DAUNTLESS PRESS GUARDIAN, FOE OF ALL ENEMIES OF THE PRESS

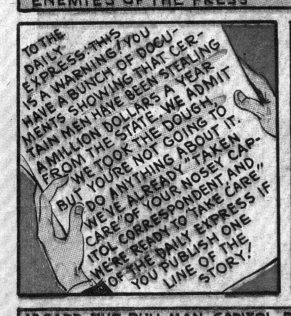

TO THE DAILY EXPRESS: THIS IS A WARNING! YOU HAVE A BUNCH OF DOCUMENTS SHOWING THAT CERTAIN MEN HAVE BEEN STEALING A MILLION DOLLARS A YEAR FROM THE STATE. WE ADMIT WE TOOK THE DOUGH, BUT YOU'RE NOT GOING TO DO ANYTHING ABOUT IT. WE'VE ALREADY "TAKEN CARE" OF YOUR NOSEY CAPITOL CORRESPONDENT AND WE'RE READY TO "TAKE CARE" OF THE DAILY EXPRESS IF YOU PUBLISH ONE LINE OF THE STORY!

SEND ME TO THE CAPITOL, DAD. I'D LIKE TO UNCOVER THE ONE MAN OUR DOCUMENTS DIDN'T NAME—THE TOP MAN.

IT MIGHT BE A GOOD IDEA. PERRY IS SO SIMPLE THE CROOKS WOULD IGNORE HIM!

IT'S AGAINST MY JUDGEMENT, BUT GO AHEAD!

A NEW TASK FOR THE PRESS GUARDIAN!

ABOARD THE PULLMAN, CAPITOL BOUND!

WE KNOW THE DAILY EXPRESS SENT YOU— MIND YOUR OWN BUSINESS AT THE CAPITOL, OR ELSE......

OR ELSE WHAT?

TAKE YOUR HANDS OFF ME WISE GUY, UNLESS YOU WANNA GET HURT!

YOU MEAN I MIGHT GET HURT, LIKE THIS?

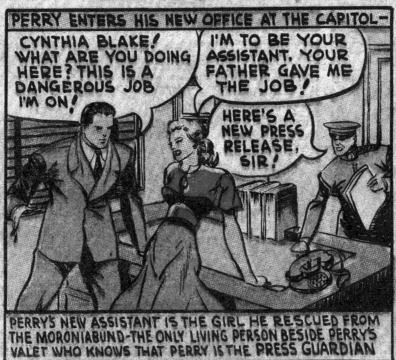

PERRY ENTERS HIS NEW OFFICE AT THE CAPITOL—

CYNTHIA BLAKE! WHAT ARE YOU DOING HERE? THIS IS A DANGEROUS JOB I'M ON!

I'M TO BE YOUR ASSISTANT. YOUR FATHER GAVE ME THE JOB!

HERE'S A NEW PRESS RELEASE, SIR!

PERRY'S NEW ASSISTANT IS THE GIRL HE RESCUED FROM THE MORONIABUND-THE ONLY LIVING PERSON BESIDE PERRY'S VALET WHO KNOWS THAT PERRY IS THE PRESS GUARDIAN

THE EXPRESS AIN'T LAID OFF LIKE YOU TOLD 'EM TO.— THEY GOT A NEW MAN HERE!

SPIES WATCH PERRY EVERY MINUTE. CAN HE OUTWIT THEM?

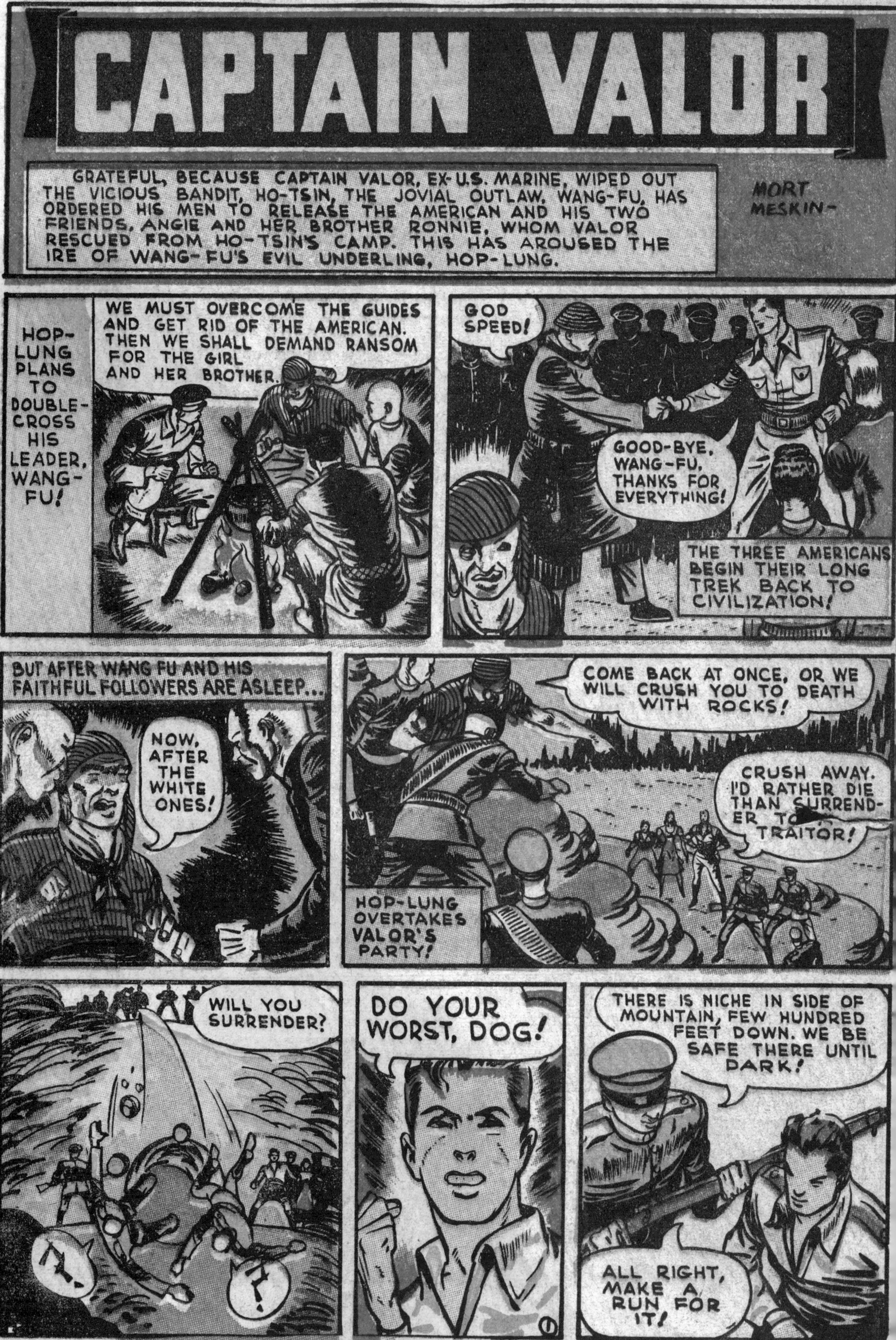
CAPTAIN VALOR
GRATEFUL, BECAUSE CAPTAIN VALOR, EX-U.S. MARINE, WIPED OUT THE VICIOUS BANDIT, HO-TSIN, THE JOVIAL OUTLAW, WANG-FU, HAS ORDERED HIS MEN TO RELEASE THE AMERICAN AND HIS TWO FRIENDS, ANGIE AND HER BROTHER RONNIE, WHOM VALOR RESCUED FROM HO-TSIN'S CAMP. THIS HAS AROUSED THE IRE OF WANG-FU'S EVIL UNDERLING, HOP-LUNG.
MORT MESKIN-
HOP-LUNG PLANS TO DOUBLE-CROSS HIS LEADER, WANG-FU!
WE MUST OVERCOME THE GUIDES AND GET RID OF THE AMERICAN. THEN WE SHALL DEMAND RANSOM FOR THE GIRL AND HER BROTHER.
GOD SPEED!
GOOD-BYE, WANG-FU, THANKS FOR EVERYTHING!
THE THREE AMERICANS BEGIN THEIR LONG TREK BACK TO CIVILIZATION!
BUT AFTER WANG FU AND HIS FAITHFUL FOLLOWERS ARE ASLEEP...
NOW, AFTER THE WHITE ONES!
COME BACK AT ONCE, OR WE WILL CRUSH YOU TO DEATH WITH ROCKS!
CRUSH AWAY. I'D RATHER DIE THAN SURRENDER TO TRAITOR!
HOP-LUNG OVERTAKES VALOR'S PARTY!
WILL YOU SURRENDER?
DO YOUR WORST, DOG!
THERE IS NICHE IN SIDE OF MOUNTAIN, FEW HUNDRED FEET DOWN. WE BE SAFE THERE UNTIL DARK!
ALL RIGHT, MAKE A RUN FOR IT!
1

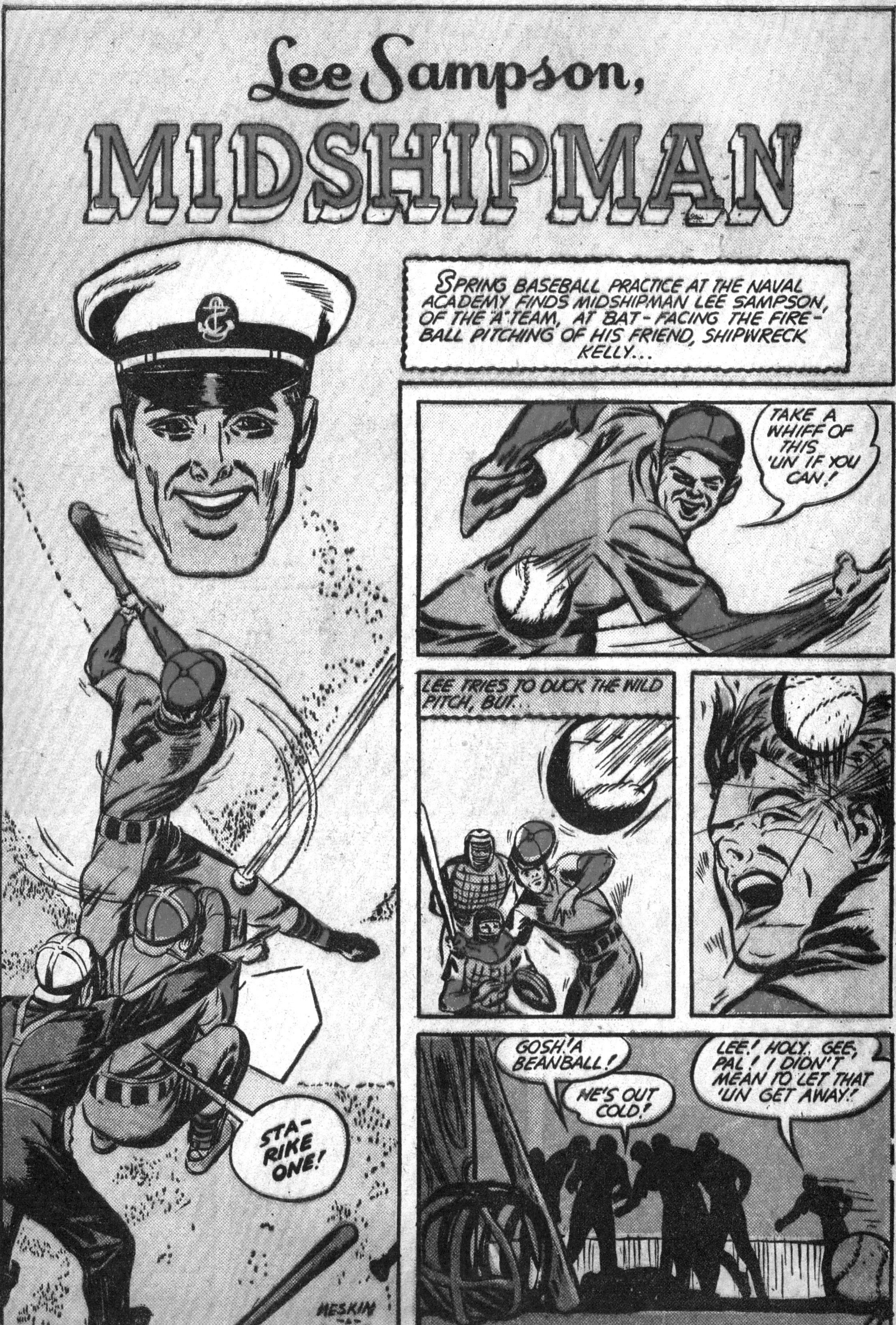
Lee Sampson,
MIDSHIPMAN
SPRING BASEBALL PRACTICE AT THE NAVAL ACADEMY FINDS MIDSHIPMAN LEE SAMPSON, OF THE "A" TEAM, AT BAT - FACING THE FIRE-BALL PITCHING OF HIS FRIEND, SHIPWRECK KELLY...
TAKE A WHIFF OF THIS 'UN IF YOU CAN!
STA-RIKE ONE!
MESKIN - BLAIR
LEE TRIES TO DUCK THE WILD PITCH, BUT...
GOSH! A BEANBALL!
HE'S OUT COLD!
LEE! HOLY GEE, PAL! I DIDN'T MEAN TO LET THAT 'UN GET AWAY!

There he worked on such features as *Bob Phantom*, *Doc Strong*, *Hercules*, and *Ty-Gor, Son of the Tiger*.

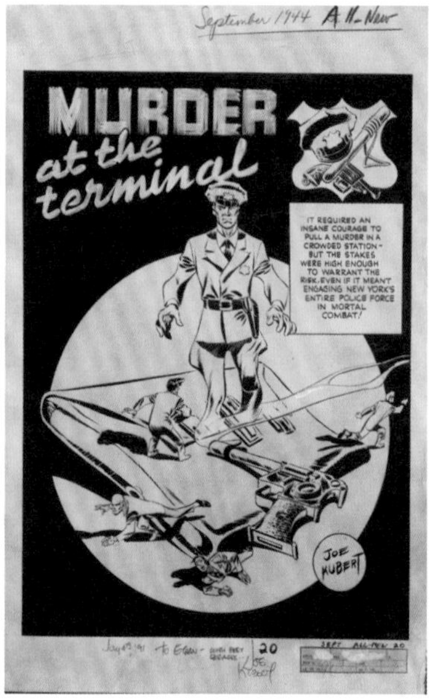
September 1944 All-New
MURDER
at the terminal
IT REQUIRED AN INSANE COURAGE TO PULL A MURDER IN A CROWDED STATION - BUT THE STAKES WERE HIGH ENOUGH TO WARRANT THE RISK, EVEN IF IT MEANT ENGAGING NEW YORK'S ENTIRE POLICE FORCE IN MORTAL COMBAT!
JOE KUBERT
20

A teenage Joe Kubert shows Meskin's influence in this splash page from *All-New Comics*, 1944. (Collection of Ethan Roberts.)

These comics soon caught the eye of young Joe Kubert, from Brooklyn, who made the pilgrimage by subway to MLJ after school one day. "I was perhaps twelve. I lived in East New York, in Brooklyn, and I had a friend of mine who went to Junior High School with me, one of his relatives he said was a comic book publisher. And the guy that I went to school with knew that I was doing muscle guy cartoons since I was a kid. He said 'Joe, you do all this stuff all the time, why don't you go up and get a job, you're doing all this funny comic book stuff, you could do that.' That happened to be MLJ, before Archie Comics. And I found out where their office was, in downtown New York, around Chambers Street and Canal. And I packed my stuff up, sketches and so on that I did with pencil or whatever, wrapped it up in a newspaper, and I took the subway from Brooklyn into Manhattan, which was a nickel at the time, I could just swing that, and I went up and jeez, the guys that were there were terrific. I remember what the office looked like. There was a banister that separated the entranceway, inside the office, from where the artists were working, there was a row of art desks. I had never seen anything like that, it was brand new to me. One of the guys up there was Mort. Mort was sitting at a table, Charlie Biro was up there at the time, Plastino, a whole bunch of guys were there. I never had met them or knew them, or knew anything about them. They allowed me to come into the bullpen area and watch the guys work. It was the first time I saw the size of the paper, the kind of paper that was being used, the fact that it was being inked, I had no knowledge of that at all.

"Mort was shy, I think he was even more shy then he was later on in life, he was kind of laid back. The drawings that he was doing just knocked me out. What really impressed me more than anything else was his ability to do foreshortening. You must understand, for anyone starting to draw, you can do a stick figure, you can do them straight up and down, but when you take a figure and have a guy jumping out at you, and he has one leg in front of another, in a foreshorten positioned, that is a *difficult* thing for a novice artist to do, that was an impossibility for me. Those things just amazed me, and I loved the stuff that Mort was doing.

"A little bit of an aside: Harry Shorten was a writer, it was Shorten, there was an editor up there, and he allowed me to come in and see the guys working and Mort was sitting in a corner, next to the window looking over Canal Street. I said, 'Gee, I love the work you are doing' and he said, 'You know, kid, why don't you go over and tell the editor.' That's what he told me. I went over and tried to do it as innocuously as possible and said, 'Gee, I love that guy's work.' The editor shouted out, 'Mort, thanks for sending the kid over.' So that was my first meeting with Mort and the guys, all of them. I don't remember precisely who it was, but they gave me brushes to work with, they gave me the kind of paper to use, jeez, they were so kind to me, this obnoxious kid that came from no place. That was the opening, that was my beginning. I started my work within a year or so of that time."[2]

Following that initial meeting Kubert would head out to the studio after school, arriving at around 3:30 to hesitantly look over the artists' shoulders until departing at 5:30 to return home. He would practice his art using discarded scripts, and received feedback from the artists.

Jerry Robinson was born in Trenton, New Jersey and like Mort, was the son of a Russian immigrant father and a mother from New York City. He originally set out to become a journalist, and at age 17 was enrolled in Columbia University School of Journalism. He never made it. While he was staying at a Catskill resort the previous summer, his hand-illustrated tennis jacket caught the eye of fellow player Bob Kane, who had just begun producing *Batman* with Bill Finger. Already needing assistance, Kane hired Robinson on the spot.

After a year or so of working on *Batman*, Robinson attended a party in his hometown of Trenton. "All my friends still there, I was 18 or 19 at this time and had gone to Columbia to study journalism, I was kind of a local celebrity going back, drawing Batman and had an article in the home town paper. I went to a New Year's Eve party at a friend's house, New Year's 1940. One of the friends I knew said there was a young artist that is so anxious to meet you, and I've invited him to the party, and my friend said let me introduce you. So he was very excited about meeting me and getting some tips on how to break into cartooning. We got along famously right from the go. His name was Bernie Klein. I took an immediate liking to him. Very intelligent, very warm, and nice, a refreshing personality. A tough guy, but very endearing, a sweet guy. He said 'I don't know how to break into the business.' So I told him what to do, how to draw up the sample pages, the size, everything I could tell him. I said, 'As soon as you are ready come to New York call me and I'll introduce you around.' So I promptly went back to New York and I had forgotten all about him, maybe its wasn't for a few weeks, maybe a few months later, I was working a couple of months and all of a sudden I got a call, 'Hello?' 'I'm in the city.' I said, 'Bernie?' He said, 'You remember your friend?' I said, 'Oh yes. Come on over. We'll have some lunch or dinner.' So we became very best friends. He had gotten a job at MLJ, he didn't want to put me out and

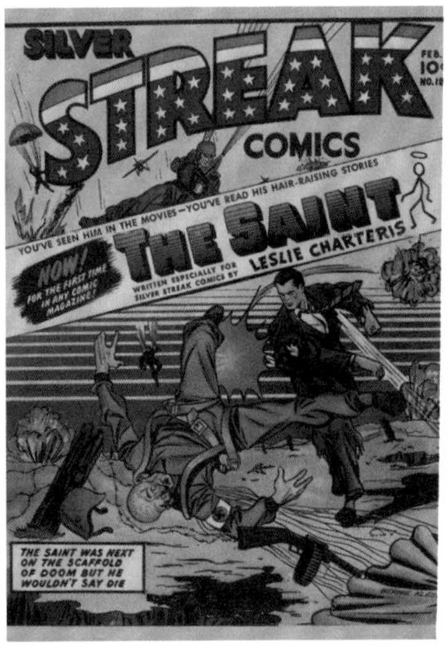
SILVER
STREAK
COMICS
FEB.
10¢
YOU'VE SEEN HIM IN THE MOVIES—YOU'VE READ HIS HAIR-RAISING STORIES
NOW! FOR THE FIRST TIME IN ANY COMIC MAGAZINE!
THE SAINT
WRITTEN ESPECIALLY FOR SILVER STREAK COMICS BY
LESLIE CHARTERIS
THE SAINT WAS NEXT ON THE SCAFFOLD OF DOOM BUT HE WOULDN'T SAY DIE

Silver Streak #18, cover art by Bernie Klein, 1942.

wanted to make it on his own. His art was so good that he was hired right away. It was very shortly after that I went down to see him at MLJ, and he was there. So there was Charlie Biro, Bob Wood, Irv Novick, Mort Meskin, and Bernie Klein, they were on staff, so that's when I met Mort.[3]

"In a very short time Mort and Bernie and I decided to get an apartment together. I was sharing an apartment with another artist in the West 70s and Bernie was living in a real hole in the wall that he had just managed to get, he was getting practically nothing from MLJ. So I invited him to join us. We had a one-bedroom apartment that had a sleeping couch in the living room and two beds in the bedroom. The other fellow drifted off somewhere and it was just Bernie and I. And then Mort joined us in the apartment because he was living in some hole somewhere. Mort, Bernie, and I became good friends at the time, that was in early 1942."[4]

The three were soon sharing another apartment on 33rd Street between Second and Third Avenues. "We used to kid ourselves that we lived on turdy turd and turd. It was also a one-bedroom apartment, it was nicer, convenient, and completely furnished, with maid service, as some apartments had in those days, and it was $75 a month.

"We went to Socialist/Communist meetings," continued Robinson, "and local bars and argued with anybody who was to the right of us. The three of us were very, very close. Bernie went off and then Mort and I shared the apartment for many years. He was an incredible guy; funny thing, he was a good singer. I remember one time Mort bought a recording machine, very primitive, and we would sing and record our voices. That was a phase we went through. And we looked at art, films, like anybody else would when there was something interesting. He had a passion for fine art. And then Mort got his own apartment, very nearby."[5]

BELOW: Meskin super-hero pencil sketches.

DC COMICS

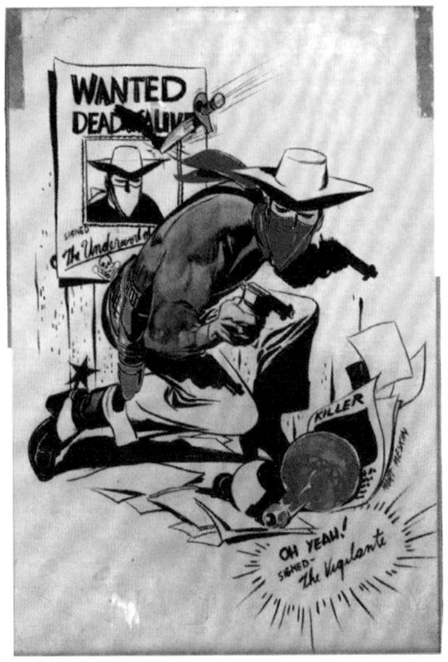
WANTED
OH YEAH!
SIGNED-
The Vigilante
KILLER

"I brought Bernie up to DC, to [editor] Whitney Ellsworth," Robinson continued, "and he was hired, and then I brought Mort up to DC."[6] Soon Meskin was working alongside Robinson, while Bernie Klein chose to work at home. "It was a fantastic time, a unique group of artists who happened to land at DC's bullpen at the same time. I met Jack [Kirby] when I was 18. Jack was five years older. On one side of me was Joe Shuster, on the other Jack Kirby, Fred Ray, Mort Meskin. We were all side-by-side, learning from each other. We all benefited from that unique experience."[6]

The environment at 480 Lexington Avenue, right in mid-town, was a step up from both Eisner-Iger and Chesler. The offices opened into a waiting room adorned with a painting of Superman that reached the height of the cathedral ceiling. Although freelance, the artists found it convenient to work at the DC offices rather than rent a workspace. Meskin worked alongside Robinson, Joe Siegel, Mac Raboy, and they were soon joined by Jack Kirby after his partner Joe Simon left for the Coast Guard and the two gave up their studio space.

As noted by Robinson, Kirby and Meskin were a wonder to behold: two of the fastest and most prolific artists in the business. "Meskin was the more careful of the two," Robinson recalls.[7] According to DC editor Jack Schiff, "We once had a sort of race in the front office. We had a big artist's room. Jack [Kirby] and Mort Meskin were sitting next to each other and there was some copy we needed pretty quickly from both of them. Each of them turned out five pages of pencils. Beautifully. It was really something. After a while, people began to crowd around watching. And they would both go ahead undisturbed. Meskin was a more careful artist than Kirby..."[8] This friendly competition was short-lived, however, as Kirby was soon drafted into the army.

Over time, comics historians and fans have debated which way the influence flowed between Kirby and Meskin. Robinson has a different take: "They were both very well advanced in their styles, their storytelling, their theories about the comics. I knew both of their thinking, so I don't think either one influenced [the other] to a degree to change their style or change their vision, they were already advanced. We all picked up things from each other. Not to the extent that Mort and I did, because we worked so closely together."[9]

ABOVE LEFT: *Vigilante* character design sketch by Mort Meskin (collection of Ethan Roberts). OVERLEAF: *Vigilante* splash pages, *Action Comics* #47, 1942 (left), and 61 (right), inks by Charles Paris, 1943. SPREAD FOLLOWING: *Action Comics* #61. (© DC Comics. All Rights Reserved. Used with Permission).

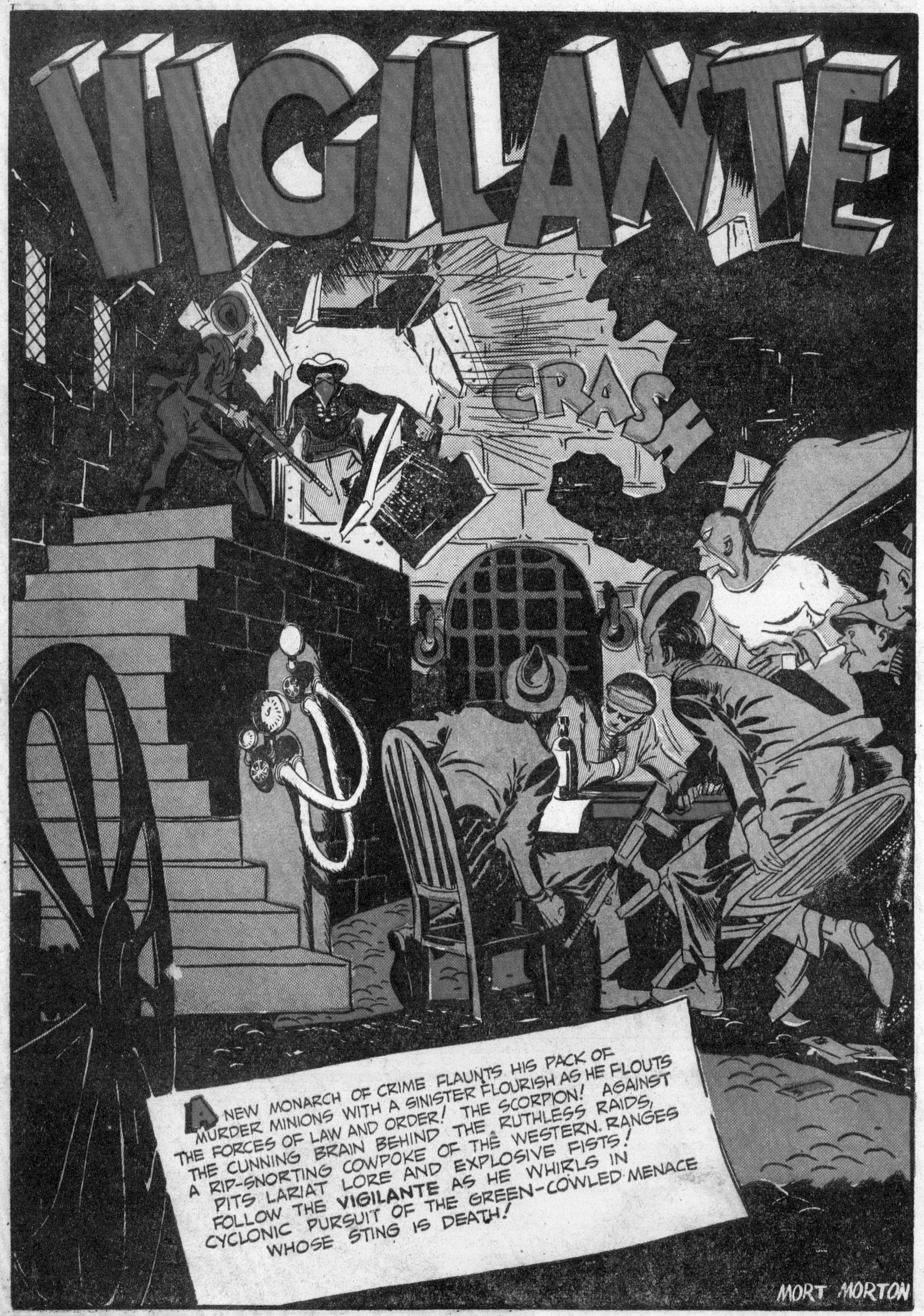
VIGILANTE
CRASH
A NEW MONARCH OF CRIME FLAUNTS HIS PACK OF MURDER MINIONS WITH A SINISTER FLOURISH AS HE FLOUTS THE FORCES OF LAW AND ORDER! THE SCORPION! AGAINST THE CUNNING BRAIN BEHIND THE RUTHLESS RAIDS, A RIP-SNORTING COWPOKE OF THE WESTERN RANGES PITS LARIAT LORE AND EXPLOSIVE FISTS! FOLLOW THE **VIGILANTE** AS HE WHIRLS IN CYCLONIC PURSUIT OF THE GREEN-COWLED MENACE WHOSE STING IS DEATH!
MORT MORTON

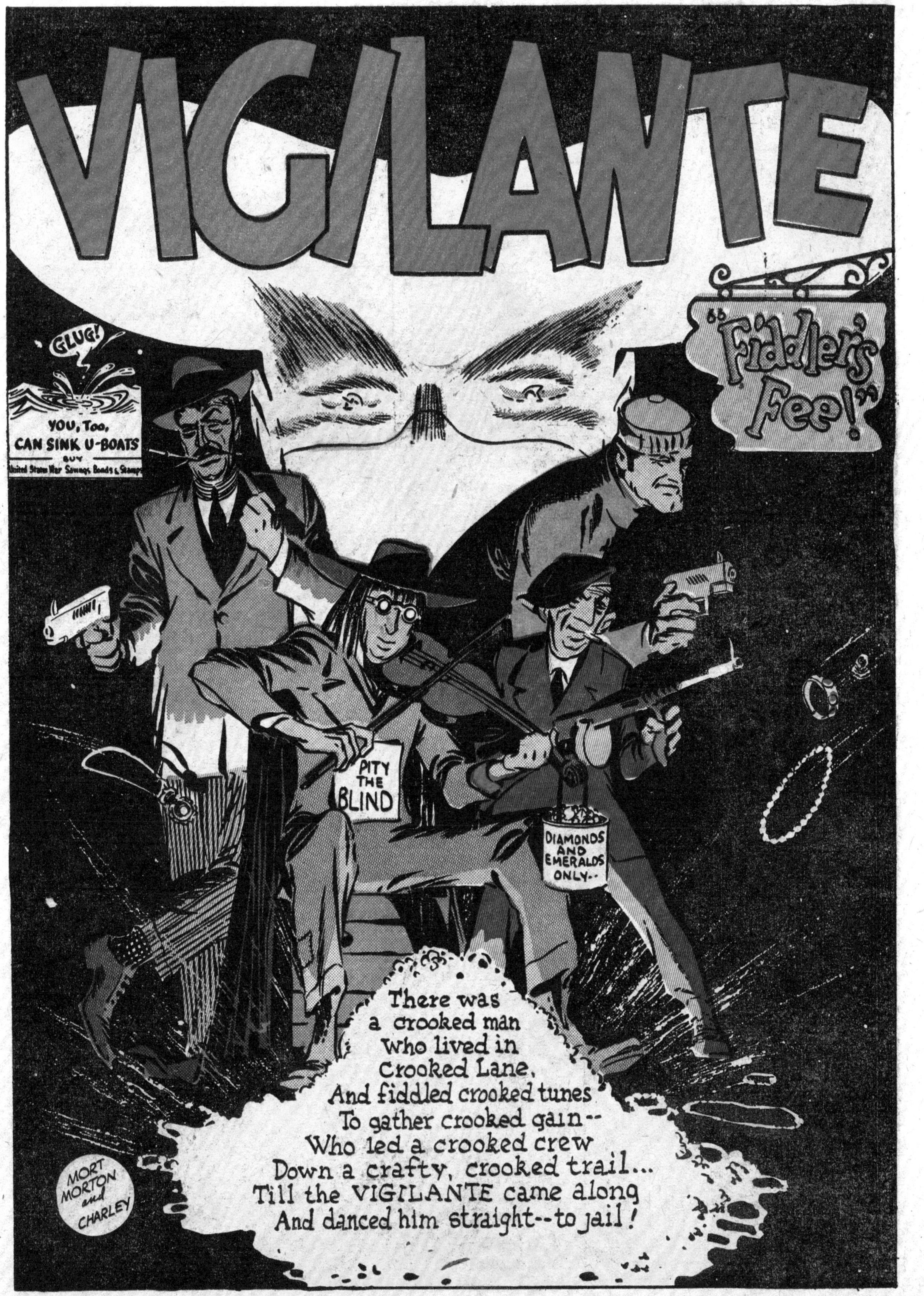
VIGILANTE
"Fiddler's Fee!"
GLUG!
YOU, Too, CAN SINK U-BOATS
BUY
United States War Savings Bonds & Stamps
PITY THE BLIND
DIAMONDS AND EMERALDS ONLY--
There was a crooked man
Who lived in Crooked Lane,
And fiddled crooked tunes
To gather crooked gain--
Who led a crooked crew
Down a crafty, crooked trail...
Till the VIGILANTE came along
And danced him straight--to jail!
MORT MORTON and CHARLEY

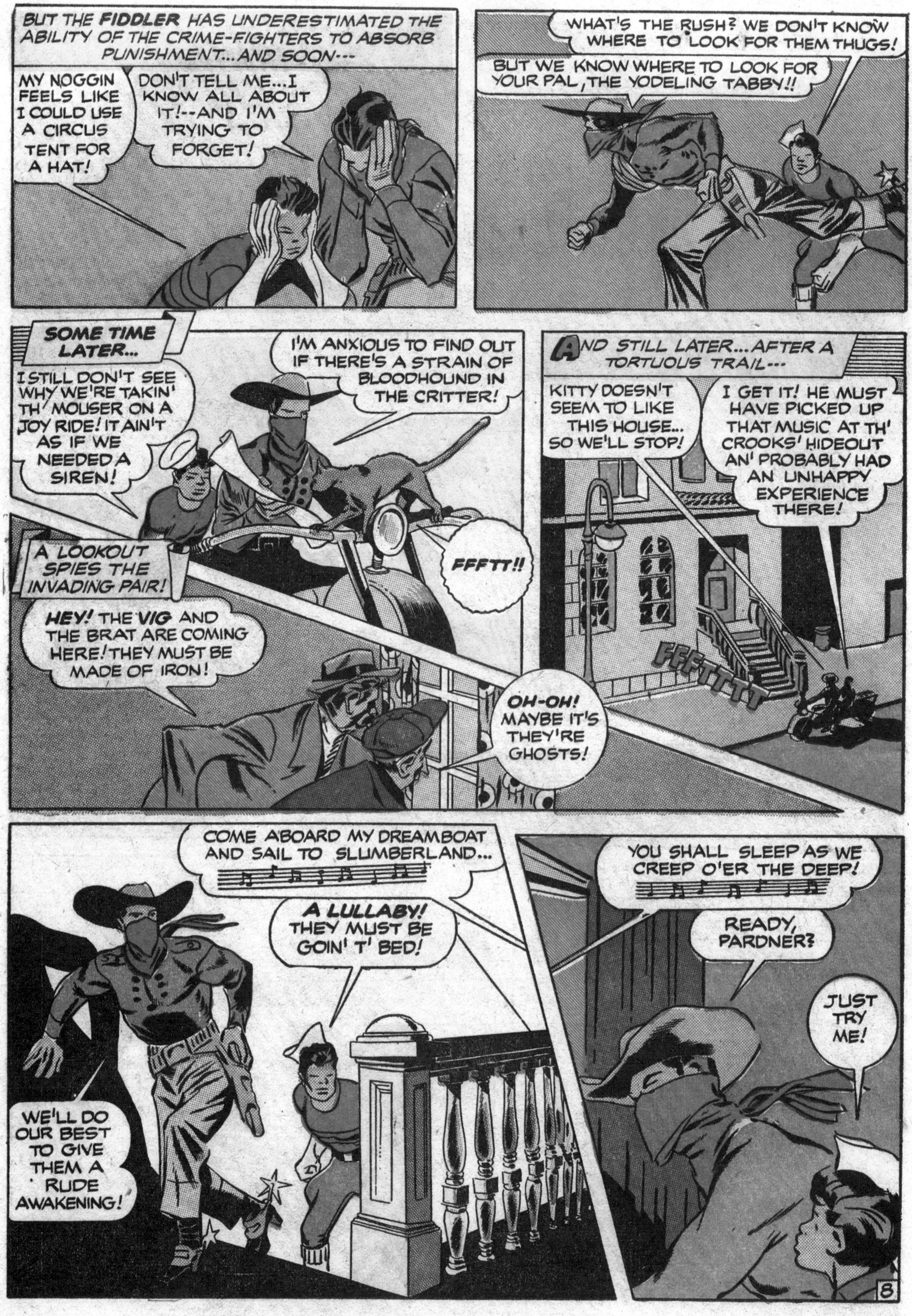
BUT THE FIDDLER HAS UNDERESTIMATED THE ABILITY OF THE CRIME-FIGHTERS TO ABSORB PUNISHMENT... AND SOON---
MY NOGGIN FEELS LIKE I COULD USE A CIRCUS TENT FOR A HAT!
DON'T TELL ME...I KNOW ALL ABOUT IT!--AND I'M TRYING TO FORGET!
WHAT'S THE RUSH? WE DON'T KNOW WHERE TO LOOK FOR THEM THUGS!
BUT WE KNOW WHERE TO LOOK FOR YOUR PAL, THE YODELING TABBY!!
SOME TIME LATER...
I STILL DON'T SEE WHY WE'RE TAKIN' TH' MOUSER ON A JOY RIDE! IT AIN'T AS IF WE NEEDED A SIREN!
I'M ANXIOUS TO FIND OUT IF THERE'S A STRAIN OF BLOODHOUND IN THE CRITTER!
FFFTT!!
A LOOKOUT SPIES THE INVADING PAIR!
HEY! THE VIG AND THE BRAT ARE COMING HERE! THEY MUST BE MADE OF IRON!
OH-OH! MAYBE IT'S THEY'RE GHOSTS!
AND STILL LATER... AFTER A TORTUOUS TRAIL---
KITTY DOESN'T SEEM TO LIKE THIS HOUSE... SO WE'LL STOP!
I GET IT! HE MUST HAVE PICKED UP THAT MUSIC AT TH' CROOKS' HIDEOUT AN' PROBABLY HAD AN UNHAPPY EXPERIENCE THERE!
FFFTTTTT
COME ABOARD MY DREAMBOAT AND SAIL TO SLUMBERLAND...
A LULLABY! THEY MUST BE GOIN' T' BED!
WE'LL DO OUR BEST TO GIVE THEM A RUDE AWAKENING!
YOU SHALL SLEEP AS WE CREEP O'ER THE DEEP!
READY, PARDNER?
JUST TRY ME!
8

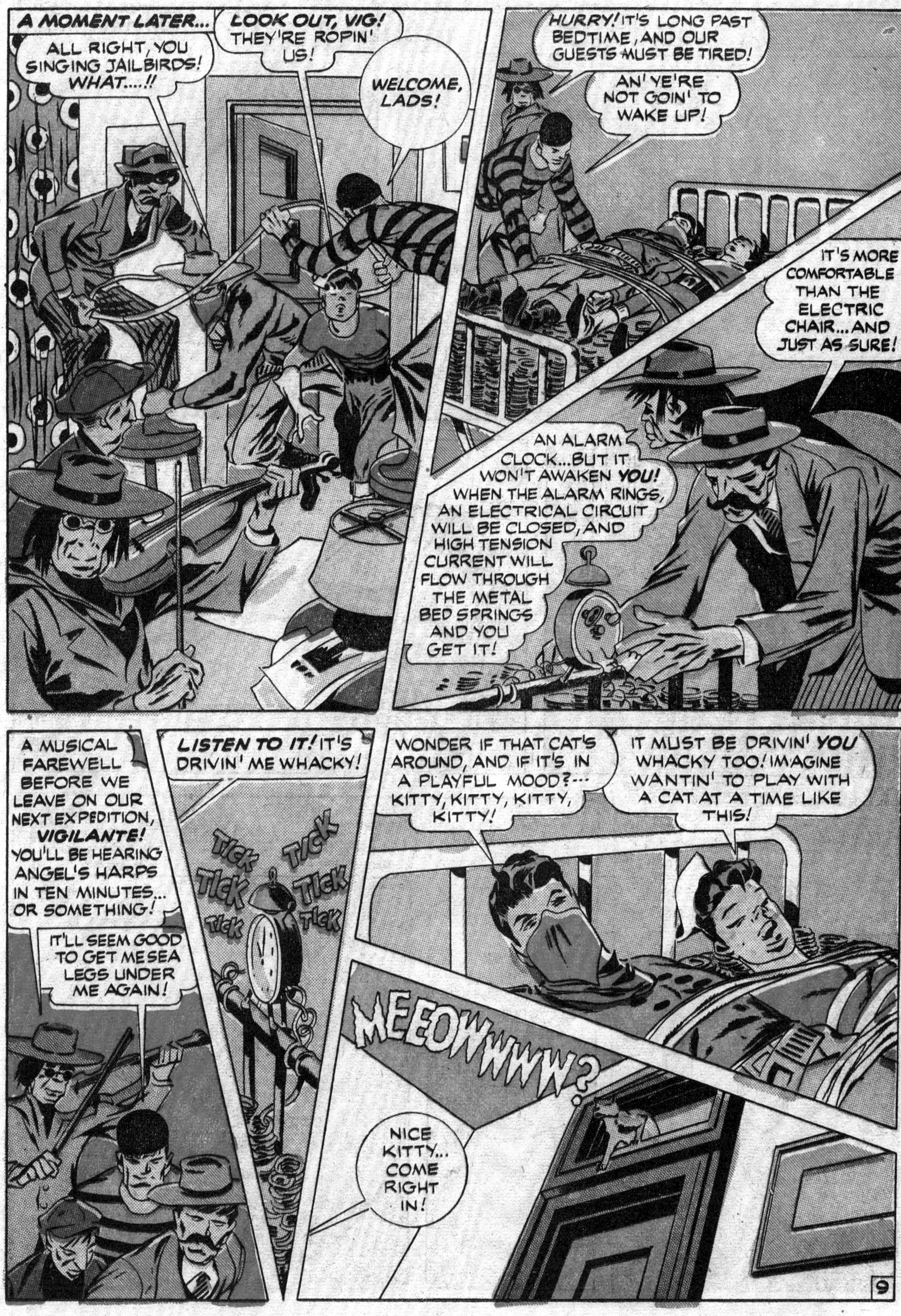

A MOMENT LATER...
ALL RIGHT, YOU SINGING JAILBIRDS! WHAT....!!
LOOK OUT, VIG! THEY'RE ROPIN' US!
WELCOME, LADS!
HURRY! IT'S LONG PAST BEDTIME, AND OUR GUESTS MUST BE TIRED!
AN' YE'RE NOT GOIN' TO WAKE UP!
IT'S MORE COMFORTABLE THAN THE ELECTRIC CHAIR...AND JUST AS SURE!
AN ALARM CLOCK...BUT IT WON'T AWAKEN YOU! WHEN THE ALARM RINGS, AN ELECTRICAL CIRCUIT WILL BE CLOSED, AND HIGH TENSION CURRENT WILL FLOW THROUGH THE METAL BED SPRINGS AND YOU GET IT!
A MUSICAL FAREWELL BEFORE WE LEAVE ON OUR NEXT EXPEDITION, VIGILANTE! YOU'LL BE HEARING ANGEL'S HARPS IN TEN MINUTES... OR SOMETHING!
IT'LL SEEM GOOD TO GET ME SEA LEGS UNDER ME AGAIN!
LISTEN TO IT! IT'S DRIVIN' ME WHACKY!
TICK TICK TICK TICK TICK TICK
WONDER IF THAT CAT'S AROUND, AND IF IT'S IN A PLAYFUL MOOD?... KITTY, KITTY, KITTY, KITTY!
IT MUST BE DRIVIN' YOU WHACKY TOO! IMAGINE WANTIN' TO PLAY WITH A CAT AT A TIME LIKE THIS!
MEEOWWWWW?
NICE KITTY... COME RIGHT IN!

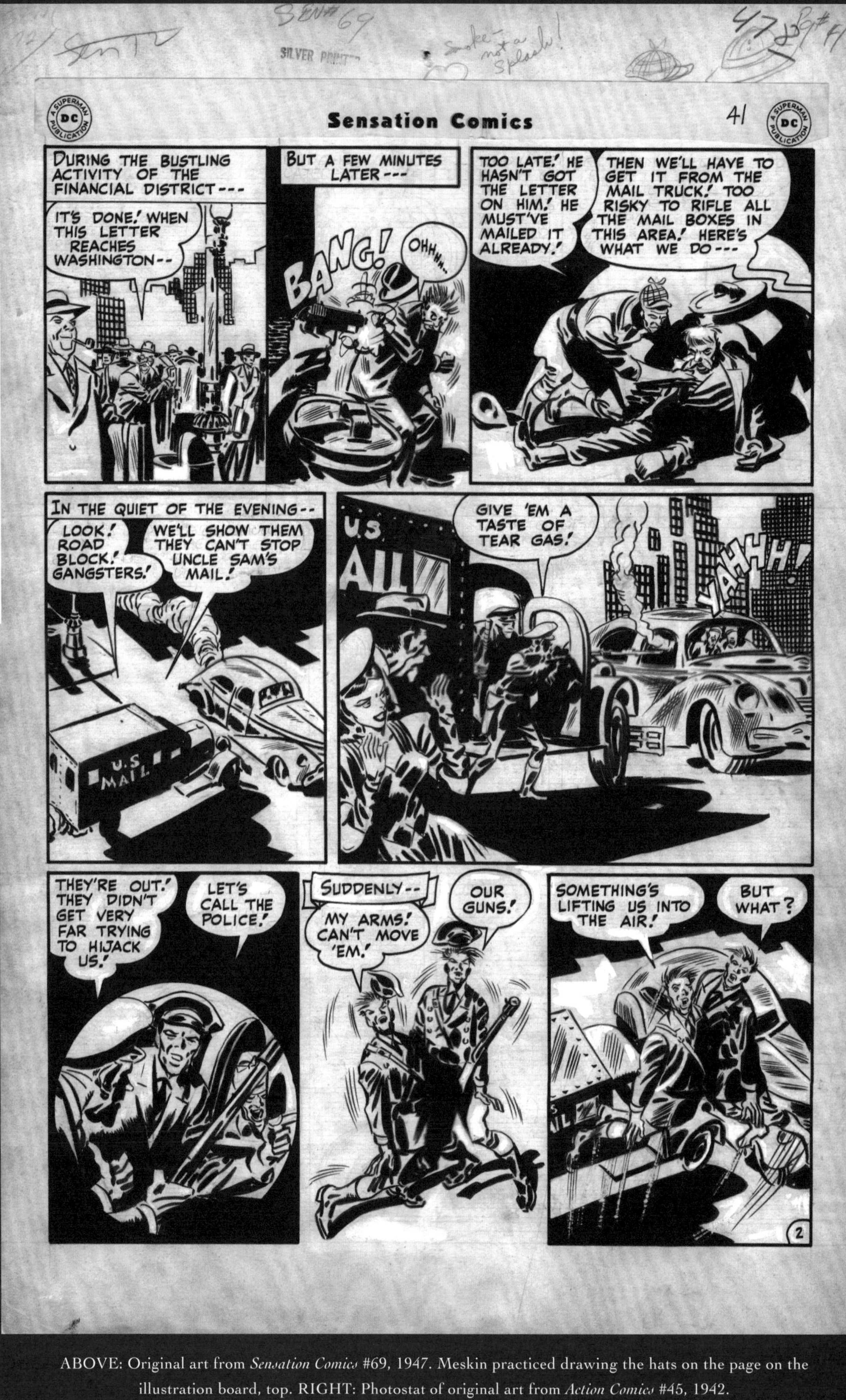
Sensation Comics
41
DURING THE BUSTLING ACTIVITY OF THE FINANCIAL DISTRICT---
IT'S DONE! WHEN THIS LETTER REACHES WASHINGTON--
BUT A FEW MINUTES LATER---
BANG!
OHHH...
TOO LATE! HE HASN'T GOT THE LETTER ON HIM! HE MUST'VE MAILED IT ALREADY!
THEN WE'LL HAVE TO GET IT FROM THE MAIL TRUCK! TOO RISKY TO RIFLE ALL THE MAIL BOXES IN THIS AREA! HERE'S WHAT WE DO---
IN THE QUIET OF THE EVENING--
LOOK! ROAD BLOCK! GANGSTERS!
WE'LL SHOW THEM THEY CAN'T STOP UNCLE SAM'S MAIL!
U.S. MAIL
GIVE 'EM A TASTE OF TEAR GAS!
YAHHH!
THEY'RE OUT! THEY DIDN'T GET VERY FAR TRYING TO HIJACK US!
LET'S CALL THE POLICE!
SUDDENLY--
MY ARMS! CAN'T MOVE 'EM!
OUR GUNS!
SOMETHING'S LIFTING US INTO THE AIR!
BUT WHAT?
2

ABOVE: Original art from *Sensation Comics* #69, 1947. Meskin practiced drawing the hats on the page on the illustration board, top. RIGHT: Photostat of original art from *Action Comics* #45, 1942.

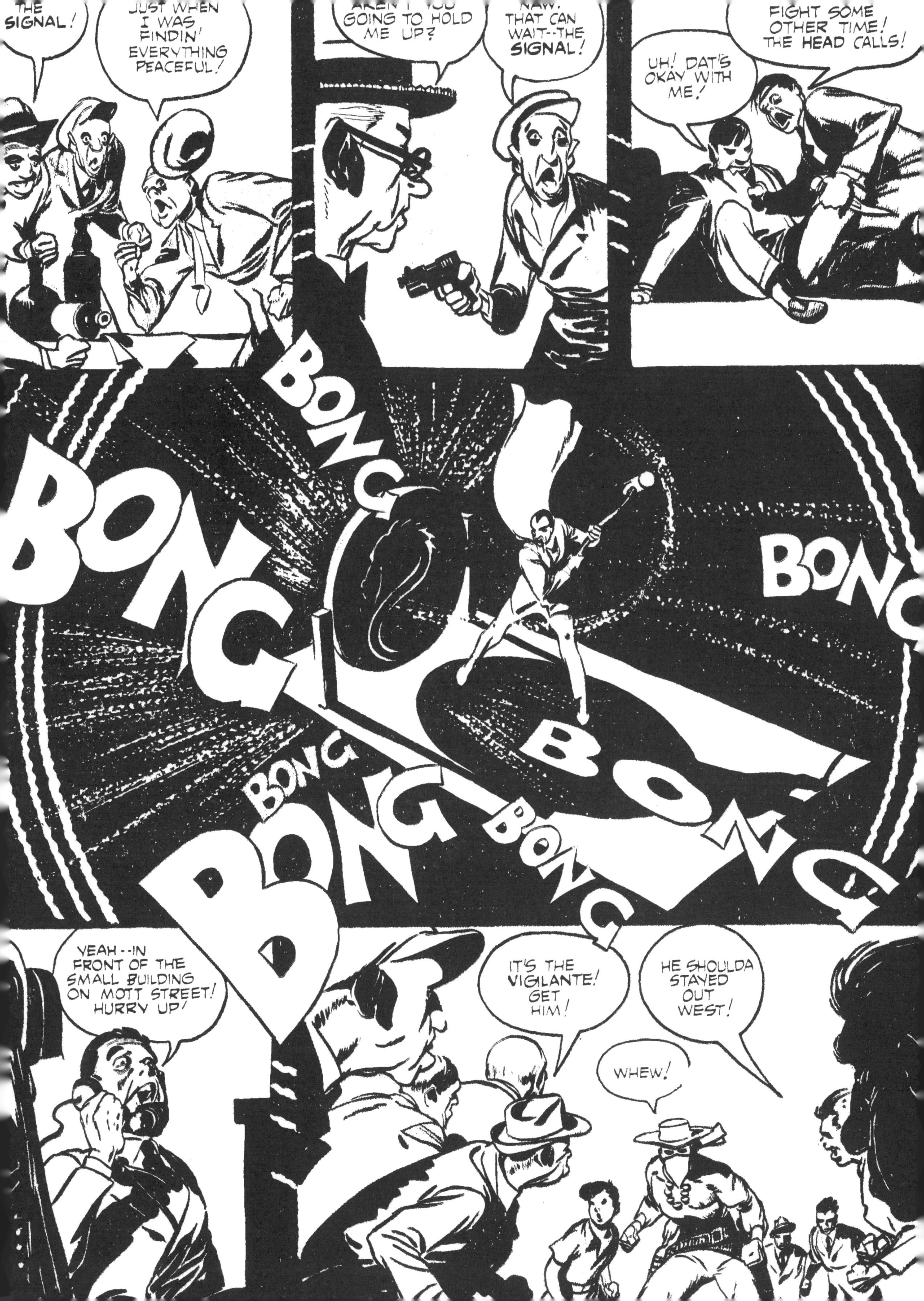

THE SIGNAL!
JUST WHEN I WAS FINDIN' EVERYTHING PEACEFUL!
GOING TO HOLD ME UP?
THAT CAN WAIT--THE SIGNAL!
FIGHT SOME OTHER TIME! THE HEAD CALLS!
UH! DAT'S OKAY WITH ME!
BONG
BONG
BONG
BONG
BONG
BONG
BONG
BONG
BONG
YEAH--IN FRONT OF THE SMALL BUILDING ON MOTT STREET! HURRY UP!
IT'S THE VIGILANTE! GET HIM!
HE SHOULDA STAYED OUT WEST!
WHEW!

In *Action Comics* #42, Meskin, with editor-writer Mort Weisinger, co-created the Western-garbed modern-day hero The Vigilante. (Meskin, who often signed his art, would playfully sign these collaborations "Mort Morton, Jr.") Soon afterwards, he created another feature, *Johnny Quick*, DC's second speedster after *The Flash*, for *More Fun Comics*. Through these features, Meskin established himself among his peers as a unique and dynamic storyteller, utilizing dramatic lighting, varying points of view, and deep space. His unique use of shadow and negative space as major design elements, and his arrangements of groups of figures along with the overall page design, greatly advanced the nascent art form. The good guys in these stories always smiled, the bad grimaced, as if inviting the reader to join in the fun.

"When [DC Comics] hired Mort Meskin to do *Vigilante*," Golden Age artist Gil Kane would later recall, "he had come over from MLJ and he was hired because some of the writers from MLJ recommended him and the first thing he did for them was Vigilante and it turned out to be a smash. He was a brilliant artist then, who hit like a ton of dynamite."[10]

"[Mort] was also one of the few artists in our time who studied art," Robinson adds; "he went to Pratt. And so he knew from an academic point of view what composition was, and anatomy, and drapery; the rest of us were faking it. I learned a lot about composing just watching him, and movement. I wanted to do things I wasn't ready to do, how to visualize something, I would say to Mort, 'How do you do this, what muscle is this?' And he would say, 'Work it out.' I would say, 'But Mort, I'm working it out. I can't work it,' and then I would watch him. And after some time I learned by doing. He was a genius of the medium, he was in full command of all the [elements], storytelling, composition, in command of the medium at the birth of it. Working with him was quite an education.

"He was a comics genius, he was a superior composer. I learned a lot about composition from Mort and the things that we did together. There are not too many who think about the composition today, and the flow of the page, from page to page. I tried to do that within my capabilities with *Batman*, but I think I did more later on. And I'm sure a lot of that was influenced by Mort. His ability to tell a story, which is in the final analysis what we're trying to do, tell a story interestingly. He could move around space and he knew how to use the space so well, white space, which is so important.[11]

"Mort was a thinking artist. He made it look very easy, but he was an intellectual in terms of his art. There was a purpose to everything."[12]

BELOW: Special small size coverless souvenir edition of *Action Comics* to publicize the release of the *Vigilante* movie serial, 1947. RIGHT: *Leading Comics* #5, Winter 1942-1943, cover art by Mort Meskin. (© DC Comics. All Rights Reserved. Used with Permission.)

FREE SOUVENIR EDITION
ACTION COMICS
IN HONOR OF Columbia's THRILLING NEW MOVIE SERIAL
"The VIGILANTE"

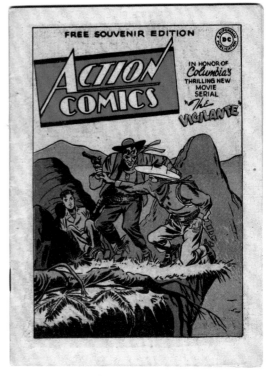

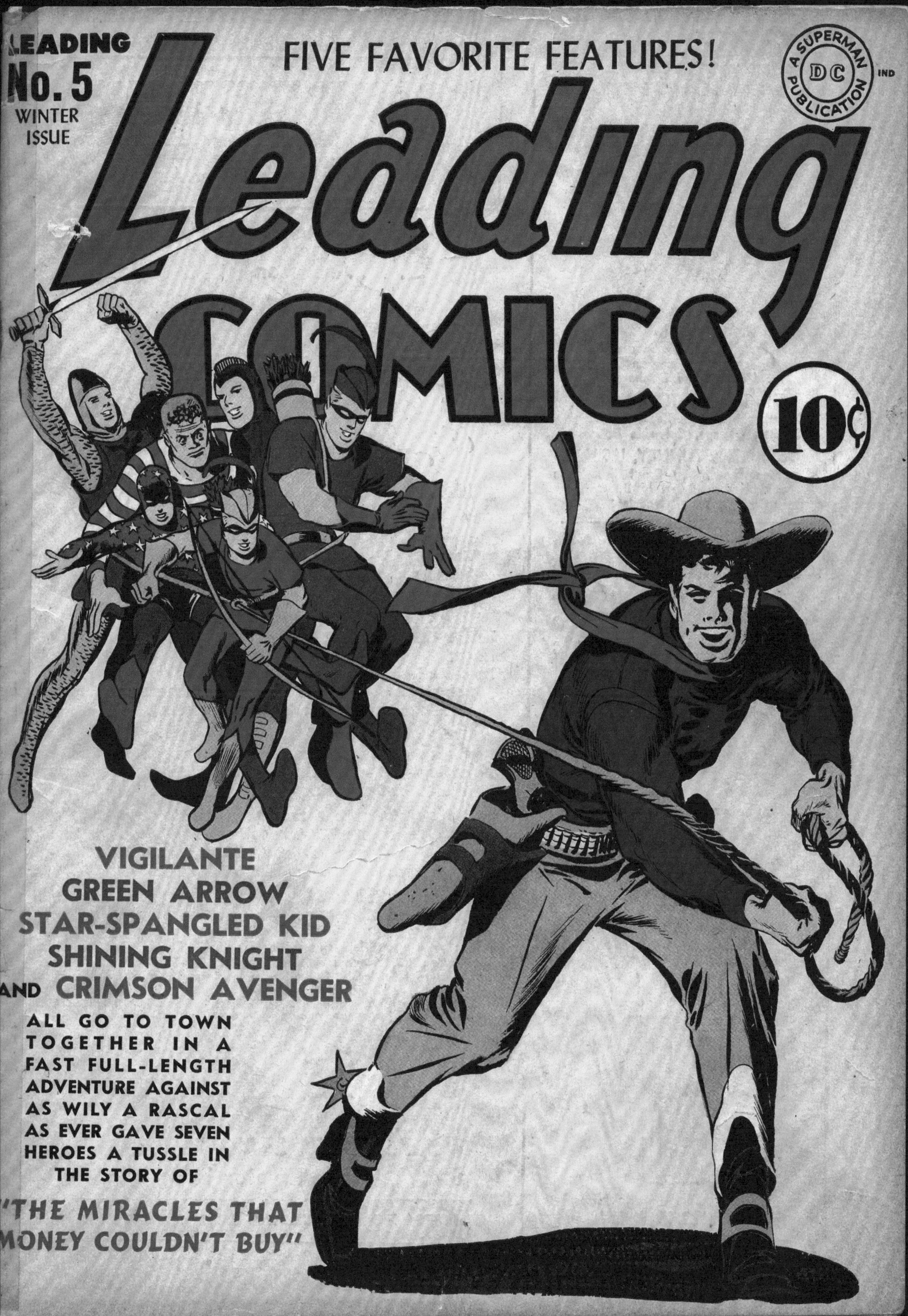

FIVE FAVORITE FEATURES!
LEADING No. 5 WINTER ISSUE
A SUPERMAN DC PUBLICATION IND
Leading COMICS
10¢
VIGILANTE
GREEN ARROW
STAR-SPANGLED KID
SHINING KNIGHT
AND CRIMSON AVENGER
ALL GO TO TOWN TOGETHER IN A FAST FULL-LENGTH ADVENTURE AGAINST AS WILY A RASCAL AS EVER GAVE SEVEN HEROES A TUSSLE IN THE STORY OF
"THE MIRACLES THAT MONEY COULDN'T BUY"

Many of the editors at DC seemed oblivious to the talent pool they had on hand. Despite his reticent nature, Meskin figured out ways to survive. George Roussos recalls, "They got along with Mort. Mort was very clever in getting around people. He was a Gemini. Mort [Weisinger] used to come in when he was younger, he would bring girls up there, and Mort [Meskin] would go out there, see the girls and make compliments about Mort [Weisinger], that he was some 'big cheese.' Mort [Meskin] was a very ingenious, very intelligent guy, a very gentle guy. Weisinger was a bulldozer."[13]

Dozens of new comic book publishers appeared around town. Many an entrepreneur jumped into this new market feet first. Soon there were myriad supermen and ensuing lawsuits for copyright infringement. In the early 1940s, Lev Gleason was a former paper salesman and newly-cast publisher with access to a pulp paper reserve and the desire to enter the fray. The catch: He had to use it up immediately or his distributor wouldn't front him the money to pay the bill. He hired artist Charles Biro with two stipulations: he wanted the comic to feature his hero Daredevil, and he had to complete a 64-page comic by Monday morning. It was Friday.

Biro shared studio space with two other comics creators, writer Bob Wood and a moonlighting Jerry Robinson. Wood in turn brought in his brothers Dave and Dick, while Jerry turned to his roommates Bernie and Mort, who brought in *Batman* inker and letterer George Roussos as well. They set up shop, two at a table, one on the floor, smoking and drinking as they worked into the night.

After Biro's *Daredevil* feature, backup stories were needed. Robinson invented "London" on the spot, the first comic book hero to take on the real-life events of the war in England. Roussos followed suit with "Blackout." They worked through the evening hours, the camaraderie dimming as the hours wore on, while the worst blizzard to hit New York in years raged outside.

By Sunday morning there was a five-foot snowdrift against the door and they had run out of food. It was decided one of them would have to venture out and bring back supplies. Straws were drawn, the short one by Klein. They dug away the snow from the front door so Klein could go off in search of an open market or grocery store.

He was gone for hours. The others kept working away, their hunger and fatigue growing.

When he returned he had little to show for his efforts: two bottles of milk and a dozen eggs, the remaining stock of the only open dairy he could find. The studio had no kitchen; there was no way to cook the eggs. They took to the bathroom, where they pried off the floor tiles with knives, lit scrap paper in waste paper baskets, and fried the eggs on the tiles. This got them through the rest of Sunday, and when Monday hit the issue of *Daredevil* was complete.

Sadly, Klein was soon drafted and killed in Anzio, Italy. "That was the most tragic thing." Robinson recalls. "He was one of my best friends; Mort was too. But Bernie especially, he was closer to my age, I guess, [and] from my hometown. Mort was older, he was my protector. But that was terrible. I dreamt about Bernie almost every night for about 20 or 30 years. Every night. It was always a variation of the same dream. Which was that Bernie went and died, and I get a phone call either from him or from a mutual friend, and I thought it was him and it was basically that he was alive and he was in Trenton... I tried to call him, I drive to Trenton and go from place to place, and I'm told "No, he's not here, he just left." The whole dream was frustration that I couldn't catch up with him. Never found him. One time he came to New York and he tried to contact me and he never made it. In retrospect apparently I could never accept the fact that he died, and he was still coming back. And one day, after several decades had ensued, I had a dream, it's now quite a few years ago, and as I recall the dream was I get a phone call, the bell rang in the apartment and I went to the door and it was Bernie and I woke up and it was the last dream I had of Bernie. I finally accepted the fact that he was dead and he was finally coming back to me. I haven't had that dream since." Unlike Robinson, despite their close relationship, Meskin rarely discussed Bernie's passing.[14]

Meskin would cut entire panels off finished artboards and rework them. Perhaps this was due to editorial dictate at DC, yet he thought enough of the unused panels to save them.

A TOUCH OF WELLES

"Create your own visual style... let it be unique for yourself and yet
identifiable for others. " —*Orson Welles*

"*Citizen Kane* influenced us a great deal, all of us. We were very excited about it and spent quite a
bit of time discussing it, employing its elements in our work. There was a contest as to who saw it
the most times," Meskin told Jim Steranko for his *History of Comics*.

In his Pulitzer Prize-winning novel *The Amazing Adventures of Kavalier & Clay*, Michael Chabon's
character Joseph Kavalier bears a marked resemblance to Mort Meskin, sharing not only an
Eastern European birthplace but a past as a gymnast. A turning point for the fictional Joseph
Kavalier is the release of the 24-year-old Orson Welles's *Citizen Kane* in 1941. Chabon writes, "It

was that *Citizen Kane* represented, more than
any other movie Joe had ever seen, the total
blending of narration and image that was...
the fundamental principle of comic book story
telling... Without the witty, potent dialog and
the puzzling shape of the story, the movie
would have merely been an American version
of the kind of brooding, shadow-filled Ufa-
style expressionist stuff that Joe had grown
up watching in Prague. Without the brooding
shadows and bold adventurings of the camera,
without the theatrical lighting and queasy
angles, it would have been merely a clever movie about a rich bastard. It was more, much more,
than any movie really needed to be. In this one crucial regard—its inextricable braiding of image
and narrative—*Citizen Kane* was like a comic book. "Though fiction, Chabon here touches on a
fact, the symbiotic relationship between Orson Welles and the birth of the American comic book.
In fact, the mutual interactions and influences between Welles and the comic book pioneers were
plentiful and profound. Not surprisingly, they shared a trio of inspirations: German Expressionism,
the pulps, and newspaper comic strips had a lasting effect on their respective media and our
culture.

As a youngster, Welles's original desire was to become a musician or artist, but his father
ruled against it. "...He was bitterly opposed to my interest in music and painting and everything
like that. As far as he was concerned, if I was going to be an artist, it'd be better to be a cartoonist,
like his friend George McManus, who drew 'Jiggs and Maggie,' otherwise known as *Bringing Up
Father*—that's where the money was."[15] Welles maintained a love for cartoon strips, and later on,
comic books, throughout his life.

This love of popular writing and art extended to the pulps, and in 1933, at the age of eighteen, he began writing for them while living in Morocco and Spain, and was eventually published in the well-known *Ellery Queen* magazine. His radio career began with the Walter B. Gibson character born of the pulps and comic books, The Shadow, in 1937. And it was Edd Cartier who brought The Shadow to visual life, which in turn had a lasting effect on the young Mort Meskin. "I never missed an issue of *The Shadow*," Meskin said.

Welles remained true to his populist roots throughout his life. A 1942 press release written by the publicity department of RKO Radio Pictures, with whom he was under contract, states: "Welles is a big man, well over six feet, who tips the scales around 200 pounds. He has no hobbies, considers working at his chosen professions enough to keep his mind occupied... He is an avid reader of comic strips and is particularly fond of *Terry and the Pirates*. He believes comic strips mirror contemporary American life."

He applied dramatic devices taken directly from comics to his films. For example, the clock tower ending of *The Stranger* was a device used many times in the early 1940s by Batman writer and co-creator Bill Finger. As Welles notes, "[It was] pure *Dick Tracy*. I had to fight for it. Everybody felt, 'Well, it's bad taste and Orson's going too far,' but I wanted a straight comic-strip finish."[16] Another comic book mainstay that Welles utilized to great effect in the famous mirror sequence of *Lady From Shanghai* was the carnival setting, also right out of the pages of *Batman*. And the overall milieu of a sailor and femme fatale had a direct antecedent in *Terry and the Pirates*.

Thus it is clear that Welles was not only a connoisseur of the comic strip and comic book as a visual and literary form, but actively engaged it in his work. Visually, his odd, edgy, upward proscenium-like angles and forced perspectives owed much to the comic strip and early comic books, which was reciprocated on their part, and back and forth, creating an interplay between the media that reached its zenith in Welles's work in *Mr. Arkadin* and *Touch of Evil*.

If Welles drew on comic strips and comic books for inspiration, one group of comic creators readily countered. Bob Kane, Jerry Robinson, Bill Finger, Fred Ray and Mort Meskin engaged in a contest to see who could view it the most times. With 15 viewings, Mort wasn't the winner; Ray was, with 30.

It was Bob Kane's *Batman* (soon with assistance by Jerry Robinson) that introduced the world to the odd angles and deep shadows on the comic book page, displaying directly the influence of German Expressionism as well as the horror pictures of Hollywood. Cartoonist Jules Feiffer summed up the differences this way: "Batman's world was more cinematic than Superman's.

Kane was one of the early experimenters with angle shots... though he was not compulsively avant-garde in his use of the worm's eye, the bird's eye, the shot through the wine glass. [17]

In fact, Batman's most famous villain, The Joker, co-created by Robinson and Finger, was directly inspired by a German film. As Robinson notes, "When Bill came back with a script, he brought in a picture of Conrad Veidt... Bill knew about Veidt because he was into German Expressionist films and had seen the movie [*The Man Who Laughs*, 1928, Directed by Paul Leni]."

Jerry Robinson: "We saw (*Citizen Kane*) endlessly, literally dozens of times. And invariably knew every line, while we were drawing, we could recite whole scenes of dialog. We were particularly delighted because he did a lot of things in that medium that comics would do."[18]

RIGHT: *Wildcat* art page from *Sensation Comics* number 65, 1947 (collection of Ethan Roberts).
(© DC Comics. All Rights Reserved. Used with Permission).

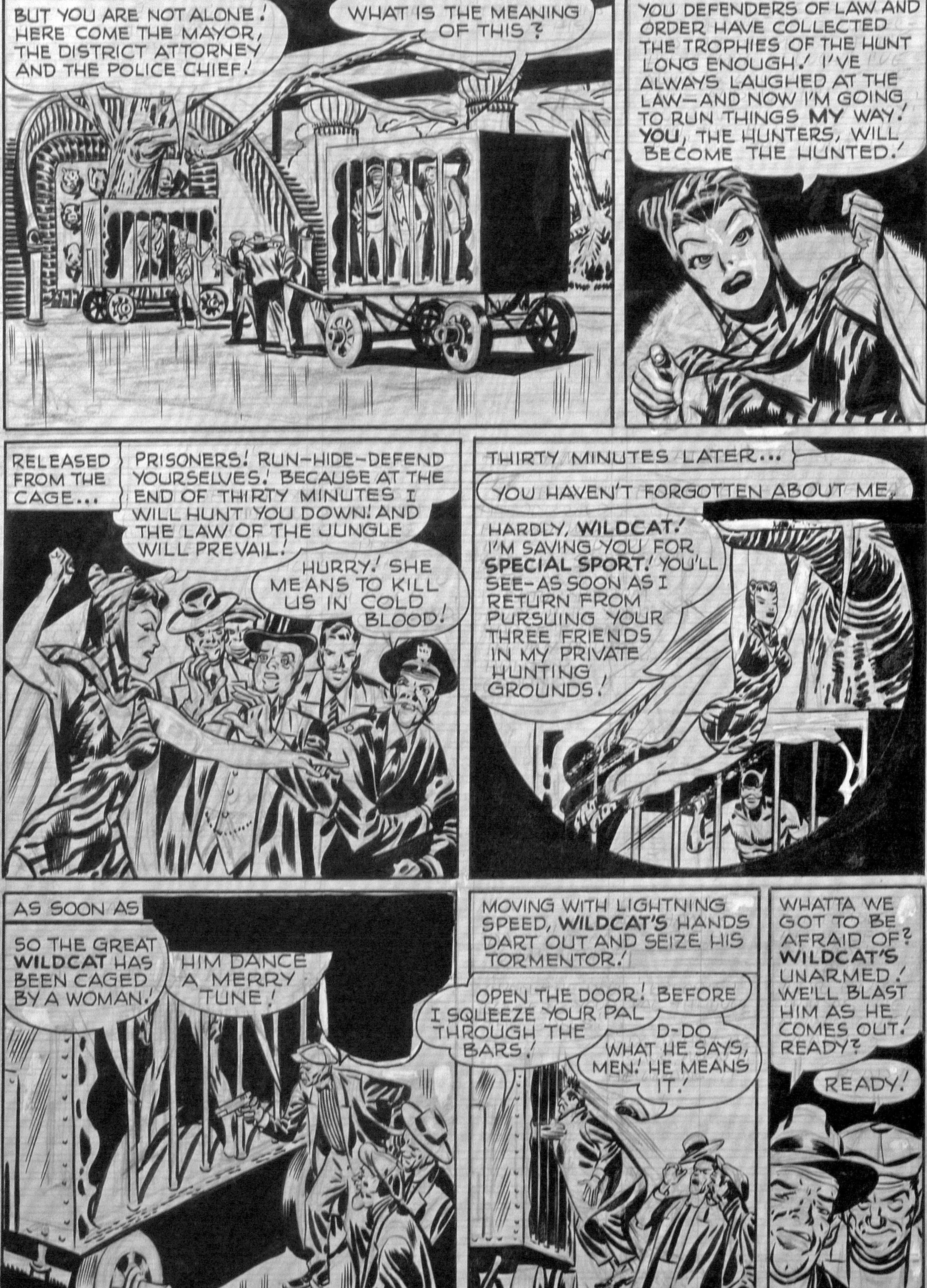
BUT YOU ARE NOT ALONE! HERE COME THE MAYOR, THE DISTRICT ATTORNEY AND THE POLICE CHIEF!
WHAT IS THE MEANING OF THIS?
YOU DEFENDERS OF LAW AND ORDER HAVE COLLECTED THE TROPHIES OF THE HUNT LONG ENOUGH! I'VE ALWAYS LAUGHED AT THE LAW—AND NOW I'M GOING TO RUN THINGS MY WAY! YOU, THE HUNTERS, WILL BECOME THE HUNTED!
RELEASED FROM THE CAGE...
PRISONERS! RUN-HIDE-DEFEND YOURSELVES! BECAUSE AT THE END OF THIRTY MINUTES I WILL HUNT YOU DOWN! AND THE LAW OF THE JUNGLE WILL PREVAIL!
HURRY! SHE MEANS TO KILL US IN COLD BLOOD!
THIRTY MINUTES LATER...
YOU HAVEN'T FORGOTTEN ABOUT ME.
HARDLY, WILDCAT! I'M SAVING YOU FOR SPECIAL SPORT! YOU'LL SEE-AS SOON AS I RETURN FROM PURSUING YOUR THREE FRIENDS IN MY PRIVATE HUNTING GROUNDS!
AS SOON AS
SO THE GREAT WILDCAT HAS BEEN CAGED BY A WOMAN!
HIM DANCE A MERRY TUNE!
MOVING WITH LIGHTNING SPEED, WILDCAT'S HANDS DART OUT AND SEIZE HIS TORMENTOR!
OPEN THE DOOR! BEFORE I SQUEEZE YOUR PAL THROUGH THE BARS!
D-DO WHAT HE SAYS, MEN! HE MEANS IT!
WHATTA WE GOT TO BE AFRAID OF? WILDCAT'S UNARMED! WE'LL BLAST HIM AS HE COMES OUT! READY?
READY!

ONE HUNDRED PERCENT

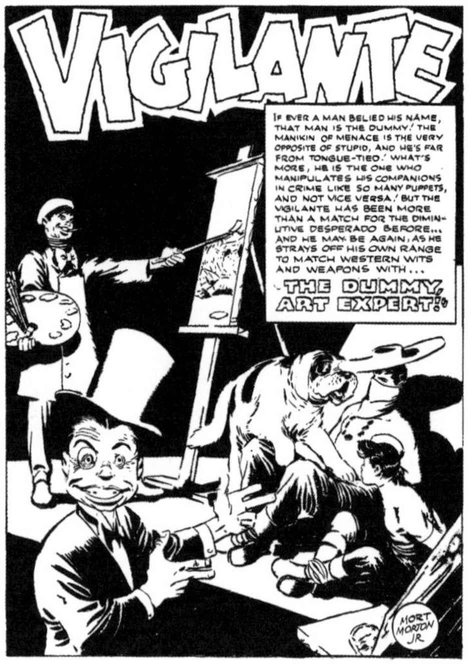
VIGILANTE
IF EVER A MAN BELIED HIS NAME, THAT MAN IS THE DUMMY! THE MANIKIN OF MENACE IS THE VERY OPPOSITE OF STUPID, AND HE'S FAR FROM TONGUE-TIED! WHAT'S MORE, HE IS THE ONE WHO MANIPULATES HIS COMPANIONS IN CRIME LIKE SO MANY PUPPETS, AND NOT VICE VERSA! BUT THE VIGILANTE HAS BEEN MORE THAN A MATCH FOR THE DIMINUTIVE DESPERADO BEFORE... AND HE MAY BE AGAIN, AS HE STRAYS OFF HIS OWN RANGE TO MATCH WESTERN WITS AND WEAPONS WITH...
THE DUMMY, ART EXPERT!
MORT MORTON JR.

During his DC period Meskin's art took on a sinewy, moody, dramatic flavor. Shadows loomed, faces were dramatically cropped. A cinematic use of deep space was introduced, along with negative space, combined with odd angles and extreme close-ups. This shifting point of view owed as much to Orson Welles (see preceding sidebar) as it did to Caniff. At the same time his page design took a great step forward, as he focused on the page as a whole, employing circular and oddly-shaped panels to punctuate action. These action-packed pages, along with Jack Kirby's, set a new standard for how a comic book story could be told. Meskin's figures, like Simon & Kirby's, could not be contained within the panels as they leapt into action. His full splash pages in particular set a new standard for composition, drama, and detail.

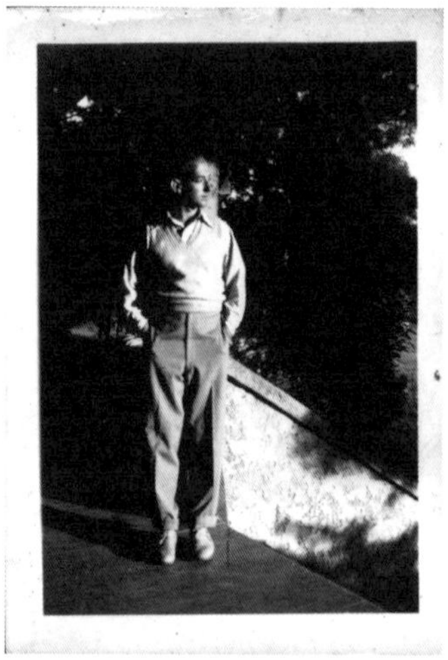

A young Mort emerges from the shadows.

According to Robinson, "Most of the things he did, he was very confident, in himself and his talent. He wasn't the hail-fellow-well-met kind, he was very shy, quiet, reticent. And *very* funny. He enjoyed dancing and enjoyed going out. You know, we did everything together, the three of us, and then Bernie went off to war, and we remained there [at National Periodicals]."

Joe Kubert soon followed the artists to DC. Joe was 16 when editor Whitney Ellsworth made the decision that Meskin's time would be better spent concentrating exclusively on pencil work. "I guess Meskin was running into a problem with deadlines," Kubert speculated. "There is a uniqueness when someone does their own work as opposed to when someone does a collaborative thing, when somebody does the figures, somebody does the penciling, somebody the inking, I think it has a tendency under those circumstances to become more generic than unique, and I think that uniqueness and quality that Mort had on his own stuff nobody came near. One of the jobs that I did, *Johnny Quick*, that Mort was doing at the time, I inked his *Vigilante*, and that was incredible because his penciling was so beautiful, he worked in an entirely different way than most artists do. He would first smudge the whole paper in a gray patina over the entire page and then he would pencil on top of that, and then with a kneaded eraser he would pick up the highlights, so that he had a dimensionality in his work that I had not seen in any other work. I was really impressed with him and when they gave me this stuff to ink, I felt kind of intimidated. When I brought it in, I showed it to Mort and he said, 'It looks fine.' I said, tell me if I can improve it. He said, 'No, you're doing good, kid, just go ahead and do what you're doing.' This was after the beautiful work that he had and I'm sure I loused the hell out of it. I loused up some of his best stuff. This also was a terrific learning experience for me.[19]

"Why I wasn't scared to death putting down a pen and brush to his work, I don't know. The blissful ignorance of youth, I guess! I just blithely went ahead and in doing so I learned an incredible series of drawing lessons from inking Mort Meskin's pencils.

"Mort was the kind of insecure person who never fully appreciated his own abilities. Often, he was pushed into doing a lot of stuff that was really beneath him. In terms of the quality of the work, he was an outstanding artist. I did a passably O.K. job on Mort's pencils, but he never put me down. I'd say, 'Gee, Mort, I'm a little unsure about this....' He'd say, 'D-don't worry k-k-kid. You're doing fine.'"[20]

George Roussos: "Mort was much more diplomatic about many things. He never liked to criticize anybody if he could help it. If he disliked something, the only way you [could] read him, [was] by not asking him but by seeing what his reaction was, [but] if he used the guy again. He never criticized anyone because he felt criticism may hurt the guy's chances of having a job, because the editors would hear that, their ears are always looking for criticism of an artist they knew nothing about, so he was very tactful."[21]

Meskin's style and storytelling had a profound effect on Kubert, and he would remain an influence throughout the latter's 60-plus year career. "When I inked [Meskin] especially I learned quite a bit about composition; in fact, I noticed that on every page he did, he would have one large illustration, and I asked him about that, I said, 'How do you decide which drawing you want to focus on and give more size to, more space to on the page?' And he said, 'Well, when I read the script, I figure out which is the most dramatic, most impactful way and I concentrate around that, I build my whole page around that,' which was a terrific idea, for several reasons: Number one, it makes a more interesting page, more interesting drawing, more impactful. I'm not sure if he explained it to me or not, but most young

[TEXT CONTINUES ON PAGE 61]

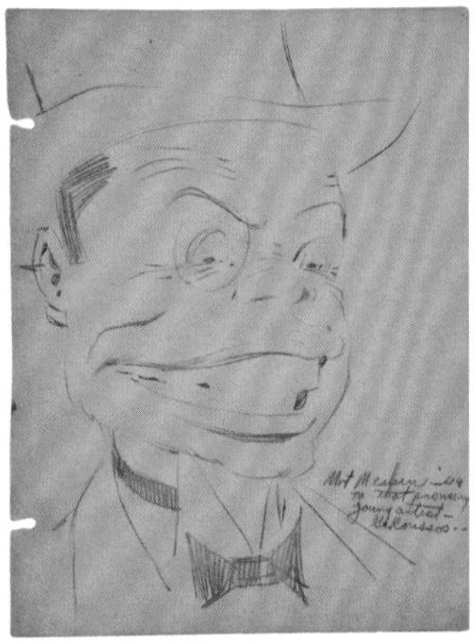

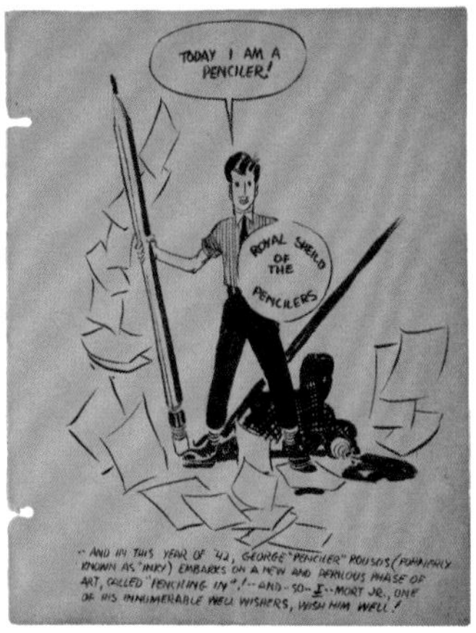
TODAY I AM A PENCILER!
ROYAL SHEILD OF THE PENCILERS
—AND IN THIS YEAR OF '42, GEORGE "PENCILER" ROUSSOS (FORMERLY KNOWN AS "INKY") EMBARKS ON A NEW AND PERILOUS PHASE OF ART, CALLED "PENCILING IN"!—AND—SO—I—MORT JR., ONE OF HIS INNUMERABLE WELL WISHERS, WISH HIM WELL!

Along with several artists, Meskin drew in George Roussos's sketchbook to congratulate him for being pormoted from inker to penciller, in 1942

OVERLEAF: *Action Comics* #56 (left), inks by George Roussos, 1943. RIGHT: *Action Comics* #61, 1943. SPREAD FOLLOWING: *Action Comics* #43, 1941 (left), *Leading Comics* #1 artboard, art by Mort Meskin and Fred Ray, Winter, 1941-1942 (collection of Jerry Robinson). (© DC Comics. All Rights Reserved. Used with Permission.)

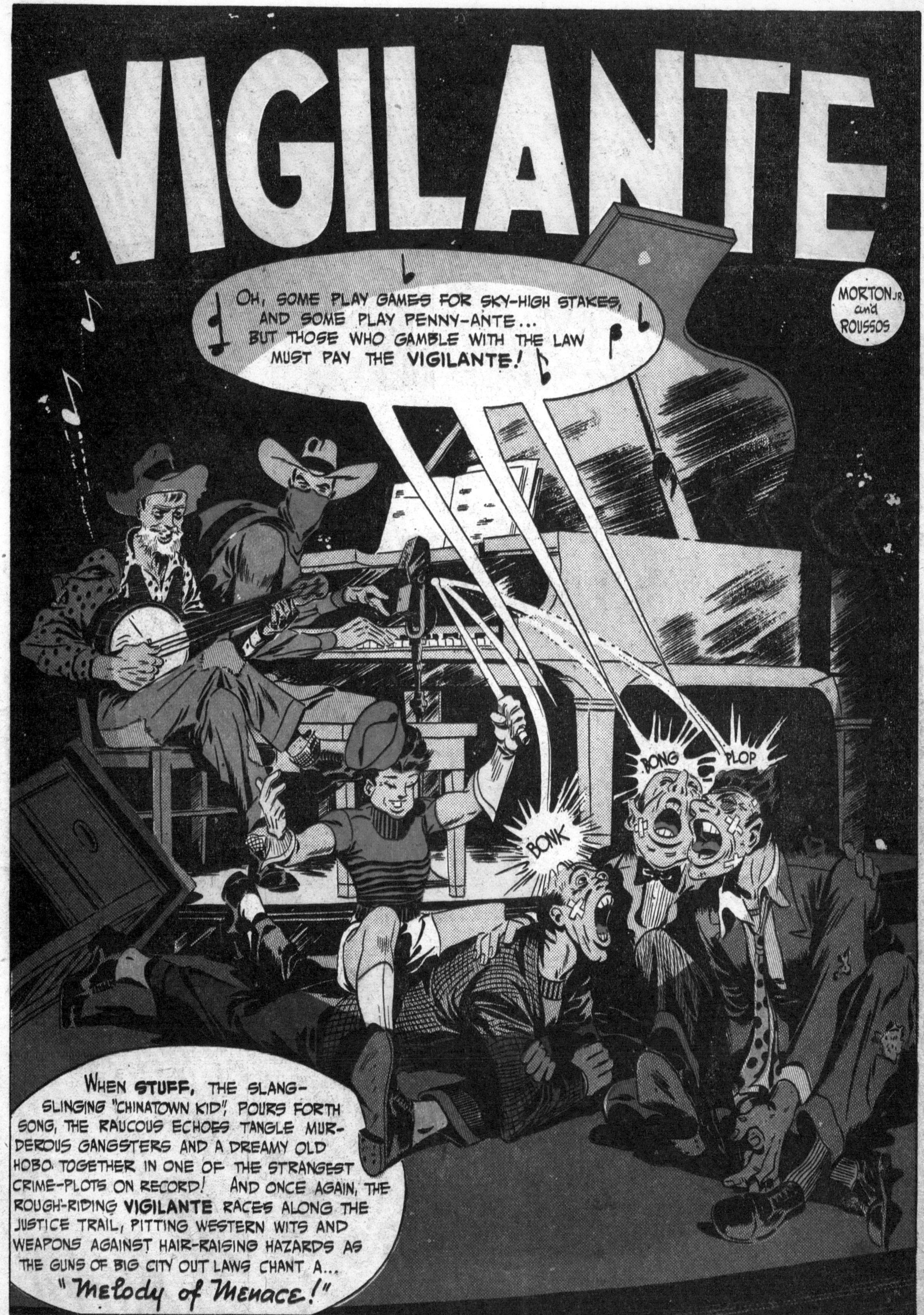
VIGILANTE
MORTON JR. and ROUSSOS
OH, SOME PLAY GAMES FOR SKY-HIGH STAKES, AND SOME PLAY PENNY-ANTE... BUT THOSE WHO GAMBLE WITH THE LAW MUST PAY THE VIGILANTE!
BONG
PLOP
BONK
WHEN STUFF, THE SLANG-SLINGING "CHINATOWN KID", POURS FORTH SONG, THE RAUCOUS ECHOES TANGLE MURDEROUS GANGSTERS AND A DREAMY OLD HOBO TOGETHER IN ONE OF THE STRANGEST CRIME-PLOTS ON RECORD! AND ONCE AGAIN, THE ROUGH-RIDING VIGILANTE RACES ALONG THE JUSTICE TRAIL, PITTING WESTERN WITS AND WEAPONS AGAINST HAIR-RAISING HAZARDS AS THE GUNS OF BIG CITY OUT LAWS CHANT A...
"Melody of Menace!"

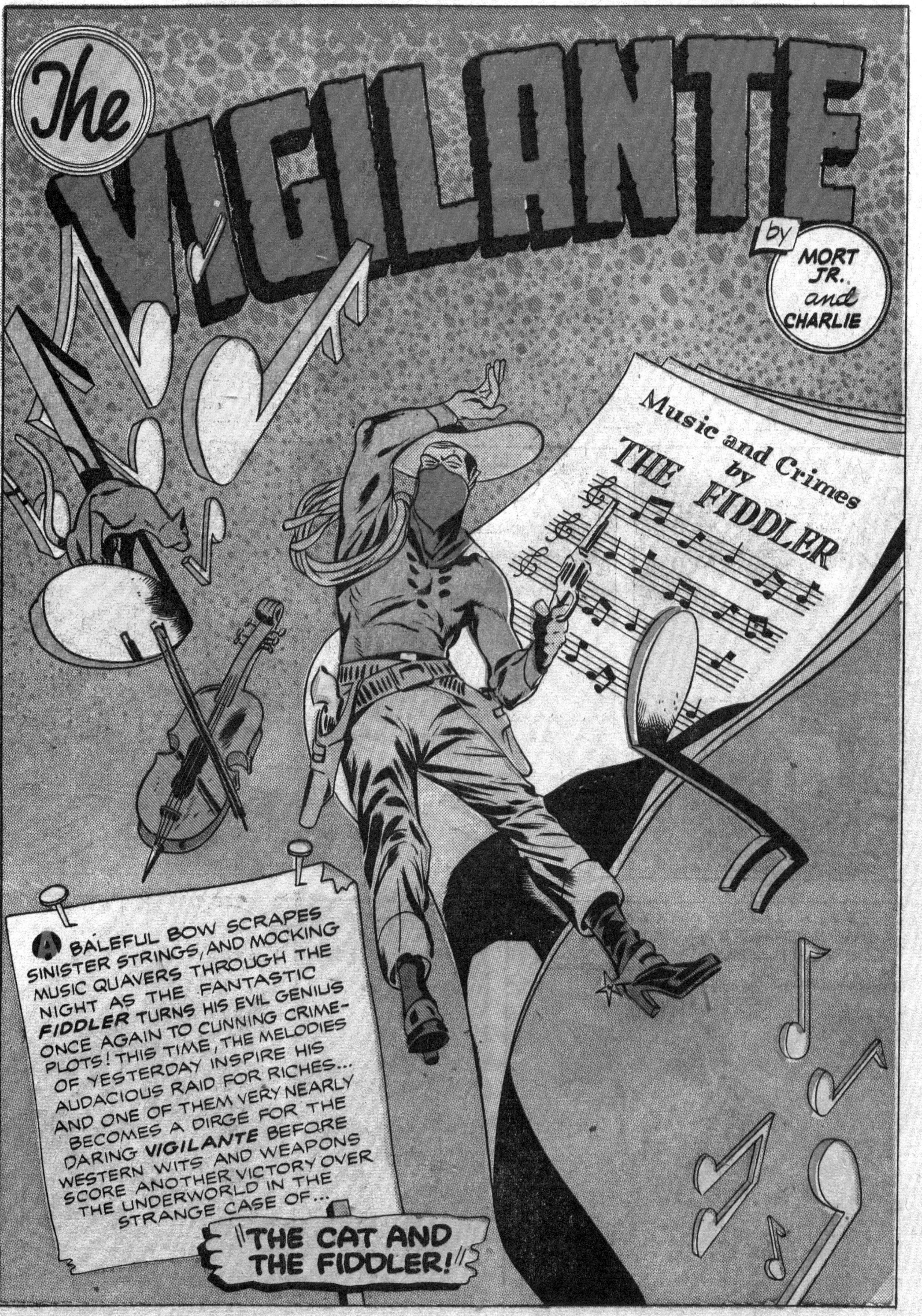
The VIGILANTE
by MORT JR., and CHARLIE
Music and Crimes by THE FIDDLER
A BALEFUL BOW SCRAPES SINISTER STRINGS, AND MOCKING MUSIC QUAVERS THROUGH THE NIGHT AS THE FANTASTIC FIDDLER TURNS HIS EVIL GENIUS ONCE AGAIN TO CUNNING CRIME-PLOTS! THIS TIME, THE MELODIES OF YESTERDAY INSPIRE HIS AUDACIOUS RAID FOR RICHES... AND ONE OF THEM VERY NEARLY BECOMES A DIRGE FOR THE DARING VIGILANTE BEFORE WESTERN WITS AND WEAPONS SCORE ANOTHER VICTORY OVER THE UNDERWORLD IN THE STRANGE CASE OF...
"THE CAT AND THE FIDDLER!"

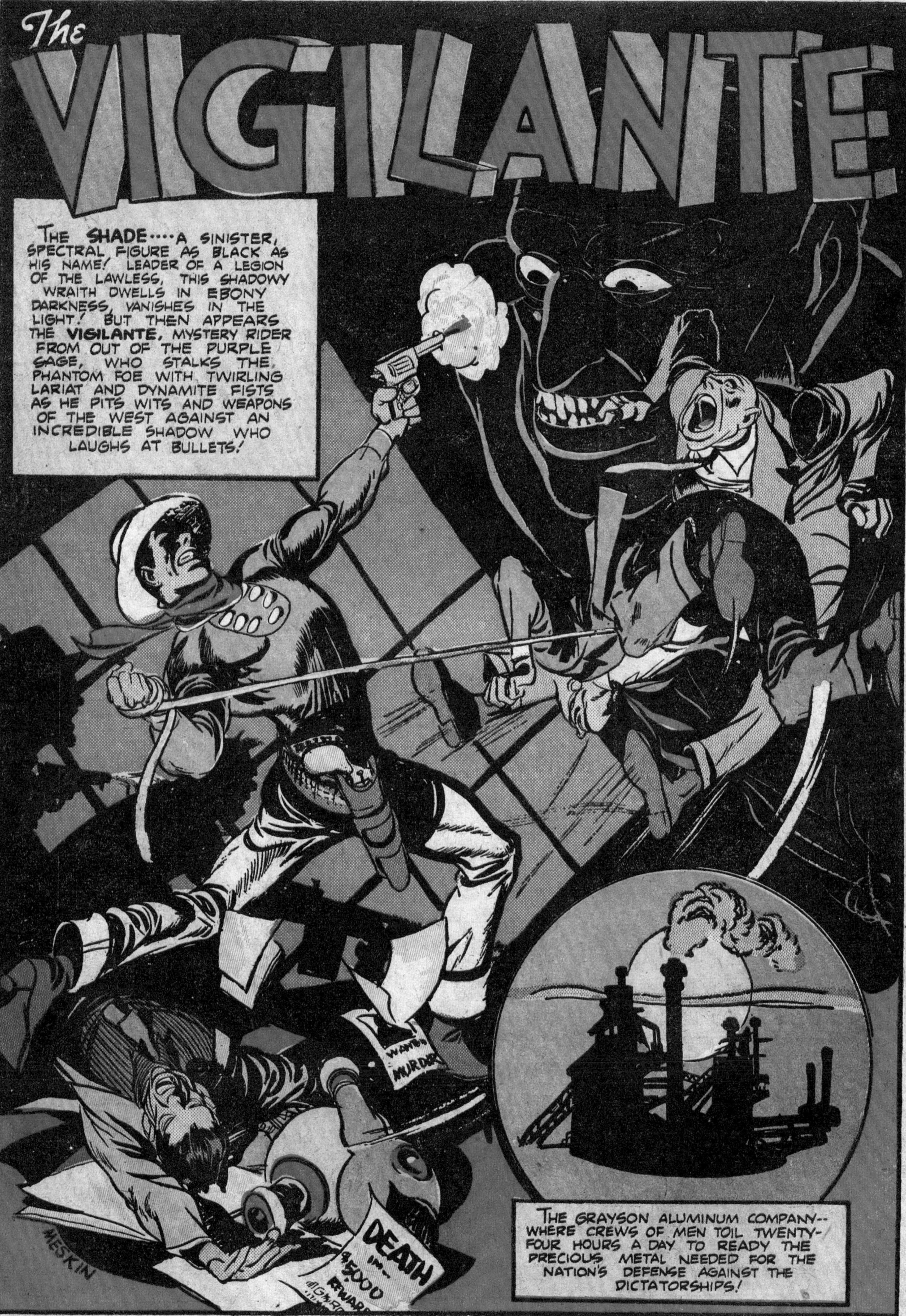

The VIGILANTE
THE SHADE.... A SINISTER, SPECTRAL FIGURE AS BLACK AS HIS NAME! LEADER OF A LEGION OF THE LAWLESS, THIS SHADOWY WRAITH DWELLS IN EBONY DARKNESS, VANISHES IN THE LIGHT! BUT THEN APPEARS THE VIGILANTE, MYSTERY RIDER FROM OUT OF THE PURPLE SAGE, WHO STALKS THE PHANTOM FOE WITH TWIRLING LARIAT AND DYNAMITE FISTS AS HE PITS WITS AND WEAPONS OF THE WEST AGAINST AN INCREDIBLE SHADOW WHO LAUGHS AT BULLETS!
MURDER
DEATH
MESKIN
THE GRAYSON ALUMINUM COMPANY-- WHERE CREWS OF MEN TOIL TWENTY-FOUR HOURS A DAY TO READY THE PRECIOUS METAL NEEDED FOR THE NATION'S DEFENSE AGAINST THE DICTATORSHIPS!

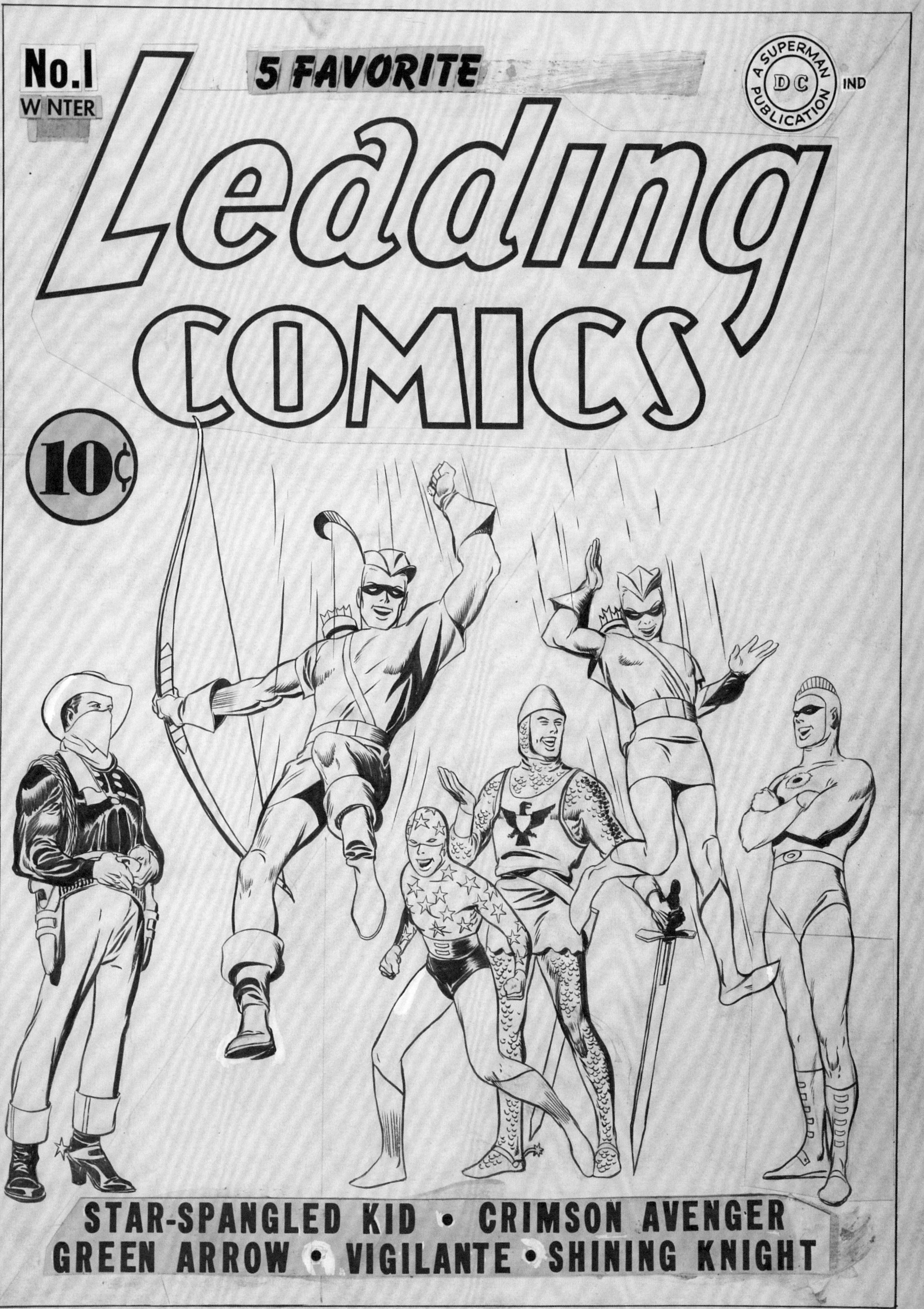
No.1
W NTER
5 FAVORITE
A SUPERMAN DC PUBLICATION
IND
Leading
COMICS
10¢
STAR-SPANGLED KID • CRIMSON AVENGER
GREEN ARROW • VIGILANTE • SHINING KNIGHT

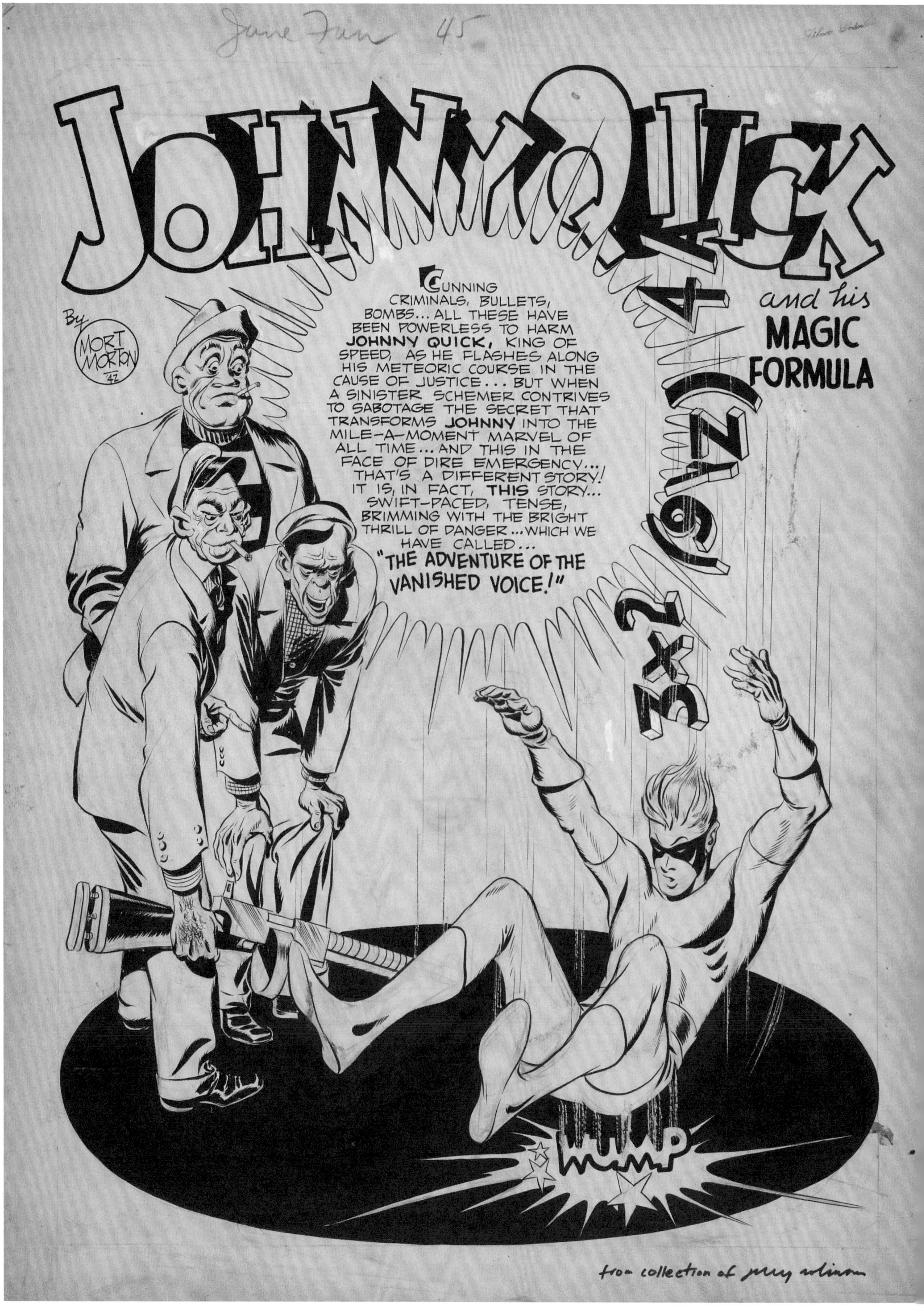
June Fun 45
JOHNNY QUICK
and his MAGIC FORMULA
By MORT MORTON '42
CUNNING CRIMINALS, BULLETS, BOMBS... ALL THESE HAVE BEEN POWERLESS TO HARM JOHNNY QUICK, KING OF SPEED, AS HE FLASHES ALONG HIS METEORIC COURSE IN THE CAUSE OF JUSTICE... BUT WHEN A SINISTER SCHEMER CONTRIVES TO SABOTAGE THE SECRET THAT TRANSFORMS JOHNNY INTO THE MILE-A-MOMENT MARVEL OF ALL TIME... AND THIS IN THE FACE OF DIRE EMERGENCY... THAT'S A DIFFERENT STORY! IT IS, IN FACT, THIS STORY... SWIFT-PACED, TENSE, BRIMMING WITH THE BRIGHT THRILL OF DANGER... WHICH WE HAVE CALLED...
"THE ADVENTURE OF THE VANISHED VOICE!"
3X2 (9YZ) 4A
WUMP
from collection of jerry robinson

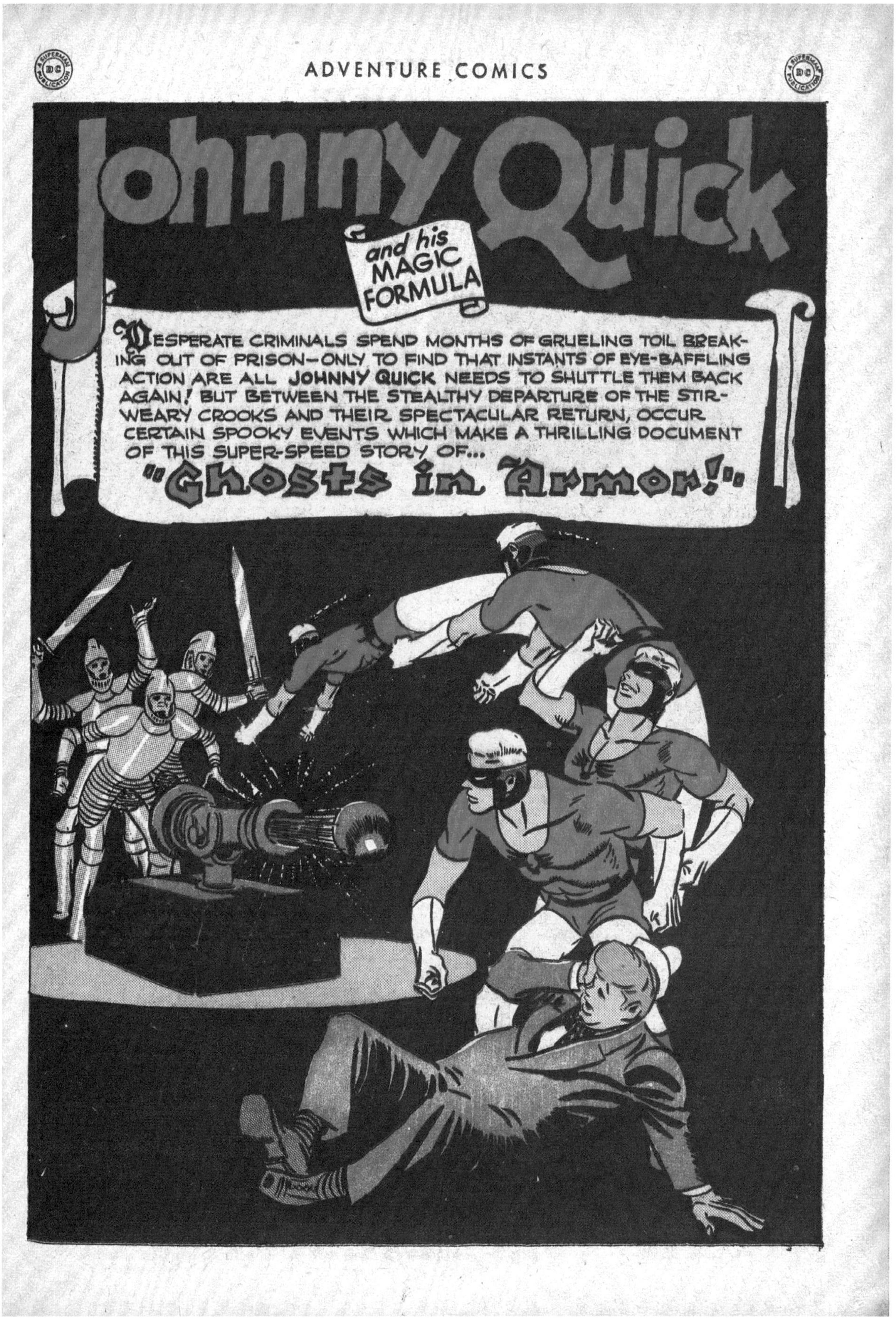
ADVENTURE COMICS
Johnny Quick
and his MAGIC FORMULA
DESPERATE CRIMINALS SPEND MONTHS OF GRUELING TOIL BREAKING OUT OF PRISON—ONLY TO FIND THAT INSTANTS OF EYE-BAFFLING ACTION ARE ALL JOHNNY QUICK NEEDS TO SHUTTLE THEM BACK AGAIN! BUT BETWEEN THE STEALTHY DEPARTURE OF THE STIR-WEARY CROOKS AND THEIR SPECTACULAR RETURN, OCCUR CERTAIN SPOOKY EVENTS WHICH MAKE A THRILLING DOCUMENT OF THIS SUPER-SPEED STORY OF...
"Ghosts in Armor!"

LEFT: Splash page from *More Fun Comics* #80, art by Mort Meskin and Jerry Robinson, 1942 (collection of Jerry Robinson). ABOVE: *Adventure Comics* #108 splash, 1946. FOLLOWING TWO SPREADS: Splash pages from *Adventure Comics*, #132, 133, respectively, both 1949. THIRD SPREAD FOLLOWING: Printed cover and artwork from *More Fun Comics* #8, 1943. Art by Mort Meskin.

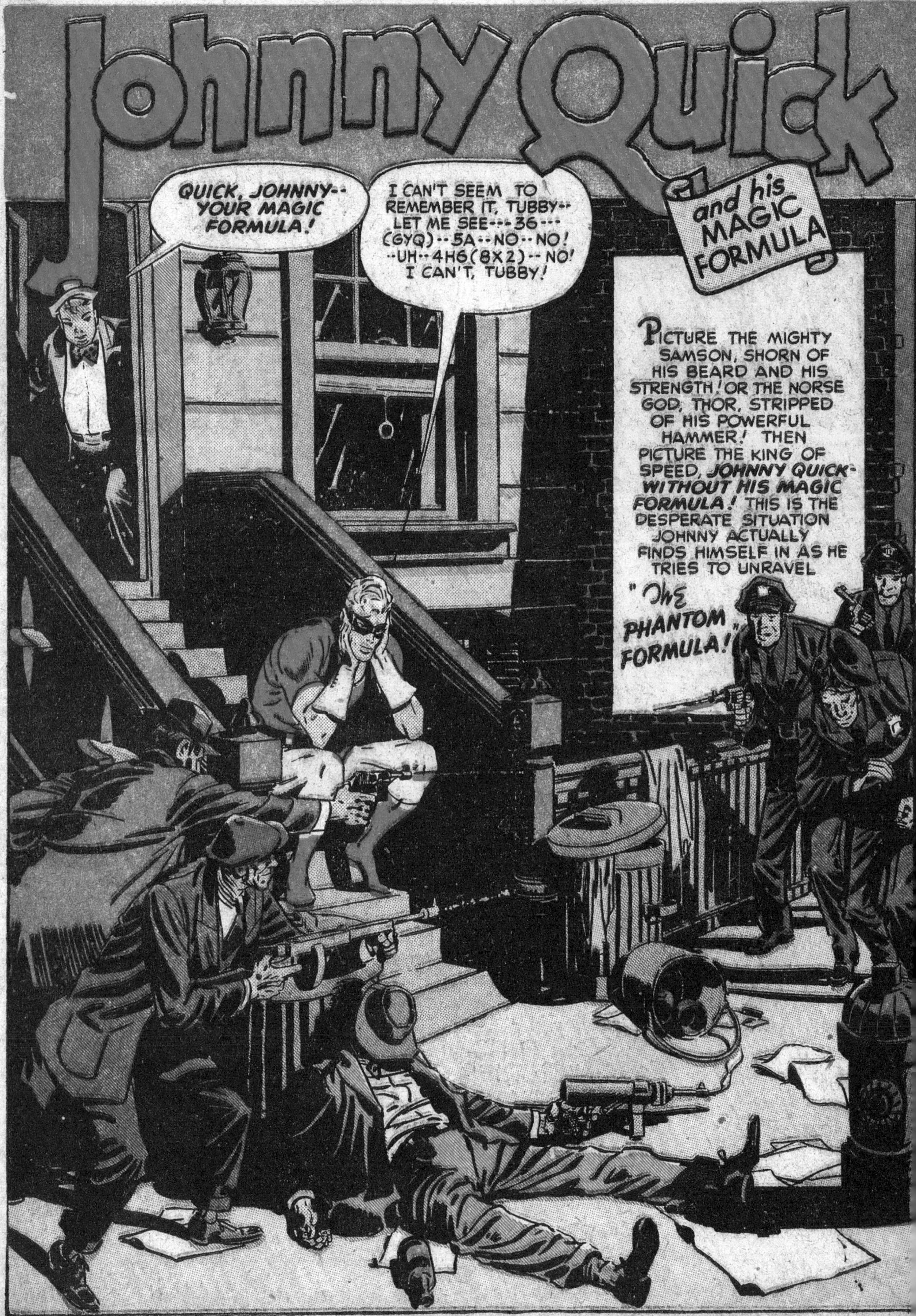
Johnny Quick
and his MAGIC FORMULA
QUICK, JOHNNY-- YOUR MAGIC FORMULA!
I CAN'T SEEM TO REMEMBER IT, TUBBY-- LET ME SEE---36---(GYQ)--5A--NO--NO! --UH--4H6(8X2)--NO! I CAN'T, TUBBY!
PICTURE THE MIGHTY SAMSON, SHORN OF HIS BEARD AND HIS STRENGTH! OR THE NORSE GOD, THOR, STRIPPED OF HIS POWERFUL HAMMER! THEN PICTURE THE KING OF SPEED, JOHNNY QUICK-WITHOUT HIS MAGIC FORMULA! THIS IS THE DESPERATE SITUATION JOHNNY ACTUALLY FINDS HIMSELF IN AS HE TRIES TO UNRAVEL "THE PHANTOM FORMULA!"

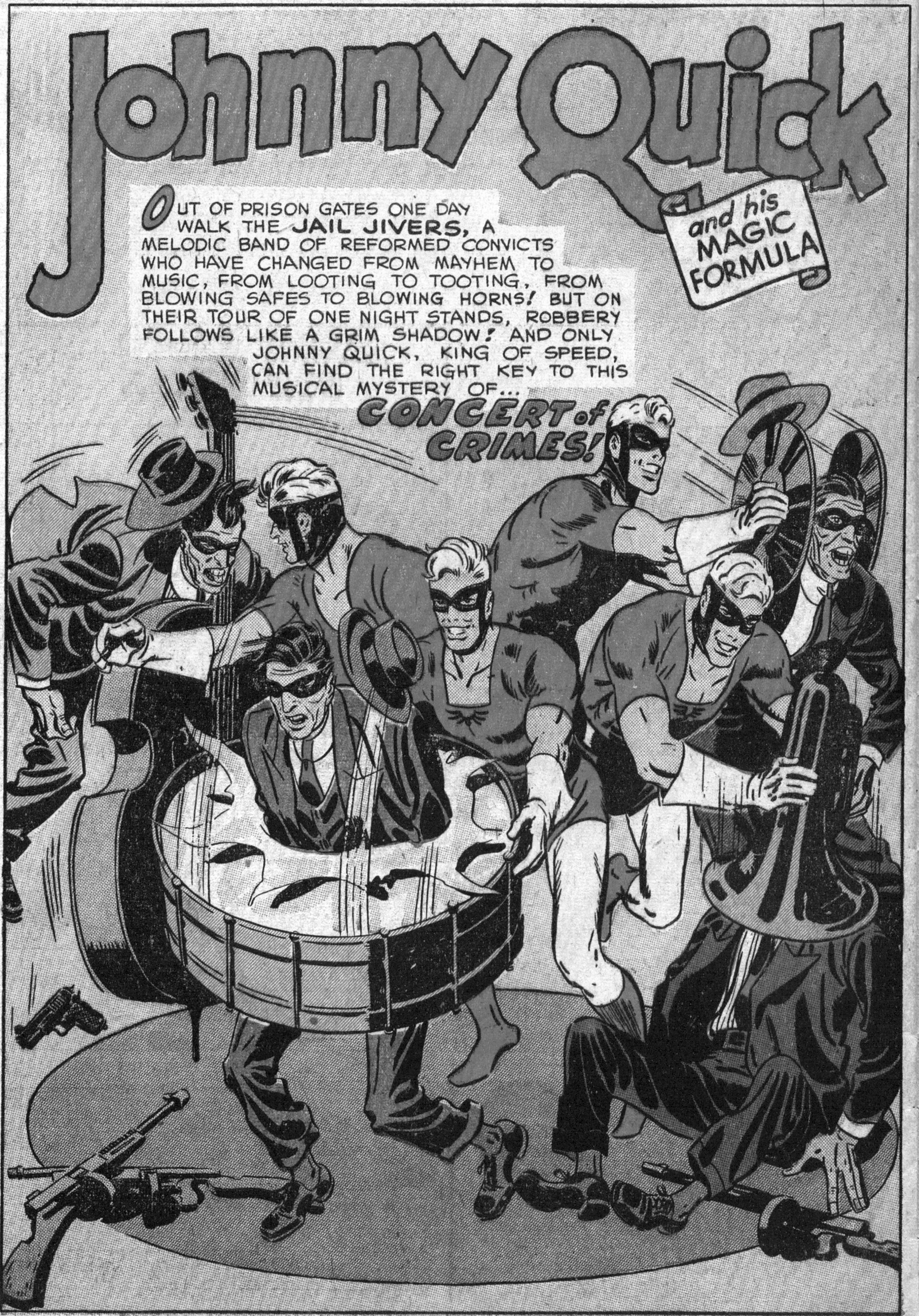

Johnny Quick
and his MAGIC FORMULA
OUT OF PRISON GATES ONE DAY WALK THE JAIL JIVERS, A MELODIC BAND OF REFORMED CONVICTS WHO HAVE CHANGED FROM MAYHEM TO MUSIC, FROM LOOTING TO TOOTING, FROM BLOWING SAFES TO BLOWING HORNS! BUT ON THEIR TOUR OF ONE NIGHT STANDS, ROBBERY FOLLOWS LIKE A GRIM SHADOW! AND ONLY JOHNNY QUICK, KING OF SPEED, CAN FIND THE RIGHT KEY TO THIS MUSICAL MYSTERY OF...
CONCERT of CRIMES!

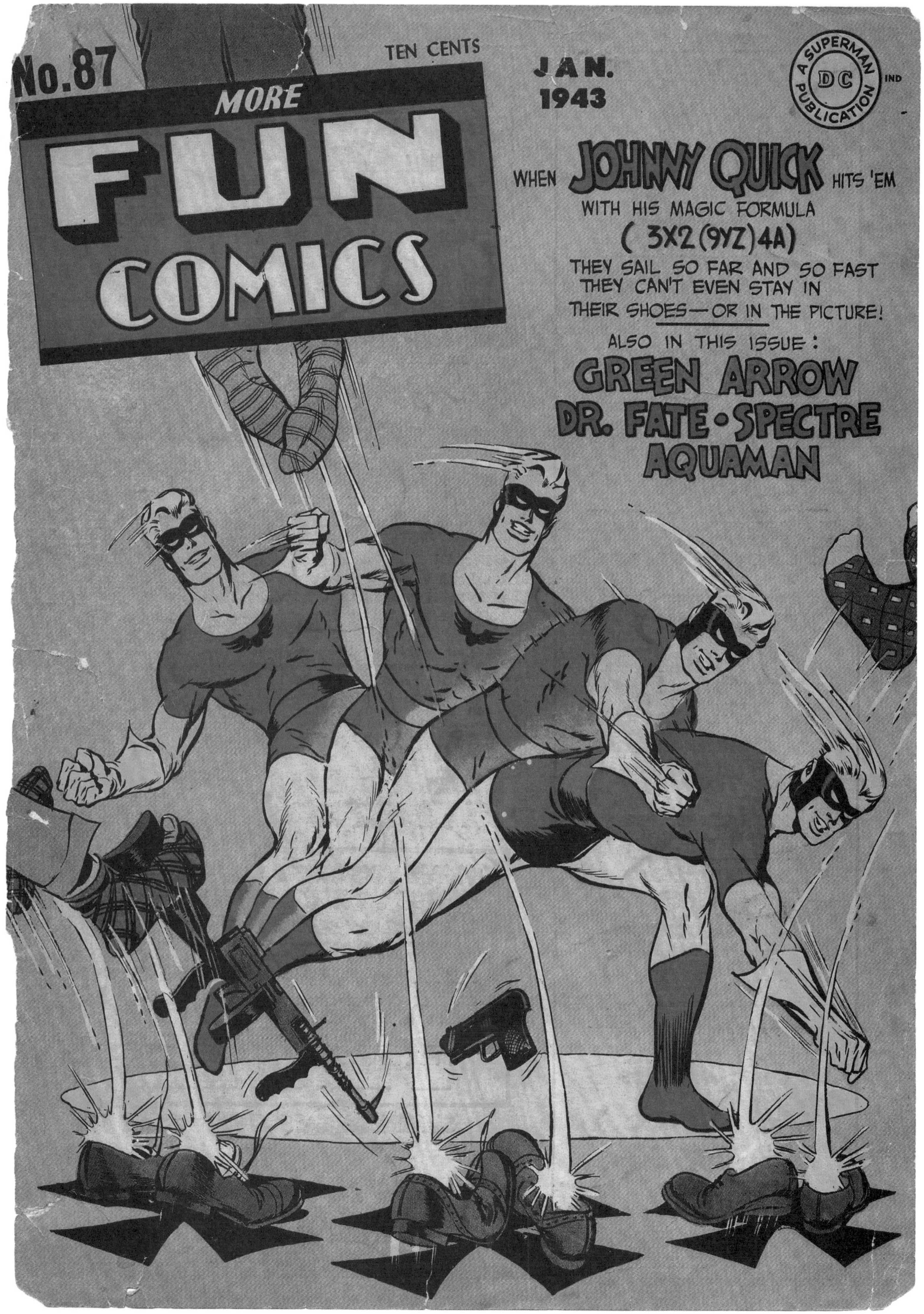
No. 87
TEN CENTS
MORE FUN COMICS
JAN. 1943
A SUPERMAN DC PUBLICATION IND
WHEN JOHNNY QUICK HITS 'EM WITH HIS MAGIC FORMULA
(3X2 (9YZ) 4A)
THEY SAIL SO FAR AND SO FAST THEY CAN'T EVEN STAY IN THEIR SHOES—OR IN THE PICTURE!
ALSO IN THIS ISSUE:
GREEN ARROW
DR. FATE • SPECTRE
AQUAMAN

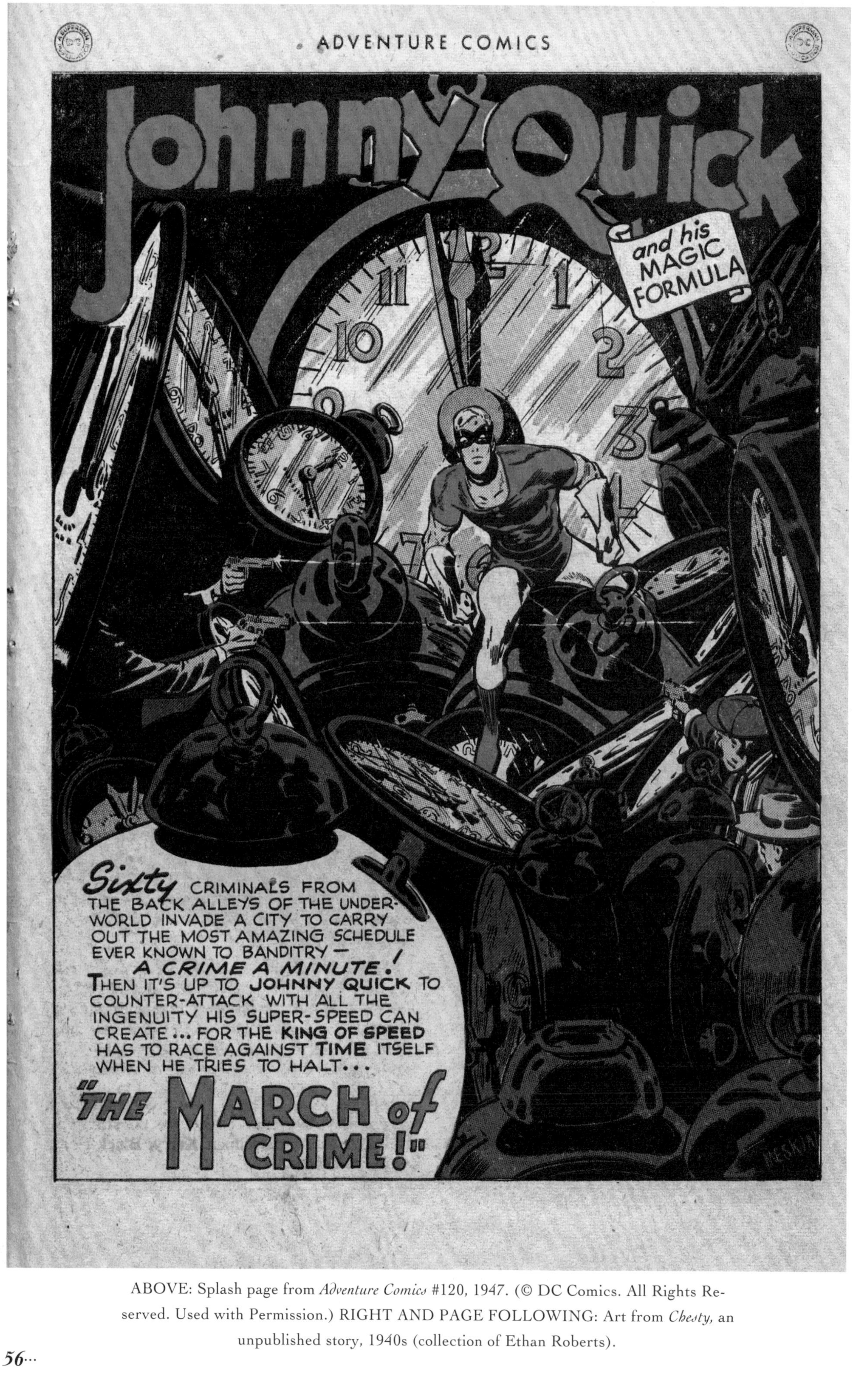
ADVENTURE COMICS
Johnny Quick
and his MAGIC FORMULA
Sixty CRIMINALS FROM THE BACK ALLEYS OF THE UNDER-WORLD INVADE A CITY TO CARRY OUT THE MOST AMAZING SCHEDULE EVER KNOWN TO BANDITRY — A CRIME A MINUTE! THEN IT'S UP TO JOHNNY QUICK TO COUNTER-ATTACK WITH ALL THE INGENUITY HIS SUPER-SPEED CAN CREATE ... FOR THE KING OF SPEED HAS TO RACE AGAINST TIME ITSELF WHEN HE TRIES TO HALT...
"THE MARCH of CRIME!"

ABOVE: Splash page from *Adventure Comics* #120, 1947. (© DC Comics. All Rights Reserved. Used with Permission.) RIGHT AND PAGE FOLLOWING: Art from *Chesty,* an unpublished story, 1940s (collection of Ethan Roberts).

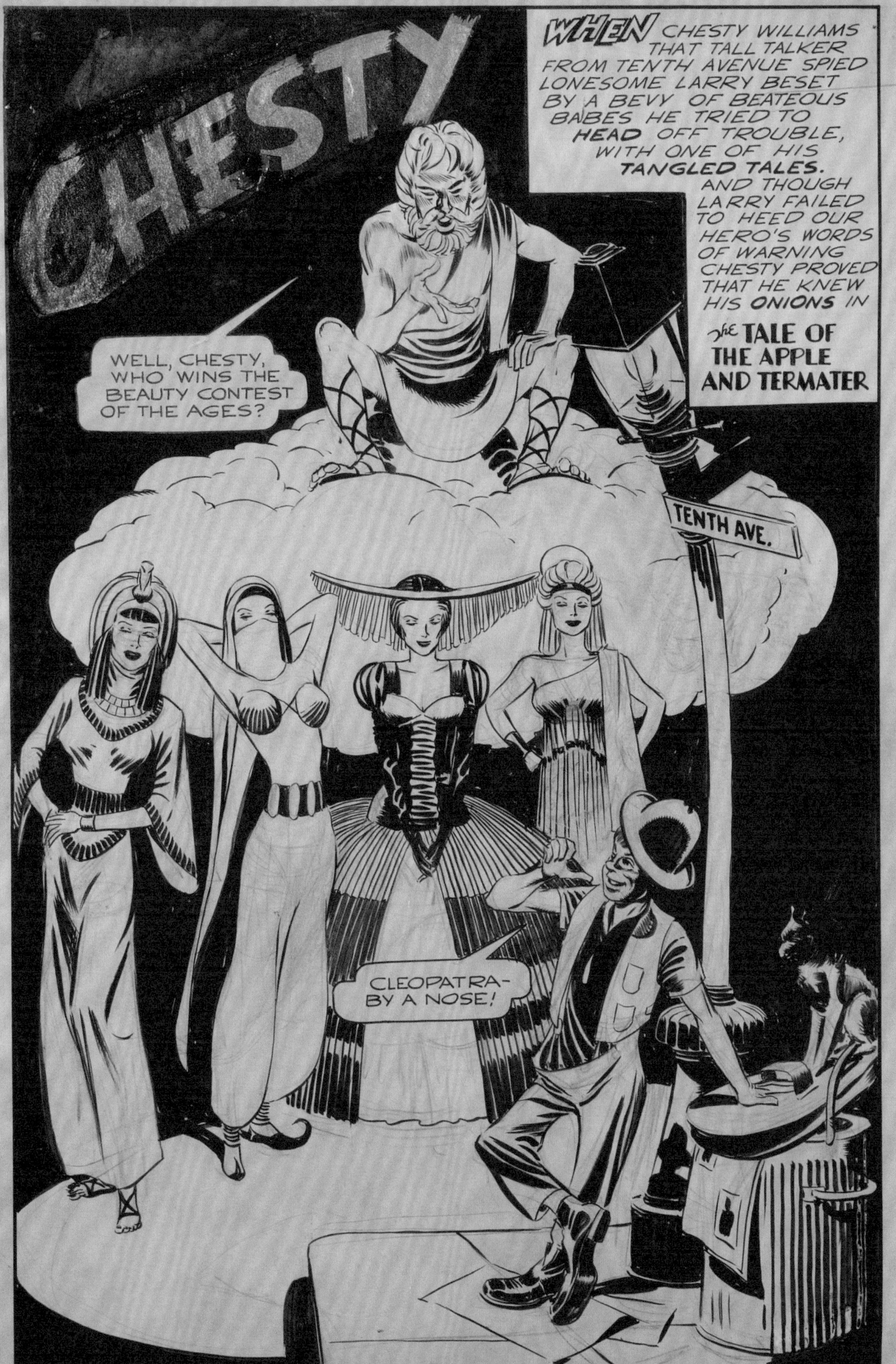
CHESTY
WHEN CHESTY WILLIAMS THAT TALL TALKER FROM TENTH AVENUE SPIED LONESOME LARRY BESET BY A BEVY OF BEATEOUS BABES HE TRIED TO HEAD OFF TROUBLE, WITH ONE OF HIS TANGLED TALES. AND THOUGH LARRY FAILED TO HEED OUR HERO'S WORDS OF WARNING CHESTY PROVED THAT HE KNEW HIS ONIONS IN
The TALE OF THE APPLE AND TERMATER
WELL, CHESTY, WHO WINS THE BEAUTY CONTEST OF THE AGES?
TENTH AVE.
CLEOPATRA- BY A NOSE!

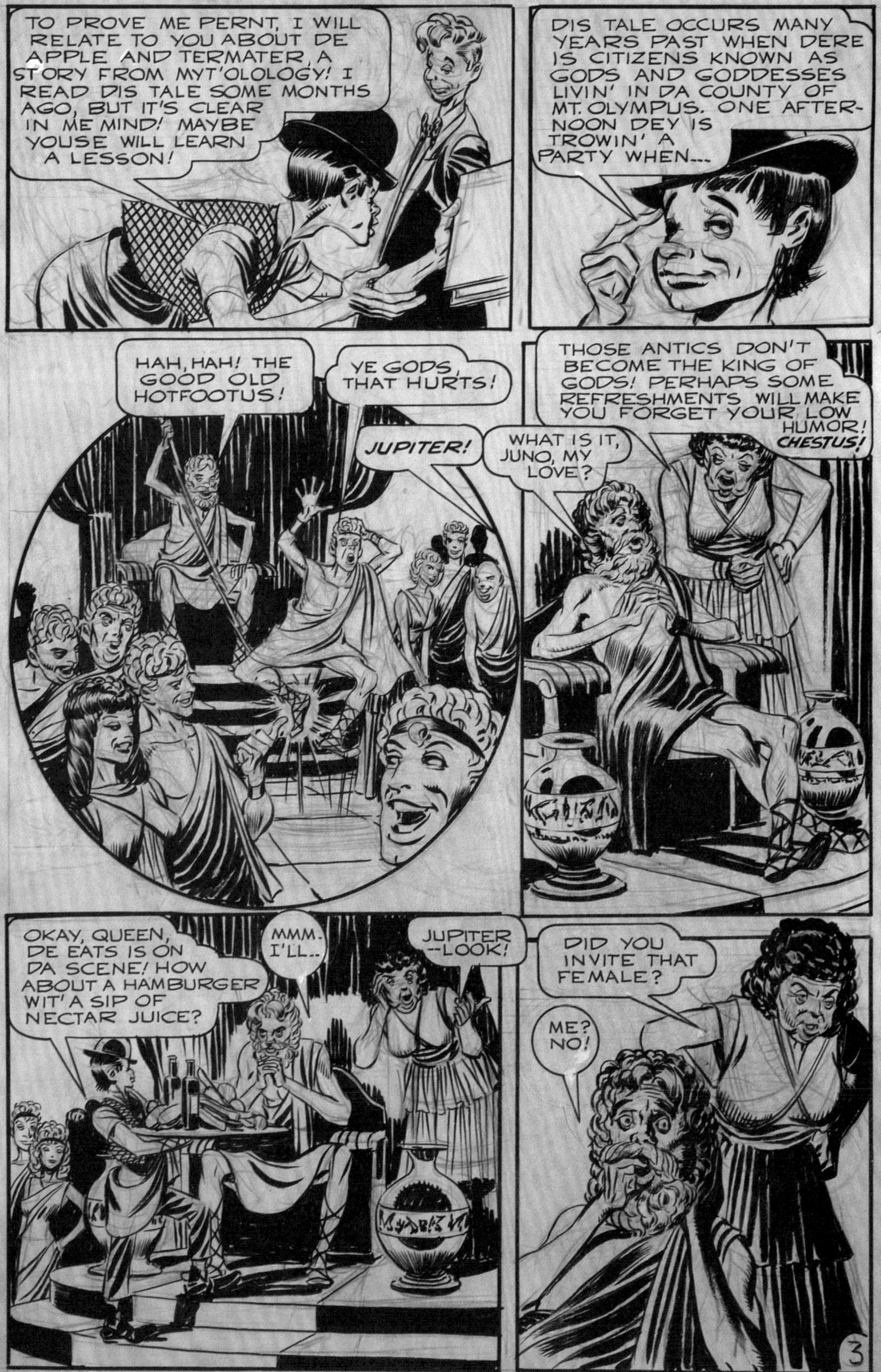
TO PROVE ME PERNT, I WILL RELATE TO YOU ABOUT DE APPLE AND TERMATER, A STORY FROM MYT'OLOLOGY! I READ DIS TALE SOME MONTHS AGO, BUT IT'S CLEAR IN ME MIND! MAYBE YOUSE WILL LEARN A LESSON!
DIS TALE OCCURS MANY YEARS PAST WHEN DERE IS CITIZENS KNOWN AS GODS AND GODDESSES LIVIN' IN DA COUNTY OF MT. OLYMPUS. ONE AFTER-NOON DEY IS TROWIN' A PARTY WHEN...
HAH, HAH! THE GOOD OLD HOTFOOTUS!
YE GODS, THAT HURTS!
JUPITER!
WHAT IS IT, JUNO, MY LOVE?
THOSE ANTICS DON'T BECOME THE KING OF GODS! PERHAPS SOME REFRESHMENTS WILL MAKE YOU FORGET YOUR LOW HUMOR! CHESTUS!
OKAY, QUEEN, DE EATS IS ON DA SCENE! HOW ABOUT A HAMBURGER WIT' A SIP OF NECTAR JUICE?
MMM. I'LL..
JUPITER --LOOK!
DID YOU INVITE THAT FEMALE?
ME? NO!
3

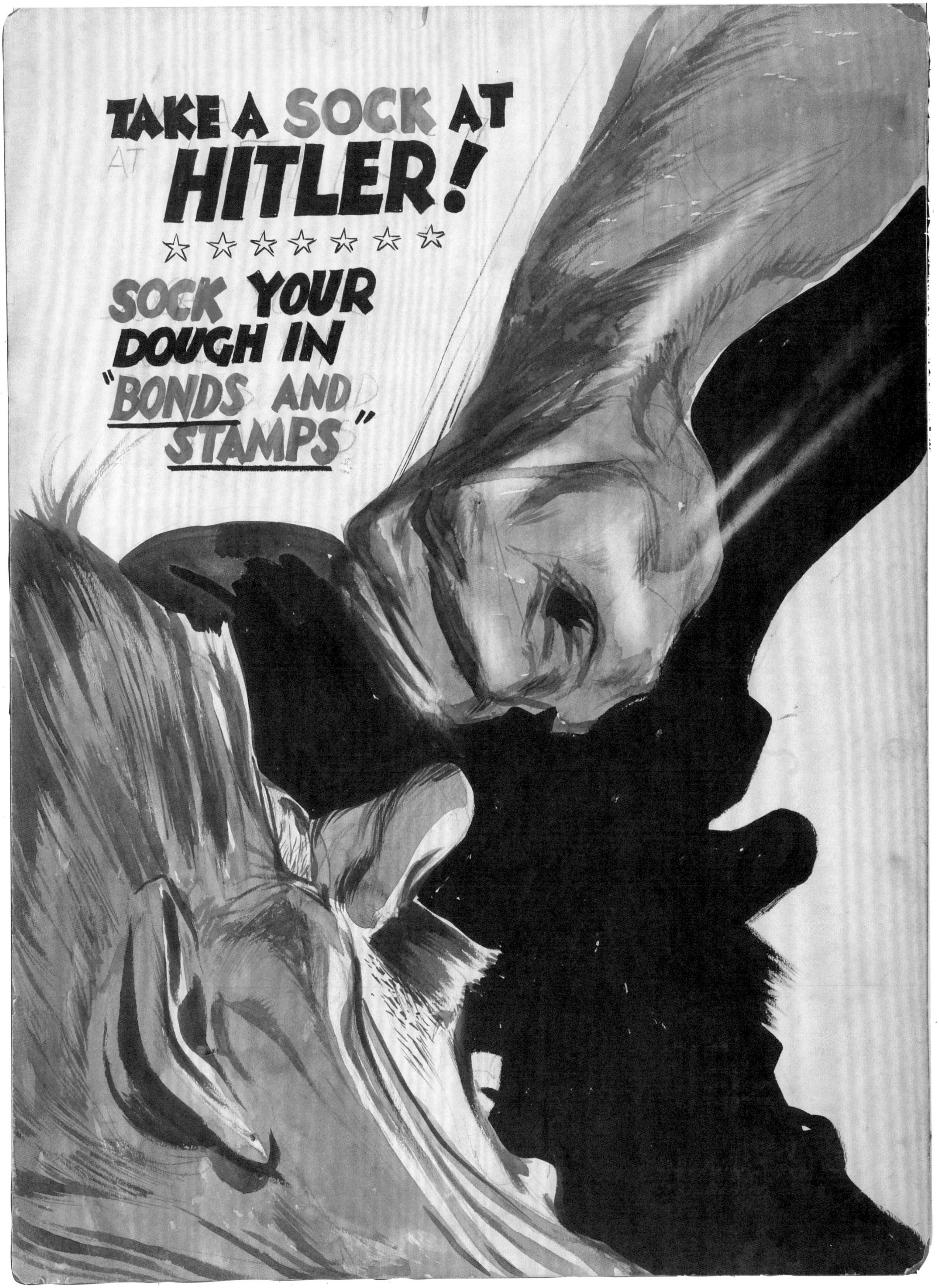
TAKE A SOCK AT
HITLER!
SOCK YOUR
DOUGH IN
"BONDS AND
STAMPS"

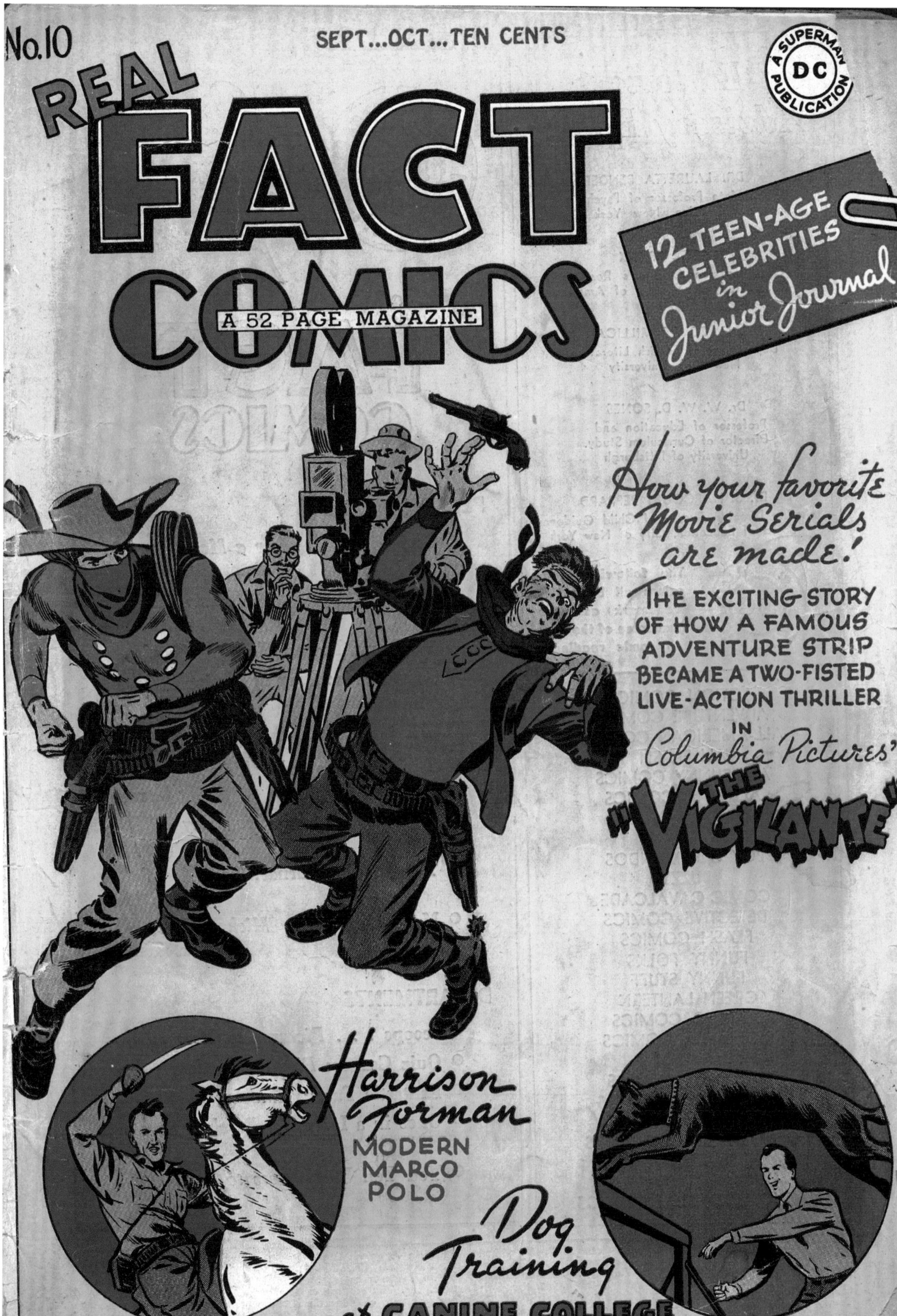
No.10
SEPT...OCT...TEN CENTS
A SUPERMAN DC PUBLICATION
REAL
FACT
COMICS
A 52 PAGE MAGAZINE
12 TEEN-AGE CELEBRITIES in Junior Journal
How your favorite Movie Serials are made!
THE EXCITING STORY OF HOW A FAMOUS ADVENTURE STRIP BECAME A TWO-FISTED LIVE-ACTION THRILLER IN
Columbia Pictures'
"THE VIGILANTE"
Harrison Forman
MODERN MARCO POLO
Dog Training
at CANINE COLLEGE

people who pick up a comic book would usually flip through the pages, and a larger panel, a more dramatic panel, catches their eye, that may be the book that they'll buy, just because of that illustration. Those are some of the things that I learned from him but there was a great deal. He was a terrific artist, terrific storyteller; beyond just being able to draw, he was able to communicate. And his characterization was so credible, so believable that he made the whole story that much more credible."[22]

Another youngster who visited the DC offices was Carmine Infantino. Carmine met Meskin for the first time when he was 16 years old and he and friend Frank Giacoia went to visit DC as fans and asked to meet the guy behind *Johnny Quick* and *The Vigilante*. As he had been with Joe Kubert earlier, Meskin was convivial and gracious. According to Infantino, Meskin's *Johnny Quick* was a great influence when he later worked on *The Flash*.

With *Johnny Quick*, Meskin introduced another innovation. Previously, within the pages of DC's flagship character *The Flash*, speed lines were used to connote rapid movement. Never one to take the easy way out, Meskin introduced the use of multiple figures to show not only how fast Quick was traveling but the path he took as well. This afforded Meskin more opportunities to develop character and humor. It was also more time-consuming; where another artist would draw one figure, Meskin was drawing ten. "In order to indicate extreme motion, I drew Johnny Quick so that he seemed to be everywhere at once," Meskin recalled.[23] Johnny Quick stood in direct contrast to the moody Vigilante, always appeared to be having a good time, smiling at the audience, inviting them along for the ride.

PREVIOUS PAGE. Although Meskin never served during the war, he used his talents to aid in the war effort. He created anti-fascist posters and visited the U.S. Naval Hospital, where he entertained wounded soldiers by drawing sketches (collection of Jerry Robinson). LEFT: *Real Fact Comics* #10 cover, 1949. (© DC Comics. All Rights Reserved. Used with Permission.)

LOVE ON PAPER

Perhaps these smiling figures represent Meskin's own happiness. He had begun dating Betty Lampel, the adopted daughter of a Hungarian tailor, in 1943 and within a year they were wed—on May 17, 1944, at city hall in Manhattan. They spent their honeymoon at Coney Island, where they were photographed at the very same spot that Meskin had spent time with his brother Nat when they were children. The couple settled in Manhattan at 124 West 86th Street, between Columbus and Amsterdam. Meskin was about to turn 28.

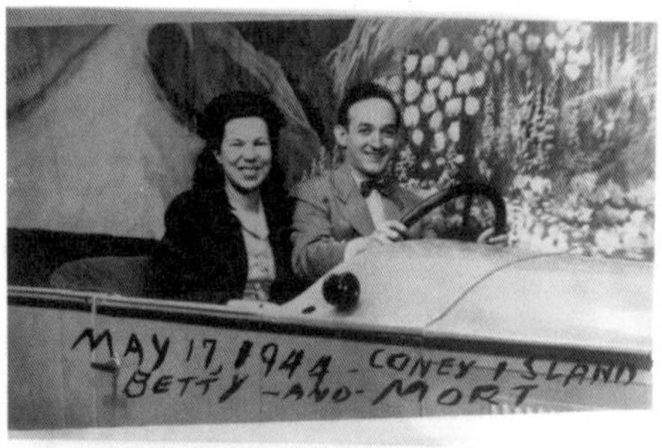
MAY 17, 1944 - CONEY ISLAND
BETTY - AND - MORT

On their wedding day. No time for a honey-moon for a working comic book artist.

Two sons soon followed: Peter in 1945 and Philip in 1949. Although he worked long hours, Meskin was a warm and attentive father. When the door opened in the evening, the boys would climb on to what seemed giant boat-like shoes (Meskin was only 5' 7") to ride around the apartment. With the boys in tow he would kiss his wife hello, and then he would extend his limbs at right angles, hands on hips, Superman fashion, and the boys would climb him like a human jungle gym. He would deposit the days' riches on a table: myriad comics, art supplies and small presents for his sons. "I know some kids are not so excited when their fathers come home," Peter remembers, "but when dad would come home, we were excited every night, 'Daddy's Home!,' and the door would open and there would be Daddy and we would climb on his feet and he would shuffle in with us wrapped around his lower legs, and he'd try to kiss Mom hello, and we just wanted all his attention, and he did his best to give all of us attention.

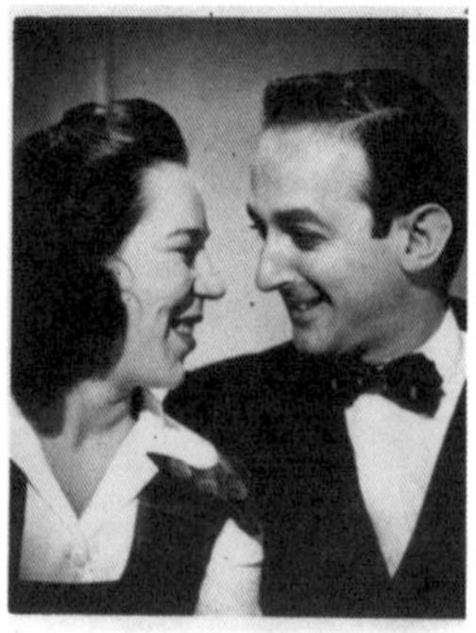

ABOVE: Mort with Betty, 1944. BELOW: Mort with son Peter.

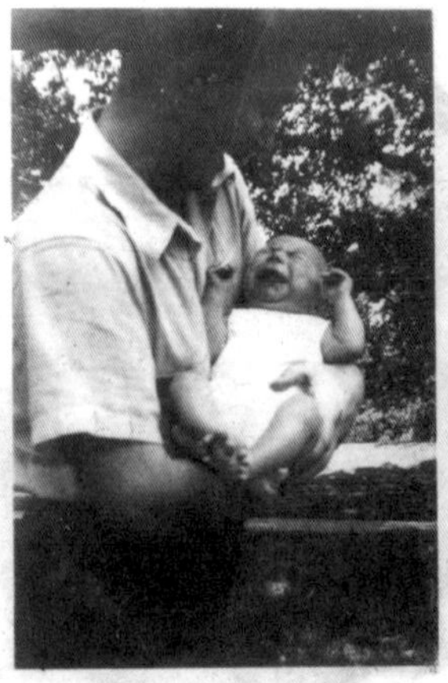

"Dad was very creative, and would build things in the house, turn the entire living room into a planetarium. I remember getting masking tape and string and we would all design stars and planets and hang them from the ceiling and do all of that. Dad built an entire rocket ship out of cardboard that we would get inside and play with all the dials, all out of cardboard and masking tape. He made a 'Knight of the Red Horse' costume for me out of poster board and masking tape and another for Philip, and one time I even handed in a carving of an Eskimo to my Cub Scout den that was blatantly too professional and my Den Mother said, 'You didn't do this,' and I proudly replied, 'No, my Daddy did it!' The fact that he had carved it for me was much more important than trying to palm it off as my own creation. When dad took a large piece of Ivory soap and held it in his left hand and carved out this beautiful Eskimo with an X-acto type knife, it was just an amazing thing to watch. As far back as I can remember I've always been totally awed by dad's artistic abilities"[24]

In the evenings Mort would tell his sons "One Hundred Percent Almost

True To Life Stories," which featured Peter and Philip ("Once upon a time, on a far-off planet Prince Peter and King Philip..."), creating them on the spot. He would sing to them, in a beautiful voice, never stuttering. Mort left the disciplinarian chores to the boys' mother. Peter recalls, "We had a nice, close, loving relationship. He never hit me, never once. My mother once told him to spank me when I had been acting up. Dad took me in another room, laid me on his lap and said, "OK, I'm going to clap my hands real loud and every time I do that, you scream. I looked at him as if to say, 'What are you talking about?' and he clapped his hands. I faked a scream but had to control the giggles because otherwise my mother would come in."[25]

ABOVE: Mort, Betty and
son Philip, Manhattan, 1951.

"Philip and I would hop up on the bureau and Dad would tighten his stomach and we would leap off into the air and land on his stomach full force. And we would say, 'Do it again!' Mom would get worried and Dad would say, 'Let the boys have their fun.' And we'd jump again, it was wonderful! We used to climb up my father. He was like our own jungle gym and he would simply stand and make muscles. I think at that point I was below his knee and now I'm climbing up, with a little help from him and now I'm getting on his shoulders, and not quite touching the ceiling." He taught both boys to play chess, allowing them to win to feel good about themselves. "For him, playing the game was more important than winning the game," Peter said. And he enjoyed taking the boys bowling, regularly scoring above 200. Meskin maintained a studio space with Jerry Robinson so he could work away from home, undistracted. Peter, recalls, "I remember Dad's studio, which was a room I loved to go in because that's where magic happened. I'd stand on my tiptoes and look up at his easel and watch him draw and paint. I could smell all the paints and inks. I loved it.

ABOVE: Mort. Betty and
Peter, summer 1951.
BELOW: Mort with Peter
and Philip, Coney Island
Beach, NY.

"I asked him once, 'How do you draw, Dad?' He shrugged and said, 'I don't know.' He'd point to his shoulder and say, 'It comes down my arm and goes out my fingers and comes out of the brush.' He never wanted to teach Philip and me how to draw. He felt it was too difficult a life. I never learned to draw because he didn't want us to."[26] Philip concurs: "That's true, though I don't think he actively discouraged it. I once asked him about that when I was in high school. He said it was a conscious decision on his part not to encourage us in art because of the bad feelings he had towards making a career out of art, the struggles you have to go through, etc."[27]

Around 1949 the family relocated to a middle-income housing

project in Brooklyn, Vanderveer Estates, built that year on the site of
the old Flatbush Water Works as a haven for working families. Barbra
Streisand, a year older than Peter, grew up in the same project.
Peter recalls, "It was a clean, lovely, nice neighborhood with six-story
attached buildings grouped around a lovely terrace area where the
kids could ride their bikes and play and not be in traffic at all. Also, I
always remember Dad encouraging us to be active, to climb up on the
rocks in Prospect Park and I felt protected, I could try to do anything.
He always felt that whenever a child was asking a question they
deserved and were ready to get an answer on their level. Now a lot of parents

say, 'Come back when you're 15,' but Dad wasn't that way. He wanted to give us
some kind of answer, and I always loved him for that. Dad always believed the
parents should sit still and the children could go wander and come back, touch
home base and go out again. At the beach, he would always be very careful
when he was teaching us how to find our way back to the umbrella. He would
stand by the water and he would point, 'Look for that umbrella, look beyond it,
line it up with this, look for the colors of it,' he was always teaching us how to
look at things, from the earliest stage. He was a protective dad.

"We had a lovely childhood. Wonderful memories of being on the beach,
looking in the Wonderland Toy Store, our special sitting place at Farragut Pool,
it was our favorite place in the world. Dad sang a lot, both Mom and Dad sang.
That was the routine every night. Two single beds, Mom and Dad, would take
turns sitting in between us, Dad would tell us 'One Hundred Percent Almost
True To Life Stories.' They were hoping we would fall asleep right away, but we
would say, 'Oh no, we've got to get a song' and Mom would sing a whole series
of songs, 'Danny Boy,' 'There's a Long, Long Trail A-Winding,' 'Somewhere Over
the Rainbow,' 'Pennies from Heaven,' 'Take Me Out to the Ballgame,' 'East Side,
West Side' and a whole bunch of others, and Dad and Mom would often read to
us. Dad was actually better at telling stories than reading to us. I think he might
have stuttered when he read. But when he told stories or sang, he didn't.

ABOVE: Peter and
Mort, Broad
Channel Day
Camp. 1952.
BELOW: Peter and
Philip, in front of
the Ferris Wheel,
Coney Island,
NY, 1958.

"Dad was a wonderful athlete, a gymnast, and of course he was a really
great swimmer. At Farragut Pool we would play 'Daddy Whale and Baby Whale'
and I would hang onto his shoulders and he would take a deep breath and
literally swim under water for the entire pool with me hanging on. At five years
old it felt to me as if I was holding on to a submarine, or a ship, or...a whale,
usually above water, and every once in a while I'm below, and I'm going 'Dad,
can you get me up on the surface!?' And I loved it. I got my love of the water
from Dad and of course I've been involved with water ever since. Both Phil and I
are good swimmers and I was on the swim team in high school and all."

Meskin worked all day and into the night and weekends as well, but still made time for family life. On the weekends Betty and Mort would take the boys to the nearby amusement parks and beaches, spending quality time together.

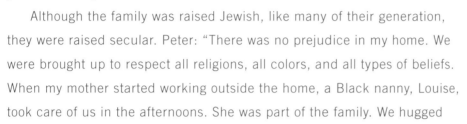

Philip, Peter and Mort, Farragut Pool, Brooklyn, NY, 1950.

"Dad took us to art museums," Peter remembers fondly. "He'd tell us about the artwork but didn't make it seem like we were in school. It was fun. He talked about what he saw in the work of art and we didn't ever want to know about them from books. We just wanted to communicate directly with the painting. Dad had a lot to say, and I don't remember him stuttering at those times."[28] Still, both Peter and Philip learned much from the many art and nature books in their parents' library.

Although the family was raised Jewish, like many of their generation, they were raised secular. Peter: "There was no prejudice in my home. We were brought up to respect all religions, all colors, and all types of beliefs. When my mother started working outside the home, a Black nanny, Louise, took care of us in the afternoons. She was part of the family. We hugged and kissed her and my parents treated her very warmly."[29]

LEFT: Peter and Mort, second from left, father and son cub-scout dinner, 1954. BELOW: Philip and Mort, Coney Island.

On occasion the Meskins would give parties, inviting over friends like the Robinsons. The boys would sneak out after bedtime to try to engage in the activities and partake in the snacks, only to be sent back to bed by their mother. They would also visit the Robinsons in their West End Avenue Apartment where the boys played with the Robinson children's rabbit on the floor.

Still, things were far from perfect. Meskin had a hard time keeping up with deadlines, a constant pressure. No longer afforded the luxury of inking his own work, he was often paired with George Roussos, although other inkers included Charles Paris, Cliff Young, and the neophyte Joe Kubert.

Leonard Starr was in his early twenties when he visited the DC offices and encountered a Meskin page. Starr recalls, "In the late '40s, working for Funnies Inc. where we had been grinding out features for various publishers to satisfy the servicemen and -women who were enriching the then young comic book industry, I felt that I was ready to graduate to DC. I arrived with a portfolio of samples one afternoon at lunch time, the editor was out, but in the wonderfully casual way things were run in those days, was told that if I felt like it I could wait in the production room till he returned. In those days many of the cartoonists worked in-house and so there were quite a few empty drawing boards in the room, some with work in progress. On one of the boards, though, was a large sheet with sketches of figures in action, instantly recognizable as The Vigilante, a favorite of mine, the panels so elegantly composed and atmospheric, rare at that time. Already awed by Mort's, work it wasn't just that the drawings were dazzling, it was the fluidity and ease with which they were done that floored me. I didn't wait any longer. I just took my unopened portfolio and left."

This early period had a profound effect on another budding artist as well: Alex Toth. Born in 1926, Toth attended the High School of Industrial Arts in Manhattan, and while still a student there began his comics career at age 15, illustrating true stories for *Heroic* magazine through Steve Douglas' Famous Funnies shop. After graduating in 1947, Toth was hired by DC editor Sheldon Mayer, and worked on myriad titles. He went on to be recognized as one of the great innovators in both the comic book and animation media, and duly noted his debt to that earlier innovator Meskin (see sidebar).

RIGHT: *Wildcat* splash page from *Sensation Comics*, #67, 1947. (© DC Comics. All Rights Reserved. Used with Permission.)

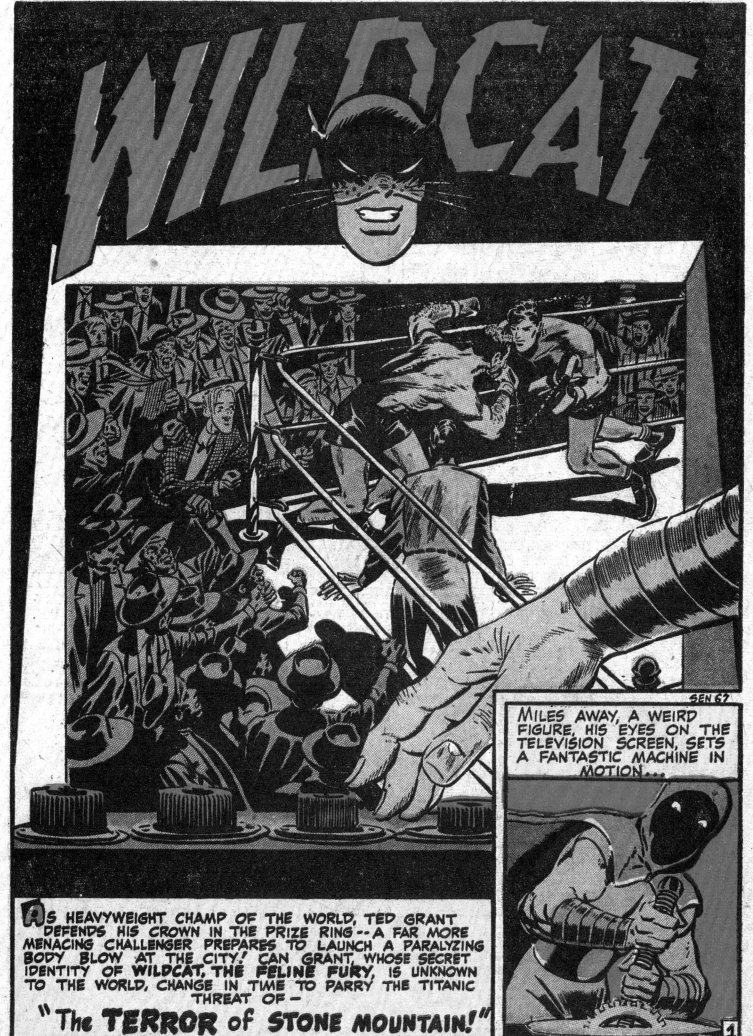

MILES AWAY, A WEIRD FIGURE, HIS EYES ON THE TELEVISION SCREEN, SETS A FANTASTIC MACHINE IN MOTION...

AS HEAVYWEIGHT CHAMP OF THE WORLD, TED GRANT DEFENDS HIS CROWN IN THE PRIZE RING -- A FAR MORE MENACING CHALLENGER PREPARES TO LAUNCH A PARALYZING BODY BLOW AT THE CITY! CAN GRANT, WHOSE SECRET IDENTITY OF WILDCAT, THE FELINE FURY, IS UNKNOWN TO THE WORLD, CHANGE IN TIME TO PARRY THE TITANIC THREAT OF --

"The TERROR of STONE MOUNTAIN!"

TOTH ON MESKIN

"Mort Meskin broke rules, created his own (and years of splendid artistry along the way) — most notably in his *Vigilante* and *Johnny Quick* series for DC Comics... His invention, daring, and subtlety were unique and exciting to us young Turks and older pros. Mort created surprises, beauty, action, mystery art through his keen talent for the unusual viewpoint, layout, composition, lighting, massing of forms and solid shapes, rich blacks, and line work, in ways deceptively simple, bold, strong (yet subtle, remember), and clearly-stated, so respected that no inker of Mort's fine pencils ever altered the character of his work, and Mort enjoyed the best of the lot at DC—Joe Kubert (first rate), Jerry Robinson, and George 'Inky' Roussos.

"Mort drew pages packed with up to 12 panels, yet through his excellent design and economy, managed to avoid the trap of clutter and confusion and delivered beautifully-constructed storytelling of dramatic quality. Students of his work will note that Mort's world was not a realistic one—guns were outsized, cars, trucks, trains, boats, planes were exaggerations and imaginative devices once-removed from the real items (akin to Jack Kirby's own personalized graphic liberties) but these distortions added to their visual impact, not unlike the stuff of gag strips, eh? Absolutely correct!

"Said students of the art could find no better model for emulation than Mort Meskin's action-filled *Johnny Quick* pages, where he proved exceptionally adept at strobe figure motion, with smooth follow-throughs of overlapping bodies of Johnny performing stunts and fistwork without parallel in comic book art. These stories by Mort are landmarks of our craft's very history; so study up! Mark well their enviable simplicity!

"...Mort's intention was to move your eyes across [and] out, not to stop your scan of dialogue and art. That was a pro, a thinking pro, at work, and Mort was that, and more. He created action, atmosphere, a sense of place, of movement, throughout his storytelling—drama, suspense, surprise, and novelty through economy. Mort edited out superfluous technique and distracting clutter. The resulting simplicity made for smoother reading flow of caption and dialogue copy as well as his art. He served his text all that much better for it, too. Also, consider that simplicity of open areas so receptive to color (the hues of which he could not possibly know in advance, save for his heroes' costumes) versus his generous sweeps of large masses and spottings of black. What those black and whites of his original art did was to ensure the integrity of his work.

"Things, in fact, haven't changed all that much, have they? But let me explain a bit about Mort's penciling method during those mid-'40s DC years—something I witnessed, firsthand, while visiting his studio flat, before I entered DC's hallowed halls at 480 Lexington as a goggle-eyed tyro. Mort was busy penciling a *Vigilante* story, despite my intruding and questioning presence, and what I saw him do that afternoon was indicative of his unique approach to every part of his creative endeavors... He took a DC page blank and rubbed soft (2B) lead across its face, smudged it, into a smooth, overall gray tone; script at hand, he took a kneaded eraser and (referring to script) proceeded to 'pick out'/erase panel borders; across, top row to bottom, from circles to squares to rectangles, in varying sizes, of course (as always, then) I was fascinated, delighted, and puzzled. Then, his eraser picked out solid white shapes of each panel's interiors—a caption panel, a balloon, a figure, another. Working in reverse, he erased shapes, forms, interlocking compositional elements, to create complete (but negative/white on gray) pictures. It was simple, efficient, and effective.

"No messy haylined penciling for Mort Meskin. His way was astoundingly basic, elementary, devoid of any concern other than to sculpt out, from a gray mass, his solid forms—damn, it was brilliant. My eyes and memory bank absorbed his every move. Pure joy, it was panel by panel, enthralled with his overall page composition. If a shape or space didn't work, he merely smudged in more gray tone, and tried again until he got it right. Working his magic there before my novice eyes, it was ruddy genius. All the while, he cautioned me not to try the same thing because I was too young, green, and ungrounded in experience to fully comprehend or utilize the procedure. Well, now, he knew that that was exactly what I intended to do, once home again—he was absolutely right, tho', absolutely 100% correct! I did try it, again and again and again—never did get it quite right, gave it up, went back to my own stumbling way of creating pictures with a pencil—in turn, with black, blue, heliotrope leads, from 2H to 4B and back again, and with charcoal smudge-stumps (for soft-shaded blocking-in of figures, etc.—did have luck with that method for some time). Years later, I finally learnt enough to use Mort's reverse method, and learnt even more for having done so, fully appreciating, if not partially-achieving, such concentration on shapes, forms, in those first movements of composition. It led me on, to deeper study of all other types of graphic art. I owe him a great debt.

"...Mort Meskin created bold, dramatic beauty in his straightforward art and storytelling devices, entertaining us all the while through always doing the unexpected, creating new delights for us. His meaning and intellect were not given the editorial, environmental, or fiscal appreciation due him, and so, as in so many other cases in our curious profession, he was distressed enough with it until his only solace was to leave it—and so he did.

"The loss was ours..."[30]

THE DYNAMIC DUO

After the war, Meskin and Robinson collaborated and worked for other companies as well as DC. From 1946 to 1949 they worked on *Black Terror* and *Fighting Yank*. "I had left *Batman* about '46 or 7, and Mort was still working there [at DC]. I took a year or more off and I went to Florida and I came back and that is when Mort and I decided to work together," said Robinson. They rented a studio on Fifth Avenue and 42nd Street. "Standard was one of our biggest accounts," continued Robinson. "So we got a studio and we decided to pool our resources. Mort came in with *Vigilante* and *Johnny Quick* and I got an account, *Black Terror* and *Fighting Yank*, and we then also did work for Simon and Kirby."

During this period they developed a true collaborative way of working, as they would both do layout, pencils and inking, changing off, sometimes from panel to panel. "After awhile that type of stuff gets boring, creating that much stuff, day after day. We were experimenting a lot. That's why we shifted back and forth; when you got blocked or tired of doing one aspect of the work it would be a pleasant relief when you looked forward to doing penciling instead of inking, and vice versa. It was to do something different, from a different perspective. Sometimes we would pencil and ink on transparent vellum, over the pencils, with the light touch of a brush on the vellum, another time we would try to do a story without pencils, and then we decided to do a story where the subject was all lit from above, all cast shadows and black and white."[31]

This work is a complete wedding of the two, although Meskin tends to dominate, making Robinson and Meskin the second most important drawing team in early comics history, behind Simon and Kirby (who were also the highest paid). They would work separately as well, Robinson on *Atoman*, Meskin on *Golden Lad* for Spark, working with writer and publisher Kendell Foster Crossen. Crossen had written hundreds of pulp detective fiction and novels and radio scripts under his own name as well as myriad pseudonyms, and believed that if you paid the artists higher wages it would attract a better pool of artists—Meskin, Robinson, Roussos, Mac Raboy, and Lou Fine among them. "Crossen was a very progressive guy and kind of an early hero of creators' rights," notes Jerry Robinson. Another writer Meskin was paired with at Spark was Joseph Greene, who also shared a leftist political inclination. Despite all their efforts, the company was short-lived.[32]

With all this freelance work, Meskin continued to work for DC as well. His sheer volume of output and the quality of his work during this period is astounding. His early DC work, as well as his collaborations with Robinson, are

RIGHT AND FOUR SPREADS FOLLOW-ING: *Fighting Yank* and *Black Terror* represenated one of the closest collaborations between two comic artists, Jerry Robinson and Mort Meskin, Nedor /Standard publishing, 1948-1949.

[TEXT CONTINUES ON PAGE 77]

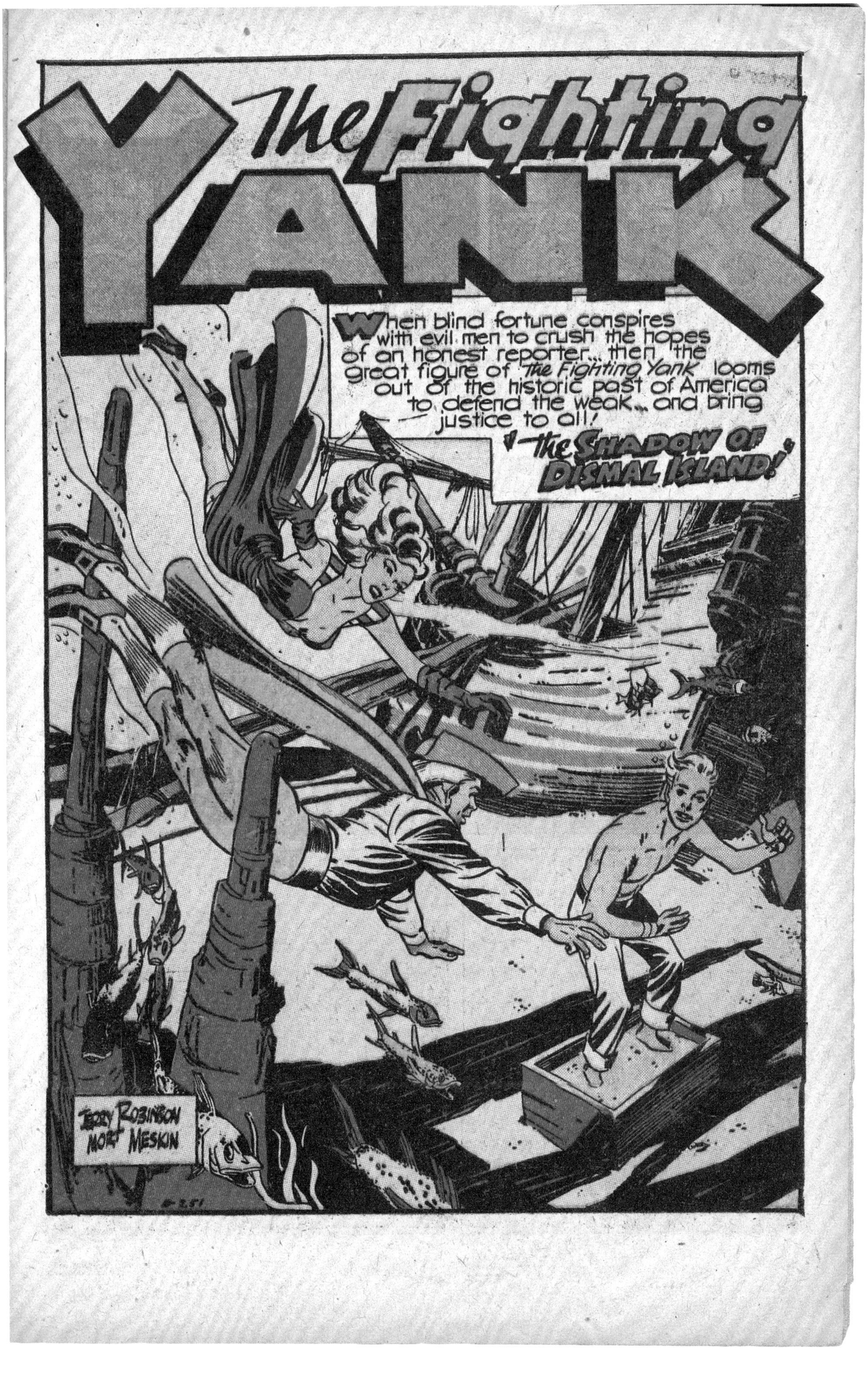
The Fighting YANK
When blind fortune conspires with evil men to crush the hopes of an honest reporter... then the great figure of The Fighting Yank looms out of the historic past of America to defend the weak... and bring justice to all!
"The Shadow of Dismal Island!"
Jerry Robinson Mort Meskin

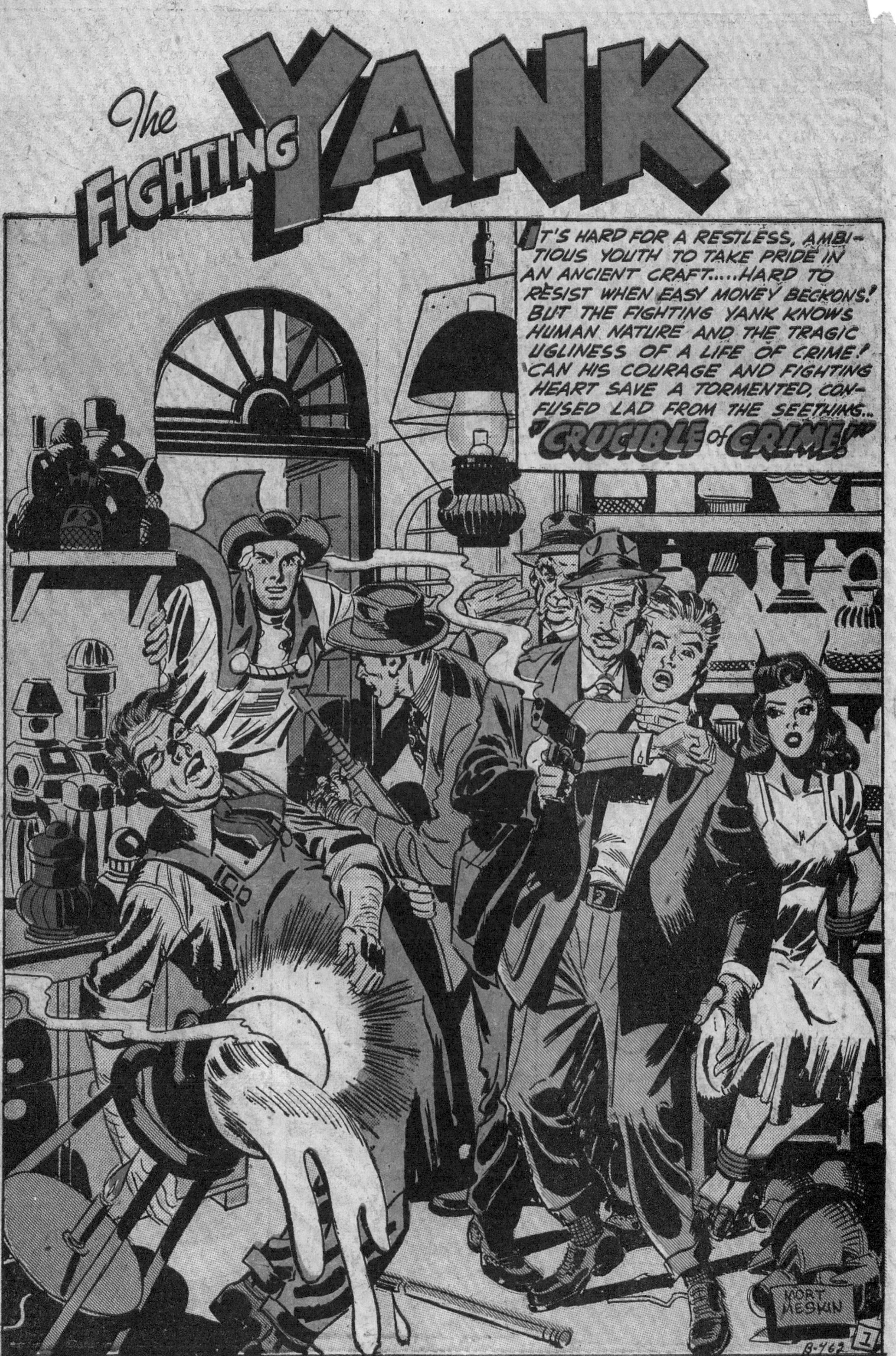
The FIGHTING YANK
IT'S HARD FOR A RESTLESS, AMBITIOUS YOUTH TO TAKE PRIDE IN AN ANCIENT CRAFT.....HARD TO RESIST WHEN EASY MONEY BECKONS! BUT THE FIGHTING YANK KNOWS HUMAN NATURE AND THE TRAGIC UGLINESS OF A LIFE OF CRIME! CAN HIS COURAGE AND FIGHTING HEART SAVE A TORMENTED, CONFUSED LAD FROM THE SEETHING...
"CRUCIBLE of CRIME!"
MORT MESKIN
B-462
1

The Fighting Yank

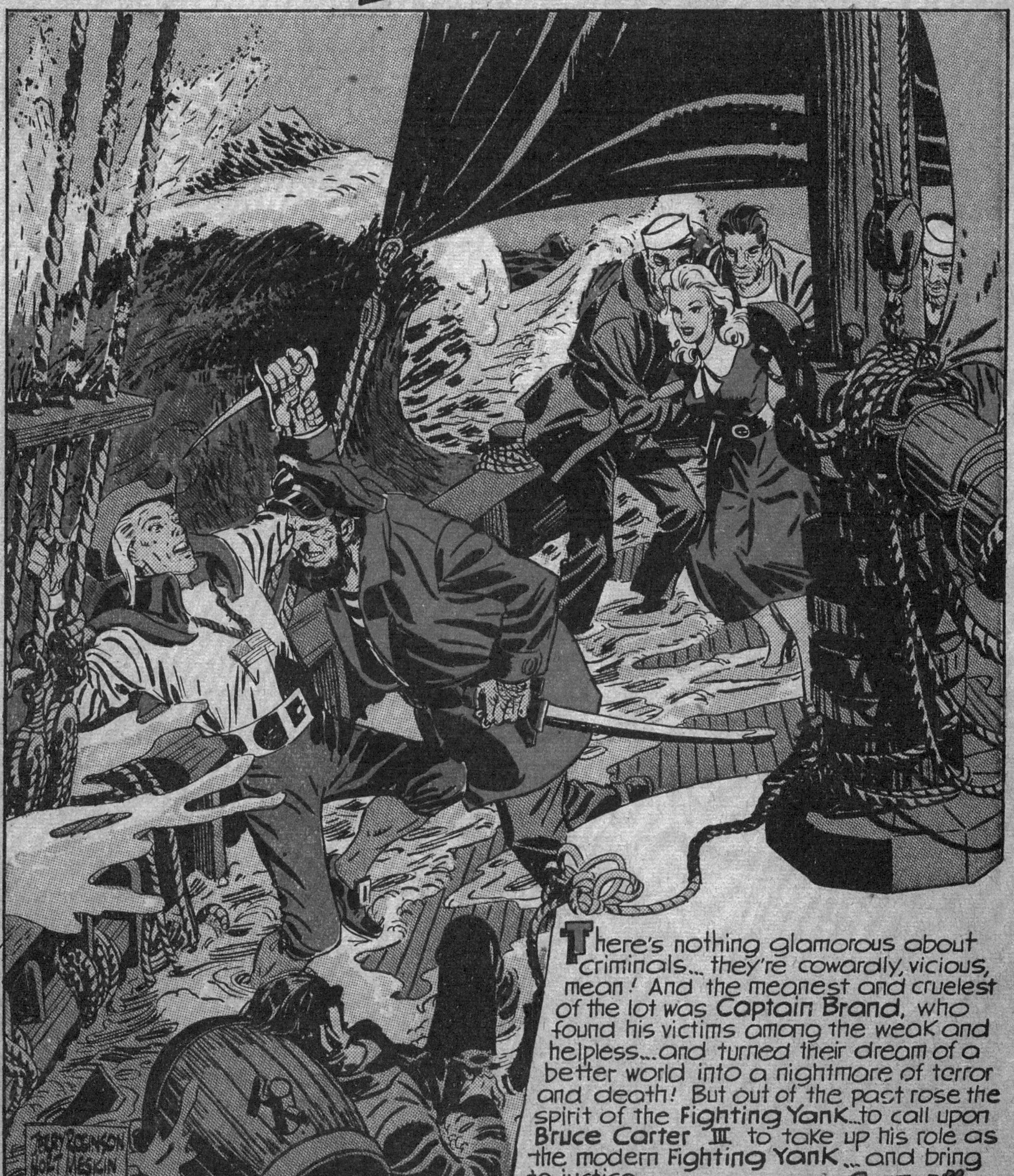

There's nothing glamorous about criminals... they're cowardly, vicious, mean! And the meanest and cruelest of the lot was Captain Brand, who found his victims among the weak and helpless...and turned their dream of a better world into a nightmare of terror and death! But out of the past rose the spirit of the Fighting Yank...to call upon Bruce Carter III to take up his role as the modern Fighting Yank... and bring to justice...
"The Beasts of the Sea!"
Jerry Robinson
Mort Meskin

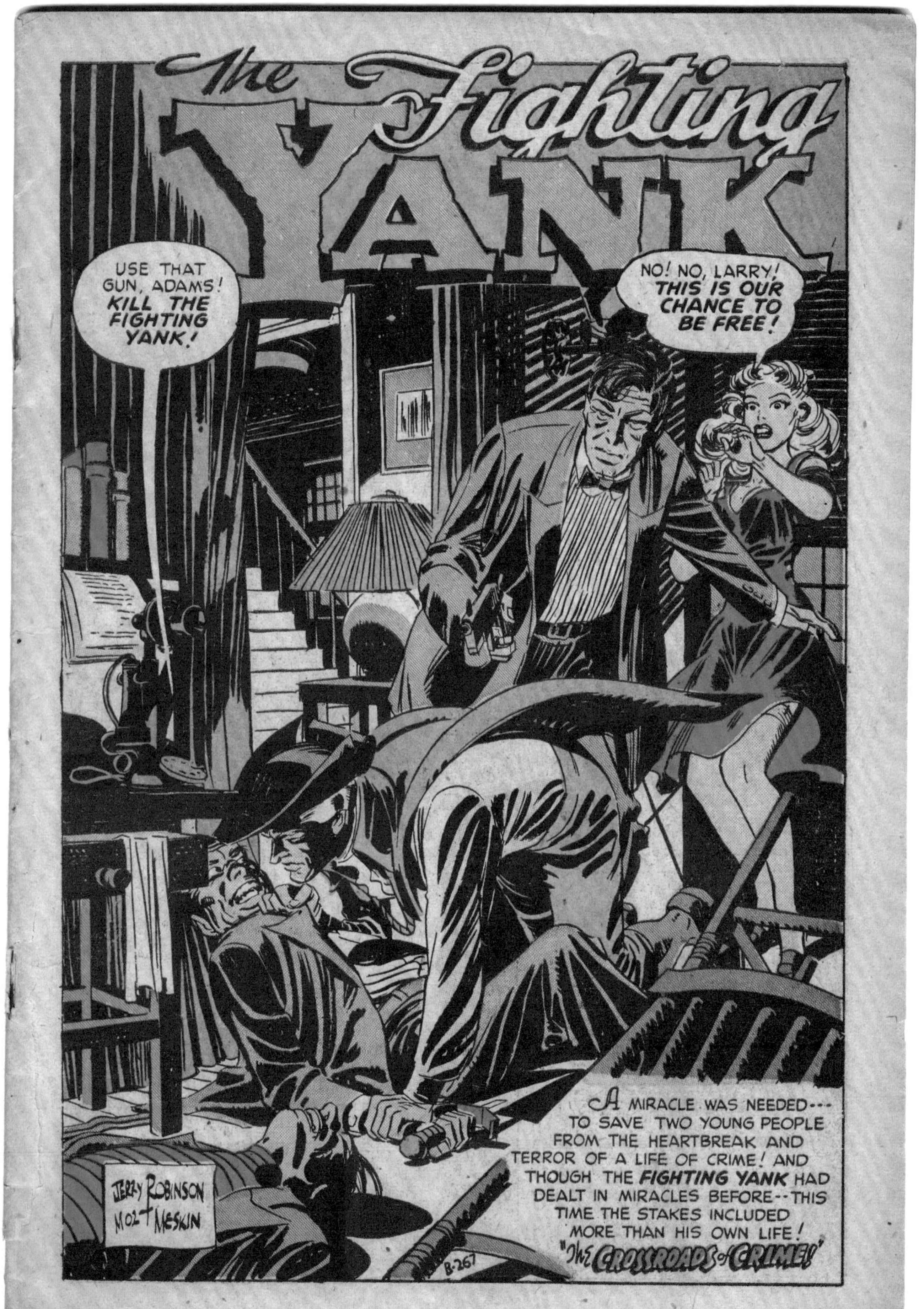
The Fighting YANK
USE THAT GUN, ADAMS! KILL THE FIGHTING YANK!
NO! NO, LARRY! THIS IS OUR CHANCE TO BE FREE!
A MIRACLE WAS NEEDED--- TO SAVE TWO YOUNG PEOPLE FROM THE HEARTBREAK AND TERROR OF A LIFE OF CRIME! AND THOUGH THE FIGHTING YANK HAD DEALT IN MIRACLES BEFORE--THIS TIME THE STAKES INCLUDED MORE THAN HIS OWN LIFE!
"THE CROSSROADS of CRIME!"
JERRY ROBINSON
MORT MESKIN
B-267

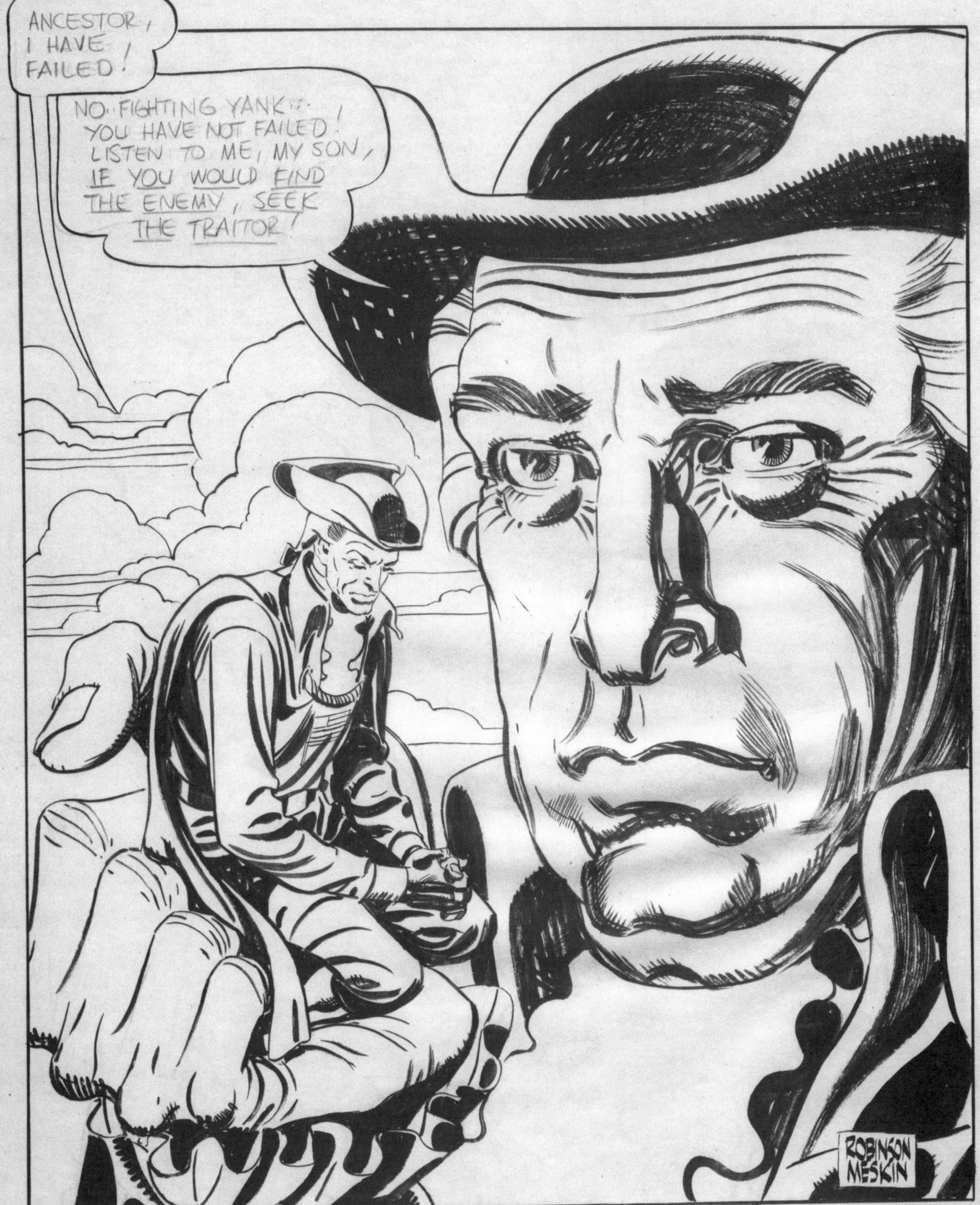
ANCESTOR, I HAVE FAILED!
NO, FIGHTING YANK... YOU HAVE NOT FAILED! LISTEN TO ME, MY SON, IF YOU WOULD FIND THE ENEMY, SEEK THE TRAITOR!
ROBINSON MESKIN

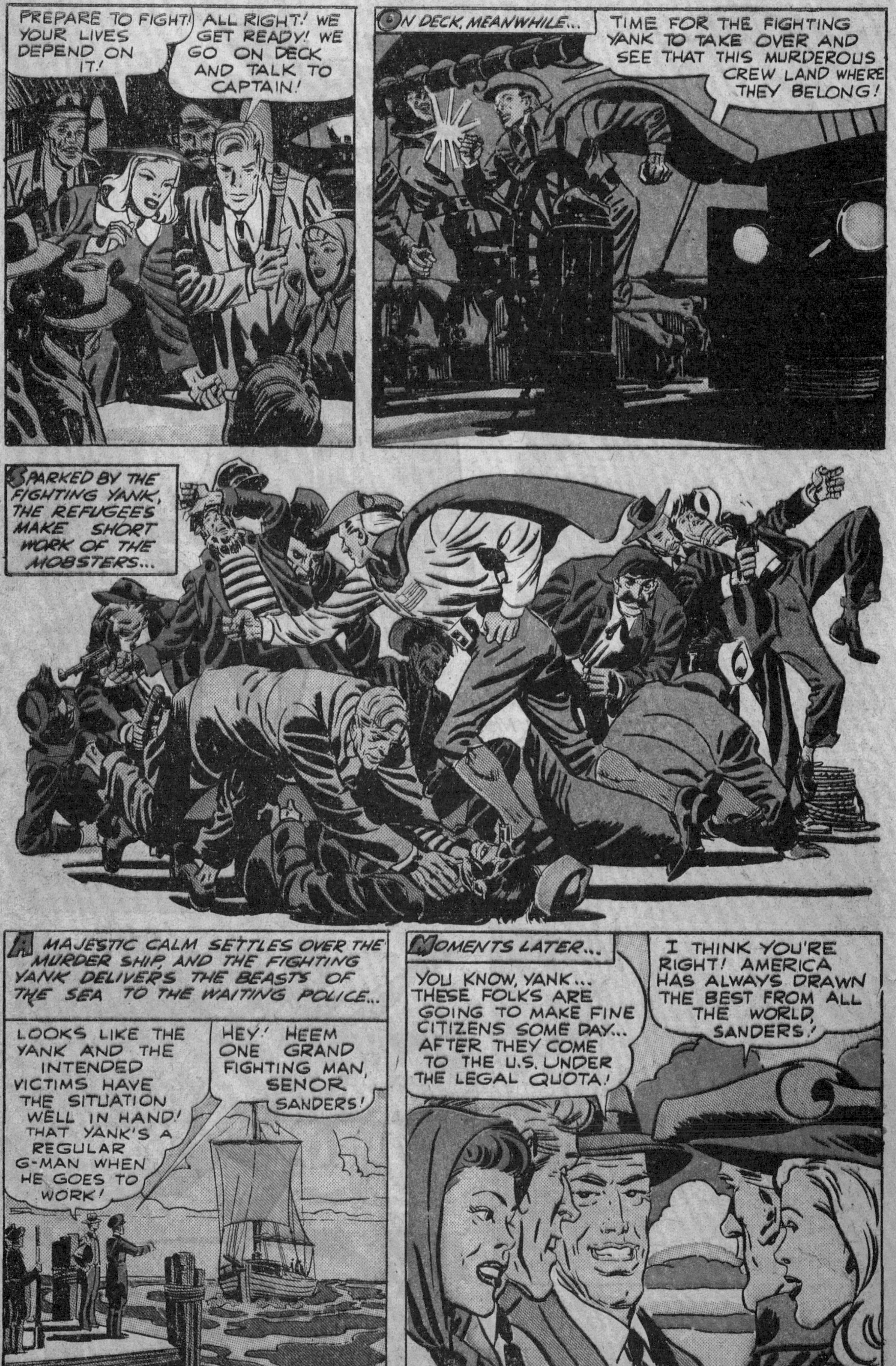
PREPARE TO FIGHT! YOUR LIVES DEPEND ON IT!
ALL RIGHT! WE GET READY! WE GO ON DECK AND TALK TO CAPTAIN!
ON DECK, MEANWHILE...
TIME FOR THE FIGHTING YANK TO TAKE OVER AND SEE THAT THIS MURDEROUS CREW LAND WHERE THEY BELONG!
SPARKED BY THE FIGHTING YANK, THE REFUGEES MAKE SHORT WORK OF THE MOBSTERS...
A MAJESTIC CALM SETTLES OVER THE MURDER SHIP, AND THE FIGHTING YANK DELIVERS THE BEASTS OF THE SEA TO THE WAITING POLICE...
LOOKS LIKE THE YANK AND THE INTENDED VICTIMS HAVE THE SITUATION WELL IN HAND! THAT YANK'S A REGULAR G-MAN WHEN HE GOES TO WORK!
HEY! HEEM ONE GRAND FIGHTING MAN, SENOR SANDERS!
MOMENTS LATER...
YOU KNOW, YANK... THESE FOLKS ARE GOING TO MAKE FINE CITIZENS SOME DAY... AFTER THEY COME TO THE U.S. UNDER THE LEGAL QUOTA!
I THINK YOU'RE RIGHT! AMERICA HAS ALWAYS DRAWN THE BEST FROM ALL THE WORLD, SANDERS!

considered by many to be among the finest comic art produced during the Golden Age.

Robinson notes, "I used to do a lot of work in those days, [but Meskin] went further than anybody, or was capable of going further than anybody. My one biggest stretch is that I did a Batman story over a weekend, 13 pages, it nearly killed me, 48 hours in a row; that's something Mort could do

[TEXT CONTINUES ON PAGE 85]

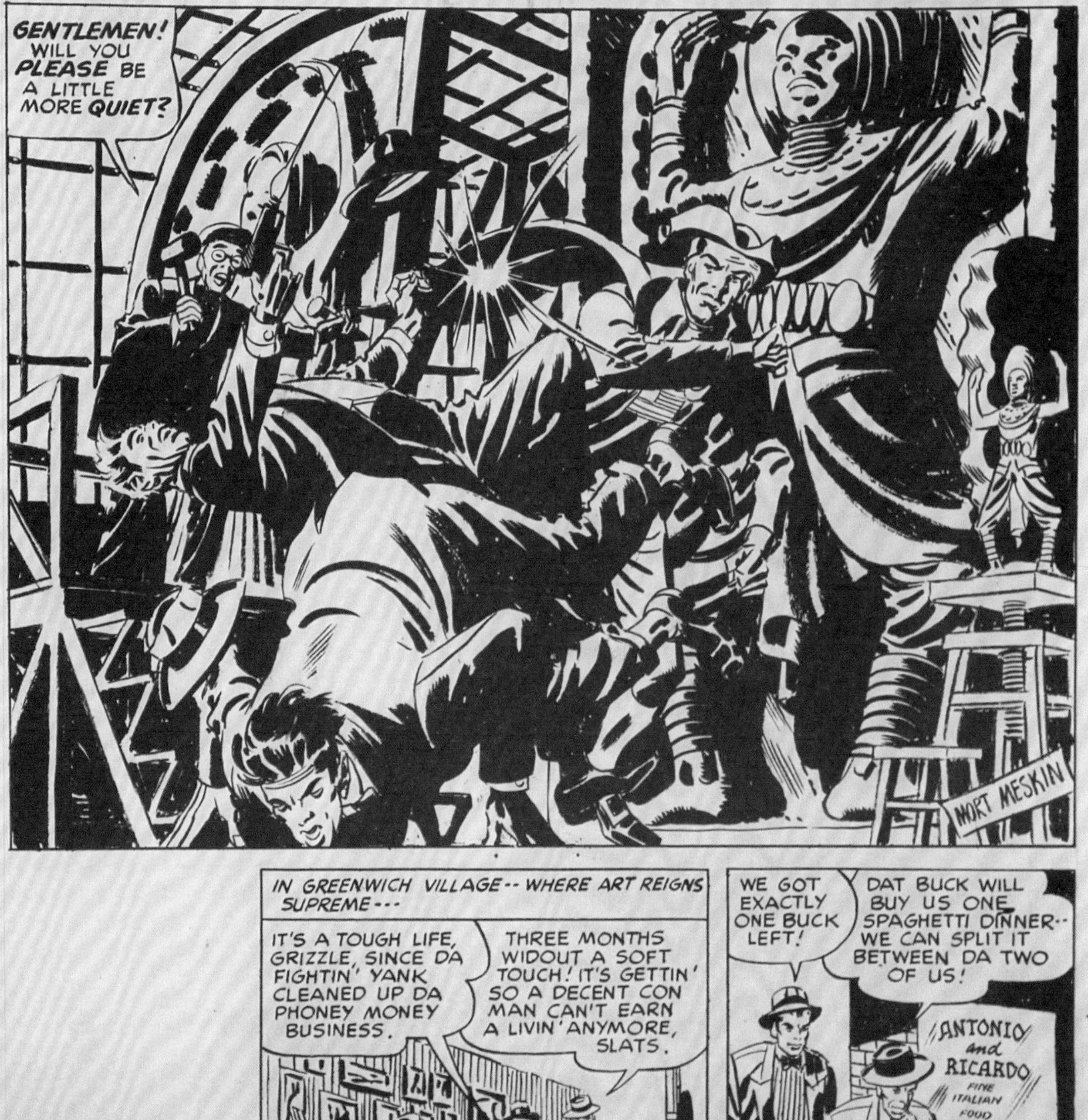
GENTLEMEN! WILL YOU PLEASE BE A LITTLE MORE QUIET?
MORT MESKIN

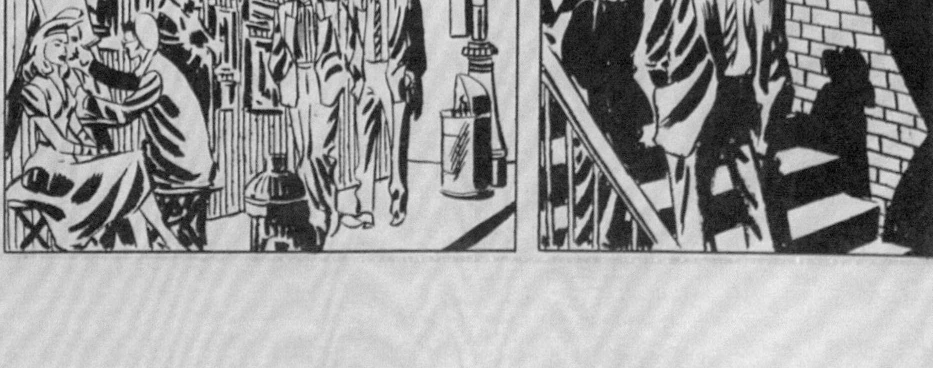
IN GREENWICH VILLAGE -- WHERE ART REIGNS SUPREME ---
IT'S A TOUGH LIFE, GRIZZLE, SINCE DA FIGHTIN' YANK CLEANED UP DA PHONEY MONEY BUSINESS.
THREE MONTHS WIDOUT A SOFT TOUCH! IT'S GETTIN' SO A DECENT CON MAN CAN'T EARN A LIVIN' ANYMORE, SLATS.
WE GOT EXACTLY ONE BUCK LEFT!
DAT BUCK WILL BUY US ONE SPAGHETTI DINNER -- WE CAN SPLIT IT BETWEEN DA TWO OF US!
ANTONIO and RICARDO
FINE ITALIAN FOOD

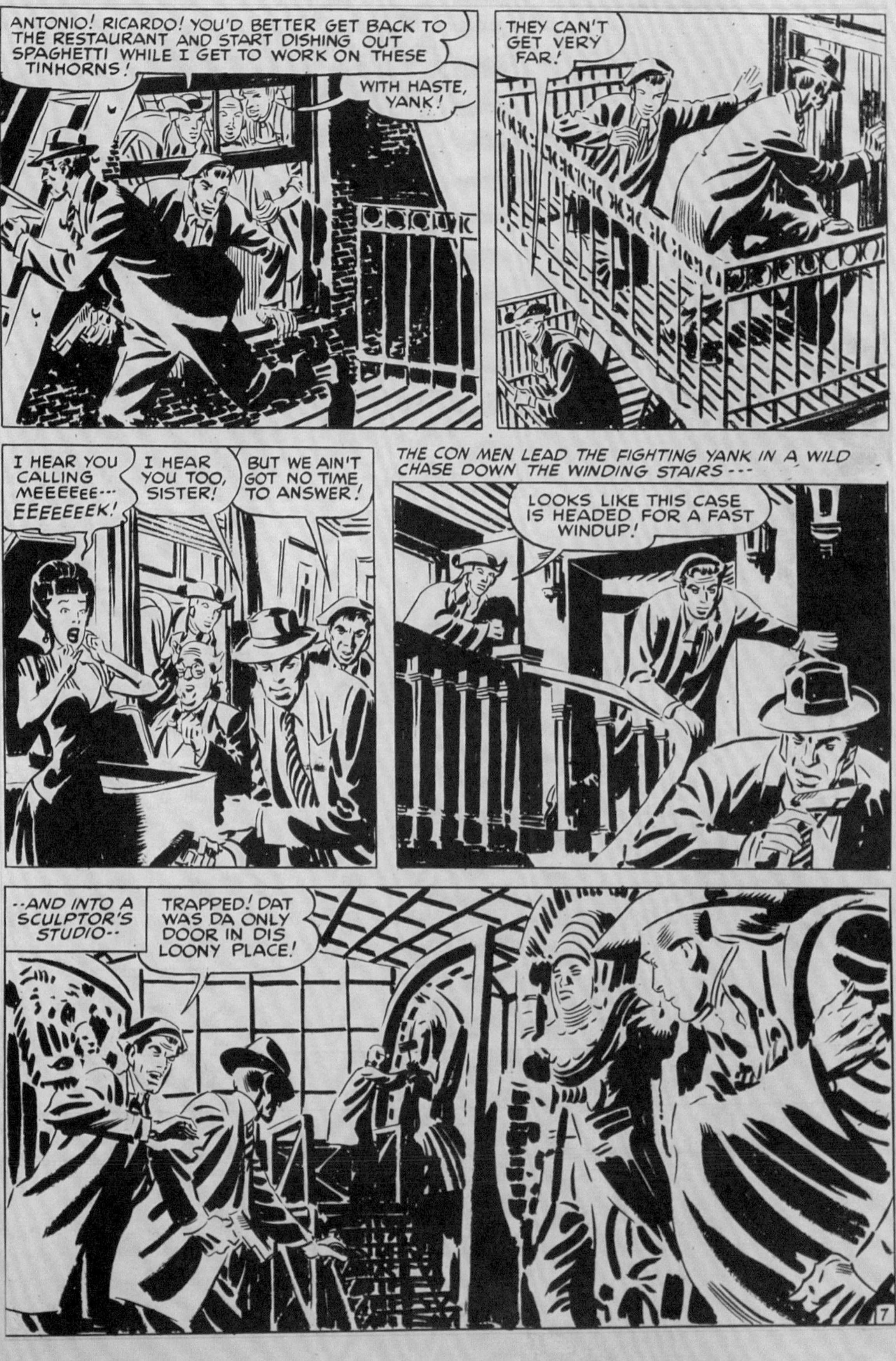
ANTONIO! RICARDO! YOU'D BETTER GET BACK TO THE RESTAURANT AND START DISHING OUT SPAGHETTI WHILE I GET TO WORK ON THESE TINHORNS!
WITH HASTE, YANK!
THEY CAN'T GET VERY FAR!
I HEAR YOU CALLING MEEEEEEE--- EEEEEEEK!
I HEAR YOU TOO, SISTER!
BUT WE AIN'T GOT NO TIME TO ANSWER!
THE CON MEN LEAD THE FIGHTING YANK IN A WILD CHASE DOWN THE WINDING STAIRS---
LOOKS LIKE THIS CASE IS HEADED FOR A FAST WINDUP!
--AND INTO A SCULPTOR'S STUDIO--
TRAPPED! DAT WAS DA ONLY DOOR IN DIS LOONY PLACE!
7

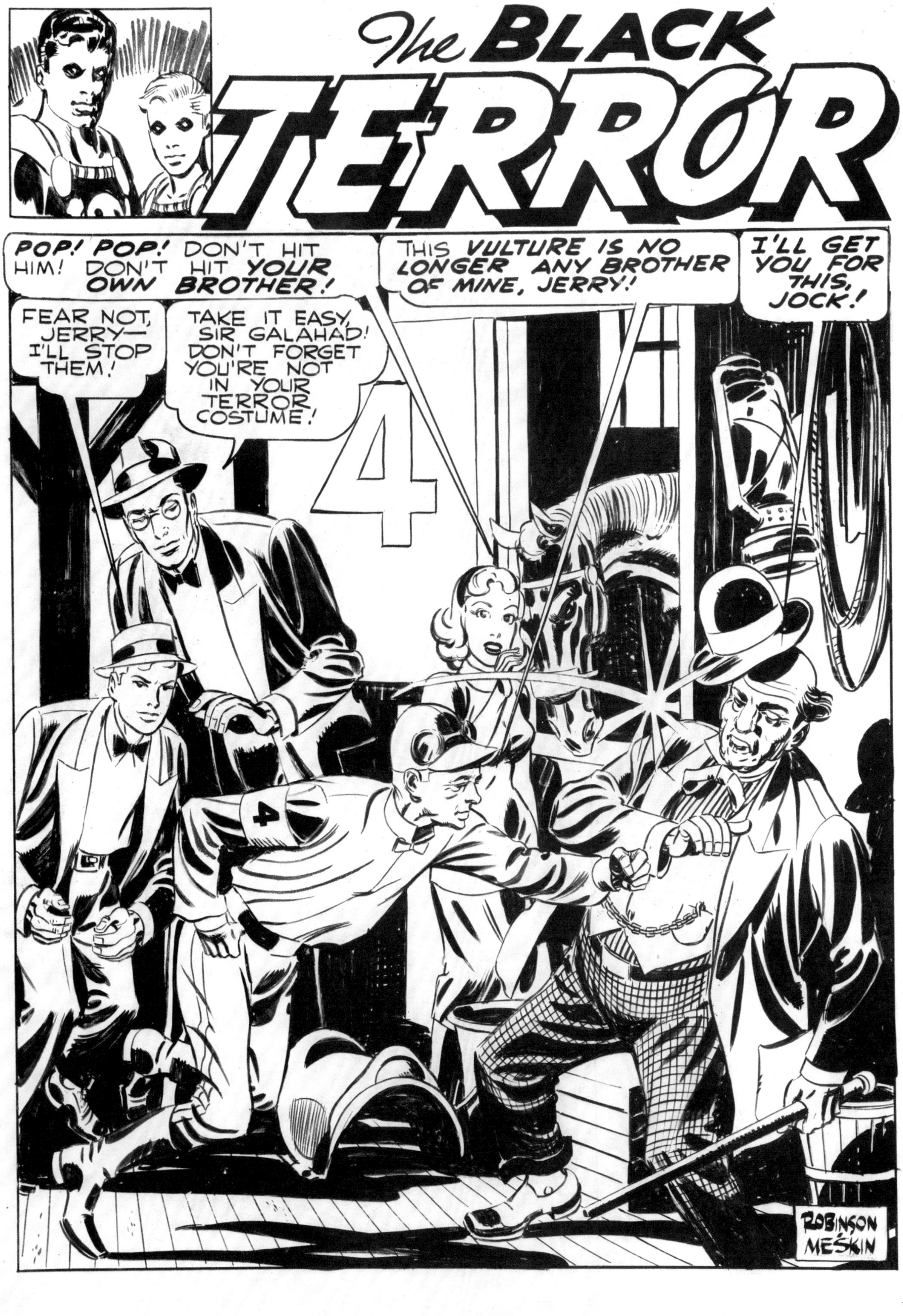
The BLACK TERROR
POP! POP! DON'T HIT HIM! DON'T HIT YOUR OWN BROTHER!
THIS VULTURE IS NO LONGER ANY BROTHER OF MINE, JERRY!
I'LL GET YOU FOR THIS, JOCK!
FEAR NOT, JERRY— I'LL STOP THEM!
TAKE IT EASY, SIR GALAHAD! DON'T FORGET YOU'RE NOT IN YOUR TERROR COSTUME!
4
4
ROBINSON MESKIN

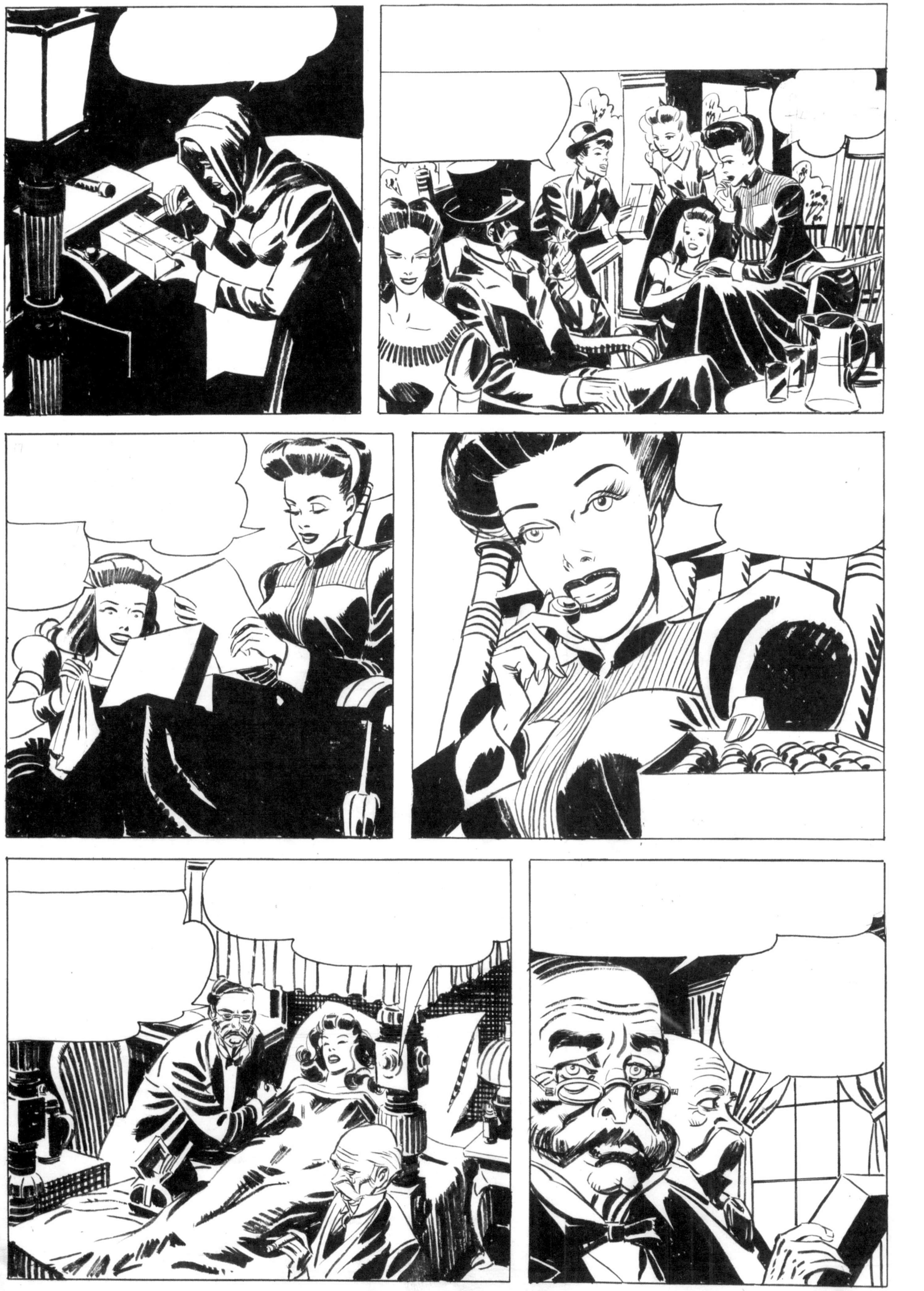

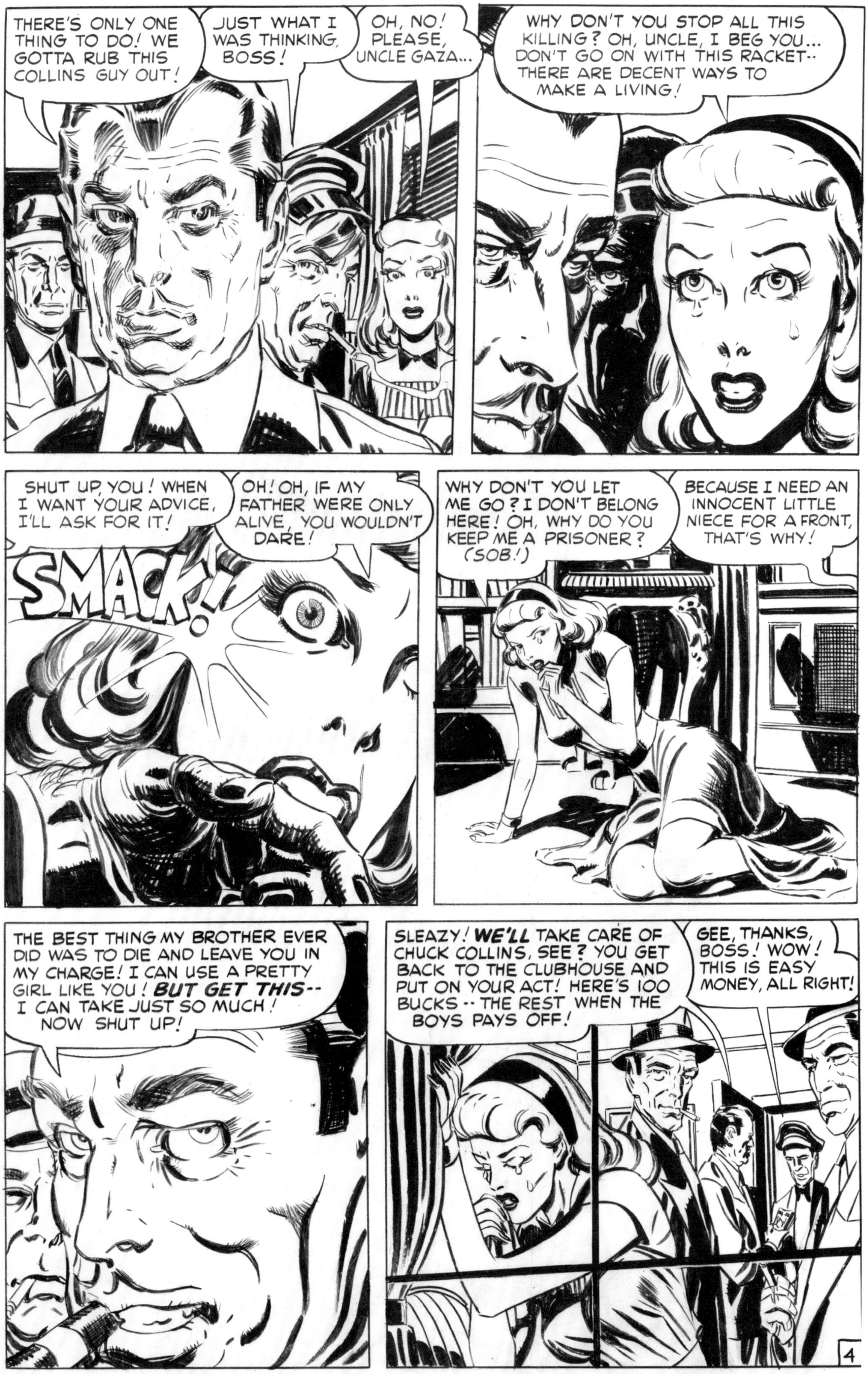
THERE'S ONLY ONE THING TO DO! WE GOTTA RUB THIS COLLINS GUY OUT!
JUST WHAT I WAS THINKING, BOSS!
OH, NO! PLEASE, UNCLE GAZA...
WHY DON'T YOU STOP ALL THIS KILLING? OH, UNCLE, I BEG YOU... DON'T GO ON WITH THIS RACKET-- THERE ARE DECENT WAYS TO MAKE A LIVING!
SHUT UP, YOU! WHEN I WANT YOUR ADVICE, I'LL ASK FOR IT!
OH! OH, IF MY FATHER WERE ONLY ALIVE, YOU WOULDN'T DARE!
SMACK!!
WHY DON'T YOU LET ME GO? I DON'T BELONG HERE! OH, WHY DO YOU KEEP ME A PRISONER? (SOB!)
BECAUSE I NEED AN INNOCENT LITTLE NIECE FOR A FRONT, THAT'S WHY!
THE BEST THING MY BROTHER EVER DID WAS TO DIE AND LEAVE YOU IN MY CHARGE! I CAN USE A PRETTY GIRL LIKE YOU! BUT GET THIS-- I CAN TAKE JUST SO MUCH! NOW SHUT UP!
SLEAZY! WE'LL TAKE CARE OF CHUCK COLLINS, SEE? YOU GET BACK TO THE CLUBHOUSE AND PUT ON YOUR ACT! HERE'S 100 BUCKS -- THE REST WHEN THE BOYS PAYS OFF!
GEE, THANKS, BOSS! WOW! THIS IS EASY MONEY, ALL RIGHT!
4

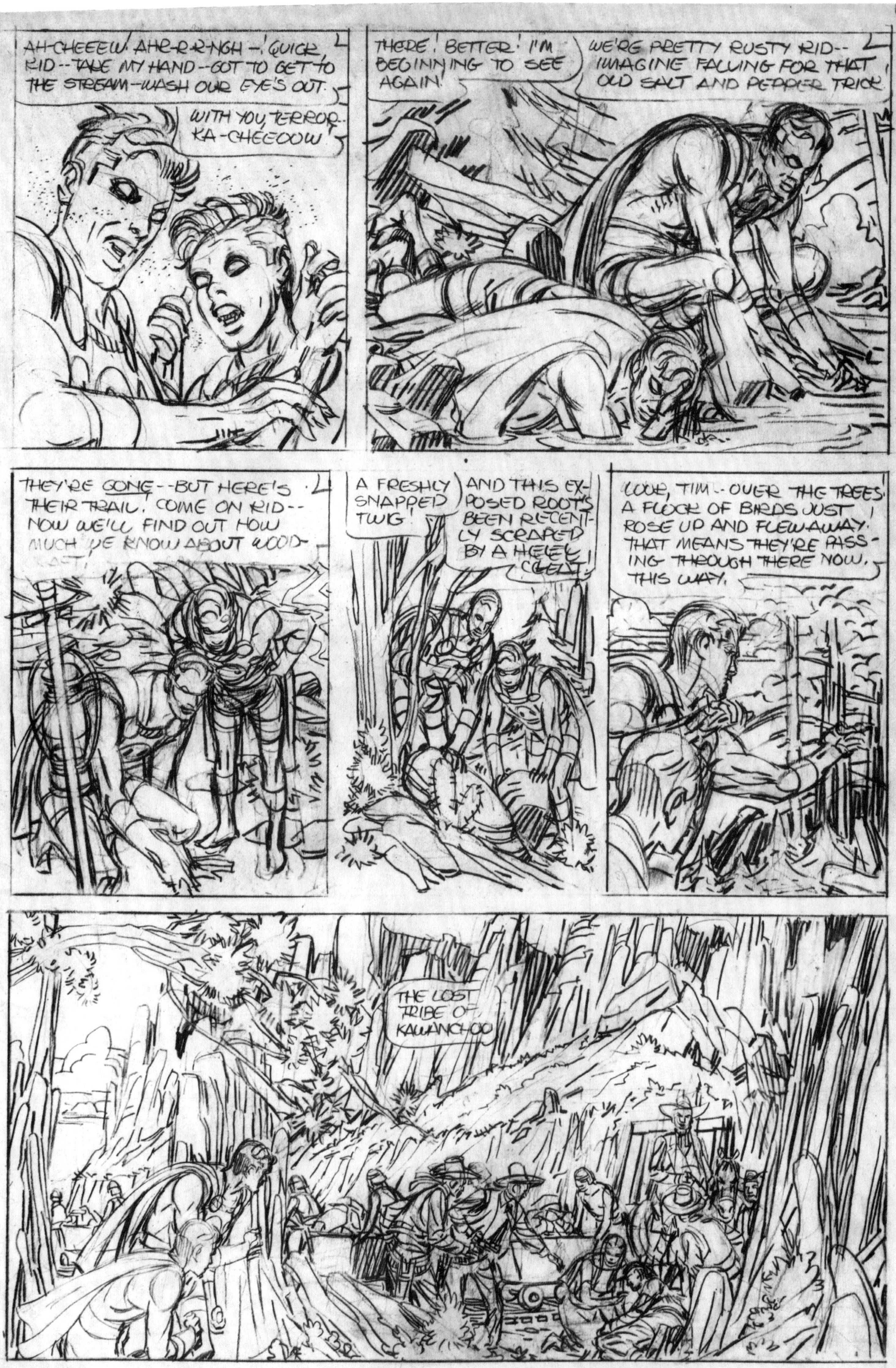
AH-CHEEEW! AHR-R-R-NGH--! QUICK, KID--TAKE MY HAND--GOT TO GET TO THE STREAM--WASH OUR EYE'S OUT.
WITH YOU, TERROR-- KA-CHEEOOW!
THERE! BETTER! I'M BEGINNING TO SEE AGAIN!
WE'RE PRETTY RUSTY KID--IMAGINE FALLING FOR THAT OLD SALT AND PEPPER TRICK!
THEY'RE GONE--BUT HERE'S THEIR TRAIL! COME ON KID--NOW WE'LL FIND OUT HOW MUCH WE KNOW ABOUT WOOD-CRAFT!
A FRESHLY SNAPPED TWIG!
AND THIS EX-POSED ROOT'S BEEN RECENT-LY SCRAPED BY A HEEL!
LOOK, TIM--OVER THE TREES! A FLOCK OF BIRDS JUST ROSE UP AND FLEW AWAY! THAT MEANS THEY'RE PASS-ING THROUGH THERE NOW. THIS WAY!
THE LOST TRIBE OF KAWANCHOO

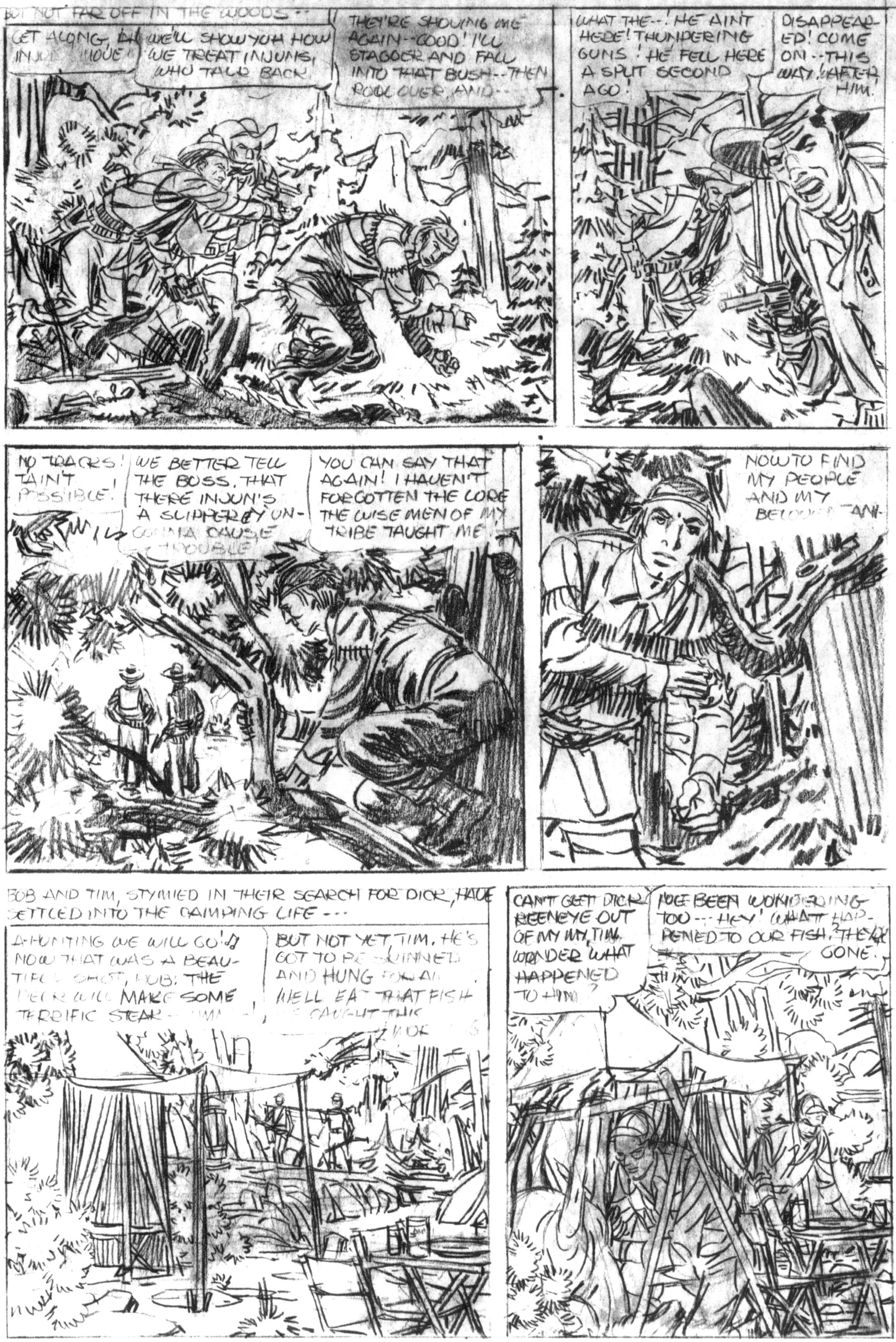
BUT NOT FAR OFF IN THE WOODS --
GET ALONG,
WE'LL SHOW YUH HOW WE TREAT INJUNS, WHO TALK BACK
THEY'RE SHOWING ME AGAIN--GOOD! I'LL STAGGER AND FALL INTO THAT BUSH--THEN ROLL OVER, AND--
WHAT THE--! HE AINT HERE! THUNDERING GUNS! HE FELL HERE A SPLIT SECOND AGO!
DISAPPEARED! COME ON--THIS WAY! AFTER HIM.
NO TRACKS! TAIN'T POSSIBLE!
WE BETTER TELL THE BOSS, THAT THERE INJUN'S A SLIPPERY UN-
YOU CAN SAY THAT AGAIN! I HAVEN'T FORGOTTEN THE LORE THE WISE MEN OF MY TRIBE TAUGHT ME
NOW TO FIND MY PEOPLE AND MY
BOB AND TIM, STYMIED IN THEIR SEARCH FOR DICK, HAVE SETTLED INTO THE CAMPING LIFE ---
A-HUNTING WE WILL GO! NOW THAT WAS A BEAU-
MAKE SOME TERRIFIC STEAK
BUT NOT YET, TIM. HE'S GOT TO BE
AND HUNG
WE'LL EAT THAT FISH
CAN'T GET DICK BEENEYE OUT OF MY MY, TIM. WONDER WHAT HAPPENED TO HIM?
I'VE BEEN WONDERING TOO--HEY! WHAT HAPPENED TO OUR FISH? THEY'RE GONE.

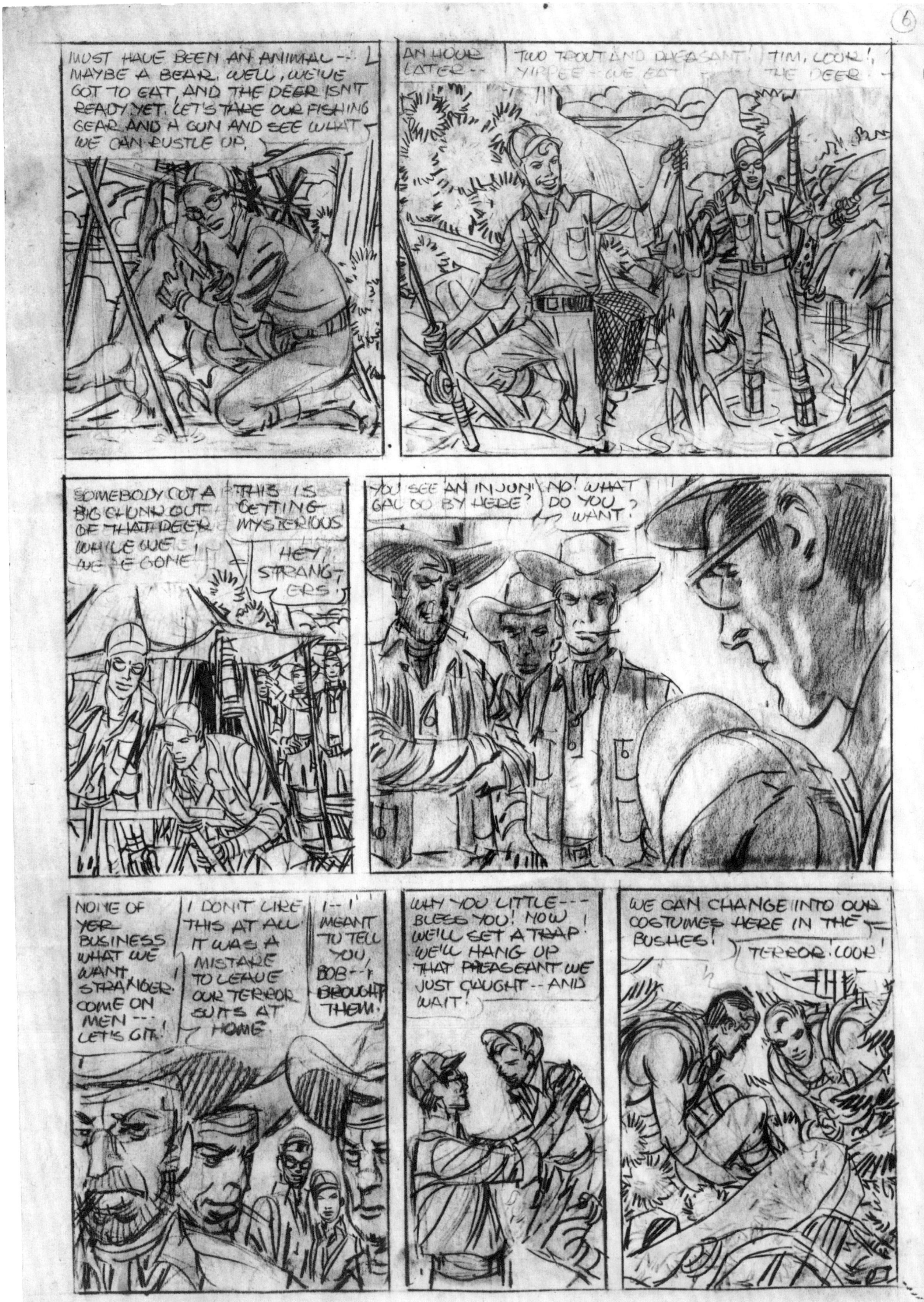
6
MUST HAVE BEEN AN ANIMAL -- MAYBE A BEAR. WELL, WE'VE GOT TO EAT, AND THE DEER ISN'T READY YET. LET'S TAKE OUR FISHING GEAR AND A GUN AND SEE WHAT WE CAN RUSTLE UP.
AN HOUR LATER --
TWO TROUT AND PHEASANT! YIPPEE -- WE EAT
TIM, LOOK! THE DEER
SOMEBODY CUT A BIG CHUNK OUT OF THAT DEER WHILE WE WERE GONE
THIS IS GETTING MYSTERIOUS
HEY, STRANGERS!
YOU SEE AN INJUN GAL GO BY HERE?
NO! WHAT DO YOU WANT?
NONE OF YER BUSINESS WHAT WE WANT, STRANGER. COME ON MEN --- LET'S GIT!
I DON'T LIKE THIS AT ALL. IT WAS A MISTAKE TO LEAVE OUR TERROR SUITS AT HOME
I -- I MEANT TO TELL YOU, BOB -- I BROUGHT THEM.
WHY YOU LITTLE --- BLESS YOU! NOW WE'LL SET A TRAP! WE'LL HANG UP THAT PHEASANT WE JUST CAUGHT -- AND WAIT!
WE CAN CHANGE INTO OUR COSTUMES HERE IN THE BUSHES!
TERROR, LOOK!

day after day, week after week, month after month."[33]

As he had as a small child, he climbed higher and higher, reaching, striving, until it all came crashing down. The story told is that Meskin jumped onto a drawing table at the DC offices, brandishing a steel ruler like a sword, challenging others to a duel. Shortly thereafter Meskin signed himself into a hospital for nervous exhaustion. Betty, now alone with the boys, left with them for a trip to Paris aboard the Queen Elizabeth. They remained there for about three months, until Meskin was released from the hospital.

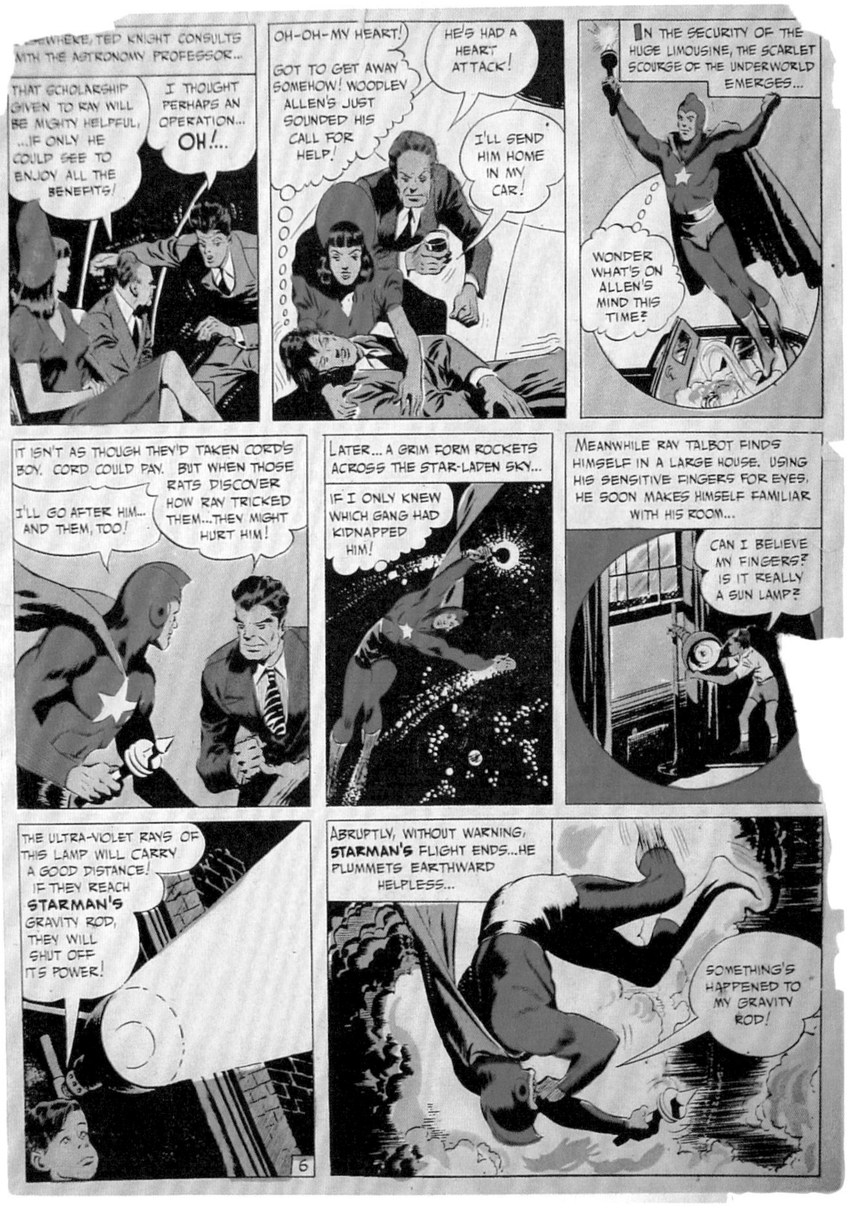
TED KNIGHT CONSULTS WITH THE ASTRONOMY PROFESSOR...
THAT SCHOLARSHIP GIVEN TO RAY WILL BE MIGHTY HELPFUL, ...IF ONLY HE COULD SEE TO ENJOY ALL THE BENEFITS!
I THOUGHT PERHAPS AN OPERATION... OH!...
OH-OH-MY HEART!
GOT TO GET AWAY SOMEHOW! WOODLEY ALLEN'S JUST SOUNDED HIS CALL FOR HELP!
HE'S HAD A HEART ATTACK!
I'LL SEND HIM HOME IN MY CAR!
IN THE SECURITY OF THE HUGE LIMOUSINE, THE SCARLET SCOURGE OF THE UNDERWORLD EMERGES...
WONDER WHAT'S ON ALLEN'S MIND THIS TIME?
IT ISN'T AS THOUGH THEY'D TAKEN CORD'S BOY. CORD COULD PAY. BUT WHEN THOSE RATS DISCOVER HOW RAY TRICKED THEM...THEY MIGHT HURT HIM!
I'LL GO AFTER HIM... AND THEM, TOO!
LATER... A GRIM FORM ROCKETS ACROSS THE STAR-LADEN SKY...
IF I ONLY KNEW WHICH GANG HAD KIDNAPPED HIM!
MEANWHILE RAY TALBOT FINDS HIMSELF IN A LARGE HOUSE. USING HIS SENSITIVE FINGERS FOR EYES, HE SOON MAKES HIMSELF FAMILIAR WITH HIS ROOM...
CAN I BELIEVE MY FINGERS? IS IT REALLY A SUN LAMP?
THE ULTRA-VIOLET RAYS OF THIS LAMP WILL CARRY A GOOD DISTANCE! IF THEY REACH STARMAN'S GRAVITY ROD, THEY WILL SHUT OFF ITS POWER!
ABRUPTLY, WITHOUT WARNING, STARMAN'S FLIGHT ENDS...HE PLUMMETS EARTHWARD HELPLESS...
SOMETHING'S HAPPENED TO MY GRAVITY ROD!
6

LEFT: Pencils for a Black Terror Page, late 1940s, art by Mort Meskin and Jerry Robinson. ABOVE: A *Starman* page, art by Mort Meskin. (© DC Comics. All Rights Reserved. Used with Permission.) FOLLOWING THREE SPREADS: *Golden Lad* covers, published by Nedor/Standard 1945-1946, art by Mort Meskin (artwork from the collection of Ethan Roberts).

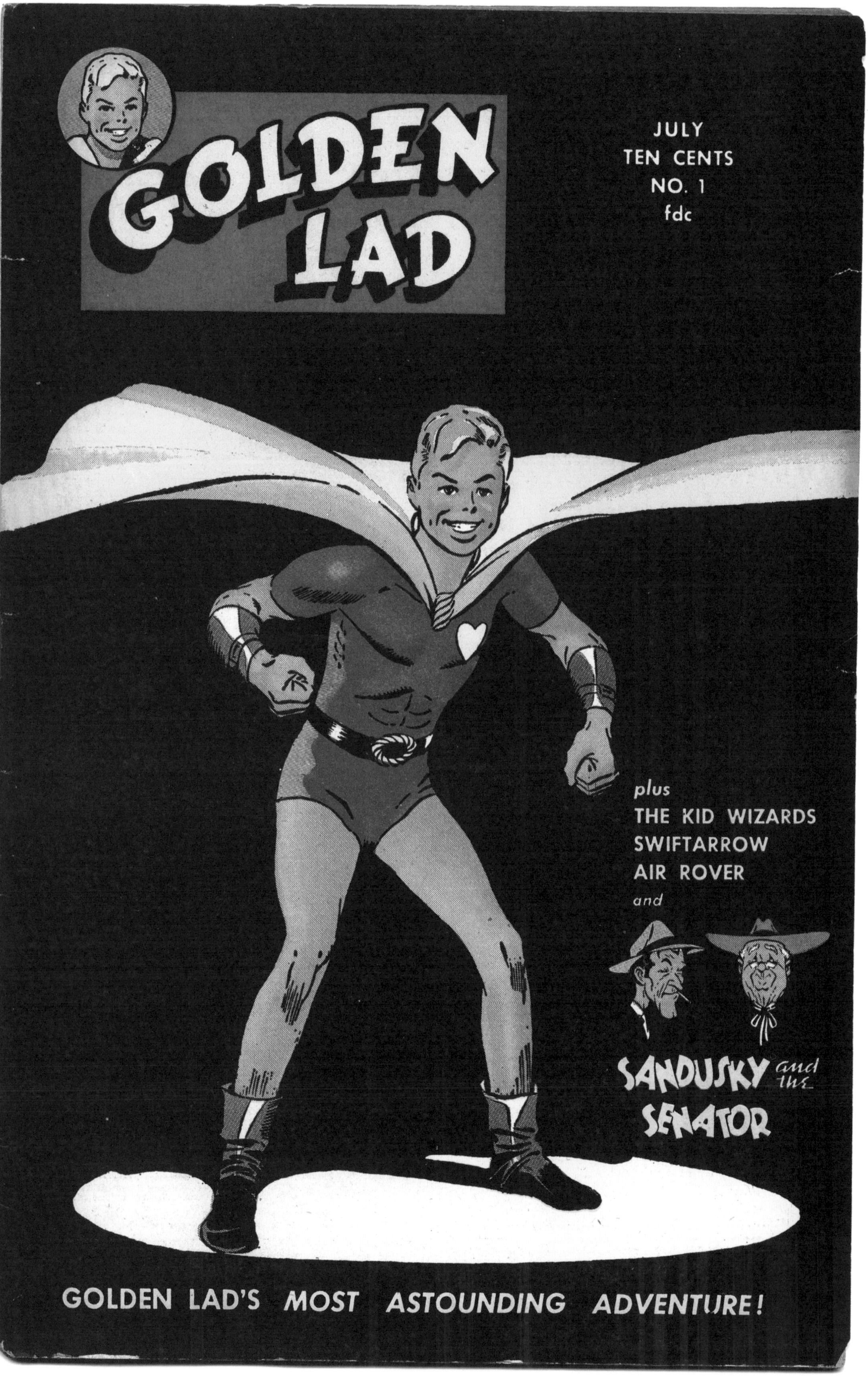

GOLDEN LAD
JULY
TEN CENTS
NO. 1
fdc
plus
THE KID WIZARDS
SWIFTARROW
AIR ROVER
and
SANDUSKY and the SENATOR
GOLDEN LAD'S MOST ASTOUNDING ADVENTURE!

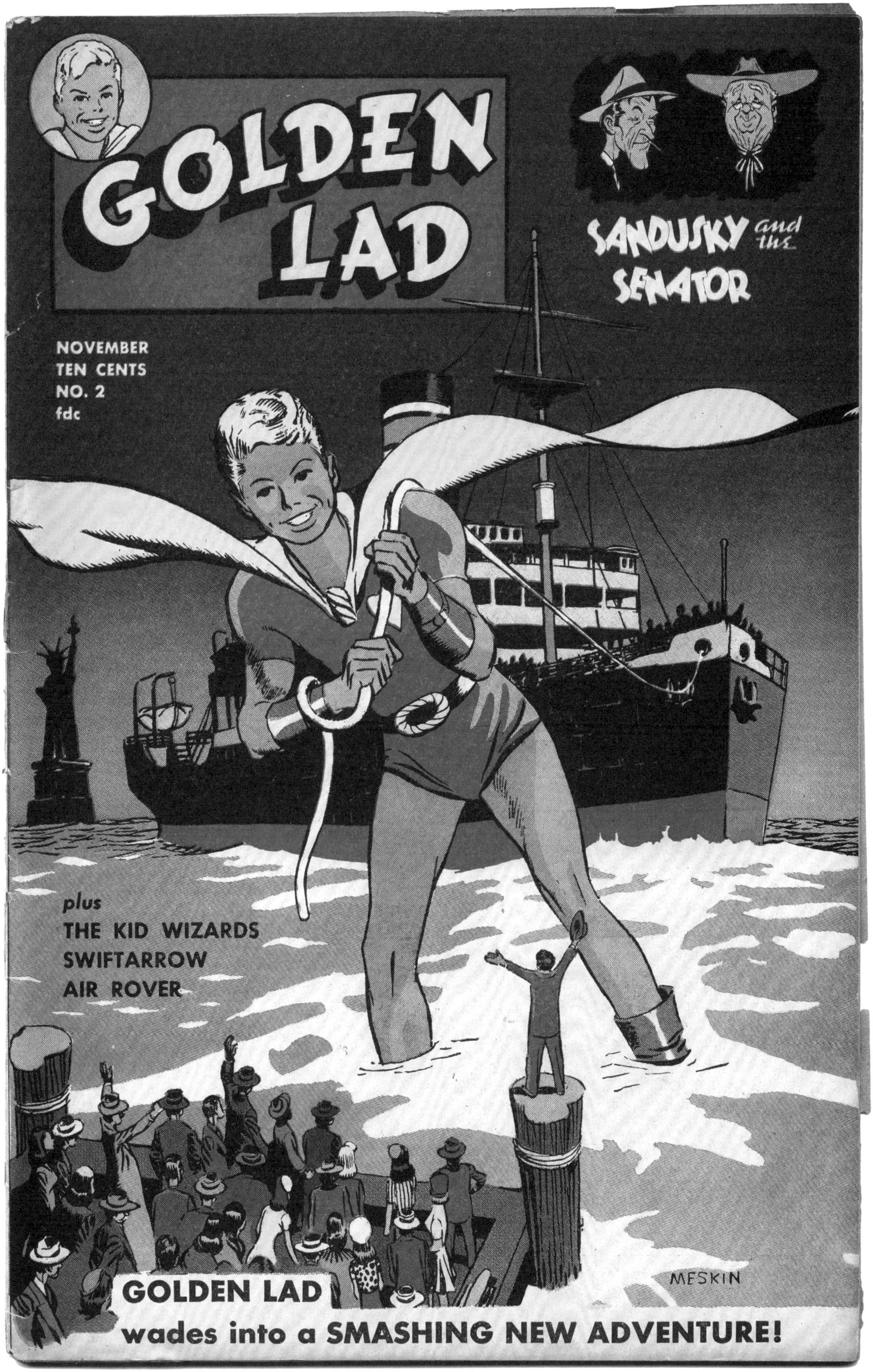
GOLDEN LAD
SANDUSKY and the SENATOR
NOVEMBER
TEN CENTS
NO. 2
fdc
plus
THE KID WIZARDS
SWIFTARROW
AIR ROVER
MESKIN
GOLDEN LAD
wades into a SMASHING NEW ADVENTURE!

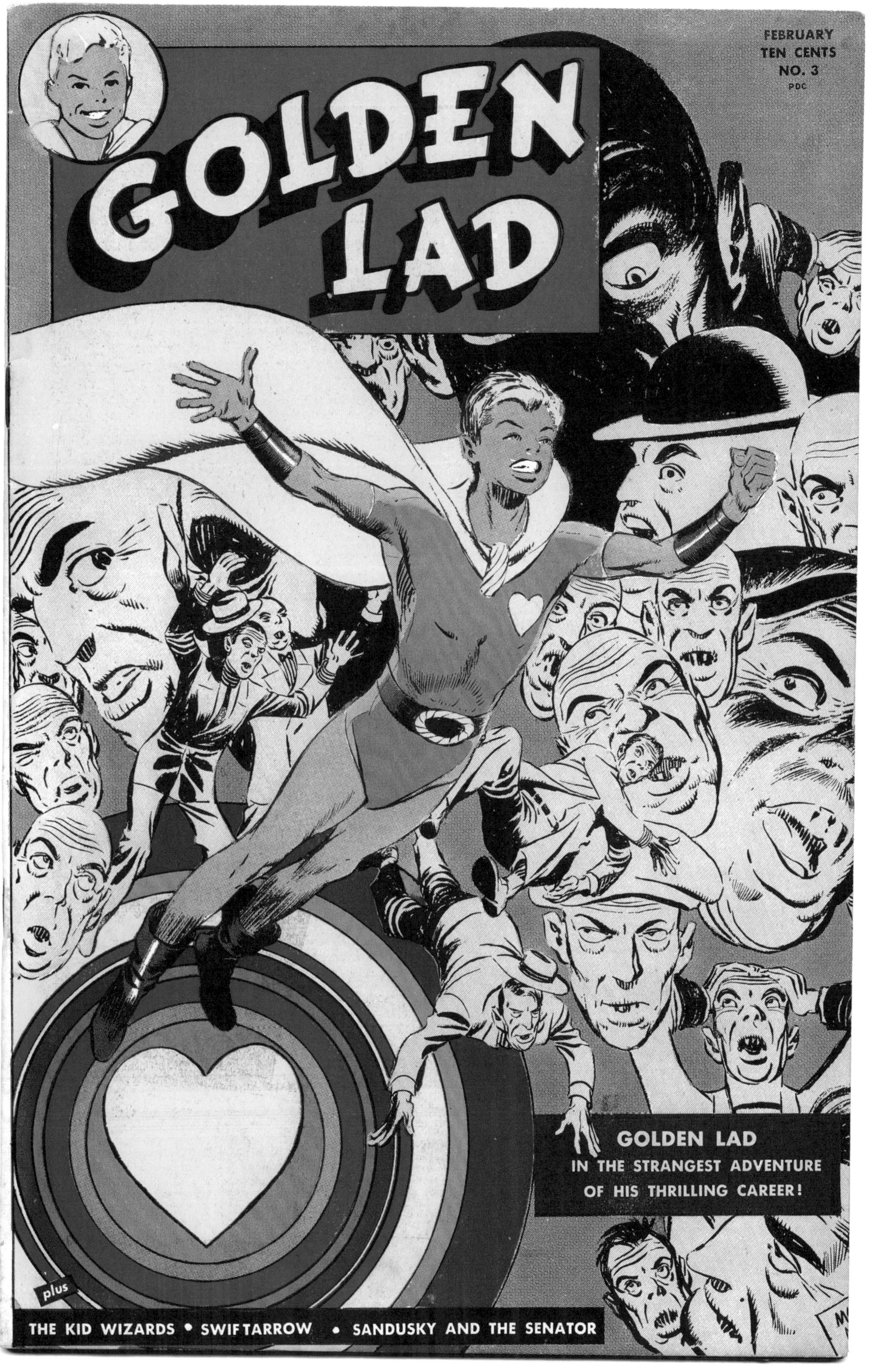
FEBRUARY
TEN CENTS
NO. 3
PDC
GOLDEN LAD
GOLDEN LAD
IN THE STRANGEST ADVENTURE
OF HIS THRILLING CAREER!
plus
THE KID WIZARDS • SWIFTARROW • SANDUSKY AND THE SENATOR

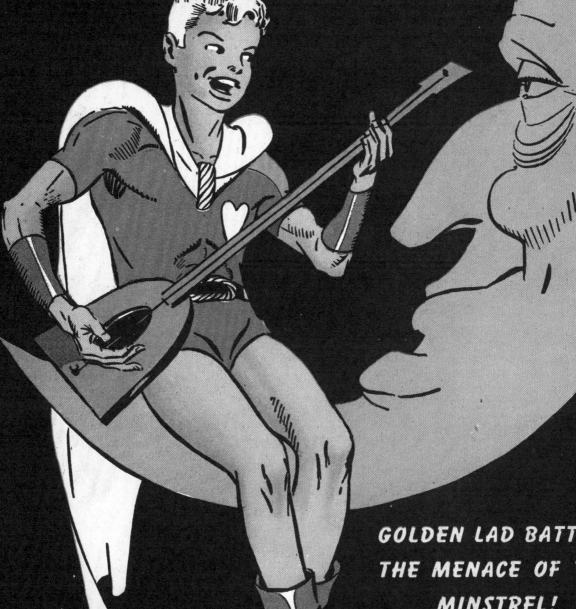

A 52-PAGE MAGAZINE

NO. 4
10¢
PDC

GOLDEN LAD

GOLDEN LAD BATTLES
THE MENACE OF THE
MINSTREL!
PLUS OTHER
EXCITING FEATURES

A CROSSEN
PUBLICATION

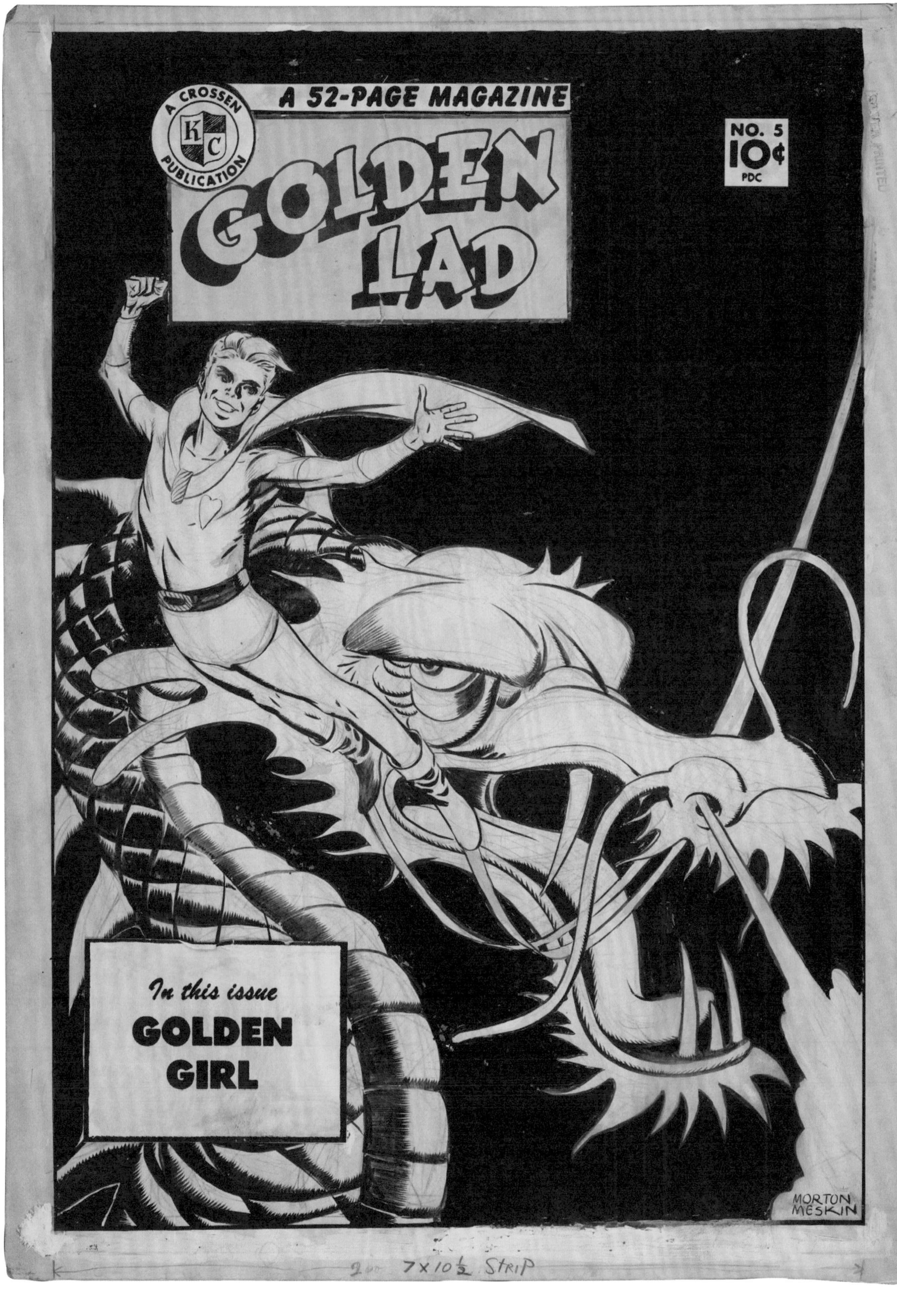
A CROSSEN
KC
PUBLICATION
A 52-PAGE MAGAZINE
GOLDEN LAD
NO. 5
10¢
PDC
In this issue
GOLDEN GIRL
MORTON MESKIN
7X10½ STRIP

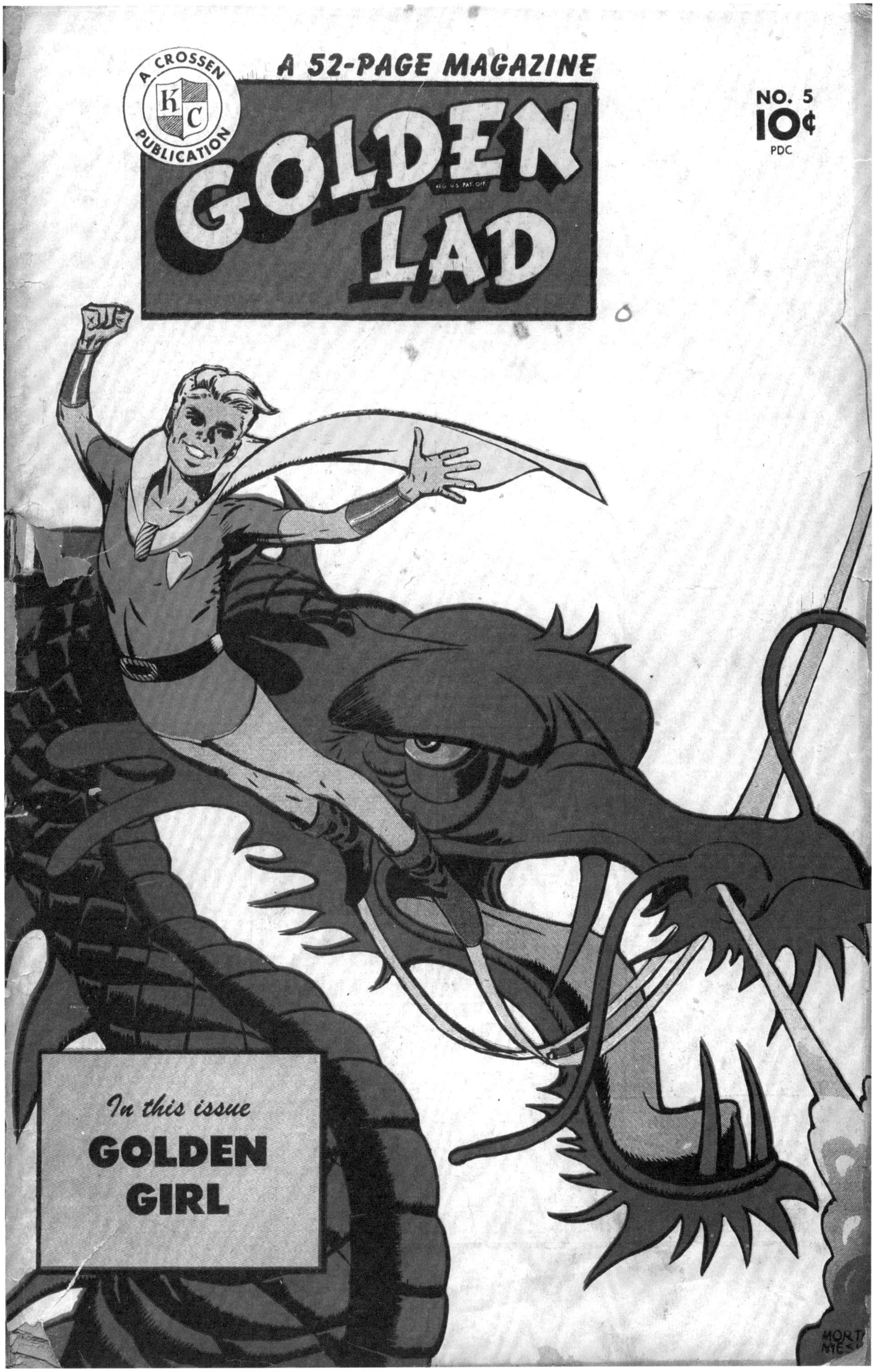
A 52-PAGE MAGAZINE
A CROSSEN PUBLICATION
KC
NO. 5
10¢
PDC
GOLDEN LAD
In this issue
GOLDEN GIRL
MORT MESK

It appears Meskin went back to this cover artwork for *Golden Lad* #5 and added the background black after publication (colllection of Ethan Roberts).

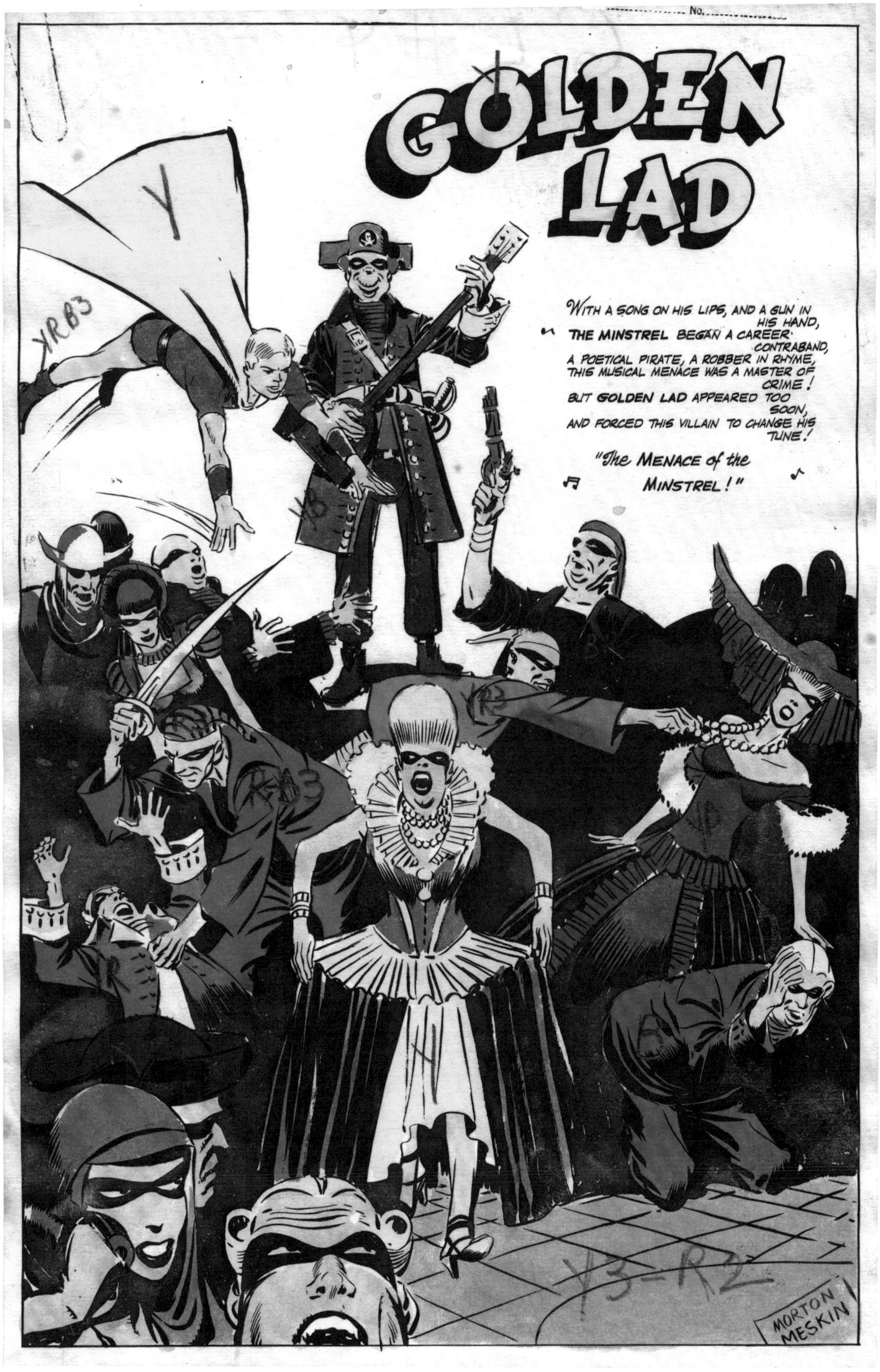
No.
GOLDEN LAD
WITH A SONG ON HIS LIPS, AND A GUN IN HIS HAND,
THE MINSTREL BEGAN A CAREER CONTRABAND,
A POETICAL PIRATE, A ROBBER IN RHYME,
THIS MUSICAL MENACE WAS A MASTER OF CRIME!
BUT GOLDEN LAD APPEARED TOO SOON,
AND FORCED THIS VILLAIN TO CHANGE HIS TUNE!
"The MENACE of the MINSTREL!"
Y3-R2
MORTON MESKIN

ABOVE: Color guide for *Golden Lad* splash. 11 PAGES FOLLOWING: Unpublished *Golden Lad* story (courtesy Greg Theakston).

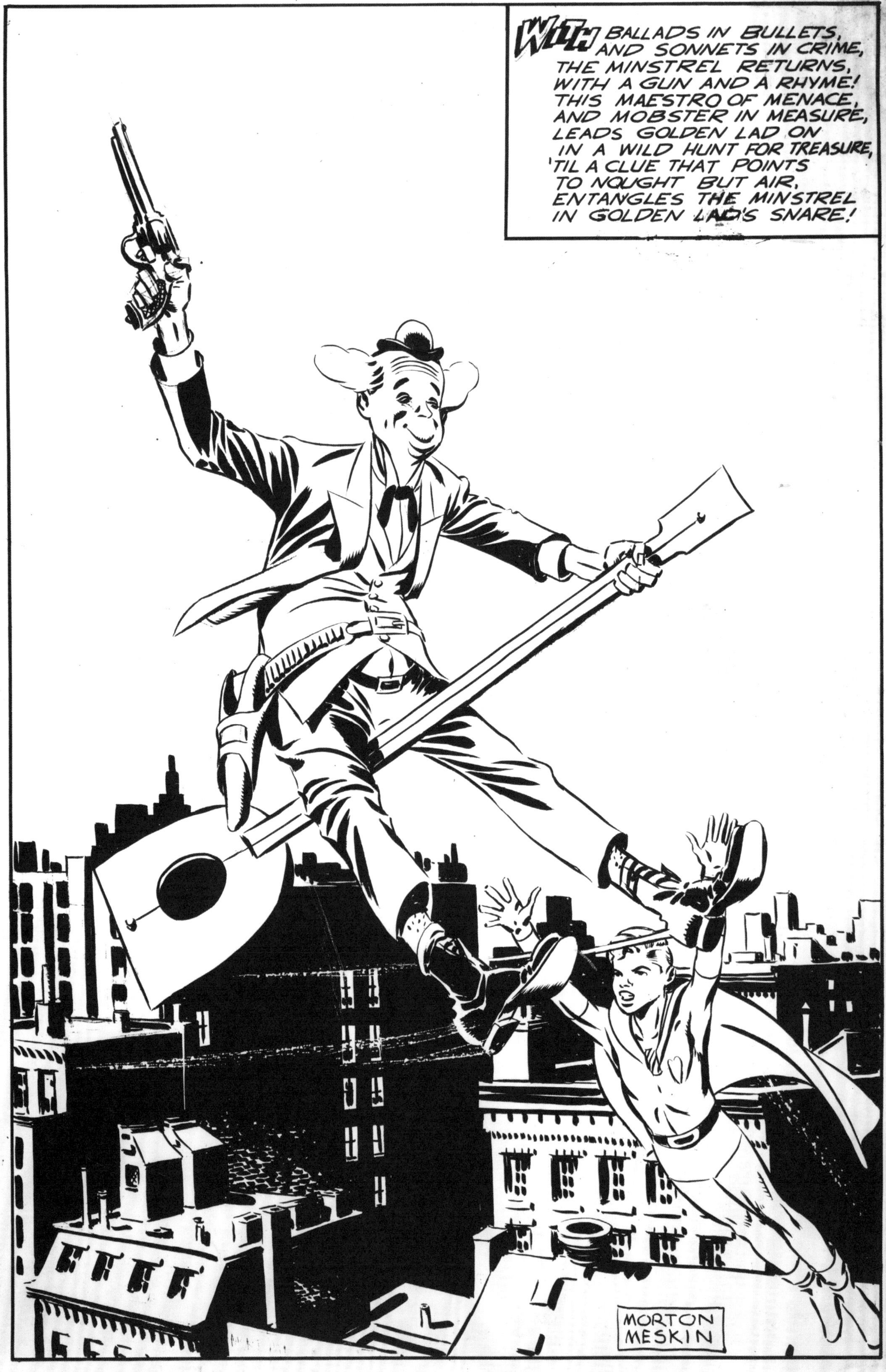
WITH BALLADS IN BULLETS, AND SONNETS IN CRIME, THE MINSTREL RETURNS, WITH A GUN AND A RHYME! THIS MAESTRO OF MENACE, AND MOBSTER IN MEASURE, LEADS GOLDEN LAD ON IN A WILD HUNT FOR TREASURE, 'TIL A CLUE THAT POINTS TO NOUGHT BUT AIR, ENTANGLES THE MINSTREL IN GOLDEN LAD'S SNARE!
MORTON MESKIN

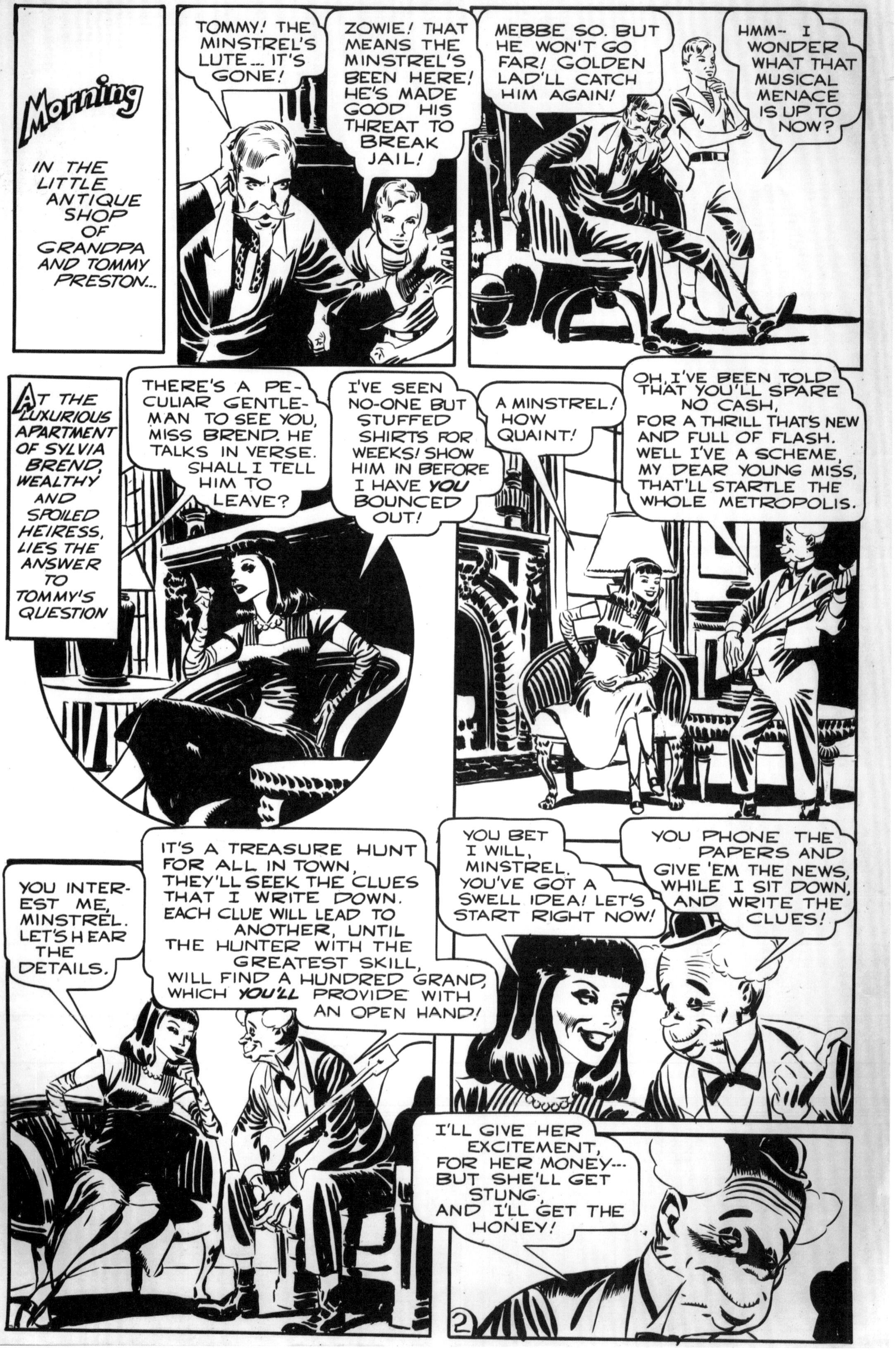
Morning
IN THE LITTLE ANTIQUE SHOP OF GRANDPA AND TOMMY PRESTON...
TOMMY! THE MINSTREL'S LUTE... IT'S GONE!
ZOWIE! THAT MEANS THE MINSTREL'S BEEN HERE! HE'S MADE GOOD HIS THREAT TO BREAK JAIL!
MEBBE SO. BUT HE WON'T GO FAR! GOLDEN LAD'LL CATCH HIM AGAIN!
HMM-- I WONDER WHAT THAT MUSICAL MENACE IS UP TO NOW?
AT THE LUXURIOUS APARTMENT OF SYLVIA BREND, WEALTHY AND SPOILED HEIRESS, LIES THE ANSWER TO TOMMY'S QUESTION
THERE'S A PECULIAR GENTLEMAN TO SEE YOU, MISS BREND. HE TALKS IN VERSE. SHALL I TELL HIM TO LEAVE?
I'VE SEEN NO-ONE BUT STUFFED SHIRTS FOR WEEKS! SHOW HIM IN BEFORE I HAVE YOU BOUNCED OUT!
A MINSTREL! HOW QUAINT!
OH, I'VE BEEN TOLD THAT YOU'LL SPARE NO CASH, FOR A THRILL THAT'S NEW AND FULL OF FLASH. WELL I'VE A SCHEME, MY DEAR YOUNG MISS, THAT'LL STARTLE THE WHOLE METROPOLIS.
YOU INTEREST ME, MINSTREL. LET'S HEAR THE DETAILS.
IT'S A TREASURE HUNT FOR ALL IN TOWN, THEY'LL SEEK THE CLUES THAT I WRITE DOWN. EACH CLUE WILL LEAD TO ANOTHER, UNTIL THE HUNTER WITH THE GREATEST SKILL, WILL FIND A HUNDRED GRAND, WHICH YOU'LL PROVIDE WITH AN OPEN HAND!
YOU BET I WILL, MINSTREL. YOU'VE GOT A SWELL IDEA! LET'S START RIGHT NOW!
YOU PHONE THE PAPERS AND GIVE 'EM THE NEWS, WHILE I SIT DOWN, AND WRITE THE CLUES!
I'LL GIVE HER EXCITEMENT, FOR HER MONEY--- BUT SHE'LL GET STUNG, AND I'LL GET THE HONEY!
2

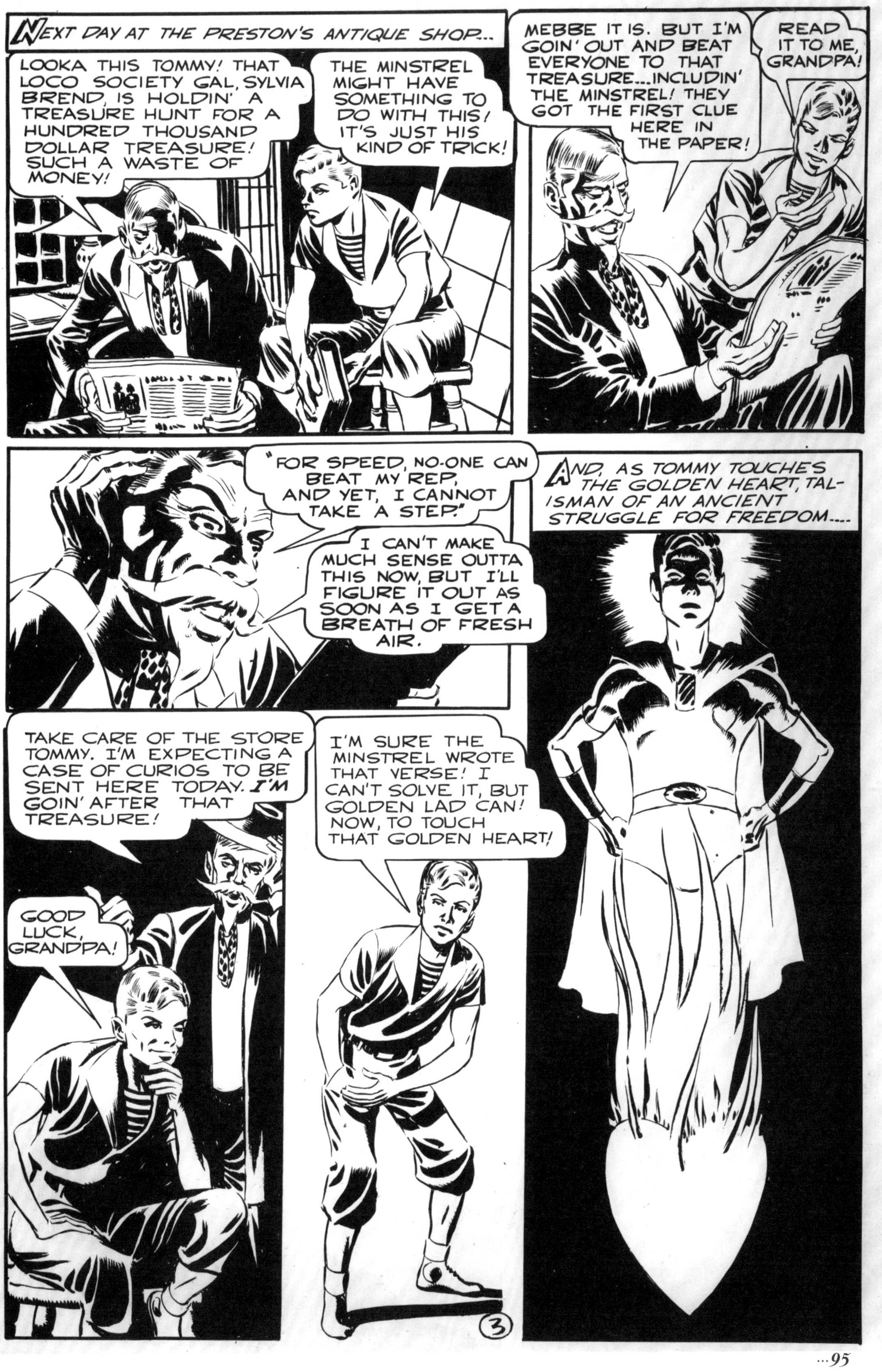
NEXT DAY AT THE PRESTON'S ANTIQUE SHOP...
LOOKA THIS TOMMY! THAT LOCO SOCIETY GAL, SYLVIA BREND, IS HOLDIN' A TREASURE HUNT FOR A HUNDRED THOUSAND DOLLAR TREASURE! SUCH A WASTE OF MONEY!
THE MINSTREL MIGHT HAVE SOMETHING TO DO WITH THIS! IT'S JUST HIS KIND OF TRICK!
MEBBE IT IS. BUT I'M GOIN' OUT AND BEAT EVERYONE TO THAT TREASURE...INCLUDIN' THE MINSTREL! THEY GOT THE FIRST CLUE HERE IN THE PAPER!
READ IT TO ME, GRANDPA!
"FOR SPEED, NO-ONE CAN BEAT MY REP, AND YET, I CANNOT TAKE A STEP."
I CAN'T MAKE MUCH SENSE OUTTA THIS NOW, BUT I'LL FIGURE IT OUT AS SOON AS I GET A BREATH OF FRESH AIR.
AND, AS TOMMY TOUCHES THE GOLDEN HEART, TALISMAN OF AN ANCIENT STRUGGLE FOR FREEDOM....
TAKE CARE OF THE STORE TOMMY. I'M EXPECTING A CASE OF CURIOS TO BE SENT HERE TODAY. I'M GOIN' AFTER THAT TREASURE!
GOOD LUCK, GRANDPA!
I'M SURE THE MINSTREL WROTE THAT VERSE! I CAN'T SOLVE IT, BUT GOLDEN LAD CAN! NOW, TO TOUCH THAT GOLDEN HEART!
3

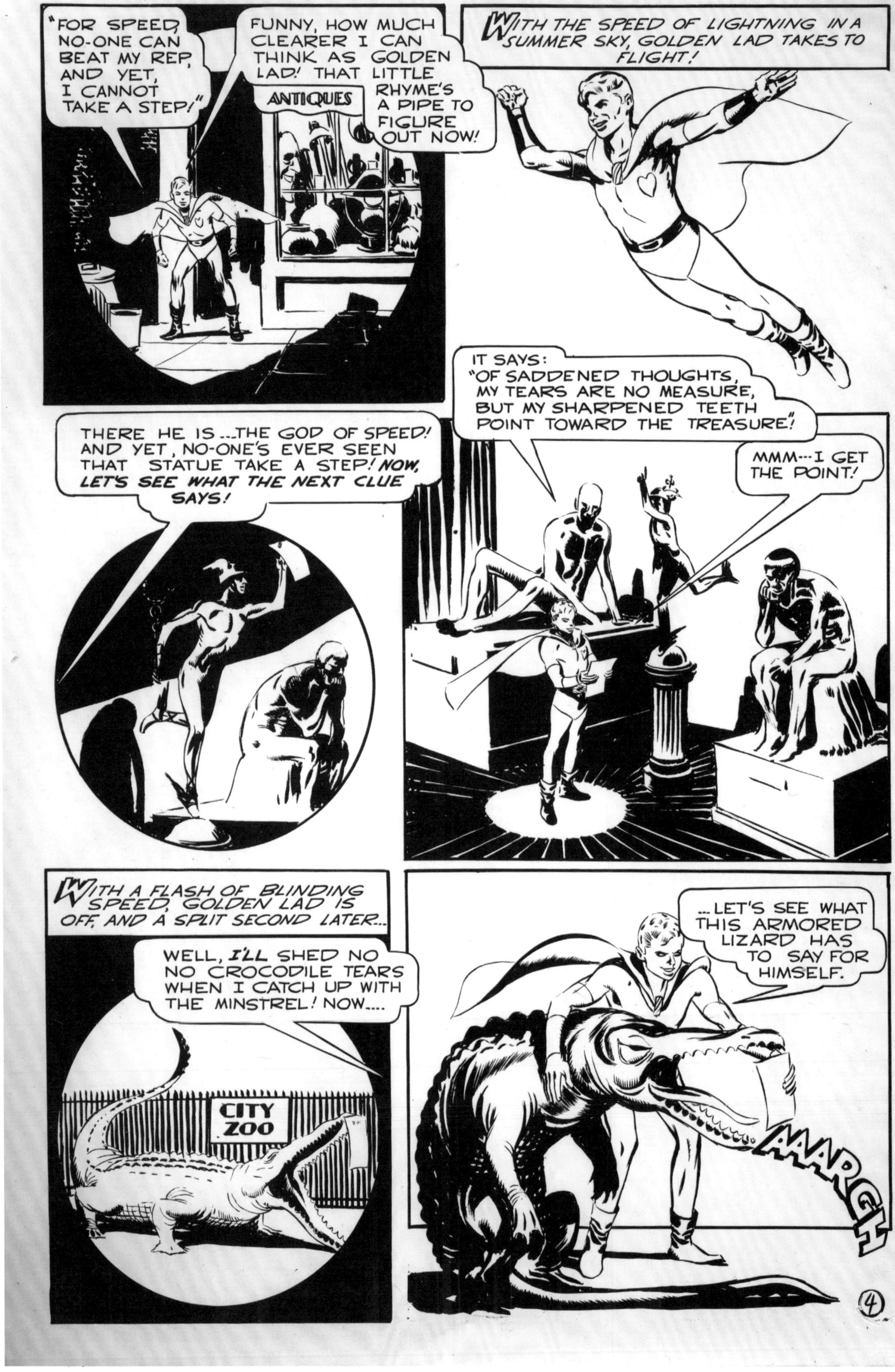
"FOR SPEED, NO-ONE CAN BEAT MY REP, AND YET, I CANNOT TAKE A STEP!"
FUNNY, HOW MUCH CLEARER I CAN THINK AS GOLDEN LAD! THAT LITTLE RHYME'S A PIPE TO FIGURE OUT NOW!
ANTIQUES
WITH THE SPEED OF LIGHTNING IN A SUMMER SKY, GOLDEN LAD TAKES TO FLIGHT!
THERE HE IS...THE GOD OF SPEED! AND YET, NO-ONE'S EVER SEEN THAT STATUE TAKE A STEP! NOW, LET'S SEE WHAT THE NEXT CLUE SAYS!
IT SAYS: "OF SADDENED THOUGHTS, MY TEARS ARE NO MEASURE, BUT MY SHARPENED TEETH POINT TOWARD THE TREASURE!"
MMM...I GET THE POINT!
WITH A FLASH OF BLINDING SPEED, GOLDEN LAD IS OFF, AND A SPLIT SECOND LATER...
WELL, I'LL SHED NO NO CROCODILE TEARS WHEN I CATCH UP WITH THE MINSTREL! NOW....
CITY ZOO
...LET'S SEE WHAT THIS ARMORED LIZARD HAS TO SAY FOR HIMSELF.
AAARGH
4

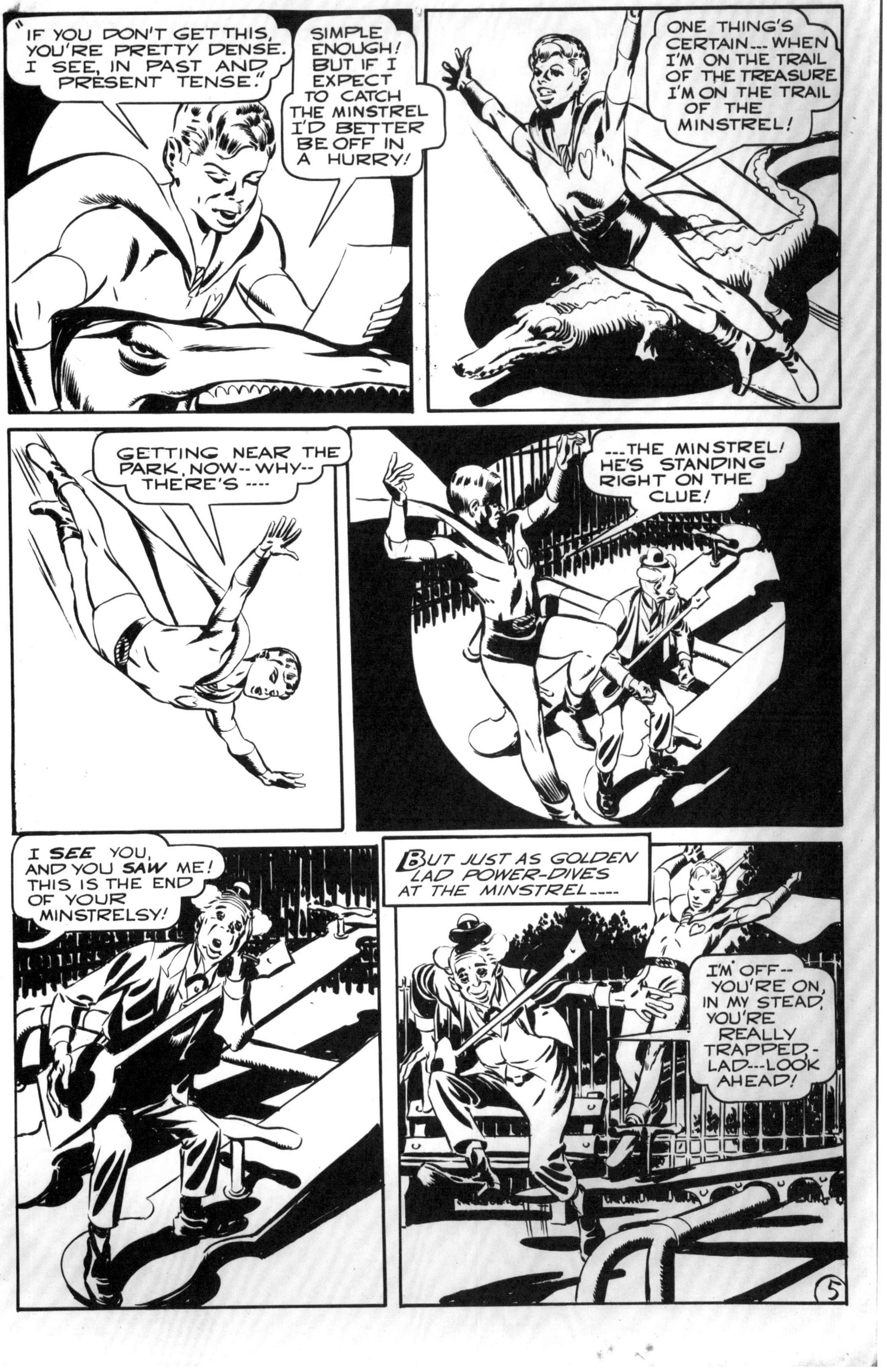
"IF YOU DON'T GET THIS, YOU'RE PRETTY DENSE. I SEE, IN PAST AND PRESENT TENSE."
SIMPLE ENOUGH! BUT IF I EXPECT TO CATCH THE MINSTREL I'D BETTER BE OFF IN A HURRY!
ONE THING'S CERTAIN--- WHEN I'M ON THE TRAIL OF THE TREASURE I'M ON THE TRAIL OF THE MINSTREL!
GETTING NEAR THE PARK, NOW-- WHY-- THERE'S ----
---THE MINSTREL! HE'S STANDING RIGHT ON THE CLUE!
I SEE YOU, AND YOU SAW ME! THIS IS THE END OF YOUR MINSTRELSY!
BUT JUST AS GOLDEN LAD POWER-DIVES AT THE MINSTREL ----
I'M OFF-- YOU'RE ON, IN MY STEAD, YOU'RE REALLY TRAPPED-LAD---LOOK AHEAD!
5

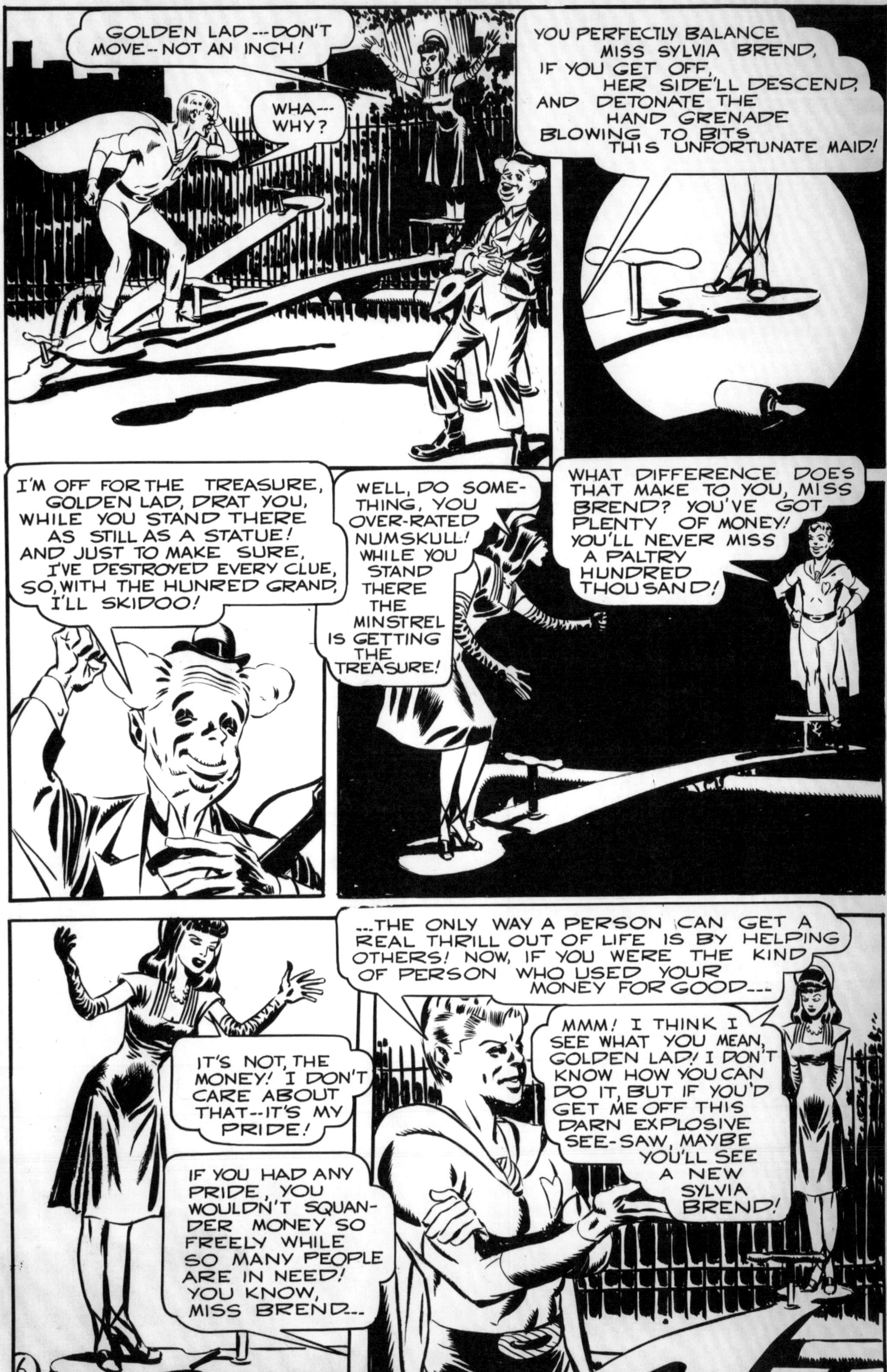
GOLDEN LAD---DON'T MOVE--NOT AN INCH!
WHA--- WHY?
YOU PERFECTLY BALANCE MISS SYLVIA BREND, IF YOU GET OFF, HER SIDE'LL DESCEND, AND DETONATE THE HAND GRENADE BLOWING TO BITS THIS UNFORTUNATE MAID!
I'M OFF FOR THE TREASURE, GOLDEN LAD, DRAT YOU, WHILE YOU STAND THERE AS STILL AS A STATUE! AND JUST TO MAKE SURE, I'VE DESTROYED EVERY CLUE, SO, WITH THE HUNRED GRAND, I'LL SKIDOO!
WELL, DO SOME-THING, YOU OVER-RATED NUMSKULL! WHILE YOU STAND THERE THE MINSTREL IS GETTING THE TREASURE!
WHAT DIFFERENCE DOES THAT MAKE TO YOU, MISS BREND? YOU'VE GOT PLENTY OF MONEY! YOU'LL NEVER MISS A PALTRY HUNDRED THOUSAND!
IT'S NOT, THE MONEY! I DON'T CARE ABOUT THAT--IT'S MY PRIDE!
IF YOU HAD ANY PRIDE, YOU WOULDN'T SQUANDER MONEY SO FREELY WHILE SO MANY PEOPLE ARE IN NEED! YOU KNOW, MISS BREND--
...THE ONLY WAY A PERSON CAN GET A REAL THRILL OUT OF LIFE IS BY HELPING OTHERS! NOW, IF YOU WERE THE KIND OF PERSON WHO USED YOUR MONEY FOR GOOD---
MMM! I THINK I SEE WHAT YOU MEAN, GOLDEN LAD! I DON'T KNOW HOW YOU CAN DO IT, BUT IF YOU'D GET ME OFF THIS DARN EXPLOSIVE SEE-SAW, MAYBE YOU'LL SEE A NEW SYLVIA BREND!
6

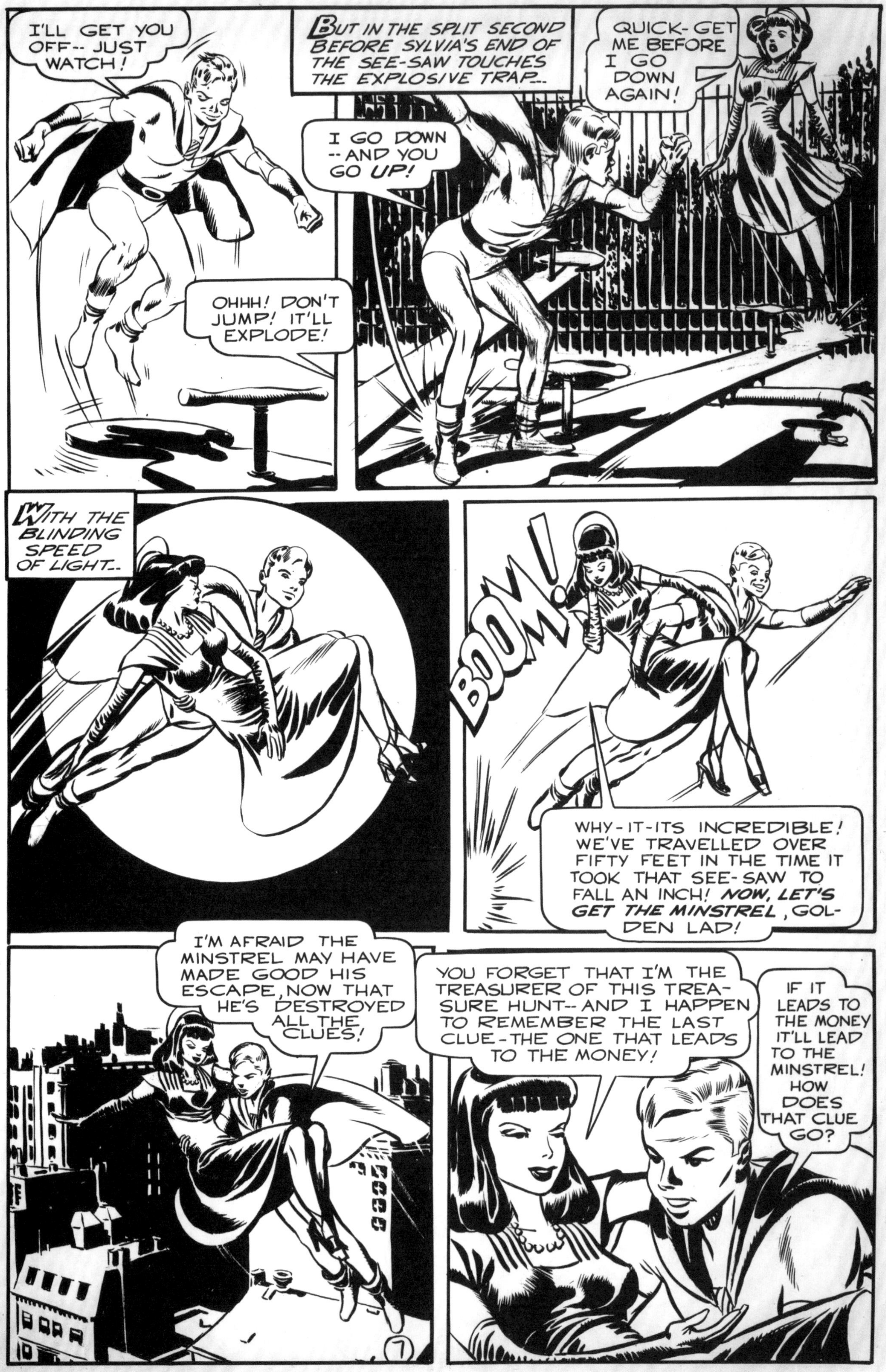
I'LL GET YOU OFF-- JUST WATCH!
OHHH! DON'T JUMP! IT'LL EXPLODE!
BUT IN THE SPLIT SECOND BEFORE SYLVIA'S END OF THE SEE-SAW TOUCHES THE EXPLOSIVE TRAP--
QUICK- GET ME BEFORE I GO DOWN AGAIN!
I GO DOWN --AND YOU GO UP!
WITH THE BLINDING SPEED OF LIGHT--
BOOM!
WHY-IT-ITS INCREDIBLE! WE'VE TRAVELLED OVER FIFTY FEET IN THE TIME IT TOOK THAT SEE-SAW TO FALL AN INCH! NOW, LET'S GET THE MINSTREL, GOLDEN LAD!
I'M AFRAID THE MINSTREL MAY HAVE MADE GOOD HIS ESCAPE, NOW THAT HE'S DESTROYED ALL THE CLUES!
YOU FORGET THAT I'M THE TREASURER OF THIS TREASURE HUNT-- AND I HAPPEN TO REMEMBER THE LAST CLUE-THE ONE THAT LEADS TO THE MONEY!
IF IT LEADS TO THE MONEY IT'LL LEAD TO THE MINSTREL! HOW DOES THAT CLUE GO?
7

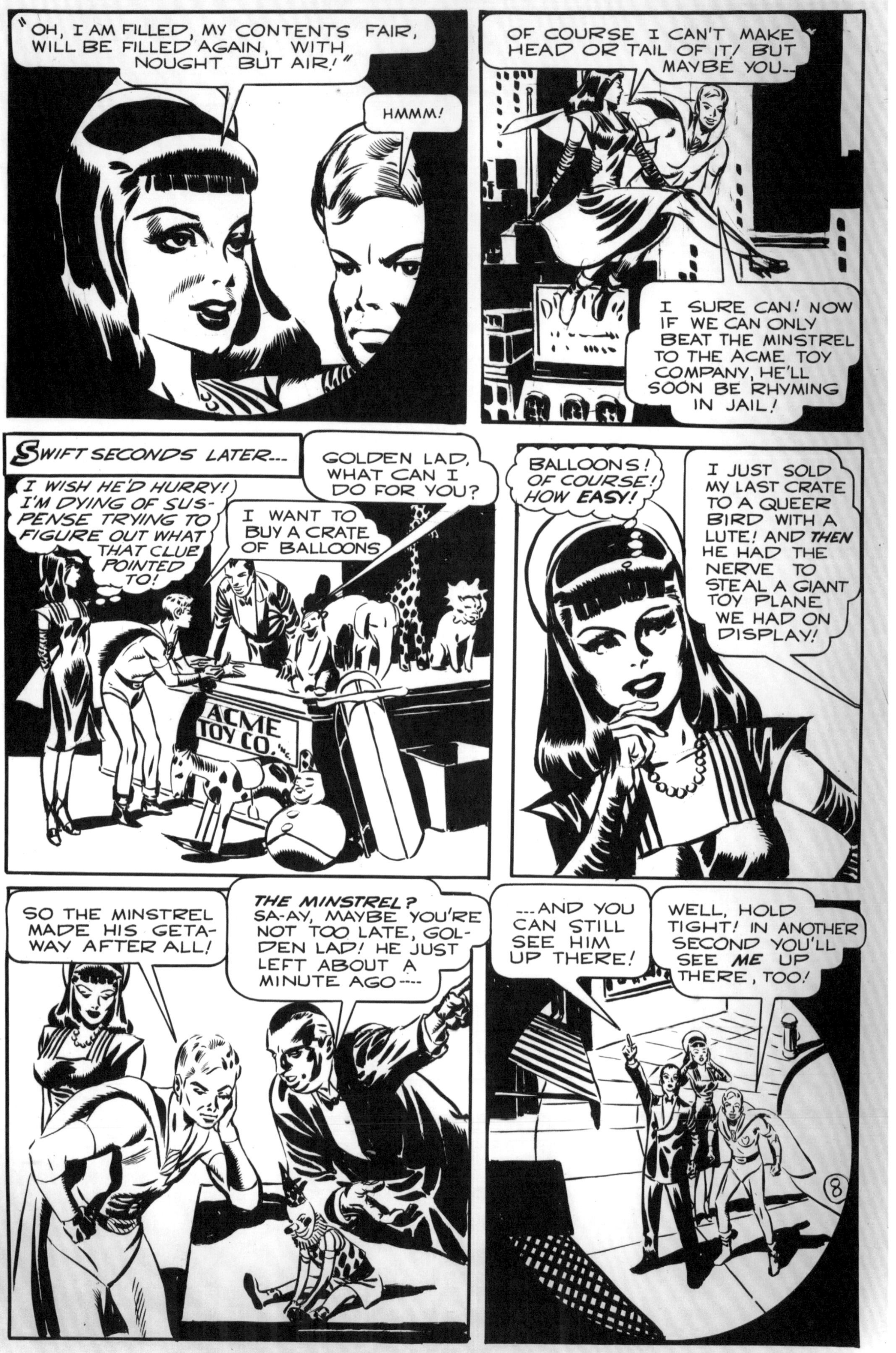
"OH, I AM FILLED, MY CONTENTS FAIR, WILL BE FILLED AGAIN, WITH NOUGHT BUT AIR!"
HMMM!
OF COURSE I CAN'T MAKE HEAD OR TAIL OF IT! BUT MAYBE YOU--
I SURE CAN! NOW IF WE CAN ONLY BEAT THE MINSTREL TO THE ACME TOY COMPANY, HE'LL SOON BE RHYMING IN JAIL!
SWIFT SECONDS LATER---
I WISH HE'D HURRY! I'M DYING OF SUSPENSE TRYING TO FIGURE OUT WHAT THAT CLUE POINTED TO!
GOLDEN LAD, WHAT CAN I DO FOR YOU?
I WANT TO BUY A CRATE OF BALLOONS
ACME TOY CO. INC.
BALLOONS! OF COURSE! HOW EASY!
I JUST SOLD MY LAST CRATE TO A QUEER BIRD WITH A LUTE! AND THEN HE HAD THE NERVE TO STEAL A GIANT TOY PLANE WE HAD ON DISPLAY!
SO THE MINSTREL MADE HIS GETAWAY AFTER ALL!
THE MINSTREL? SA-AY, MAYBE YOU'RE NOT TOO LATE, GOLDEN LAD! HE JUST LEFT ABOUT A MINUTE AGO----
---AND YOU CAN STILL SEE HIM UP THERE!
WELL, HOLD TIGHT! IN ANOTHER SECOND YOU'LL SEE ME UP THERE, TOO!
8

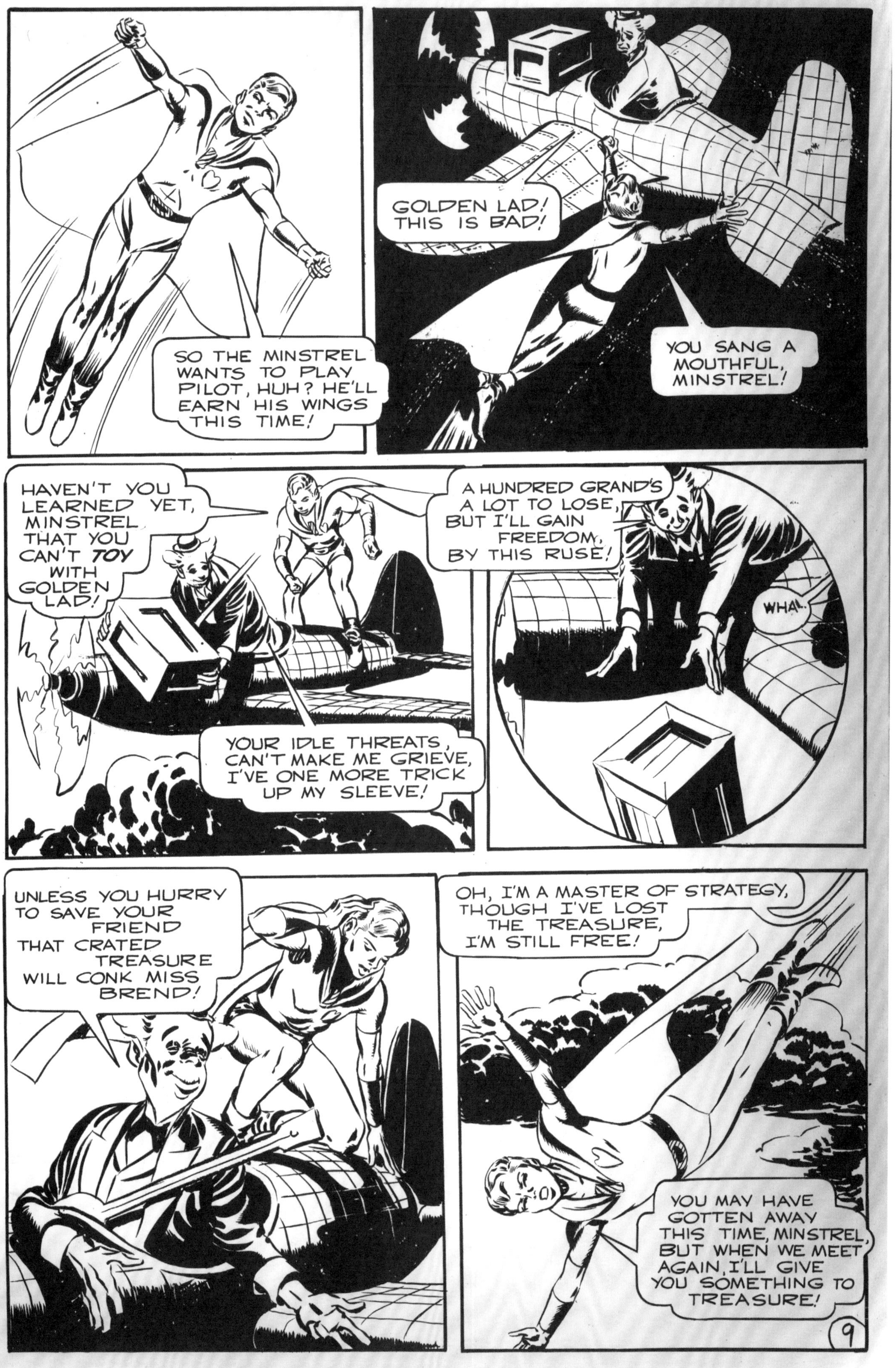
SO THE MINSTREL WANTS TO PLAY PILOT, HUH? HE'LL EARN HIS WINGS THIS TIME!
GOLDEN LAD! THIS IS BAD!
YOU SANG A MOUTHFUL, MINSTREL!
HAVEN'T YOU LEARNED YET, MINSTREL THAT YOU CAN'T TOY WITH GOLDEN LAD!
YOUR IDLE THREATS, CAN'T MAKE ME GRIEVE, I'VE ONE MORE TRICK UP MY SLEEVE!
A HUNDRED GRAND'S A LOT TO LOSE, BUT I'LL GAIN FREEDOM, BY THIS RUSE!
WHA..
UNLESS YOU HURRY TO SAVE YOUR FRIEND THAT CRATED TREASURE WILL CONK MISS BREND!
OH, I'M A MASTER OF STRATEGY, THOUGH I'VE LOST THE TREASURE, I'M STILL FREE!
YOU MAY HAVE GOTTEN AWAY THIS TIME, MINSTREL, BUT WHEN WE MEET AGAIN, I'LL GIVE YOU SOMETHING TO TREASURE!
9

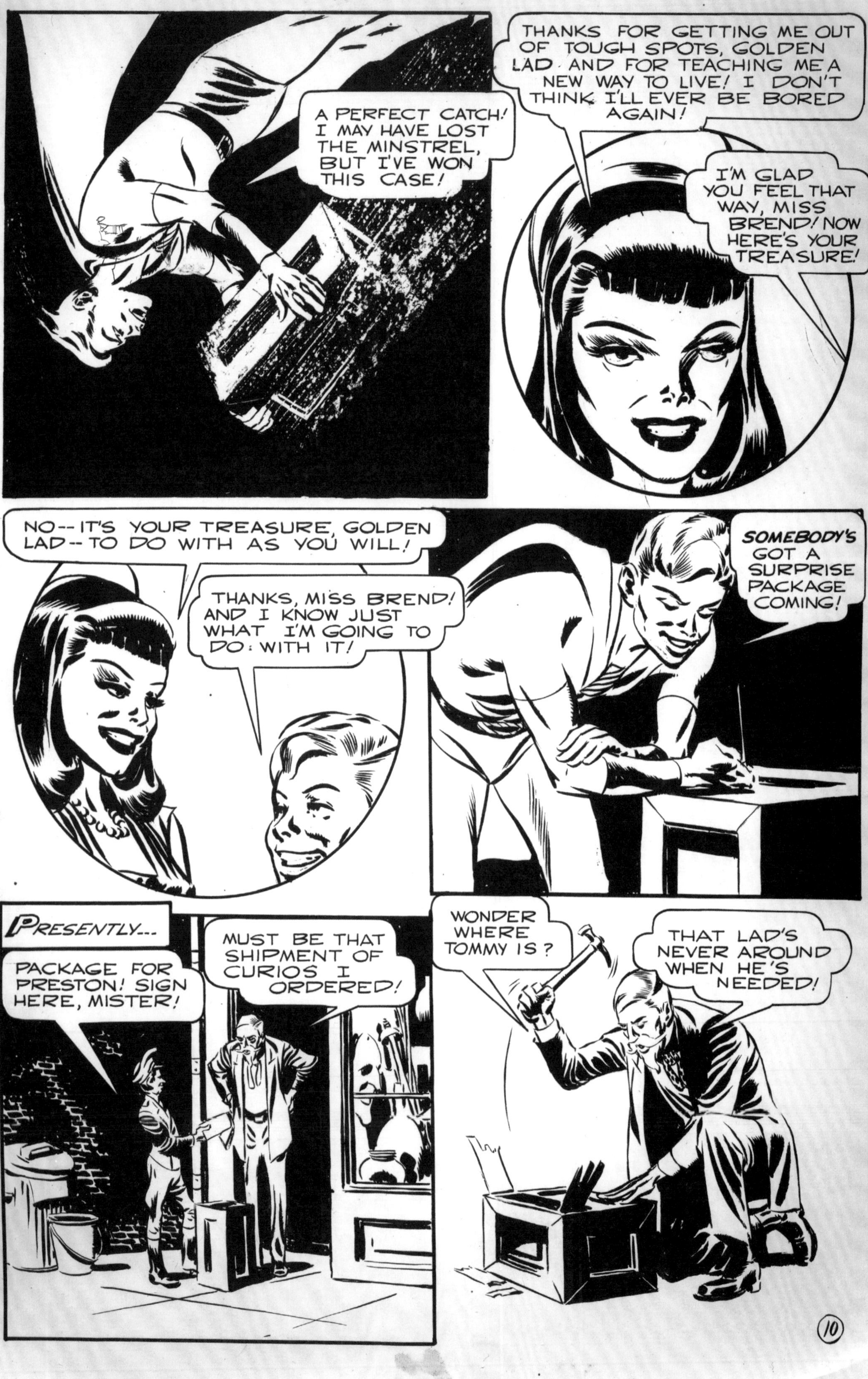
A PERFECT CATCH! I MAY HAVE LOST THE MINSTREL, BUT I'VE WON THIS CASE!
THANKS FOR GETTING ME OUT OF TOUGH SPOTS, GOLDEN LAD AND FOR TEACHING ME A NEW WAY TO LIVE! I DON'T THINK I'LL EVER BE BORED AGAIN!
I'M GLAD YOU FEEL THAT WAY, MISS BREND! NOW HERE'S YOUR TREASURE!
NO--IT'S YOUR TREASURE, GOLDEN LAD--TO DO WITH AS YOU WILL!
THANKS, MISS BREND! AND I KNOW JUST WHAT I'M GOING TO DO WITH IT!
SOMEBODY'S GOT A SURPRISE PACKAGE COMING!
PRESENTLY...
PACKAGE FOR PRESTON! SIGN HERE, MISTER!
MUST BE THAT SHIPMENT OF CURIOS I ORDERED!
WONDER WHERE TOMMY IS?
THAT LAD'S NEVER AROUND WHEN HE'S NEEDED!

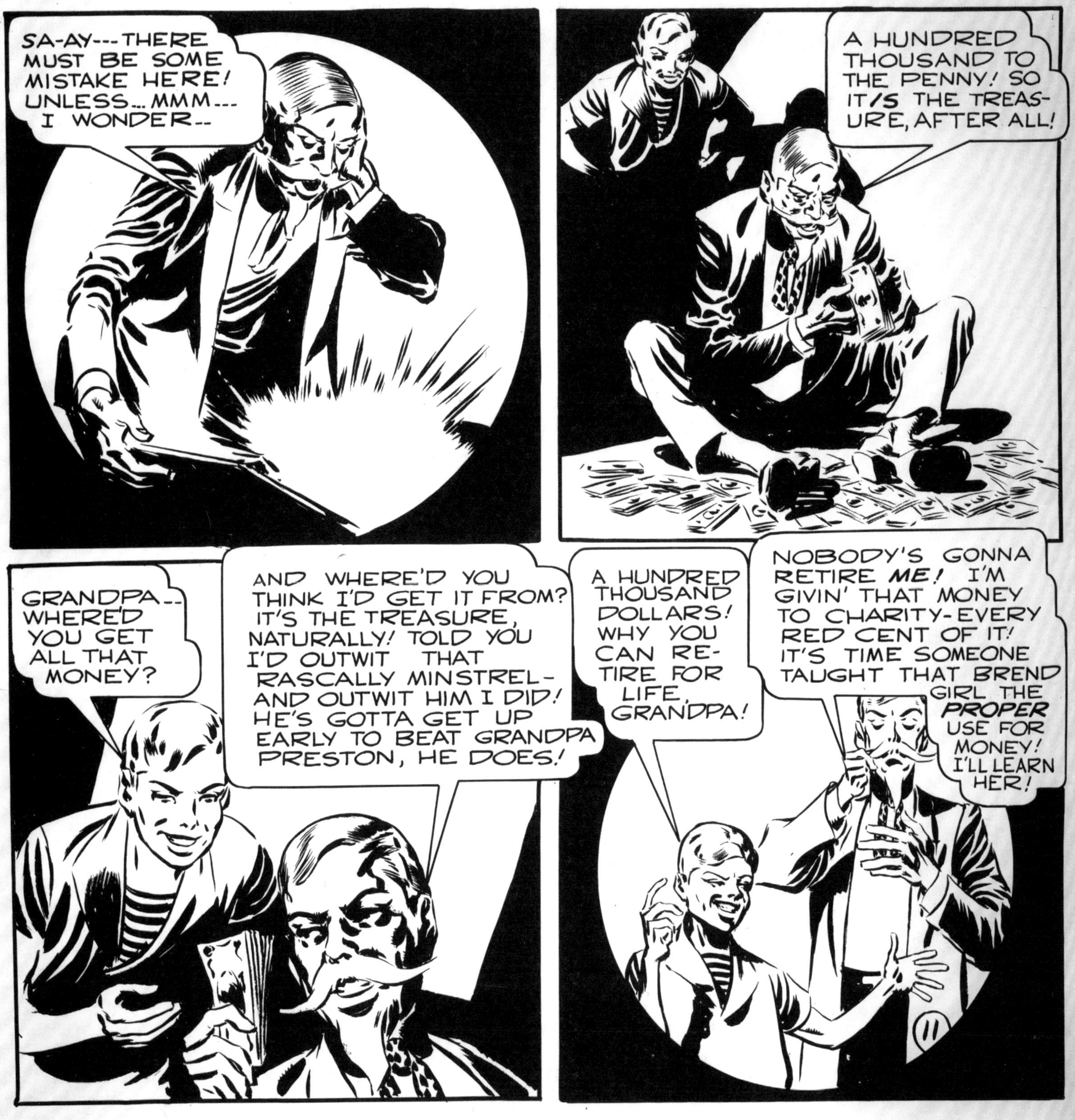
SA-AY---THERE MUST BE SOME MISTAKE HERE! UNLESS... MMM--- I WONDER--
A HUNDRED THOUSAND TO THE PENNY! SO IT IS THE TREASURE, AFTER ALL!
GRANDPA-- WHERE'D YOU GET ALL THAT MONEY?
AND WHERE'D YOU THINK I'D GET IT FROM? IT'S THE TREASURE, NATURALLY! TOLD YOU I'D OUTWIT THAT RASCALLY MINSTREL- AND OUTWIT HIM I DID! HE'S GOTTA GET UP EARLY TO BEAT GRANDPA PRESTON, HE DOES!
A HUNDRED THOUSAND DOLLARS! WHY YOU CAN RETIRE FOR LIFE, GRANDPA!
NOBODY'S GONNA RETIRE ME! I'M GIVIN' THAT MONEY TO CHARITY-EVERY RED CENT OF IT! IT'S TIME SOMEONE TAUGHT THAT BREND GIRL THE PROPER USE FOR MONEY! I'LL LEARN HER!
11

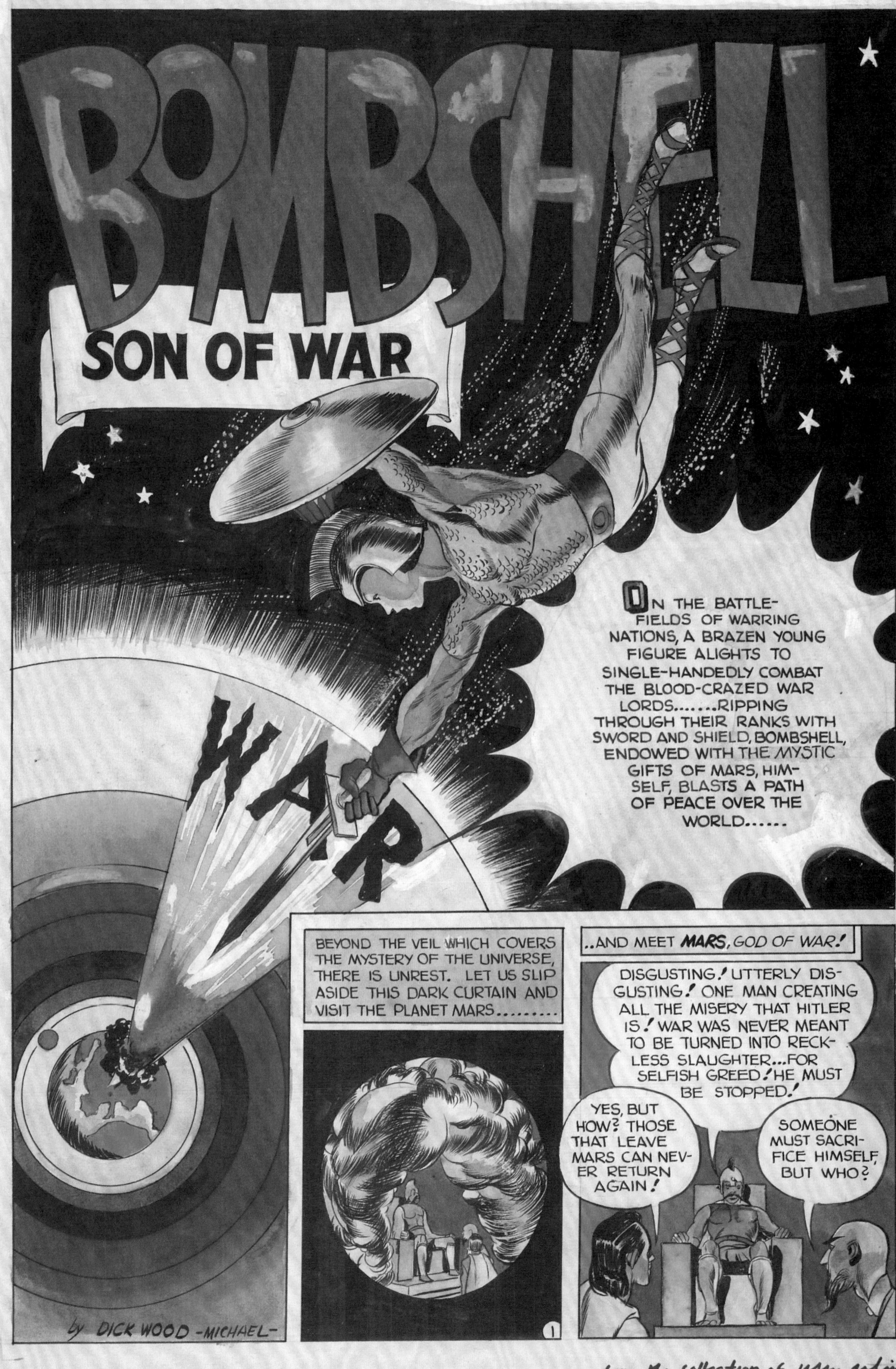
BOMBSHELL
SON OF WAR
ON THE BATTLE-FIELDS OF WARRING NATIONS, A BRAZEN YOUNG FIGURE ALIGHTS TO SINGLE-HANDEDLY COMBAT THE BLOOD-CRAZED WAR LORDS.......RIPPING THROUGH THEIR RANKS WITH SWORD AND SHIELD, BOMBSHELL, ENDOWED WITH THE MYSTIC GIFTS OF MARS, HIM-SELF, BLASTS A PATH OF PEACE OVER THE WORLD......
WAR
by DICK WOOD -MICHAEL-
BEYOND THE VEIL WHICH COVERS THE MYSTERY OF THE UNIVERSE, THERE IS UNREST. LET US SLIP ASIDE THIS DARK CURTAIN AND VISIT THE PLANET MARS.........
1
..AND MEET MARS, GOD OF WAR!
DISGUSTING! UTTERLY DIS-GUSTING! ONE MAN CREATING ALL THE MISERY THAT HITLER IS! WAR WAS NEVER MEANT TO BE TURNED INTO RECK-LESS SLAUGHTER...FOR SELFISH GREED! HE MUST BE STOPPED!
YES, BUT HOW? THOSE THAT LEAVE MARS CAN NEV-ER RETURN AGAIN!
SOMEONE MUST SACRI-FICE HIMSELF, BUT WHO?
from the collection of jerry robinson

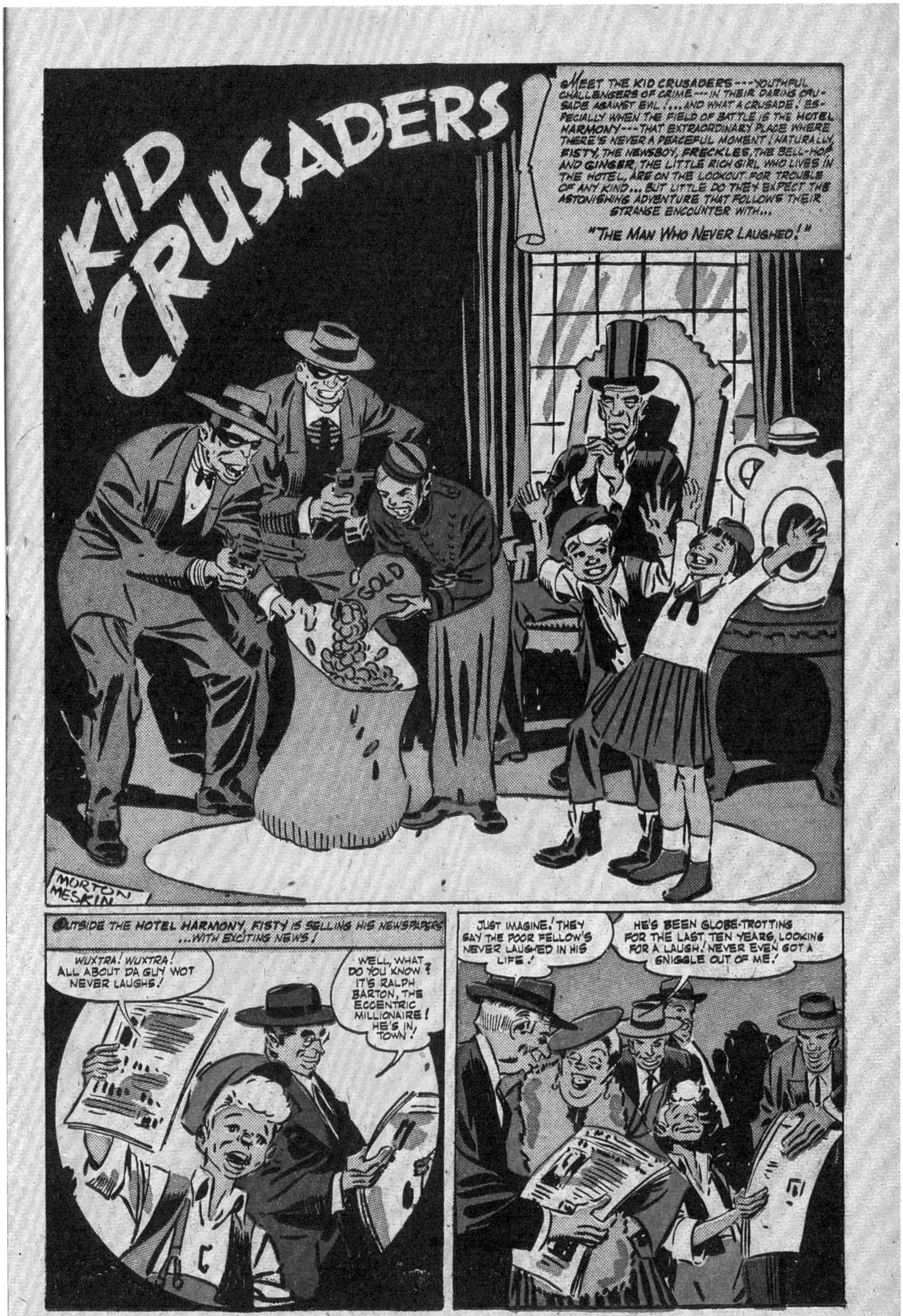
KID CRUSADERS
MEET THE KID CRUSADERS---YOUTHFUL CHALLENGERS OF CRIME---IN THEIR DARING CRUSADE AGAINST EVIL!...AND WHAT A CRUSADE! ESPECIALLY WHEN THE FIELD OF BATTLE IS THE HOTEL HARMONY---THAT EXTRAORDINARY PLACE WHERE THERE'S NEVER A PEACEFUL MOMENT! NATURALLY FISTY, THE NEWSBOY, FRECKLES, THE BELL-HOP AND GINGER, THE LITTLE RICH GIRL WHO LIVES IN THE HOTEL, ARE ON THE LOOKOUT FOR TROUBLE OF ANY KIND... BUT LITTLE DO THEY EXPECT THE ASTONISHING ADVENTURE THAT FOLLOWS THEIR STRANGE ENCOUNTER WITH...
"THE MAN WHO NEVER LAUGHED!"
GOLD
MORTON MESKIN
OUTSIDE THE HOTEL HARMONY, FISTY IS SELLING HIS NEWSPAPERS ...WITH EXCITING NEWS!
WUXTRA! WUXTRA! ALL ABOUT DA GUY WOT NEVER LAUGHS!
WELL, WHAT DO YOU KNOW? IT'S RALPH BARTON, THE ECCENTRIC MILLIONAIRE! HE'S IN TOWN!
JUST IMAGINE! THEY SAY THE POOR FELLOW'S NEVER LAUGHED IN HIS LIFE!
HE'S BEEN GLOBE-TROTTING FOR THE LAST TEN YEARS, LOOKING FOR A LAUGH! NEVER EVEN GOT A SNIGGLE OUT OF ME!

LEFT: *Bombshell, Son of War* splash page from *Boy Comics*, Gleason/Comic House, 1945. Hand colored by Mort Meskin (collection of Jerry Robinson). ABOVE: Splash from *Atoman* #1.

S&K STUDIOS

The Mort Meskin who emerged was a different man. Although never outgoing, he was now withdrawn. "Mort was a very uncertain guy, extremely sensitive," recalled George Roussos.[39] Returning to DC was not an option, and his freelance accounts had slipped. After the war Joe Simon and Jack Kirby resumed their partnership, at first working for Harvey, and then Crestwood/ Feature Publications/Prize. They had a studio on far West 42 Street in the Tudor City apartments where they employed several artists. "He just came in from out of the cold. He was a little ill at the time. And he came out of this little rest home and he got a job there, just freelancing, he preferred workspace. I had workspace there, that's where I met him," recalled fellow S&K artist (as well as Brooklynite and Pratt graduate) Marvin Stein.[34]

Mort in Central Park
with Peter, 1949.

Meskin went to see them and was hired. He was given a drawing board and a script. For the following week, while others worked around him, he stared at the blank illustration board. Simon recalls, "He was sitting at his drawing table and there was this blank sheet of board in front of him, and he's sitting there all day looking at the board and then he went home. We all went home. We came in the next day and Mort was sitting at the same blank board and he kept looking at it. And he did it for another day." At the end of the week Simon distributed paychecks. Meskin questioned where his was. Simon responded that he hadn't done any work. Meskin replied, "Joe, I just can't look at this board—I can't get started."

Simon stood up, walked over to Meskin's board, grabbed a pencil and put some scribbles on the board and said, "Here, now you can get started. "Meskin sat down and began to draw. From that point on, every morning someone would draw a few marks on Mort's board so he could begin working. Simon continues, "He was the fastest artist in the place. He'd do two, three pages a day there and other guys were struggling at half a page; couldn't stop him."[35]

His art appeared to have changed somewhat. Gone were the thin sinewy lines, replaced by bolder strokes. The backgrounds, rather than airy space, were now filled in with crosshatching. Panels were compacted, with little breathing space between characters. Perhaps this was in part influenced by the poorer printing quality compared to National's, but Meskin's work, still endlessly inventive, began to take on a compressed, claustrophobic feel.

Yet Meskin made efforts to overcome his emotional problems. He entered into a friendly competition with the equally prolific Kirby to see who could pencil the most pages in a day. Meskin produced an astounding number of pages for Simon & Kirby Studios, second only to Kirby himself. One day Meskin walked up to Kirby and said:

"I'm a better artist than you are."

"Yeah, you are," Kirby replied.

"You really mean that, don't you?" said Meskin.

"Sure I mean it."

"Well, then why are your books selling better than mine?"

"Because I tell a better story than you do. You're concentrating more on your art than you are on your story." [43]

Meskin admired Kirby greatly: "Jack never gave you the impression he was a fast artist. I've watched him pencil on a number of occasions, and I never got the impression of animated movement. Jack's secret was he could concentrate very hard and drew at a steady rate. He started at one end of a story and worked straight through, never going back.

"It's one of the reasons I don't know Jack better. He was always working. He could concentrate like nobody I ever knew. People were always running around, screaming, and there was Jack, drawing, smoking a cigar, and never looking up."[36]

Likewise, Simon said of Meskin, "He was probably the fastest, most inspired artist in the room, and certainly one of the most dependable." Kirby called him "our most valuable man."[37]

Meskin drew a pornographic version of Nancy Hale, the advice columnist in *Young Romance*, on how to sexually please your man, for everyone's amusement. At lunchtime they would all go bowling. "Mort was an excellent bowler," recalls Simon.[38]

Soon, Meskin, who was in therapy, suggested a new idea for a comic, *Strange World of Your Dreams*, which portrayed tales of dreams in a surrealistic, often nightmarish manner. Meskin was given the title of

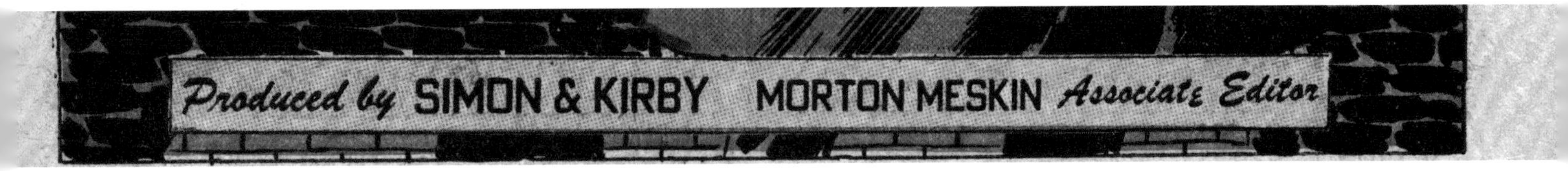
Produced by SIMON & KIRBY MORTON MESKIN Associate Editor

"Associate Editor" on the opening splash page of every comic, the only other member of the Simon and Kirby Studio to receive such status other than the two principals. "Mort had great nightmares. He'd come in, talk about them, and we'd get story ideas," recalled Kirby. "[39] Perhaps too cerebral for the

[TEXT CONTINUES ON PAGE 121]

OVERLEAF: Artwork from *Western Tales* #32, 1955 (collection of Ethan Roberts). (Copyright © 2010 Simon and Kirby. All rights reserved. Reproduced with permission from Joseph Simon and the Estate of Jack Kirby.) SPREAD FOLLOWING: Unpublished romance pencils.

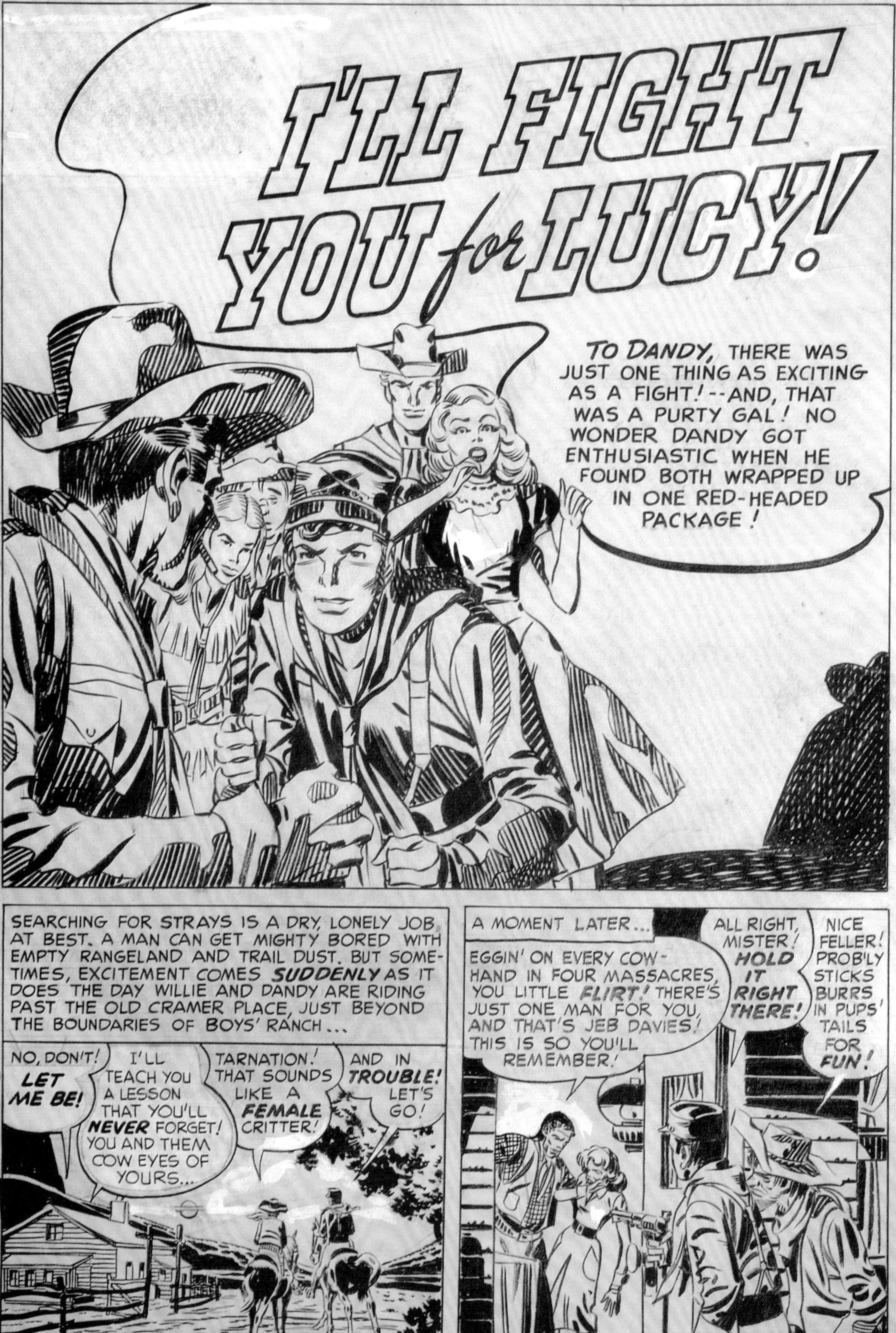
I'LL FIGHT YOU for LUCY!
TO DANDY, THERE WAS JUST ONE THING AS EXCITING AS A FIGHT! --AND, THAT WAS A PURTY GAL! NO WONDER DANDY GOT ENTHUSIASTIC WHEN HE FOUND BOTH WRAPPED UP IN ONE RED-HEADED PACKAGE!
SEARCHING FOR STRAYS IS A DRY, LONELY JOB AT BEST. A MAN CAN GET MIGHTY BORED WITH EMPTY RANGELAND AND TRAIL DUST. BUT SOMETIMES, EXCITEMENT COMES SUDDENLY AS IT DOES THE DAY WILLIE AND DANDY ARE RIDING PAST THE OLD CRAMER PLACE, JUST BEYOND THE BOUNDARIES OF BOYS' RANCH...
NO, DON'T! LET ME BE!
I'LL TEACH YOU A LESSON THAT YOU'LL NEVER FORGET! YOU AND THEM COW EYES OF YOURS...
TARNATION! THAT SOUNDS LIKE A FEMALE CRITTER!
AND IN TROUBLE! LET'S GO!
A MOMENT LATER...
EGGIN' ON EVERY COW-HAND IN FOUR MASSACRES, YOU LITTLE FLIRT! THERE'S JUST ONE MAN FOR YOU, AND THAT'S JEB DAVIES! THIS IS SO YOU'LL REMEMBER!
ALL RIGHT, MISTER! HOLD IT RIGHT THERE!
NICE FELLER! PROB'LY STICKS BURRS IN PUPS' TAILS FOR FUN!
FORGET...

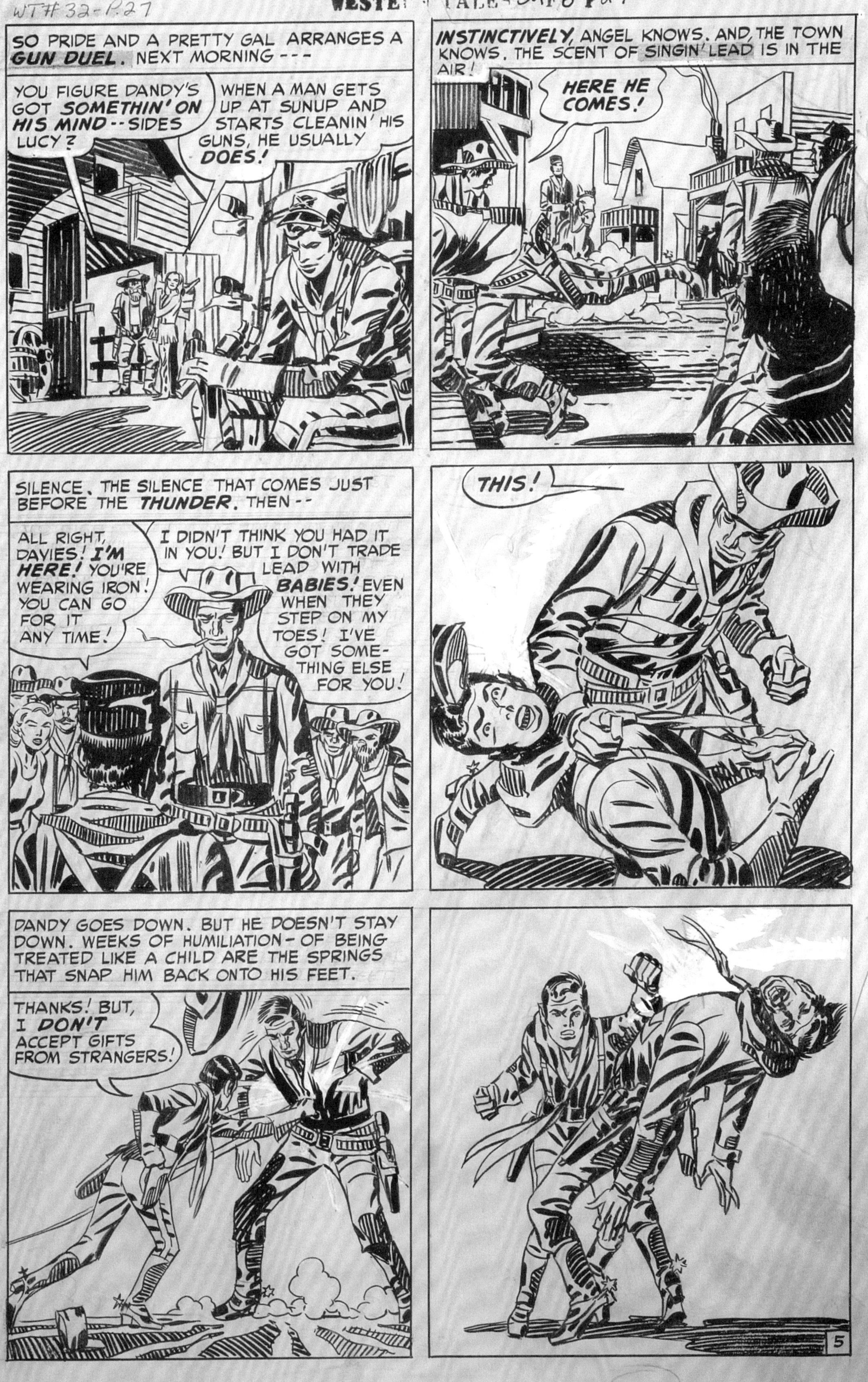
WT#32-P.27
WESTERN TALES #32 F6 P27
SO PRIDE AND A PRETTY GAL ARRANGES A GUN DUEL. NEXT MORNING---
YOU FIGURE DANDY'S GOT SOMETHIN' ON HIS MIND--SIDES LUCY?
WHEN A MAN GETS UP AT SUNUP AND STARTS CLEANIN' HIS GUNS, HE USUALLY DOES!
INSTINCTIVELY, ANGEL KNOWS. AND, THE TOWN KNOWS. THE SCENT OF SINGIN' LEAD IS IN THE AIR!
HERE HE COMES!
SILENCE. THE SILENCE THAT COMES JUST BEFORE THE THUNDER. THEN--
ALL RIGHT, DAVIES! I'M HERE! YOU'RE WEARING IRON! YOU CAN GO FOR IT ANY TIME!
I DIDN'T THINK YOU HAD IT IN YOU! BUT I DON'T TRADE LEAD WITH BABIES! EVEN WHEN THEY STEP ON MY TOES! I'VE GOT SOMETHING ELSE FOR YOU!
THIS!
DANDY GOES DOWN. BUT HE DOESN'T STAY DOWN. WEEKS OF HUMILIATION - OF BEING TREATED LIKE A CHILD ARE THE SPRINGS THAT SNAP HIM BACK ONTO HIS FEET.
THANKS! BUT, I DON'T ACCEPT GIFTS FROM STRANGERS!
5
496

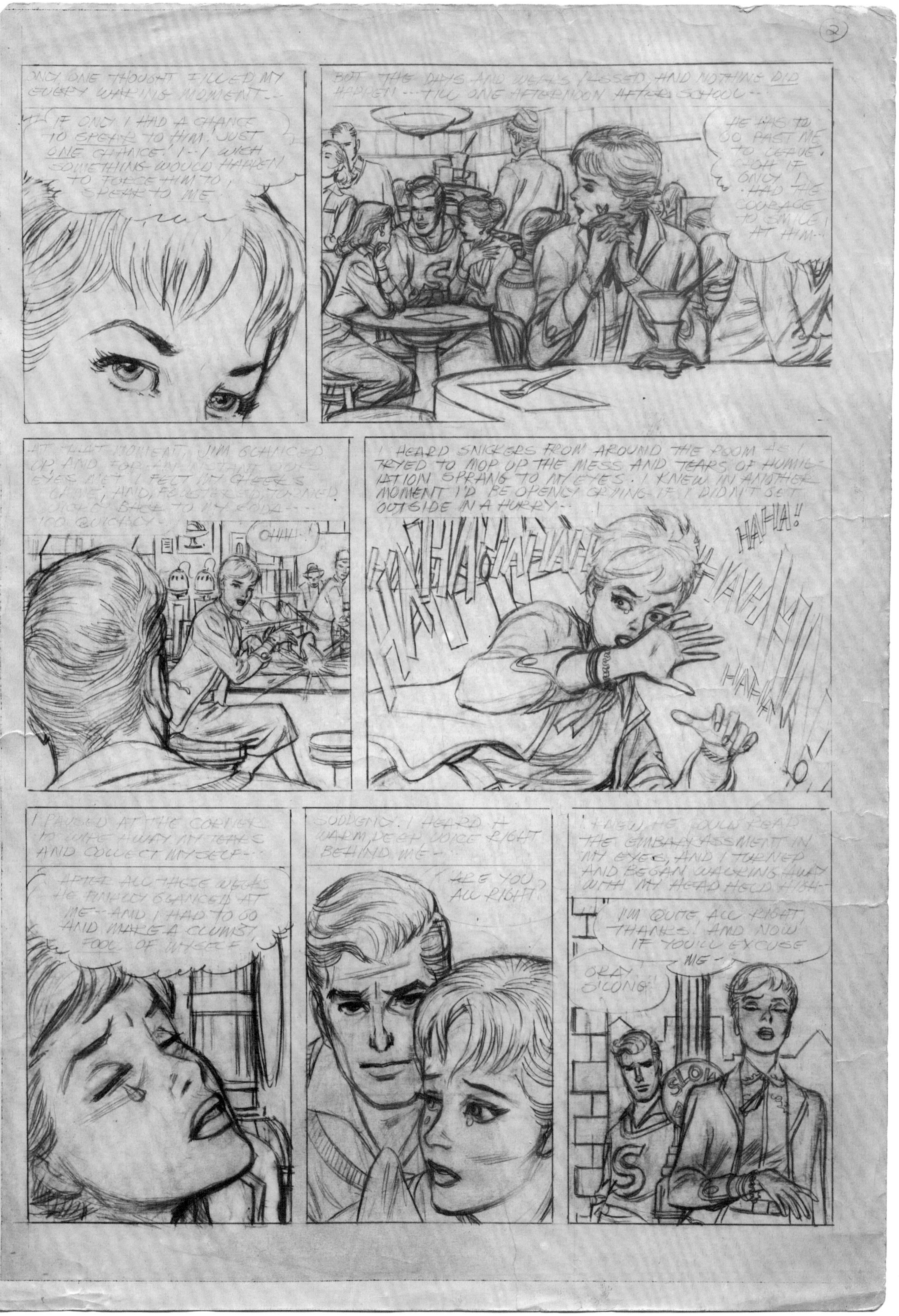

2
ONLY ONE THOUGHT FILLED MY EVERY WAKING MOMENT--
IF ONLY I HAD A CHANCE TO SPEAK TO HIM! JUST ONE CHANCE! I--I WISH SOMETHING WOULD HAPPEN TO FORCE HIM TO SPEAK TO ME!
BUT THE DAYS AND WEEKS PASSED AND NOTHING DID HAPPEN---TILL ONE AFTERNOON AFTER SCHOOL--
HE HAS TO GO PAST ME TO LEAVE. OHH IF ONLY I HAD THE COURAGE TO SMILE AT HIM--
AT THAT MOMENT, JIM GLANCED UP, AND FOR AN INSTANT OUR EYES MET. I FELT MY CHEEKS FLAME, AND, FLUSTERED, TURNED QUICKLY BACK TO MY SODA--- TOO QUICKLY--
OHH!
I HEARD SNICKERS FROM AROUND THE ROOM AS I TRYED TO MOP UP THE MESS AND TEARS OF HUMILIATION SPRANG TO MY EYES. I KNEW IN ANOTHER MOMENT I'D BE OPENLY CRYING IF I DIDN'T GET OUTSIDE IN A HURRY--
HAHA!!
I PAUSED AT THE CORNER TO WIPE AWAY MY TEARS AND COLLECT MYSELF--
AFTER ALL THESE WEEKS HE FINALLY GLANCED AT ME--AND I HAD TO GO AND MAKE A CLUMSY FOOL OF MYSELF
SUDDENLY I HEARD A WARM, DEEP VOICE RIGHT BEHIND ME--
ARE YOU ALL RIGHT?
I KNEW HE COULD READ THE EMBARRASSMENT IN MY EYES, AND I TURNED AND BEGAN WALKING AWAY WITH MY HEAD HELD HIGH--
I'M QUITE ALL RIGHT, THANKS! AND NOW IF YOU'LL EXCUSE ME--
OKAY. SO LONG!
SLOW

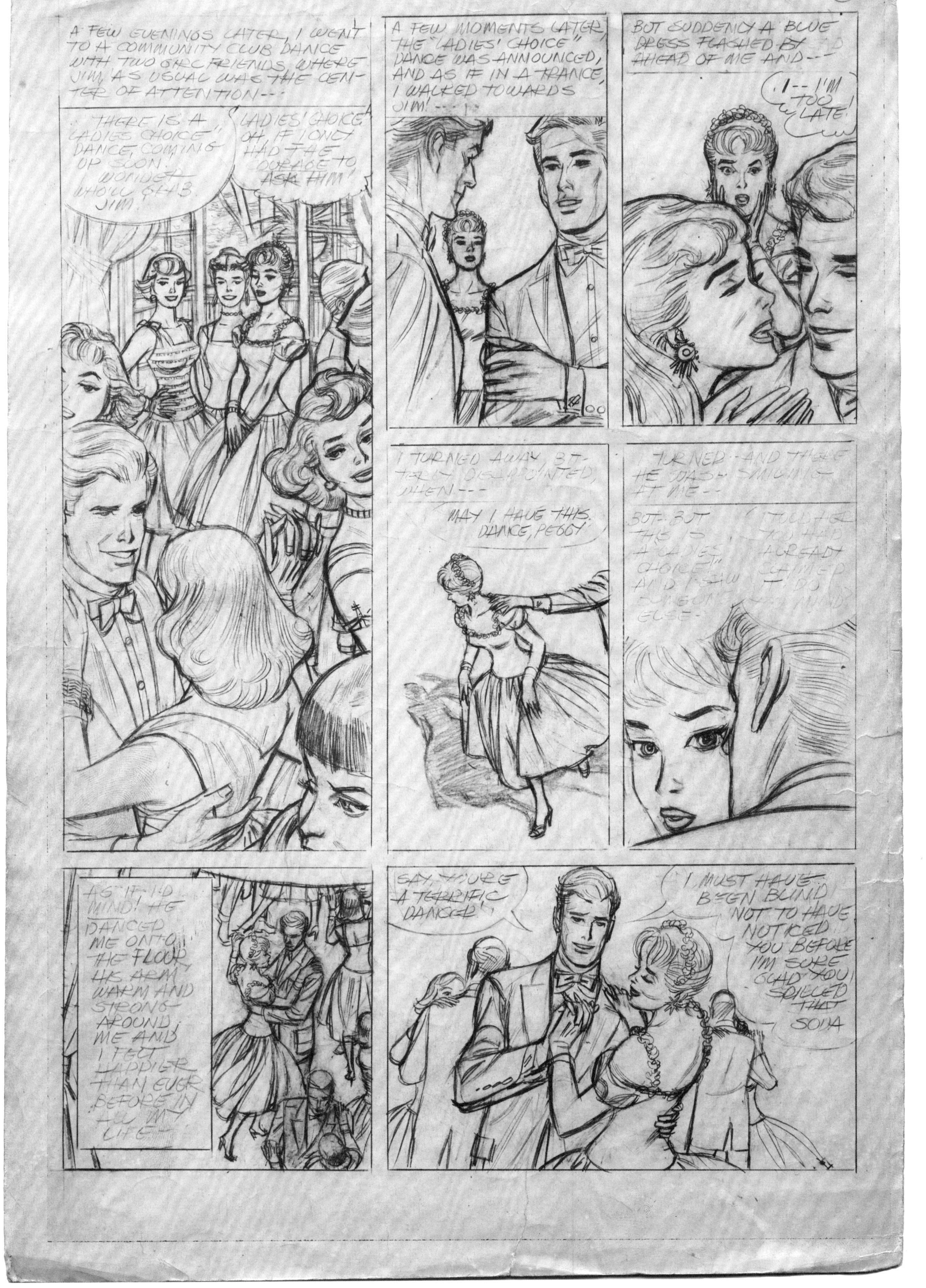
4
A FEW EVENINGS LATER, I WENT TO A COMMUNITY CLUB DANCE WITH TWO GIRL FRIENDS, WHERE JIM, AS USUAL WAS THE CENTER OF ATTENTION---
THERE IS A "LADIES CHOICE" DANCE COMING UP SOON! I WONDER WHO'LL GRAB JIM.
LADIES' CHOICE! OH, IF I ONLY HAD THE COURAGE TO ASK HIM!
A FEW MOMENTS LATER, THE "LADIES' CHOICE" DANCE WAS ANNOUNCED, AND AS IF IN A TRANCE, I WALKED TOWARDS JIM!---
BUT SUDDENLY A BLUE DRESS FLASHED BY AHEAD OF ME AND---
I-- I'M TOO LATE!
I TURNED AWAY, BITTERLY DISAPPOINTED, WHEN---
MAY I HAVE THIS DANCE, PEGGY
I TURNED--AND THERE HE WAS-- SMILING AT ME--
BUT--BUT THIS IS A "LADIES' CHOICE" AND I SAW
ELSE--
YOU HAD ALREADY CLAIMED
AS IF I'D MIND! HE DANCED ME ONTO THE FLOOR, HIS ARM WARM AND STRONG AROUND ME AND I FELT HAPPIER THAN EVER BEFORE IN ALL MY LIFE--
SAY, YOU'RE A TERRIFIC DANCER!
I MUST HAVE BEEN BLIND NOT TO HAVE NOTICED YOU BEFORE I'M SURE GLAD YOU SPILLED THAT SODA

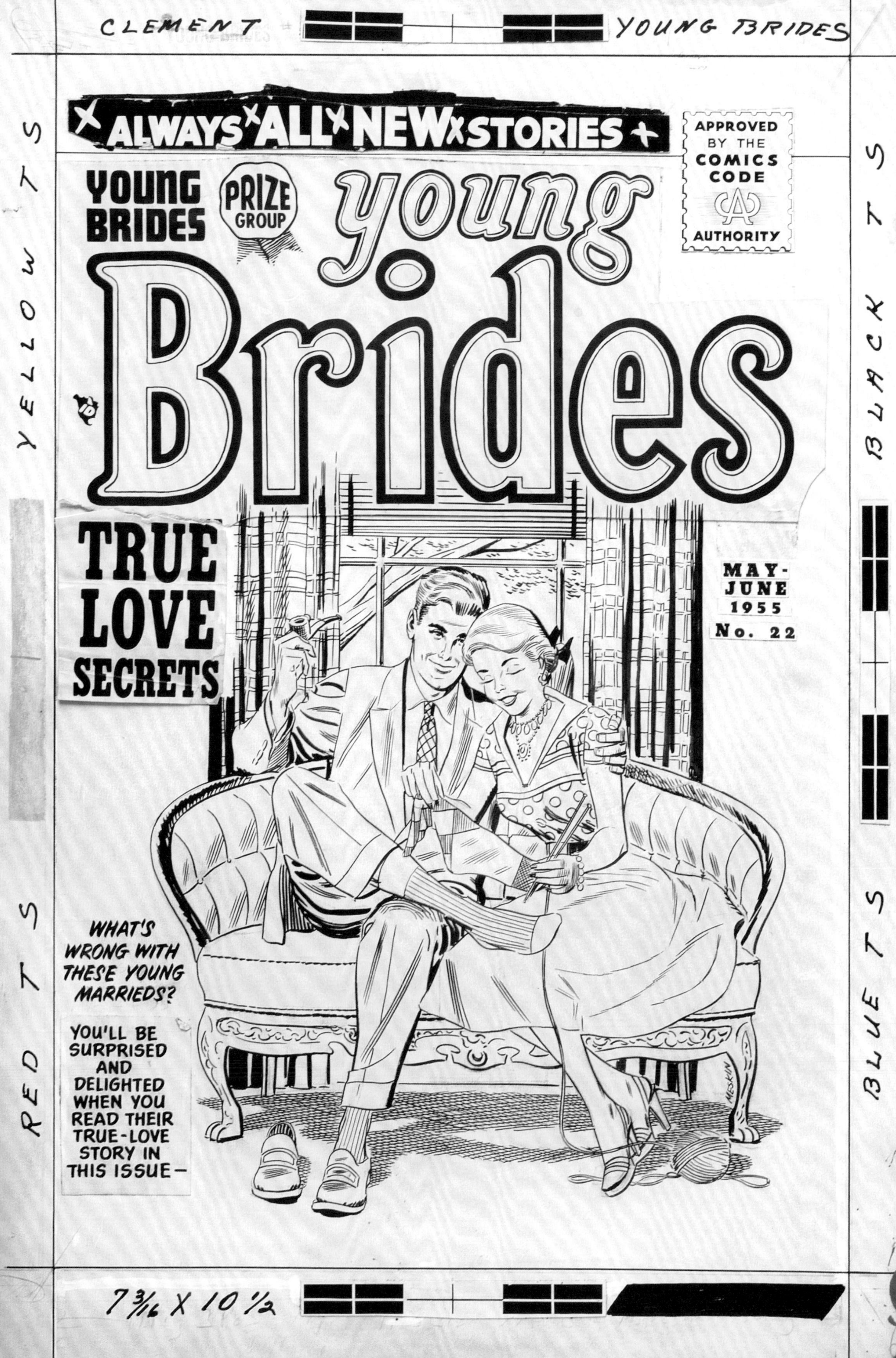
CLEMENT
YOUNG BRIDES
ALWAYS ALL NEW STORIES
APPROVED BY THE COMICS CODE AUTHORITY
YOUNG BRIDES
PRIZE GROUP
young Brides
TRUE LOVE SECRETS
MAY-JUNE 1955
No. 22
WHAT'S WRONG WITH THESE YOUNG MARRIEDS?
YOU'LL BE SURPRISED AND DELIGHTED WHEN YOU READ THEIR TRUE-LOVE STORY IN THIS ISSUE—
MESKIN
YELLOW TS
RED TS
BLACK TS
BLUE TS
7 3/16 X 10 1/2

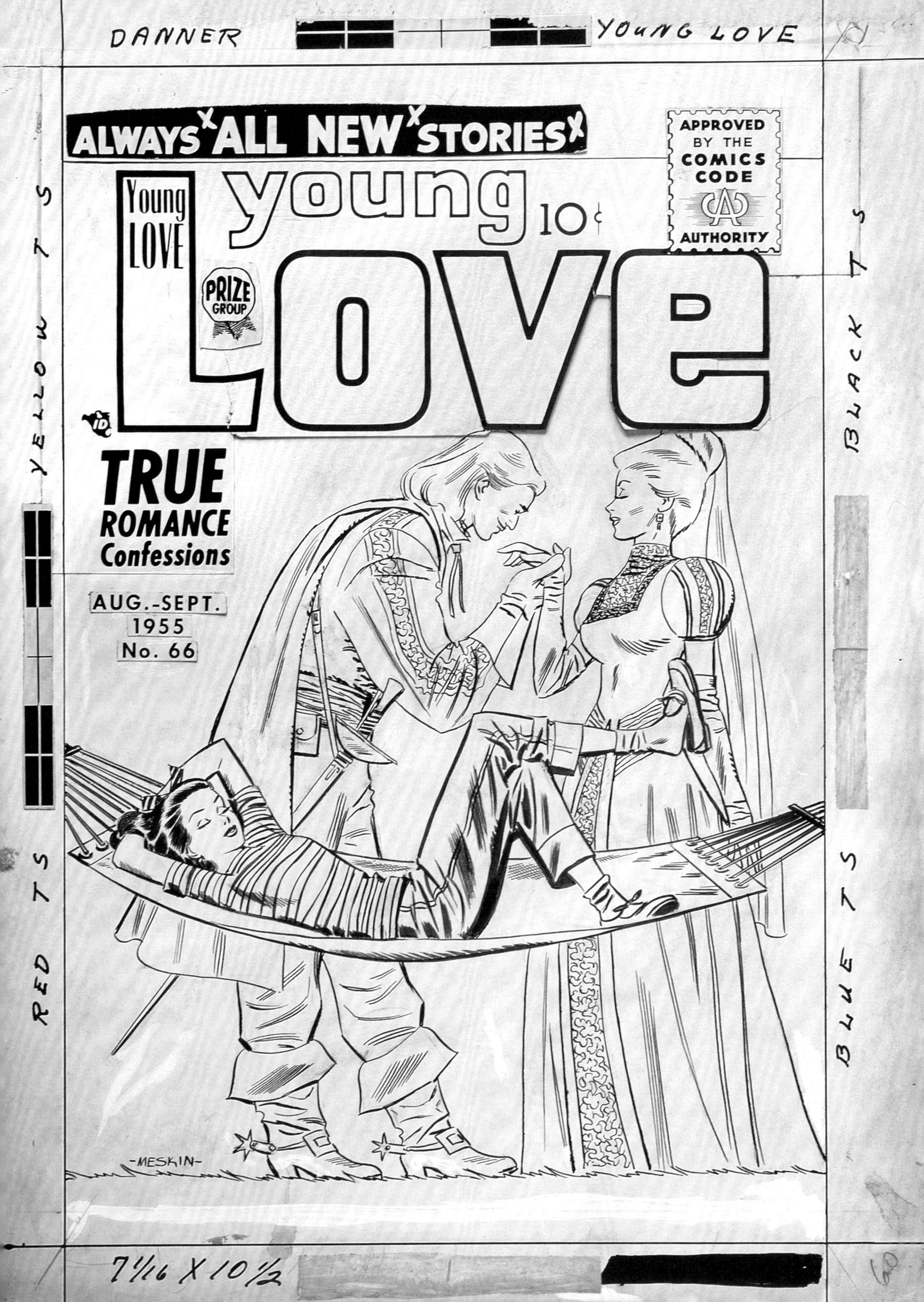
DANNER
YOUNG LOVE
ALWAYS ALL NEW STORIES
APPROVED BY THE COMICS CODE AUTHORITY
Young LOVE
young LOVE
10¢
PRIZE GROUP
TRUE ROMANCE Confessions
AUG.-SEPT. 1955
No. 66
-MESKIN-
YELLOW TS
RED TS
BLACK TS
BLUE TS
7 1/16 X 10 1/2
60

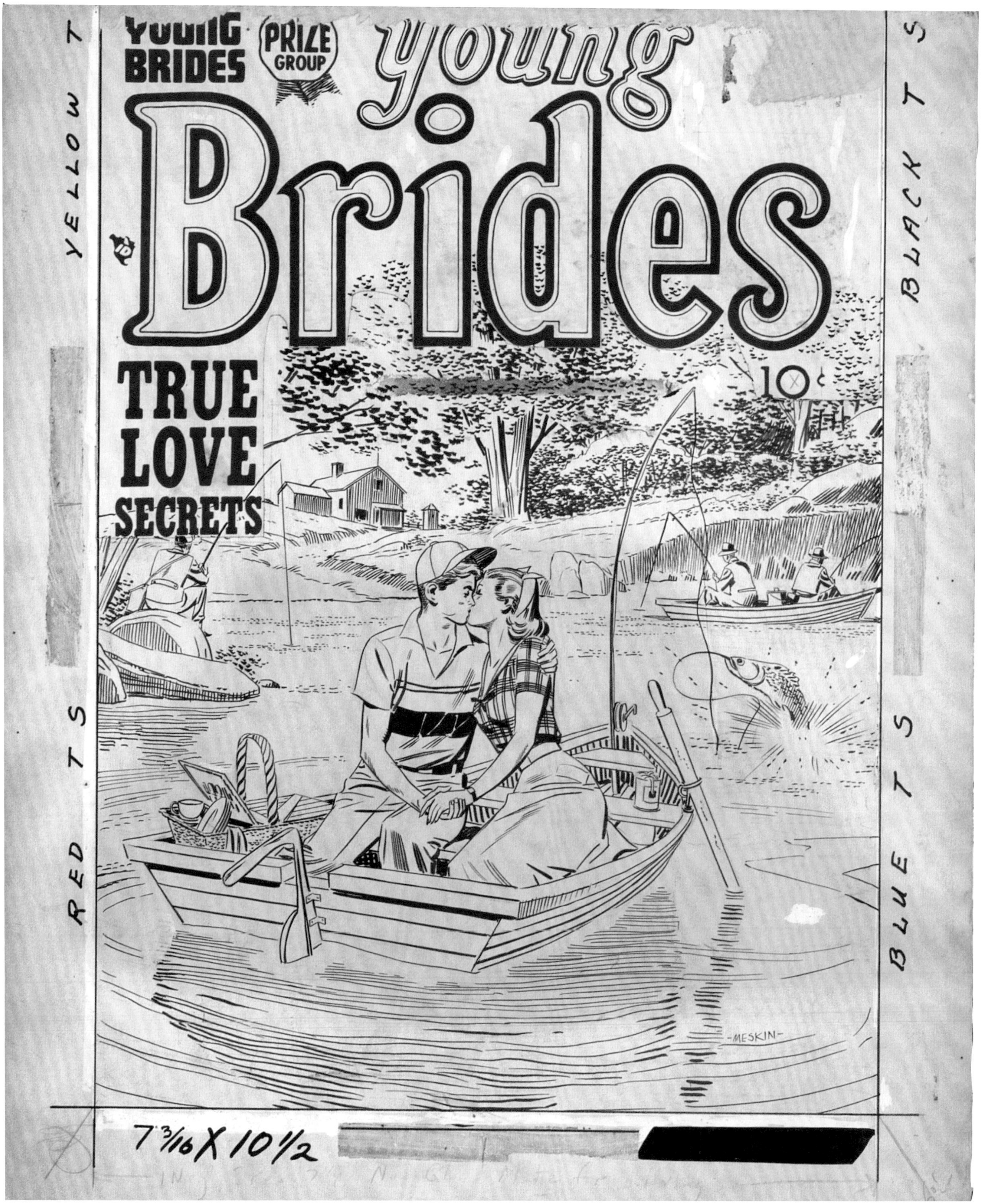
YOUNG BRIDES
PRIZE GROUP
Young Brides
10¢
TRUE LOVE SECRETS
-MESKIN-
YELLOW T
BLACK T S
RED T S
BLUE T S
7 3/16 X 10 1/2

PREVIOUS SPREAD AND ABOVE: Original art from *Young Brides* and *Young Love*, 1955. RIGHT: Original art from *Young Love*, 1955.

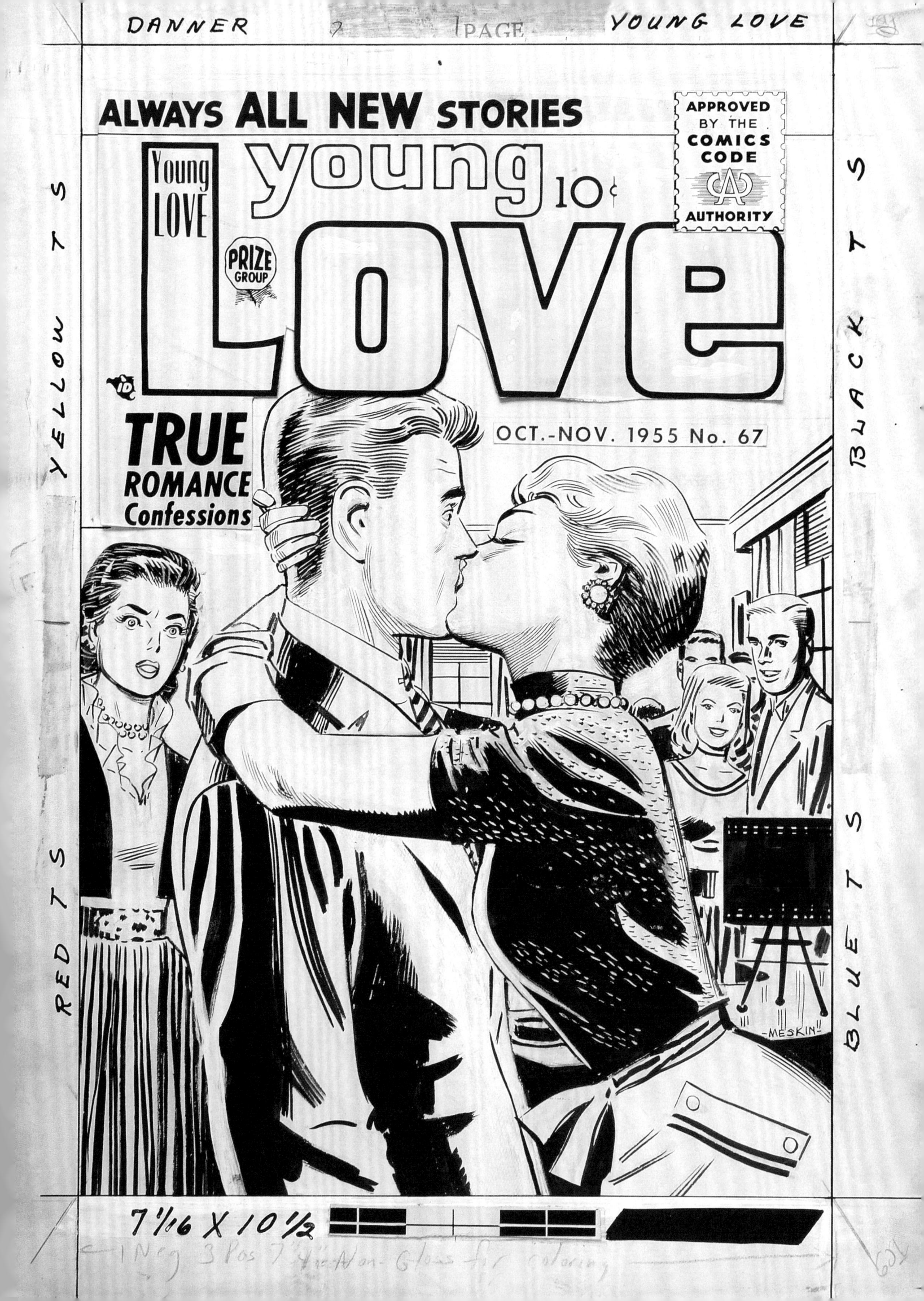

DANNER
PAGE
YOUNG LOVE
ALWAYS ALL NEW STORIES
APPROVED BY THE COMICS CODE AUTHORITY
Young LOVE
young
10¢
PRIZE GROUP
LOVE
OCT.-NOV. 1955 No. 67
TRUE ROMANCE Confessions
-MESKIN-
YELLOW TS
RED TS
BLACK TS
BLUE TS
7 1/16 X 10 1/2
1 Neg 3 Pos 7 1/4 Non-Gloss for coloring

THIS SPREAD: Unpublished pencils, most likely from *Treasure Comics*.
NEXT SPREAD: Unpublished Western strip.

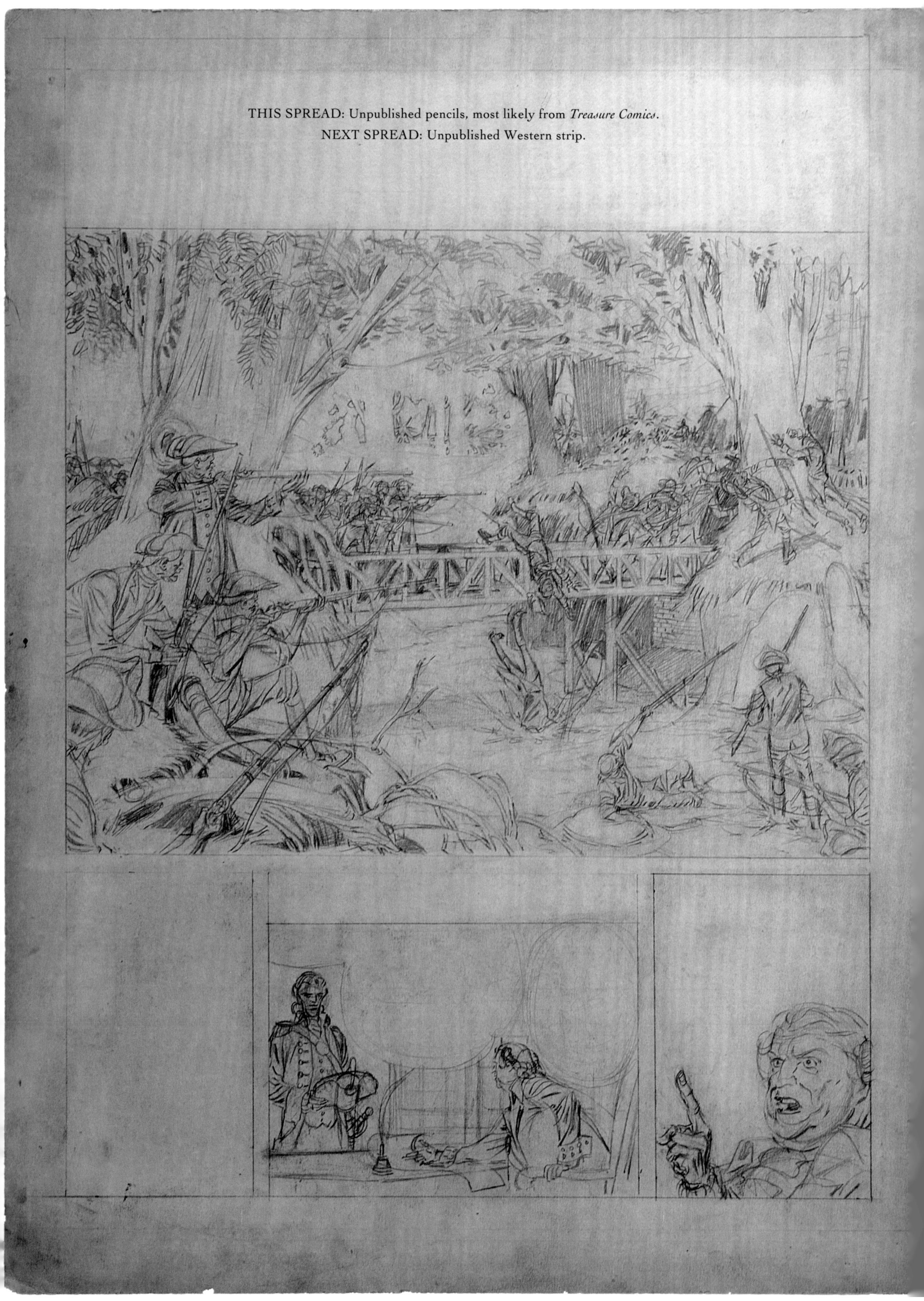

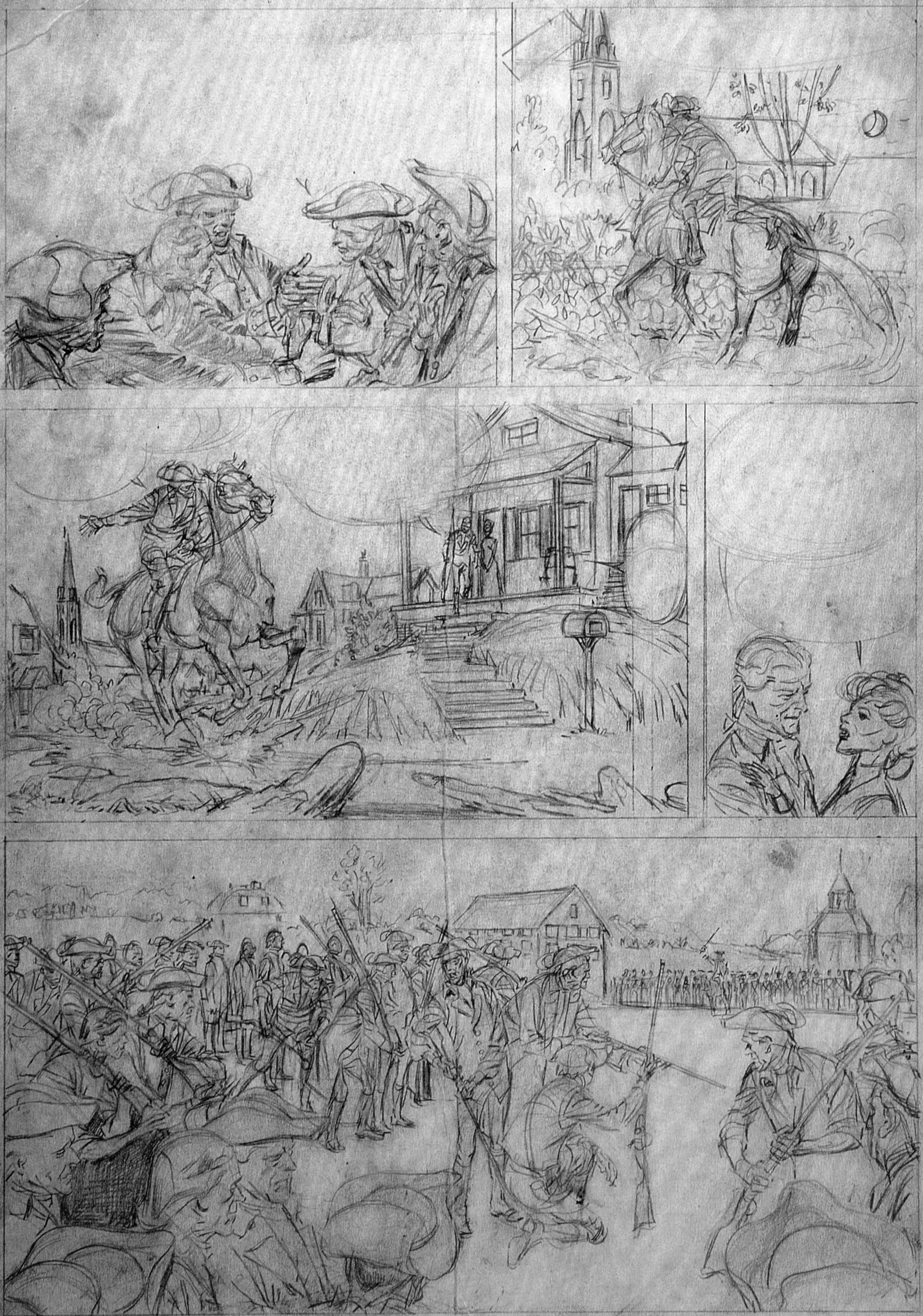

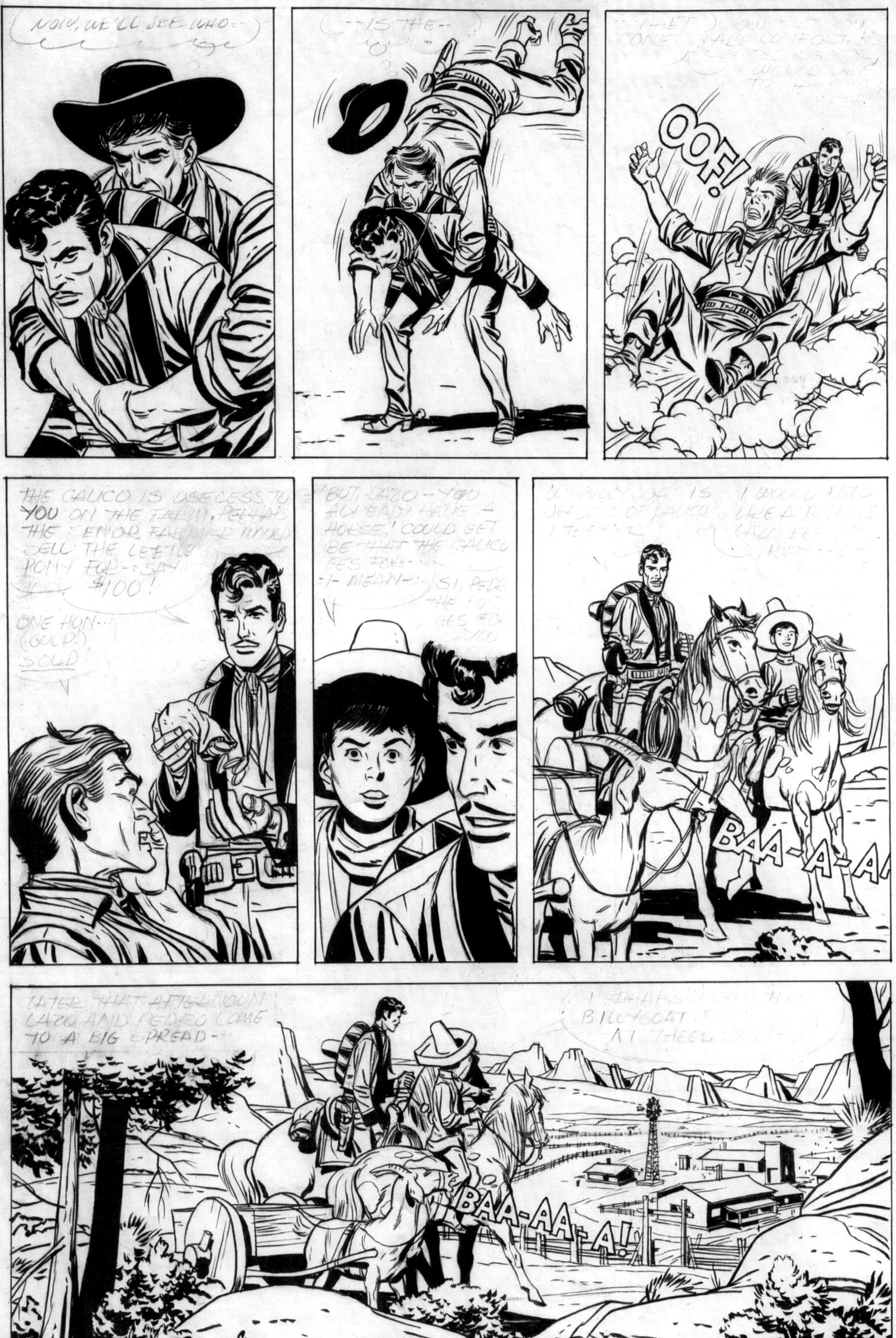
NOW, WE'LL SEE WHO--
--IS THE--
OOF!
THE CALICO IS USELESS TO YOU ON THE FARM. PERHAPS THE SEÑOR FARMER WOULD SELL THE LEETLE PONY FOR--SAY $100!
ONE HUN--
(GULP!)
SOLD!
BUT, LAZO--YOU ALREADY HAVE A HORSE!
I MEAN--
BAA-A-AA
LATER THAT AFTERNOON LAZO AND PEDRO COME TO A BIG SPREAD--
BILLYGOAT
AT THEES
BAA-AA-A!
2

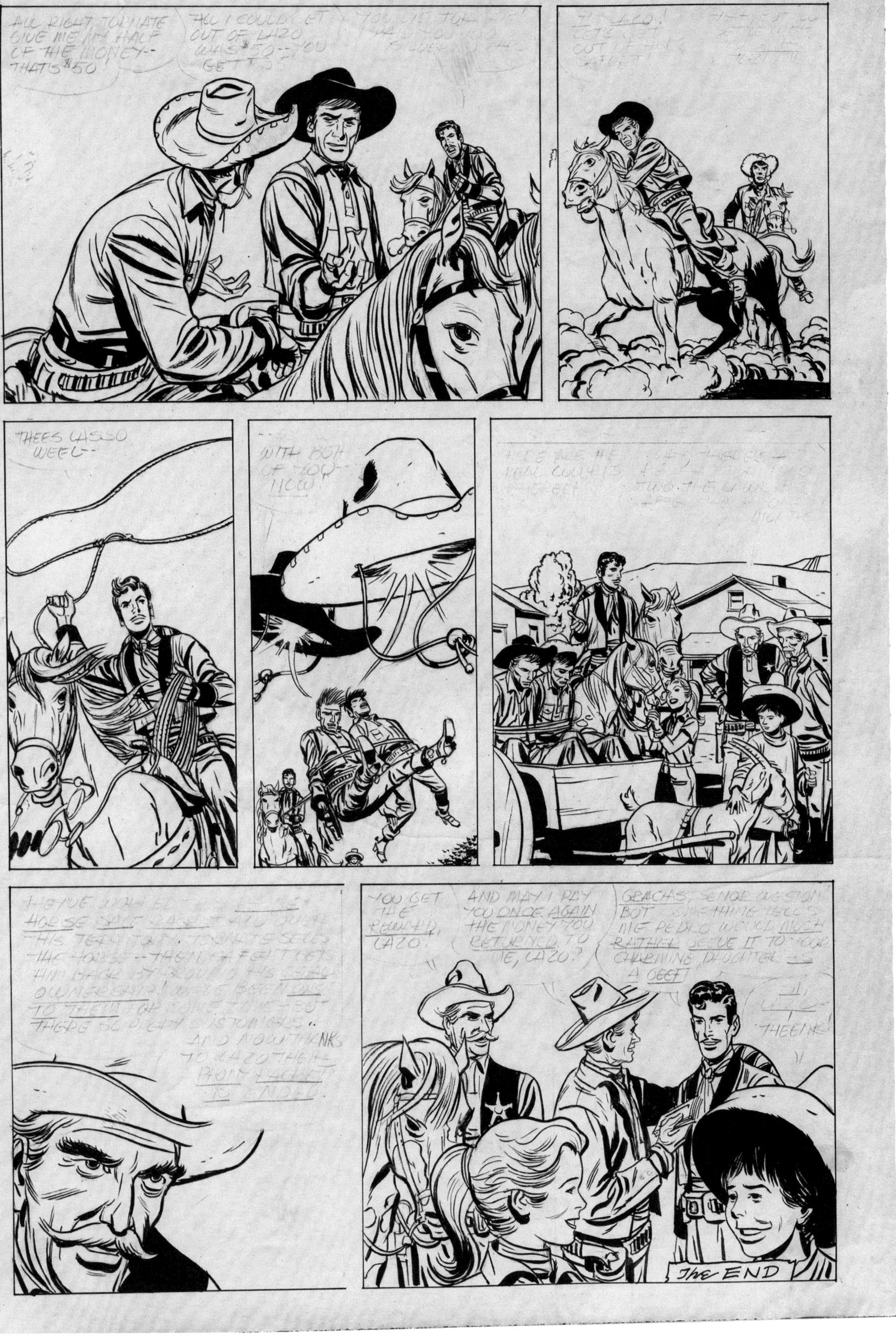

ALL RIGHT, TORNATE GIVE ME MY HALF OF THE MONEY-- THAT'S $50
ALL I COULD GET OUT OF LAZO WAS $50--YOU GET $25
THEES LASSO WEEL--
WITH BOTH OF YOU NOW!
AND NOW THANKS TO LAZO THEIR PHONY RACKET IS ENDED
YOU GET THE REWARD, LAZO.
AND MAY I PAY YOU ONCE AGAIN THE MONEY YOU RETURNED TO ME, LAZO?
GRACIAS, SENOR QUESTON BUT SOMETHING TELLS ME PEDRO WOULD MUCH RATHER SEE IT TO YOUR CHARMING DAUGHTER AS A GEEFT
THE END

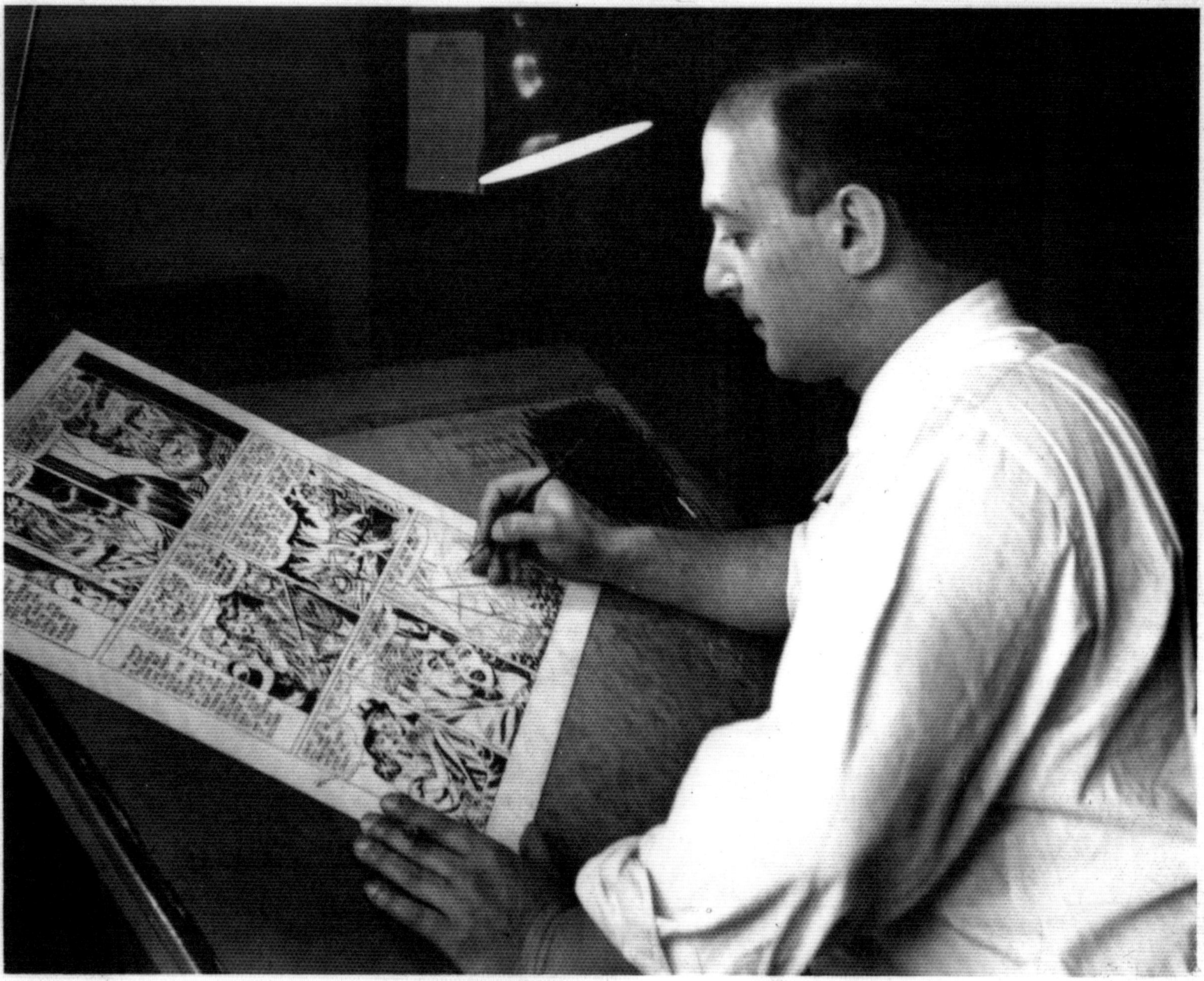

ABOVE: Meskin at work on a
Simon & Kirby Studio romance page
from *Young Love* #10, 1950.

general public, *Strange World of Your Dreams* lasted only four issues.

Still, the shop was busy, producing comics in several genres, romance (which Simon and Kirby had created), crime, horror, superhero by the dozens. Meskin found time to work for a myriad other publishers as well: Avon, Better/Nedor/Pines/Standard, Charlton, Nesbit/Sterling, Hillman, Orbit/Toytown/Patches, and for art director/editor Stan Lee over at Atlas (formerly Timely) alongside Robinson and Roussos. Both Robinson and Meskin enjoyed the freedom to take a script and run with it. Although he didn't do much work for Timely, fellow artist Dan Barry, who drew the *Tarzan* syndicated strip in the 1950s, had this to say about this period: "...nobody could get work, even Meskin couldn't get work—and I got so many scripts that I gave Mort work. I couldn't shine Mort's shoes as an artist, but I was getting work for him."[40]

With Kirby and Meskin working together again, the question of influence arose once more. According to Joe Simon, "Mort did not influence Jack. Both Jack and I loved Mort's work. He may have been influenced by Jack's work because we were seeking a similar style when they were both working on the same book. Both of them naturally used a bold, heavy brush."[41] Perhaps it was simply a matter of Meskin assuming a house style at S&K. "I did a great deal of experimenting there; concepts, blacks and whites, continuity, trying to get different effects," Meskin recalled.[43]

Evidence of the high regard in which he was held is that Meskin went on to produce more pages than any other artist for S&K Studios other than principal Kirby. Kirby, of course, was also writing and editing, but Meskin was often inking his own work. Unfortunately this included few cover designs, but his splash pages proved endlessly inventive and he experimented with vertical splash panels and unusual points of view.

Praise for Meskin's work was not confined within the studio walls. Future American popular culture historian and mystery, fantasy, and science fiction author Ron Goulart wrote him a fan letter on September 18, 1950, when he was 17:

> Dear Mr. Meskin:
>
> I have been a fan of yours for several years. Enjoying your work on "Dick Storm," "Bombshell," "Vigilante," "Johnny Quick," "Star-Man," "Golden Lad," "Black Terror," "Fighting Yank," and currently on Black Magic.
>
> In my opinion you are one of the finest cartoonists in the business. No artist has equaled the job you did on "Vigilante" and "Johnny Quick." I'm interested in cartooning and would very much like to have your autograph.
>
> Sincerely yours,
> Ronald Goulart

Next-generation comic book creator (and publisher and illustrator) Jim Steranko concurs: "Mort was among the many artists who influenced me. I always admired his design skills and smart narrative approach, always easy to comprehend and often dynamic—sometimes equaling Kirby. His *Golden Lad* was a masterpiece of simplicity and storytelling."[53]

Meskin surprisingly—perhaps as a form of therapy—began teaching at the Cartoonists and Illustrators School (now the School of Visual Arts) in Manhattan founded by Silas H. Rhodes and *Tarzan* strip artist Burne Hogarth. Robinson visited him in the classroom. "He was teaching there at night. He was a very quiet man; he would sit down with [the students] and point out things, I don't recall him lecturing as such." Mort asked Jerry to co-teach the class, and shortly afterwards said to him, "You should be doing this." "I started teaching because of Mort," Robinson says. "We already had our studio. I forget how many nights he taught. It was very difficult for him. He stuttered, that [he could teach] was surprising, but it was good for him, to get out and talk, but it became a strain, and so he asked me to fill in, in class a couple of times, and I took over, and it turned out that he was ready to leave and that's how I got to teach." It was there that Robinson taught a talented student, named Steve Ditko, whom he recommended to Simon & Kirby.[43]

Meskin paints in ink at the table in the 1950s during his S&K tenure.

The Simon & Kirby Studio has just taken on a new title for Harvey, *Captain 3-D*, to exploit the current 3D craze. Kirby penciled the first issue, with Mort inking, assisted by Ditko. "I was called in to ink the first issue with Mort," Ditko recalled, "and Mort started to pencil the second issue that I was supposed to ink myself, but the book never took off. I didn't have much faith in the process anyway: it was just a gimmick."

The work was intensive, requiring artwork on several layers of acetate to produce the color separations. It only lasted one issue. Meskin penciled a complete story for the second issue when word came down to halt production. The craze was short-lived and the Harvey warehouse was filled with unsold copies of the first issue. Still, these unfinished pages show how well Mort could draw superheroes, who were in short supply in the 1950s. Sadly, this would be the very last he would draw one. However, his influence was struck going forward, through Steve Ditko, who would go on to fame for *Spider-Man* and *Dr. Strange*. Perhaps more influenced stylistically by Meskin than any other artist was, Ditko wrote a tribute to Meskin in March 1965 for the fanzine *The Comic Reader* (see sidebar).

WHY STEVE DITKO LIKES MORT MESKIN

You asked me why I admire Mort Meskin's artwork. Well, (1) he knew how to draw good proportions, etc. and can handle any type of story well, (2) his panel compositions are consistently superior to most artists, (3) and most important he is a truly remarkable story teller.

The function of a comic artist is to TELL A STORY! He must get across an idea or point of the story and he should do it clearly so a reader knows what is going on and in this Meskin ranks very high. No one who reads a Meskin drawn story is ever in a fog as what is happening. Not only does Meskin tell a story extremely well, but he does it in the most difficult way. He does not take the easy way out or use impressive eye catching gimmicks that can confuse the story's continuity.

You want an example. Take a good look at Meskin's job in *House of Secrets* #69 "Kill the Giant Cat" and then see if other comic artists' stories are as easy to understand. Almost any of Mort's work can be used as a good example of proper story telling. Many stories are just not good picture stories to start with and you can't blame that on Mort or any artist that works from a script. If a writer has two people just talking or saying hello you can't expect the artist to put them in violent action with dramatic lighting plus a fantastic setting.

Sure there are comics artists who can draw automobiles that look like they could drive off the page, artists who use 500 lines to form an eyebrow and artists who draw every leaf on a tree or every rivet on a bridge. But if the story is not told properly, what good is a lot of detailed objects or fine lines? There is a vast difference between a comic artist who tells a story, and a comic "Technician" who draws detailed items or objects.

Anyone who has 12¢ can buy any comic or comic artist work he wants. The choice is his. I'll spend mine in Meskin or comic artists like him—The one who enjoys the "Technicians"—well that's their loss.

During this period Meskin worked independently of S&K. One such assignment was *Tom Corbett, Space Cadet*, which reunited Meskin with Joseph Greene, his *Golden Lad* co-creator. Greene, whose comics writing credits also included *The Green Lama*, and *Spunky*, parlayed his comic experience into writing for television. *Tom Corbett* had begun life as a radio show in 1949, and a newspaper syndicated strip shortly thereafter written by Greene. The television version debuted on NBC on October 2, 1950, with Tom fighting "Men from the Darkside," penned by Greene as well. Shortly thereafter a comic book was planned and Greene brought in his old friend Meskin to do the art chores. The two had much in common, and Greene, in addition to *Corbett*, hired Meskin to work on another script he penned, *Billy*

Blade, Midshipman, under a private contract. Meskin, responsible for all the lettering and inking himself, completed two full stories for which he was paid $300, but they were never published.

At S&K, Meskin continued to be the second most prolific contributor to the studio after Kirby, particularly on the crime comics *Headline* and *Justice Traps the Guilty* as well as the horror title *Black Magic*. Between 1949 and 1955 Meskin did upwards of 1,890 pages of art compared to Kirby's roughly 1,945.

George Roussos: "I liked Mort because of his sense of design, and things looked big, they never looked bitty, like most people draw a figure here and a figure there, and they're real tiny. He also had a sense of feeling that it was real, had depth to it. No one I know of was able to do that. He was very unusual, everything is big and yet it's real. He knew how to capture reality, most people don't know, they just put a table in front of them; his reason for putting something in between something is to give it space, to move it backwards. In other words there's always some object in front of you, everything was relevant to him, a desk or chair, it was the principle of Vermeer, everything he does is never the same, he has a chair, or drapery to push the scene back, he draws flat, no perspective, but he uses the elements themselves to give perspective. Mort would do the same thing. Everything he drew, that I liked about him, whether it was greatly drawn or badly drawn, it had depth to it, and more reality, a sense of space, whereas the other fellows today throw things in to fill the panel, but they have no relationship at all, no purpose, they have a desk, a light, "oh, we'll put it over here, put the desk over there," they think in those terms, they don't have the concept that Mort had. Mort's concept was the most unique in the field, from my perspective."[44]

RIGHT: Penciled page from the unpublished *Captain 3-D*. Meskin would never do another superhero comic. (Copyright © 2010 Simon and Kirby. All rights reserved. Reproduced with permission from Joseph Simon and the Estate of Jack Kirby.)

Al Williamson: "But the thing I remember about going up to Prize was, there was a fellow there, a very fine artist named Mort Meskin. Mort Meskin was one of the sweetest gentlemen I've ever met in the business. He and I got along famously. Every time I'd see him, we'd sit and talk. I was just a kid, between eighteen and twenty-four, twenty-five. I had, and still have, a Sheena Sunday page he did for Eisner and Iger back in 1938, and I asked if he'd sign it for me. He did, and I'm very proud of it. He was a damn good artist."[45]

George Roussos: "Mort's work was more graceful [than Jack Kirby's]. Jack's was exaggerated action and dramatic—one leg would be about ten feet away from the other. Mort was a gymnast so it had an influence on his Johnny Quick and Vigilante. Mort was graceful, but Jack was dynamic."[46]

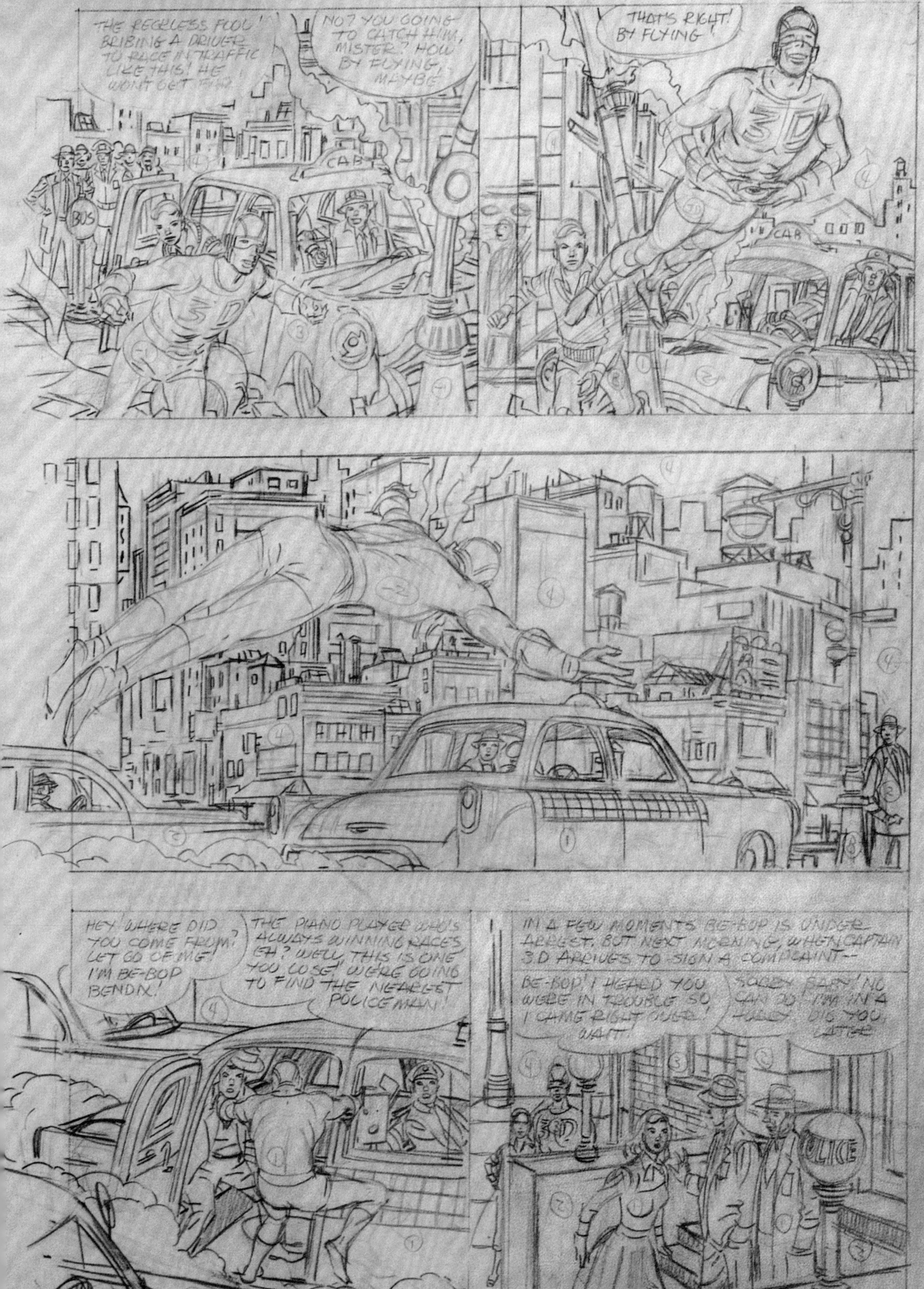
THE RECKLESS FOOL! BRIBING A DRIVER TO RACE IN TRAFFIC LIKE THIS! HE WON'T GET FAR!
NO? YOU GOING TO CATCH HIM, MISTER? HOW BY FLYING, MAYBE!
CAB
BUS
THAT'S RIGHT! BY FLYING!
3D
CAB
HEY! WHERE DID YOU COME FROM? LET GO OF ME! I'M BE-BOP BENDIX!
THE PIANO PLAYER WHO'S ALWAYS WINNING RACES EH? WELL, THIS IS ONE YOU LOSE! WE'RE GOING TO FIND THE NEAREST POLICEMAN!
IN A FEW MOMENTS BE-BOP IS UNDER ARREST. BUT NEXT MORNING, WHEN CAPTAIN 3-D ARRIVES TO SIGN A COMPLAINT--
BE-BOP! I HEARD YOU WERE IN TROUBLE SO I CAME RIGHT OVER! WAIT!
3D
POLICE

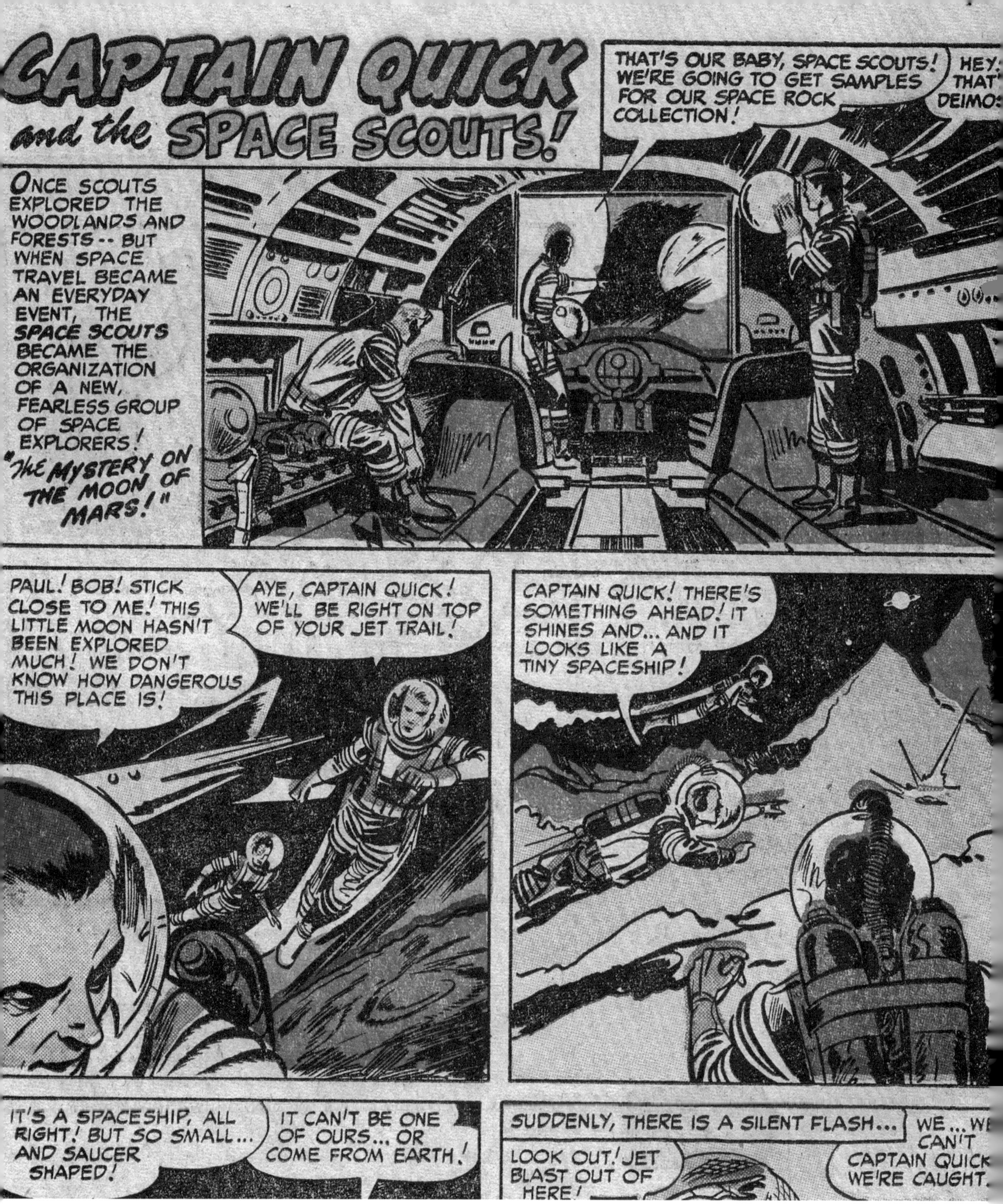
CAPTAIN QUICK and the SPACE SCOUTS!
THAT'S OUR BABY, SPACE SCOUTS! WE'RE GOING TO GET SAMPLES FOR OUR SPACE ROCK COLLECTION!
HEY! THAT DEIMO
ONCE SCOUTS EXPLORED THE WOODLANDS AND FORESTS -- BUT WHEN SPACE TRAVEL BECAME AN EVERYDAY EVENT, THE SPACE SCOUTS BECAME THE ORGANIZATION OF A NEW, FEARLESS GROUP OF SPACE EXPLORERS!
"THE MYSTERY ON THE MOON OF MARS!"
PAUL! BOB! STICK CLOSE TO ME! THIS LITTLE MOON HASN'T BEEN EXPLORED MUCH! WE DON'T KNOW HOW DANGEROUS THIS PLACE IS!
AYE, CAPTAIN QUICK! WE'LL BE RIGHT ON TOP OF YOUR JET TRAIL!
CAPTAIN QUICK! THERE'S SOMETHING AHEAD! IT SHINES AND... AND IT LOOKS LIKE A TINY SPACESHIP!
IT'S A SPACESHIP, ALL RIGHT! BUT SO SMALL... AND SAUCER SHAPED!
IT CAN'T BE ONE OF OURS... OR COME FROM EARTH!
SUDDENLY, THERE IS A SILENT FLASH...
LOOK OUT! JET BLAST OUT OF HERE!
WE... W CAN'T CAPTAIN QUICK WE'RE CAUGHT.

Tom Corbett, Space Cadet continued the working relationship between writer Joseph Greene and Mort Meskin from their Spark Comics days in the 1940s. There were several iterations of *Tom Corbett*, including a syndicated newspaper comic strip and a comic three years prior published by Dell. Meskin drew the entire issue of Volume 2, #1, published by Prize in 1955. ABOVE. Detail from #1. RIGHT: Cover art for #3. Meskin did three issues in all.

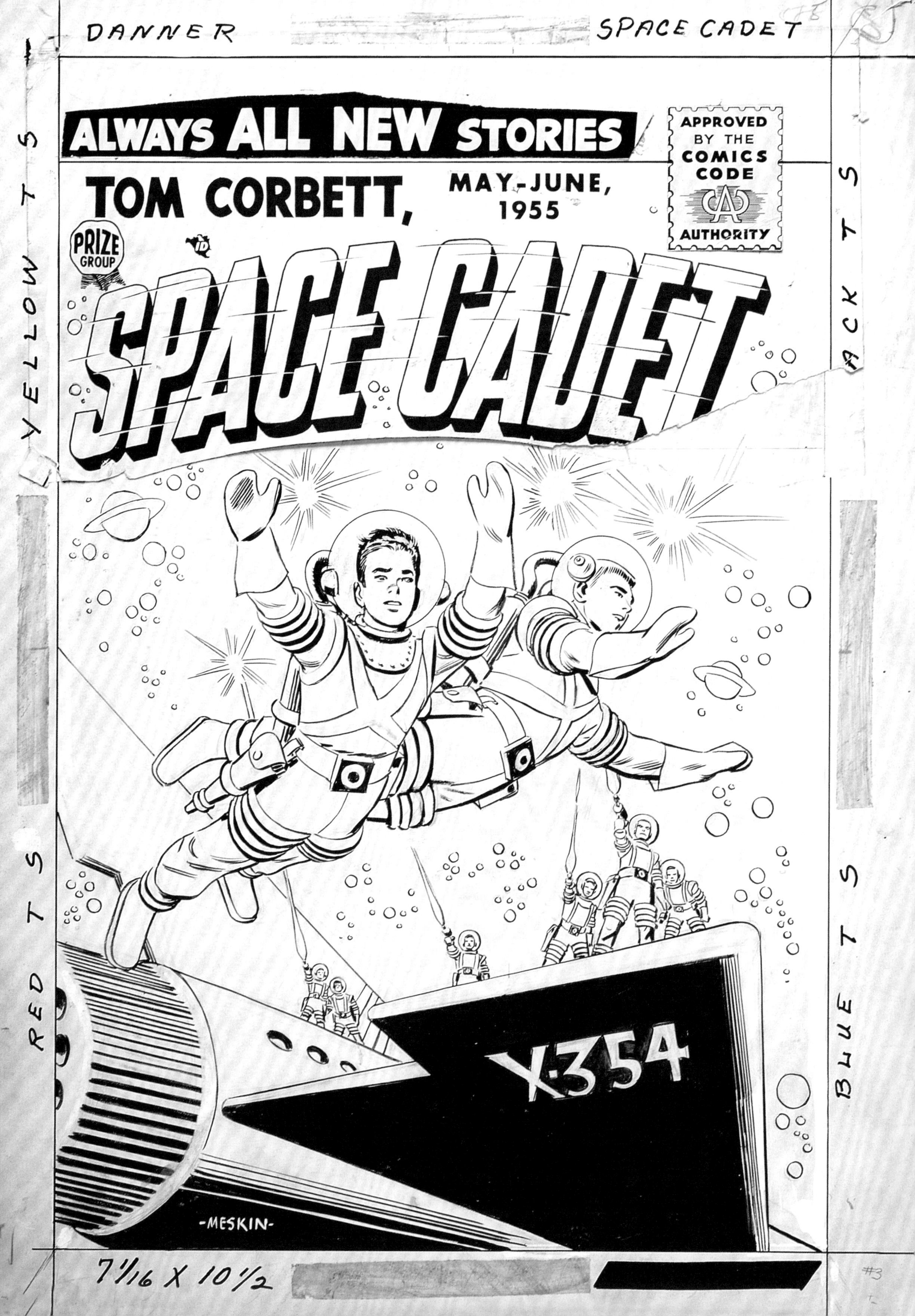
DANNER
SPACE CADET
ALWAYS ALL NEW STORIES
APPROVED BY THE COMICS CODE AUTHORITY
TOM CORBETT,
MAY-JUNE, 1955
PRIZE GROUP
SPACE CADET
X-354
-MESKIN-
7 1/16 X 10 1/2
YELLOW T S
RED T S
BLUE T S

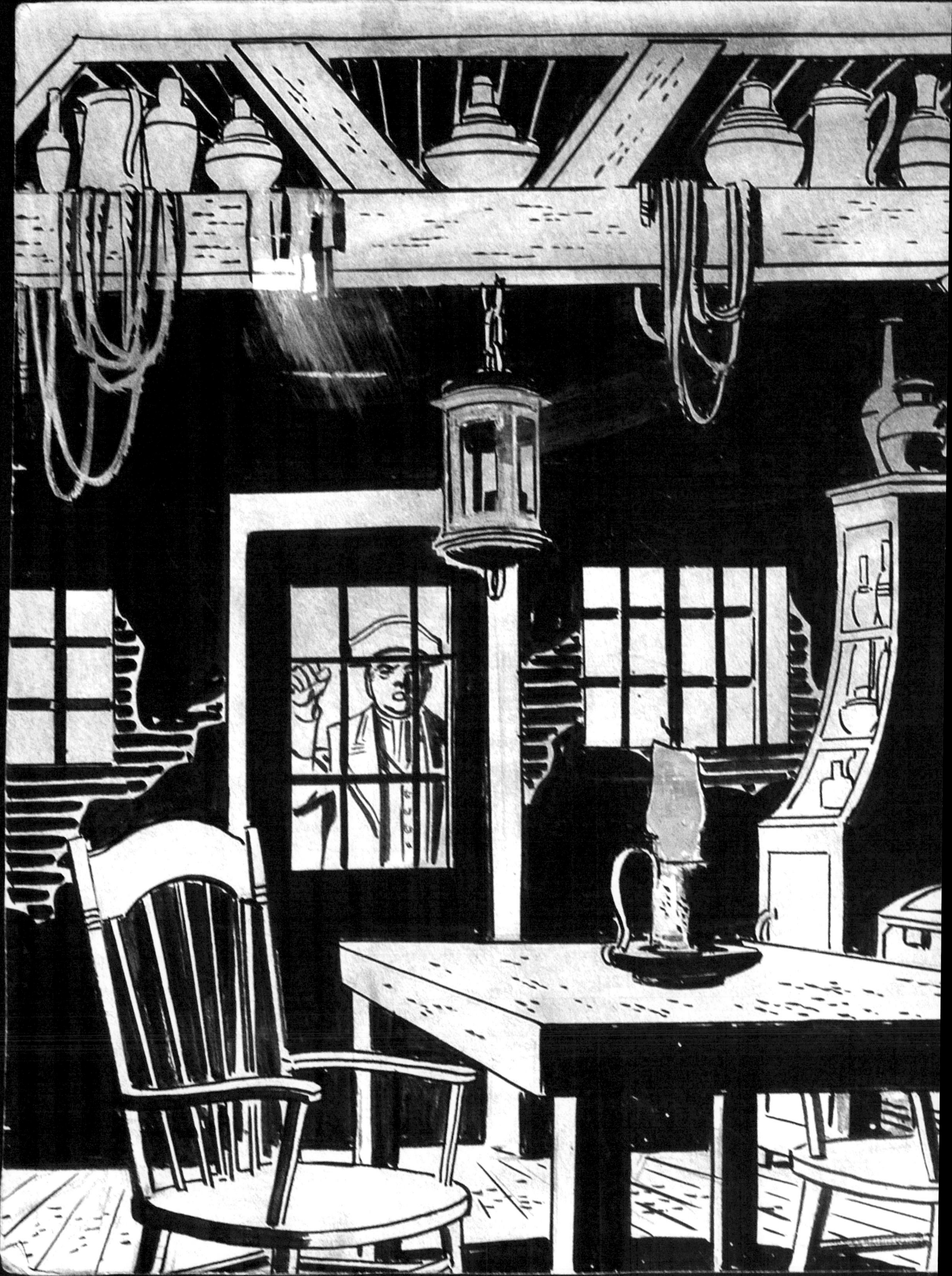

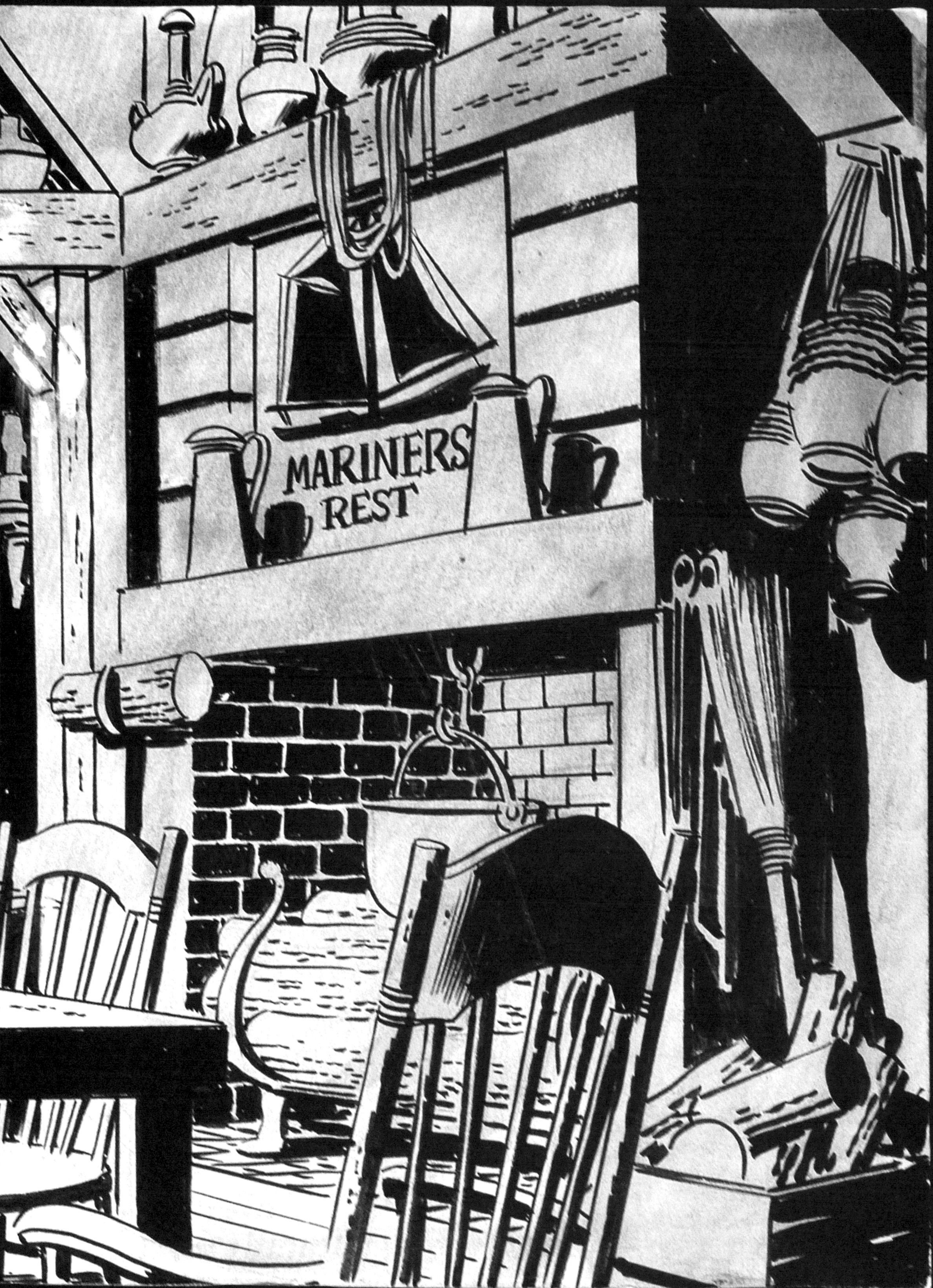
MARINERS
REST

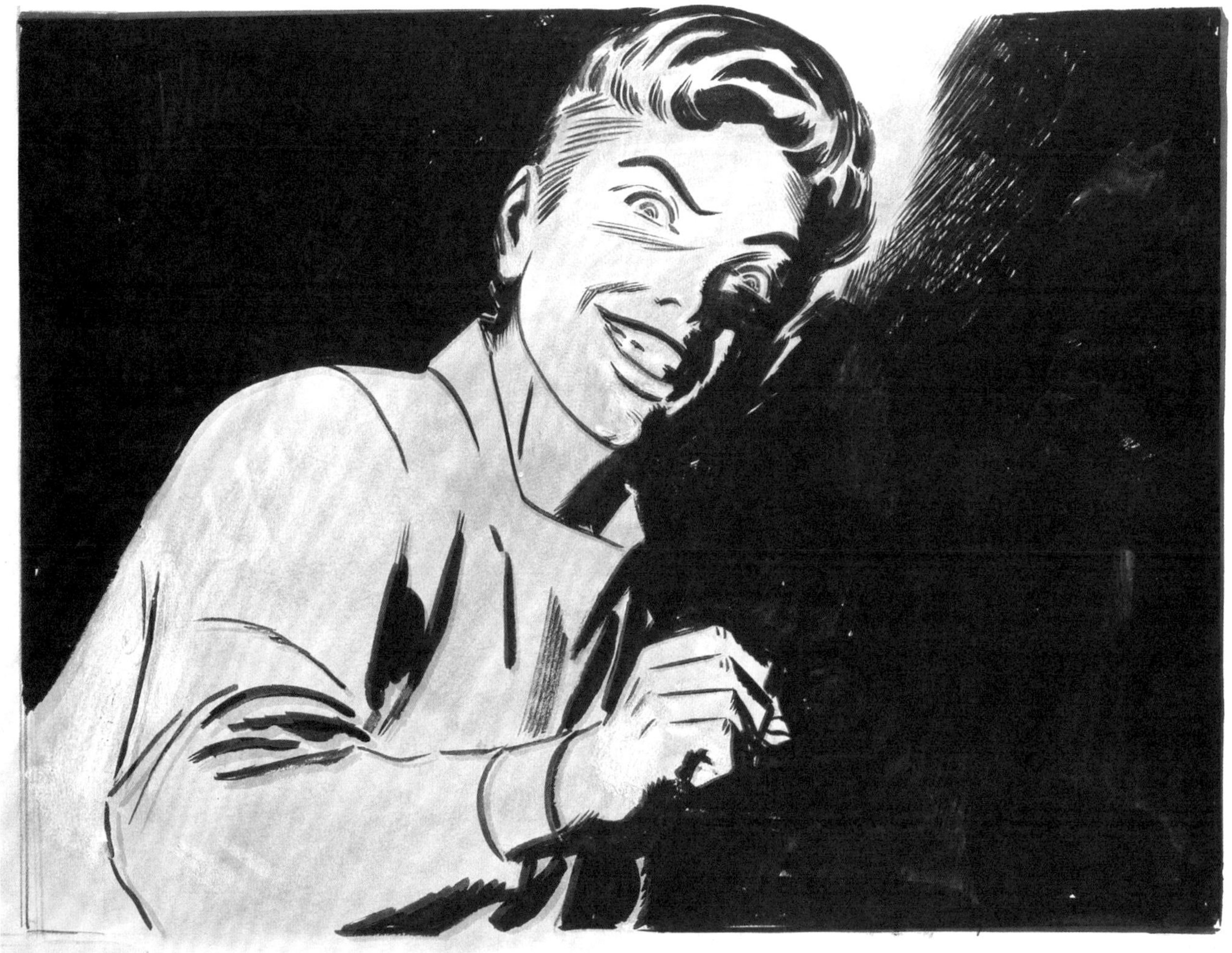

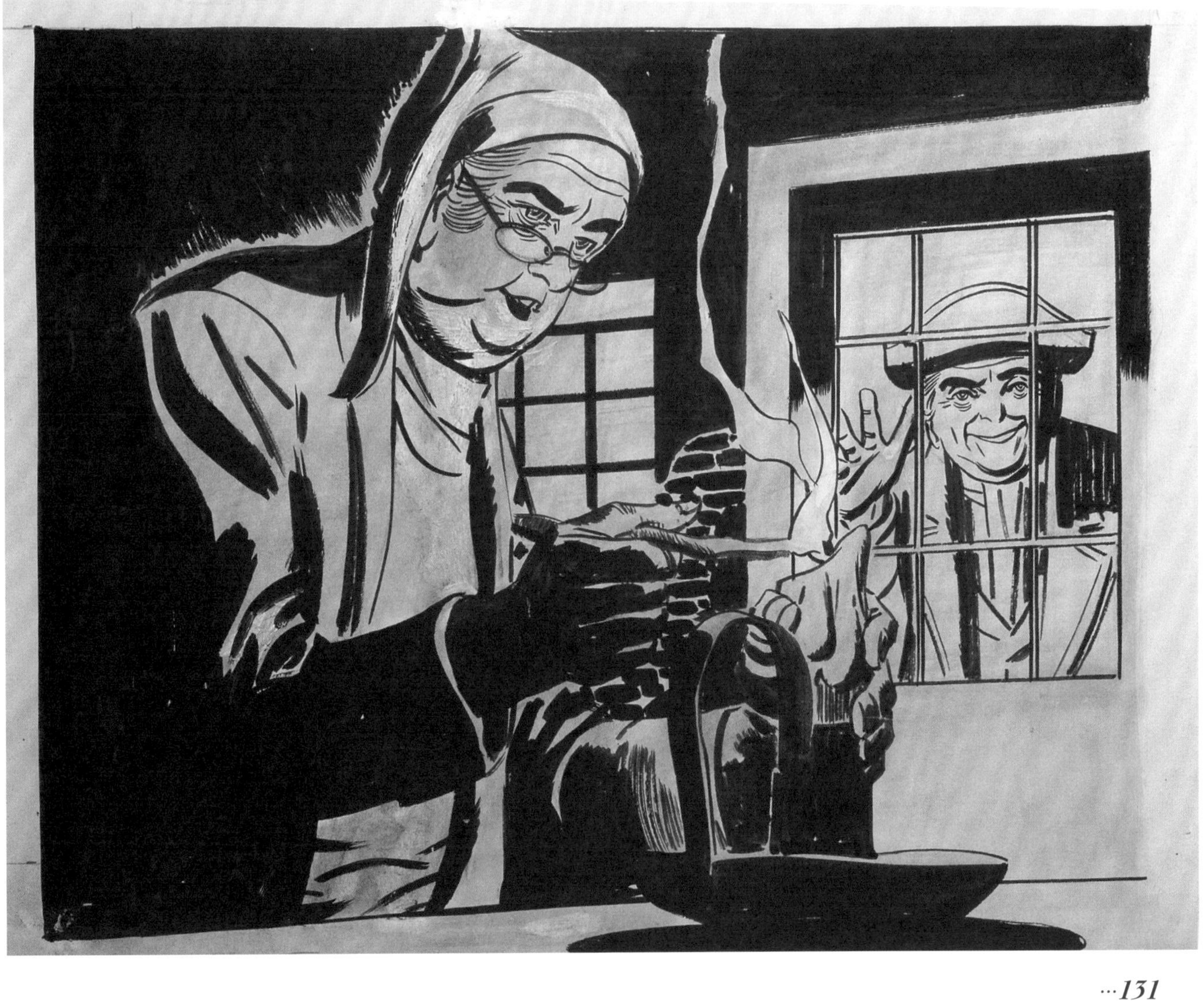

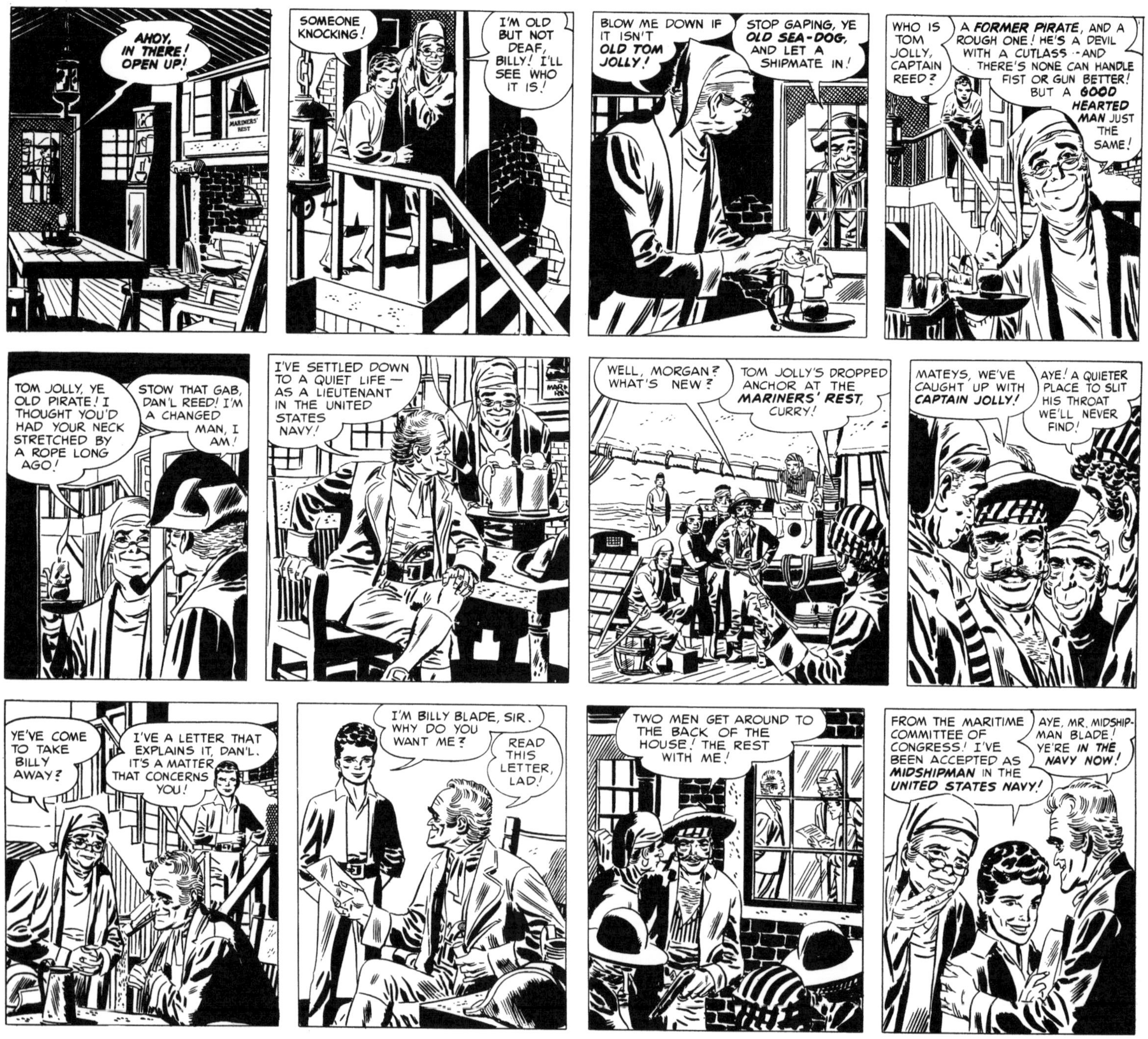
AHOY, IN THERE! OPEN UP!
MARINERS' REST
SOMEONE KNOCKING!
I'M OLD BUT NOT DEAF, BILLY! I'LL SEE WHO IT IS!
BLOW ME DOWN IF IT ISN'T OLD TOM JOLLY!
STOP GAPING, YE OLD SEA-DOG, AND LET A SHIPMATE IN!
WHO IS TOM JOLLY, CAPTAIN REED?
A FORMER PIRATE, AND A ROUGH ONE! HE'S A DEVIL WITH A CUTLASS -- AND THERE'S NONE CAN HANDLE FIST OR GUN BETTER! BUT A GOOD HEARTED MAN JUST THE SAME!
TOM JOLLY, YE OLD PIRATE! I THOUGHT YOU'D HAD YOUR NECK STRETCHED BY A ROPE LONG AGO!
STOW THAT GAB, DAN'L REED! I'M A CHANGED MAN, I AM!
I'VE SETTLED DOWN TO A QUIET LIFE — AS A LIEUTENANT IN THE UNITED STATES NAVY!
WELL, MORGAN? WHAT'S NEW?
TOM JOLLY'S DROPPED ANCHOR AT THE MARINERS' REST, CURRY!
MATEYS, WE'VE CAUGHT UP WITH CAPTAIN JOLLY!
AYE! A QUIETER PLACE TO SLIT HIS THROAT WE'LL NEVER FIND!
YE'VE COME TO TAKE BILLY AWAY?
I'VE A LETTER THAT EXPLAINS IT, DAN'L. IT'S A MATTER THAT CONCERNS YOU!
I'M BILLY BLADE, SIR. WHY DO YOU WANT ME?
READ THIS LETTER, LAD!
TWO MEN GET AROUND TO THE BACK OF THE HOUSE! THE REST WITH ME!
FROM THE MARITIME COMMITTEE OF CONGRESS! I'VE BEEN ACCEPTED AS MIDSHIPMAN IN THE UNITED STATES NAVY!
AYE, MR. MIDSHIPMAN BLADE! YE'RE IN THE NAVY NOW!

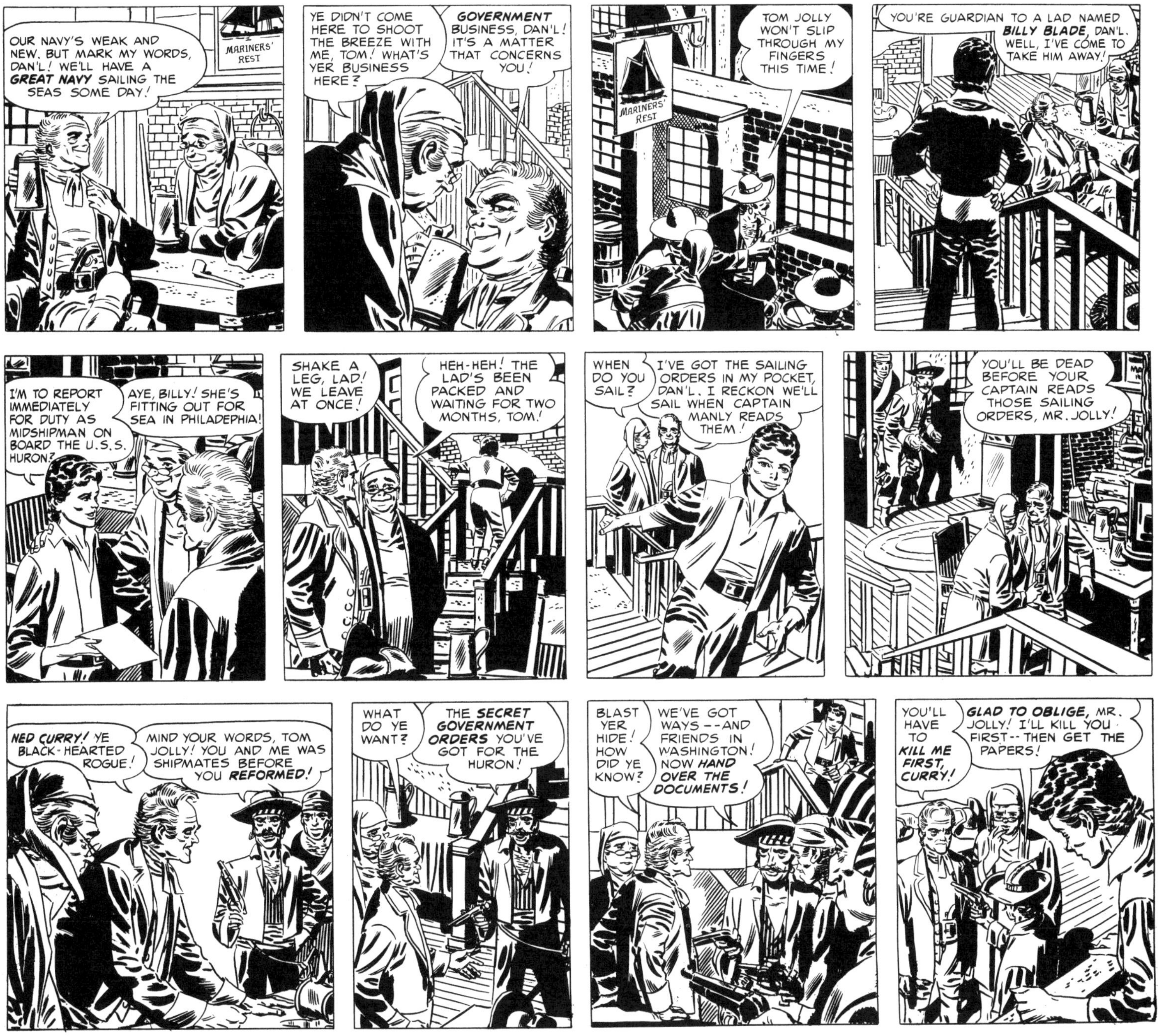

OUR NAVY'S WEAK AND NEW, BUT MARK MY WORDS, DAN'L! WE'LL HAVE A GREAT NAVY SAILING THE SEAS SOME DAY!
MARINERS' REST
YE DIDN'T COME HERE TO SHOOT THE BREEZE WITH ME, TOM! WHAT'S YER BUSINESS HERE?
GOVERNMENT BUSINESS, DAN'L! IT'S A MATTER THAT CONCERNS YOU!
MARINERS' REST
TOM JOLLY WON'T SLIP THROUGH MY FINGERS THIS TIME!
YOU'RE GUARDIAN TO A LAD NAMED BILLY BLADE, DAN'L. WELL, I'VE COME TO TAKE HIM AWAY!
I'M TO REPORT IMMEDIATELY FOR DUTY AS MIDSHIPMAN ON BOARD THE U.S.S. HURON?
AYE, BILLY! SHE'S FITTING OUT FOR SEA IN PHILADEPHIA!
SHAKE A LEG, LAD! WE LEAVE AT ONCE!
HEH-HEH! THE LAD'S BEEN PACKED AND WAITING FOR TWO MONTHS, TOM!
WHEN DO YOU SAIL?
I'VE GOT THE SAILING ORDERS IN MY POCKET, DAN'L. I RECKON WE'LL SAIL WHEN CAPTAIN MANLY READS THEM!
YOU'LL BE DEAD BEFORE YOUR CAPTAIN READS THOSE SAILING ORDERS, MR. JOLLY!
NED CURRY! YE BLACK-HEARTED ROGUE!
MIND YOUR WORDS, TOM JOLLY! YOU AND ME WAS SHIPMATES BEFORE YOU REFORMED!
WHAT DO YE WANT?
THE SECRET GOVERNMENT ORDERS YOU'VE GOT FOR THE HURON!
BLAST YER HIDE! HOW DID YE KNOW?
WE'VE GOT WAYS--AND FRIENDS IN WASHINGTON! NOW HAND OVER THE DOCUMENTS!
YOU'LL HAVE TO KILL ME FIRST, CURRY!
GLAD TO OBLIGE, MR. JOLLY! I'LL KILL YOU FIRST--THEN GET THE PAPERS!

Around the same time as *Tom Corbett*, Joseph Greene hired Meskin to illustrate another project, *Billy Blade, Midshipman.* Meskin preferred to work large, creating single panels as full-size illustrations on artboard, as wide as 16 inches. It appears that they first tried to sell this project as a newspaper strip, and later as a comic. An entire 24-page comic was produced, completely inked and lettered, which Meskin was responsible for by contract. The only thing missing was the title lettering, presumably something Meskin would have farmed out. He was paid $300 for the issue, which was never published. (Collection of Paul Greene/Estate of Joseph Greene.)

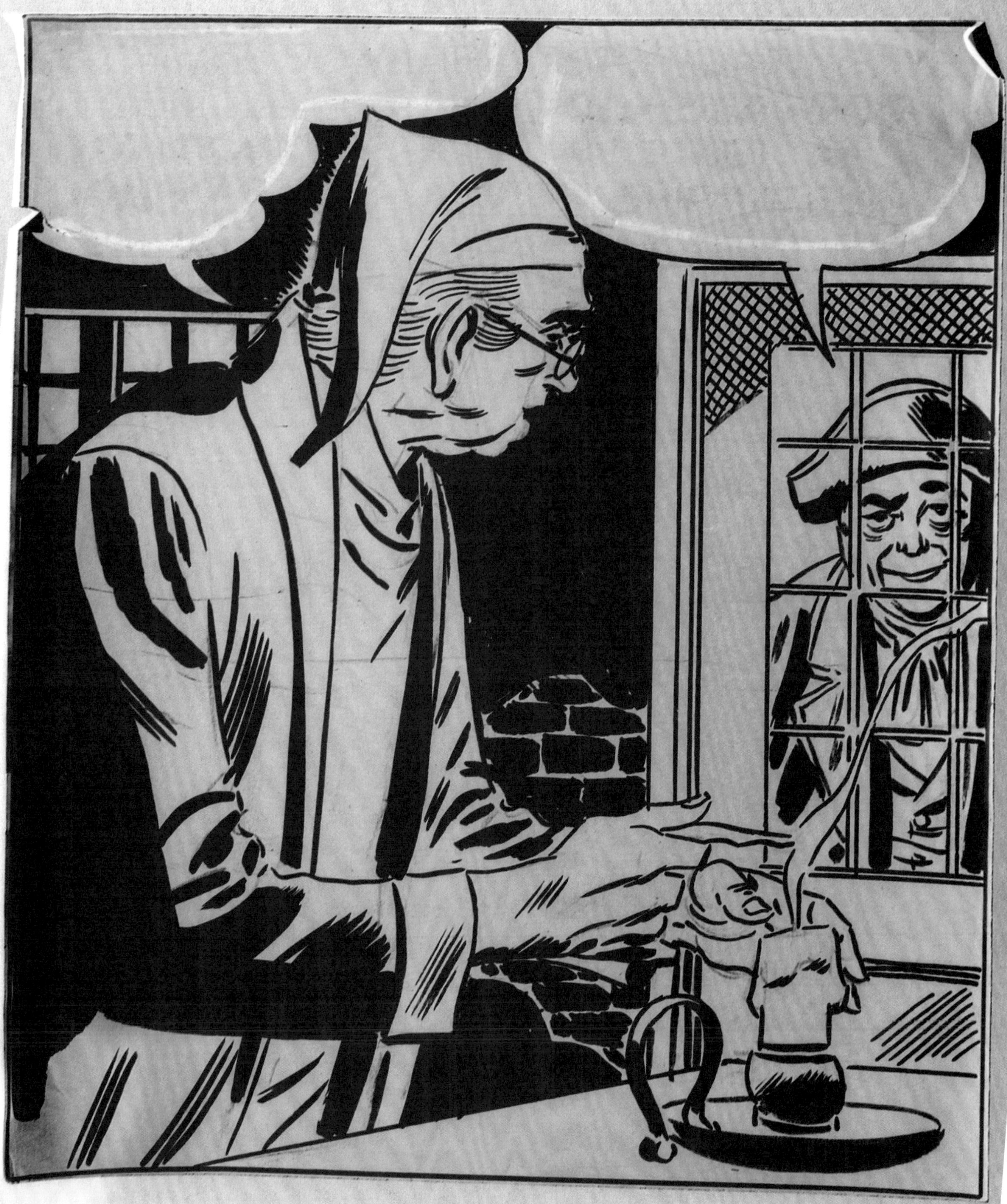

FOLLOWING EIGHT PAGES: Unpublished *Bill Blade, Midshipman* story.
(Collection of Paul Greene/The Estate of Joseph Greene.)

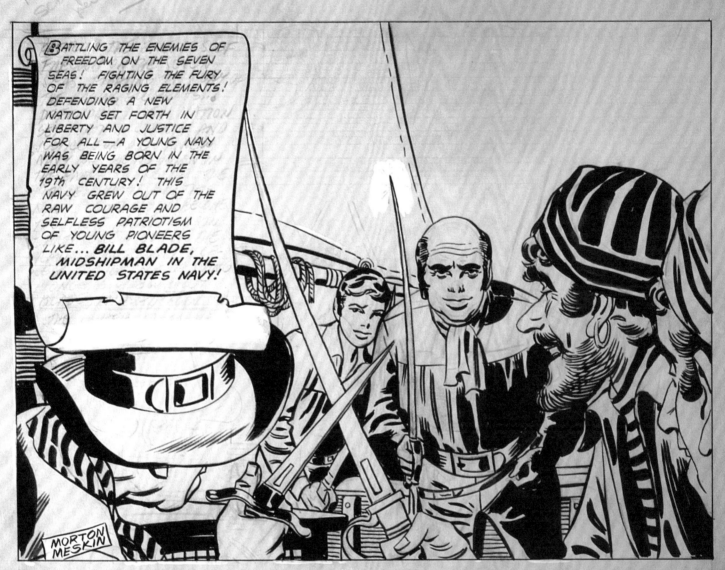

BATTLING THE ENEMIES OF FREEDOM ON THE SEVEN SEAS! FIGHTING THE FURY OF THE RAGING ELEMENTS! DEFENDING A NEW NATION SET FORTH IN LIBERTY AND JUSTICE FOR ALL—A YOUNG NAVY WAS BEING BORN IN THE EARLY YEARS OF THE 19th CENTURY! THIS NAVY GREW OUT OF THE RAW COURAGE AND SELFLESS PATRIOTISM OF YOUNG PIONEERS LIKE... BILL BLADE, MIDSHIPMAN IN THE UNITED STATES NAVY!

MORTON MESKIN

LATE AT NIGHT IN A SMALL VILLAGE ON THE SHORES OF THE DELAWARE RIVER IN NEW JERSEY...

AHOY! OPEN UP! IT'S OLD TOM JOLLY! RISE AND SHINE, CAPTAIN REED!

SO IT'S YOU, YOU OLD SEA ROGUE! WHAT DEVILRY ARE YOU UP TO, TOM?

I'VE GOT ME A COMMISSION ON BOARD THE UNITED STATES BRIG HURON. IT'S AN HONEST-TO-GOODNESS LIEUTENANT I AM!

WHAT MUST THE GOVERNMENT IN WASHINGTON BE THINKING-- BUILDING A NAVY WITH EX-PIRATES LIKE YOU! BAH!

I'VE COME HERE ON A GOVERNMENT MISSION, CAPTAIN. YOU'RE GUARDIAN TO A LAD NAMED WILLIAM BLADE. WHERE IS THE BOY?

HERE, SIR! I'M BILLY BLADE!

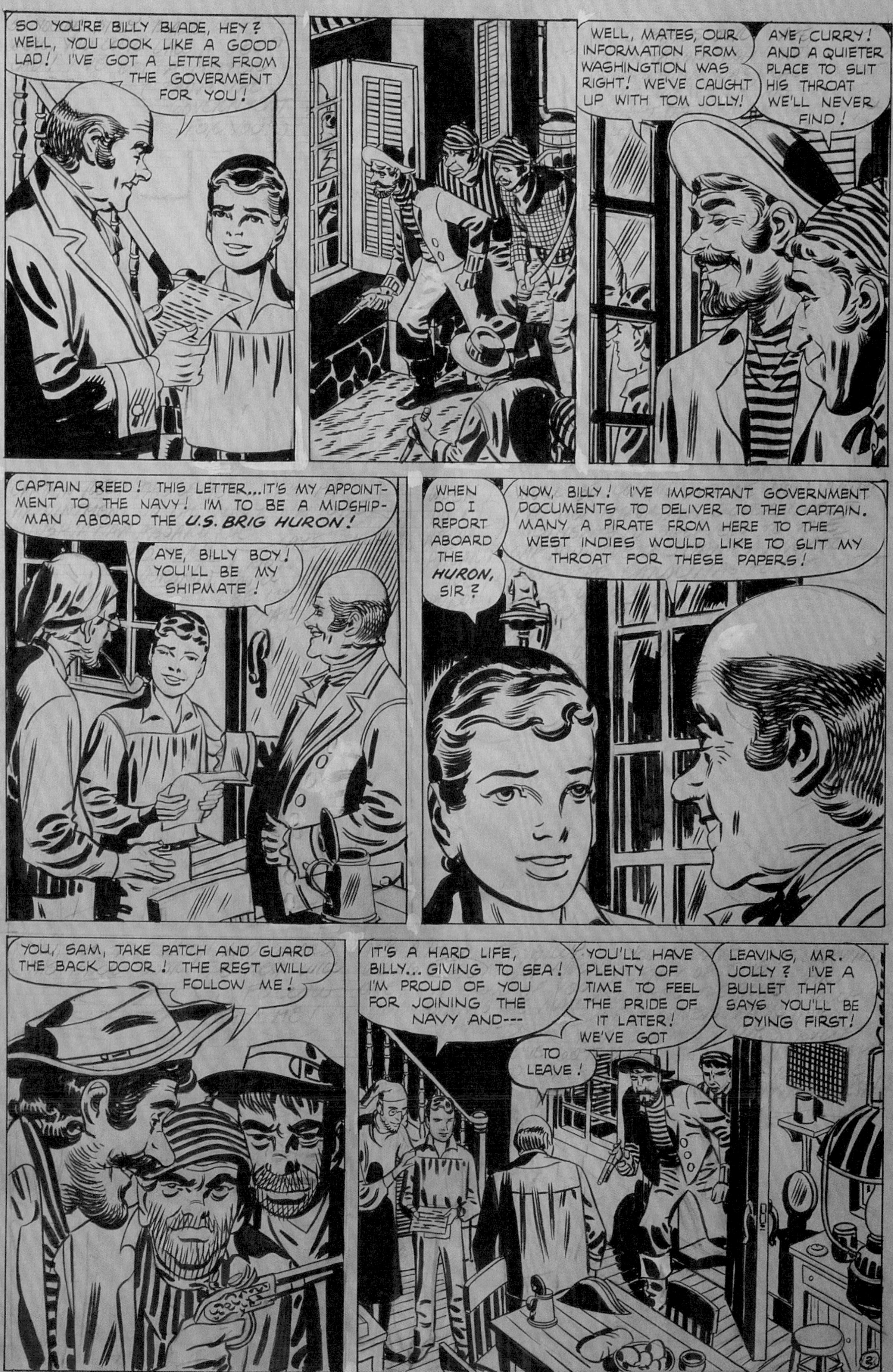

SO YOU'RE BILLY BLADE, HEY? WELL, YOU LOOK LIKE A GOOD LAD! I'VE GOT A LETTER FROM THE GOVERMENT FOR YOU!
WELL, MATES, OUR INFORMATION FROM WASHINGTION WAS RIGHT! WE'VE CAUGHT UP WITH TOM JOLLY!
AYE, CURRY! AND A QUIETER PLACE TO SLIT HIS THROAT WE'LL NEVER FIND!
CAPTAIN REED! THIS LETTER... IT'S MY APPOINTMENT TO THE NAVY! I'M TO BE A MIDSHIPMAN ABOARD THE U.S. BRIG HURON!
AYE, BILLY BOY! YOU'LL BE MY SHIPMATE!
WHEN DO I REPORT ABOARD THE HURON, SIR?
NOW, BILLY! I'VE IMPORTANT GOVERNMENT DOCUMENTS TO DELIVER TO THE CAPTAIN. MANY A PIRATE FROM HERE TO THE WEST INDIES WOULD LIKE TO SLIT MY THROAT FOR THESE PAPERS!
YOU, SAM, TAKE PATCH AND GUARD THE BACK DOOR! THE REST WILL FOLLOW ME!
IT'S A HARD LIFE, BILLY... GIVING TO SEA! I'M PROUD OF YOU FOR JOINING THE NAVY AND---
YOU'LL HAVE PLENTY OF TIME TO FEEL THE PRIDE OF IT LATER! WE'VE GOT
TO LEAVE!
LEAVING, MR. JOLLY? I'VE A BULLET THAT SAYS YOU'LL BE DYING FIRST!
2

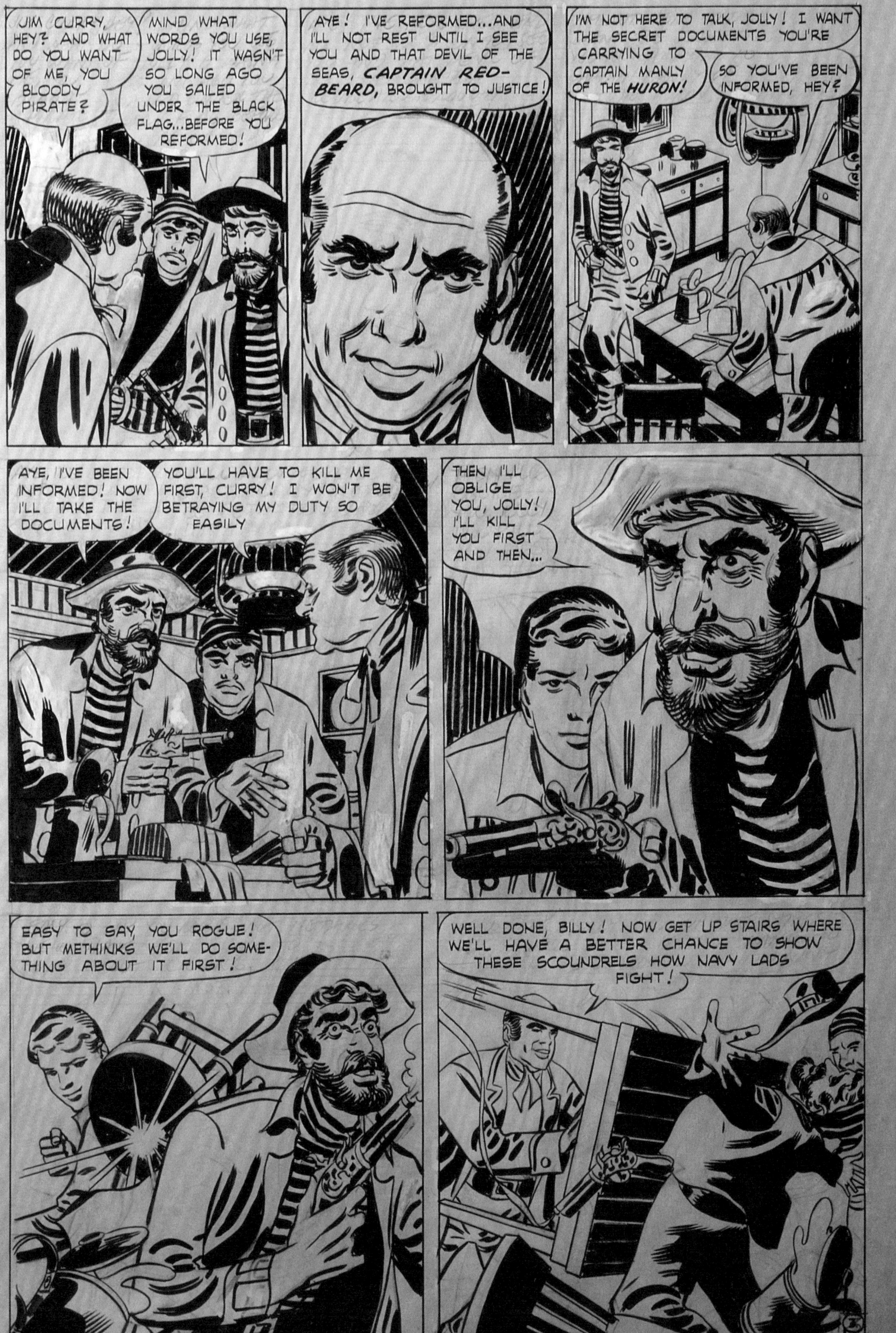
JIM CURRY, HEY? AND WHAT DO YOU WANT OF ME, YOU BLOODY PIRATE?
MIND WHAT WORDS YOU USE, JOLLY! IT WASN'T SO LONG AGO YOU SAILED UNDER THE BLACK FLAG...BEFORE YOU REFORMED!
AYE! I'VE REFORMED...AND I'LL NOT REST UNTIL I SEE YOU AND THAT DEVIL OF THE SEAS, CAPTAIN RED-BEARD, BROUGHT TO JUSTICE!
I'M NOT HERE TO TALK, JOLLY! I WANT THE SECRET DOCUMENTS YOU'RE CARRYING TO CAPTAIN MANLY OF THE HURON!
SO YOU'VE BEEN INFORMED, HEY?
AYE, I'VE BEEN INFORMED! NOW I'LL TAKE THE DOCUMENTS!
YOU'LL HAVE TO KILL ME FIRST, CURRY! I WON'T BE BETRAYING MY DUTY SO EASILY
THEN I'LL OBLIGE YOU, JOLLY! I'LL KILL YOU FIRST AND THEN...
EASY TO SAY, YOU ROGUE! BUT METHINKS WE'LL DO SOME-THING ABOUT IT FIRST!
WELL DONE, BILLY! NOW GET UP STAIRS WHERE WE'LL HAVE A BETTER CHANCE TO SHOW THESE SCOUNDRELS HOW NAVY LADS FIGHT!

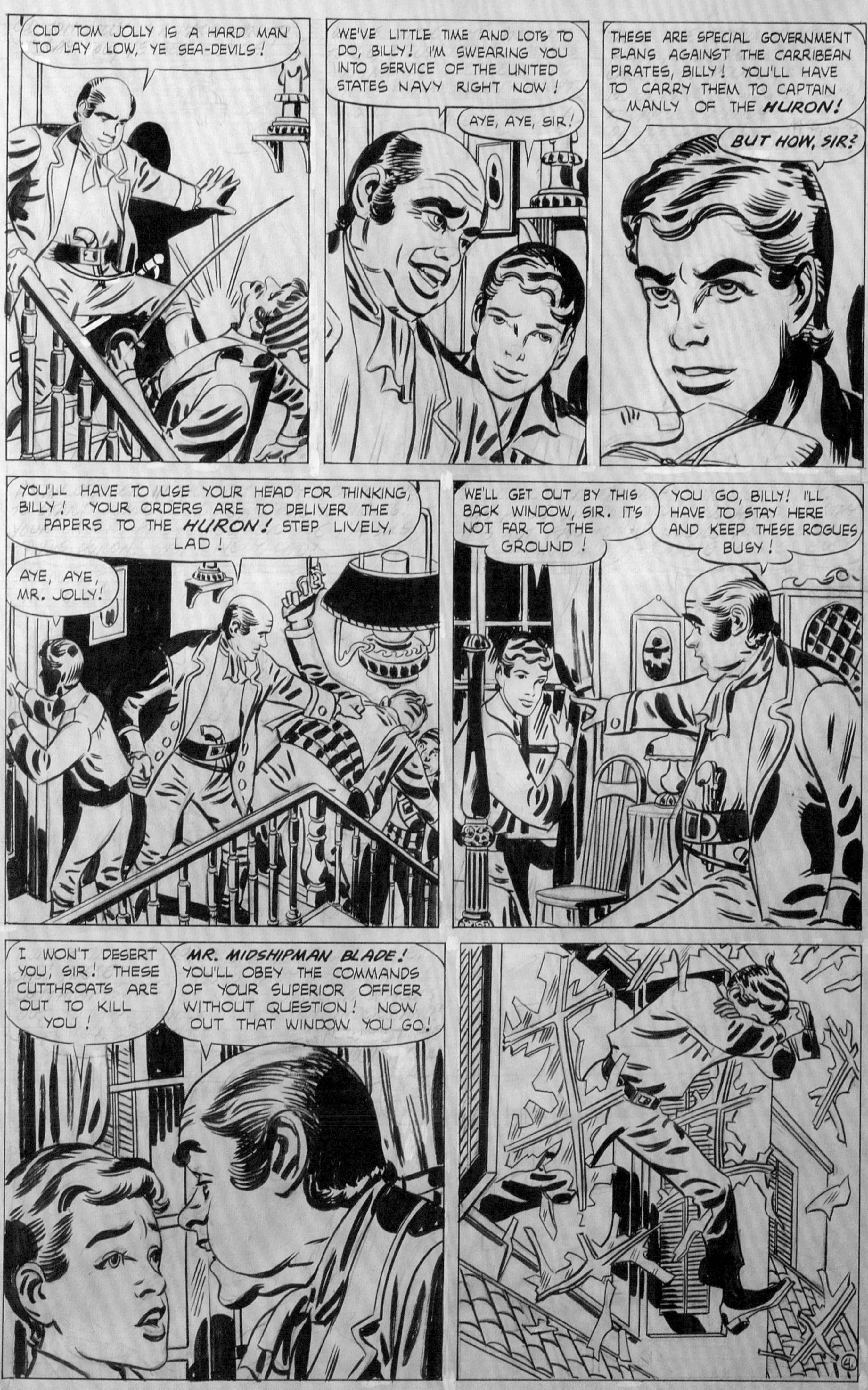
OLD TOM JOLLY IS A HARD MAN TO LAY LOW, YE SEA-DEVILS!
WE'VE LITTLE TIME AND LOTS TO DO, BILLY! I'M SWEARING YOU INTO SERVICE OF THE UNITED STATES NAVY RIGHT NOW!
AYE, AYE, SIR!
THESE ARE SPECIAL GOVERNMENT PLANS AGAINST THE CARRIBEAN PIRATES, BILLY! YOU'LL HAVE TO CARRY THEM TO CAPTAIN MANLY OF THE HURON!
BUT HOW, SIR?
YOU'LL HAVE TO USE YOUR HEAD FOR THINKING, BILLY! YOUR ORDERS ARE TO DELIVER THE PAPERS TO THE HURON! STEP LIVELY, LAD!
AYE, AYE, MR. JOLLY!
WE'LL GET OUT BY THIS BACK WINDOW, SIR. IT'S NOT FAR TO THE GROUND!
YOU GO, BILLY! I'LL HAVE TO STAY HERE AND KEEP THESE ROGUES BUSY!
I WON'T DESERT YOU, SIR! THESE CUTTHROATS ARE OUT TO KILL YOU!
MR. MIDSHIPMAN BLADE! YOU'LL OBEY THE COMMANDS OF YOUR SUPERIOR OFFICER WITHOUT QUESTION! NOW OUT THAT WINDOW YOU GO!
4

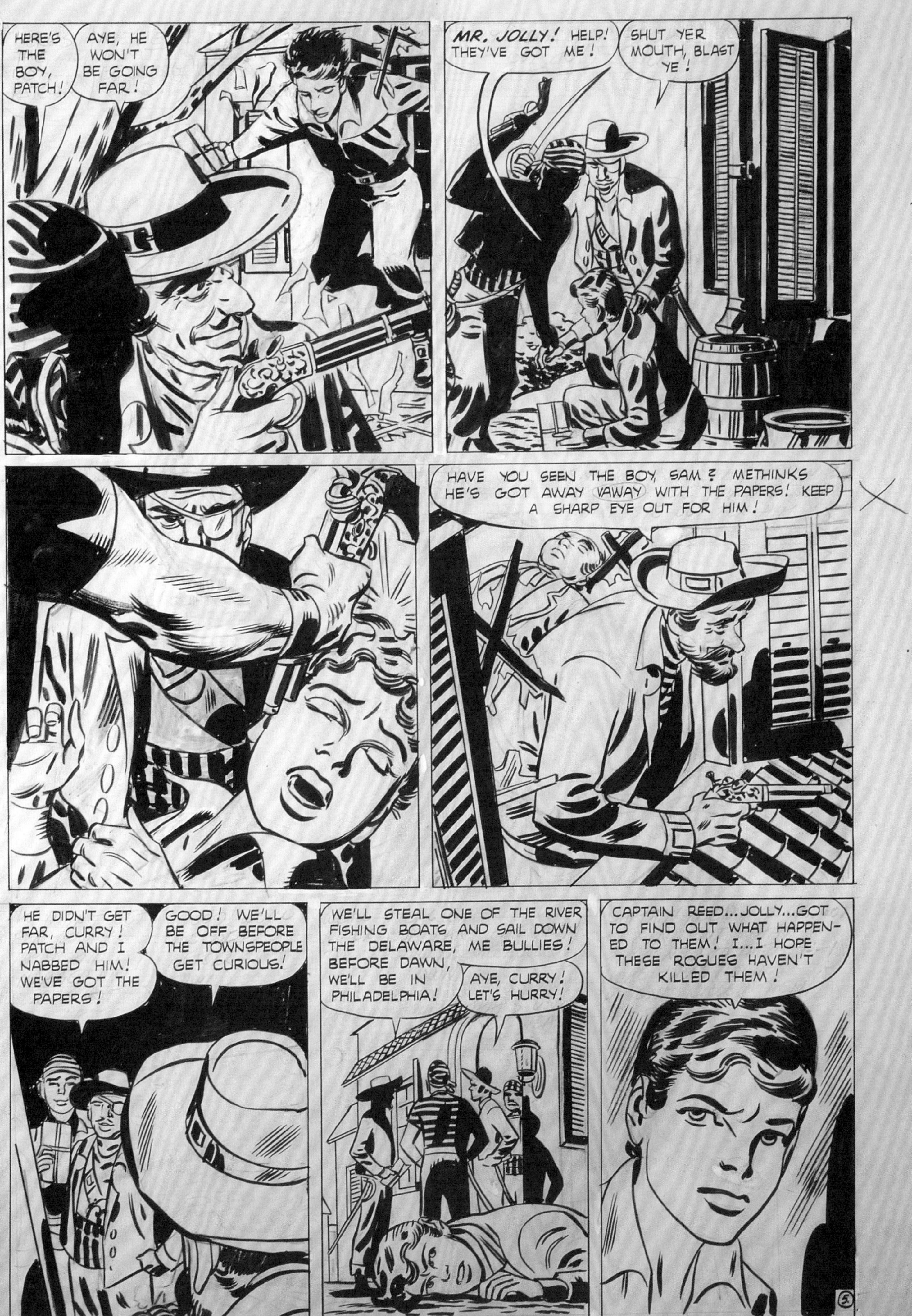
HERE'S THE BOY, PATCH!
AYE, HE WON'T BE GOING FAR!
MR. JOLLY! HELP! THEY'VE GOT ME!
SHUT YER MOUTH, BLAST YE!
HAVE YOU SEEN THE BOY, SAM? METHINKS HE'S GOT AWAY VAWAY WITH THE PAPERS! KEEP A SHARP EYE OUT FOR HIM!
HE DIDN'T GET FAR, CURRY! PATCH AND I NABBED HIM! WE'VE GOT THE PAPERS!
GOOD! WE'LL BE OFF BEFORE THE TOWNSPEOPLE GET CURIOUS!
WE'LL STEAL ONE OF THE RIVER FISHING BOATS AND SAIL DOWN THE DELAWARE, ME BULLIES! BEFORE DAWN, WE'LL BE IN PHILADELPHIA!
AYE, CURRY! LET'S HURRY!
CAPTAIN REED... JOLLY... GOT TO FIND OUT WHAT HAPPENED TO THEM! I... I HOPE THESE ROGUES HAVEN'T KILLED THEM!
5

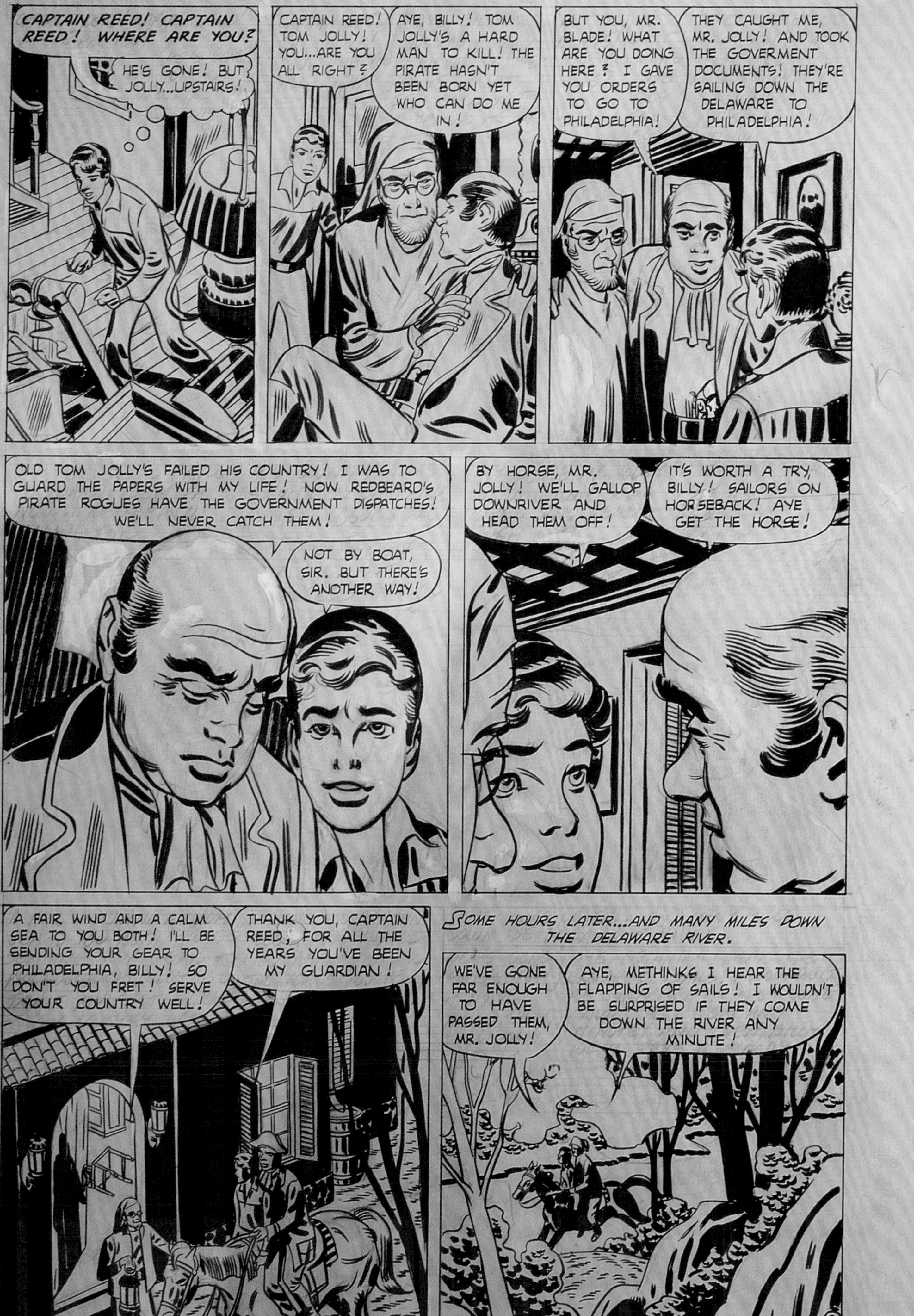
CAPTAIN REED! CAPTAIN REED! WHERE ARE YOU?
HE'S GONE! BUT JOLLY...UPSTAIRS!
CAPTAIN REED! TOM JOLLY! YOU...ARE YOU ALL RIGHT?
AYE, BILLY! TOM JOLLY'S A HARD MAN TO KILL! THE PIRATE HASN'T BEEN BORN YET WHO CAN DO ME IN!
BUT YOU, MR. BLADE! WHAT ARE YOU DOING HERE? I GAVE YOU ORDERS TO GO TO PHILADELPHIA!
THEY CAUGHT ME, MR. JOLLY! AND TOOK THE GOVERMENT DOCUMENTS! THEY'RE SAILING DOWN THE DELAWARE TO PHILADELPHIA!
OLD TOM JOLLY'S FAILED HIS COUNTRY! I WAS TO GUARD THE PAPERS WITH MY LIFE! NOW REDBEARD'S PIRATE ROGUES HAVE THE GOVERNMENT DISPATCHES! WE'LL NEVER CATCH THEM!
NOT BY BOAT, SIR. BUT THERE'S ANOTHER WAY!
BY HORSE, MR. JOLLY! WE'LL GALLOP DOWNRIVER AND HEAD THEM OFF!
IT'S WORTH A TRY, BILLY! SAILORS ON HORSEBACK! AYE GET THE HORSE!
A FAIR WIND AND A CALM SEA TO YOU BOTH! I'LL BE SENDING YOUR GEAR TO PHILADELPHIA, BILLY! SO DON'T YOU FRET! SERVE YOUR COUNTRY WELL!
THANK YOU, CAPTAIN REED, FOR ALL THE YEARS YOU'VE BEEN MY GUARDIAN!
SOME HOURS LATER...AND MANY MILES DOWN THE DELAWARE RIVER.
WE'VE GONE FAR ENOUGH TO HAVE PASSED THEM, MR. JOLLY!
AYE, METHINKS I HEAR THE FLAPPING OF SAILS! I WOULDN'T BE SURPRISED IF THEY COME DOWN THE RIVER ANY MINUTE!
6.

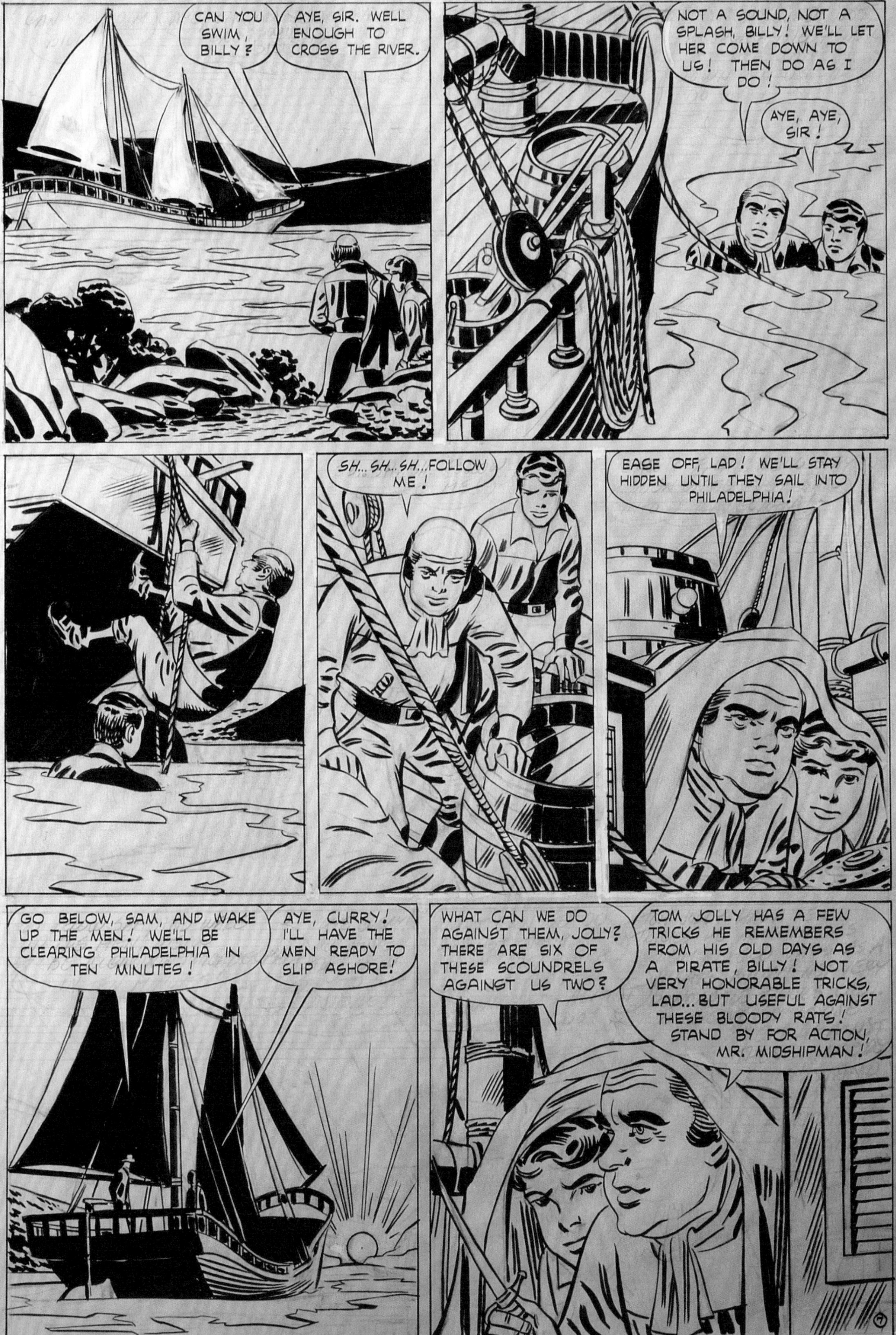
CAN YOU SWIM, BILLY?
AYE, SIR. WELL ENOUGH TO CROSS THE RIVER.
NOT A SOUND, NOT A SPLASH, BILLY! WE'LL LET HER COME DOWN TO US! THEN DO AS I DO!
AYE, AYE, SIR!
SH...SH...SH...FOLLOW ME!
EASE OFF, LAD! WE'LL STAY HIDDEN UNTIL THEY SAIL INTO PHILADELPHIA!
GO BELOW, SAM, AND WAKE UP THE MEN! WE'LL BE CLEARING PHILADELPHIA IN TEN MINUTES!
AYE, CURRY! I'LL HAVE THE MEN READY TO SLIP ASHORE!
WHAT CAN WE DO AGAINST THEM, JOLLY? THERE ARE SIX OF THESE SCOUNDRELS AGAINST US TWO?
TOM JOLLY HAS A FEW TRICKS HE REMEMBERS FROM HIS OLD DAYS AS A PIRATE, BILLY! NOT VERY HONORABLE TRICKS, LAD...BUT USEFUL AGAINST THESE BLOODY RATS! STAND BY FOR ACTION, MR. MIDSHIPMAN!
7

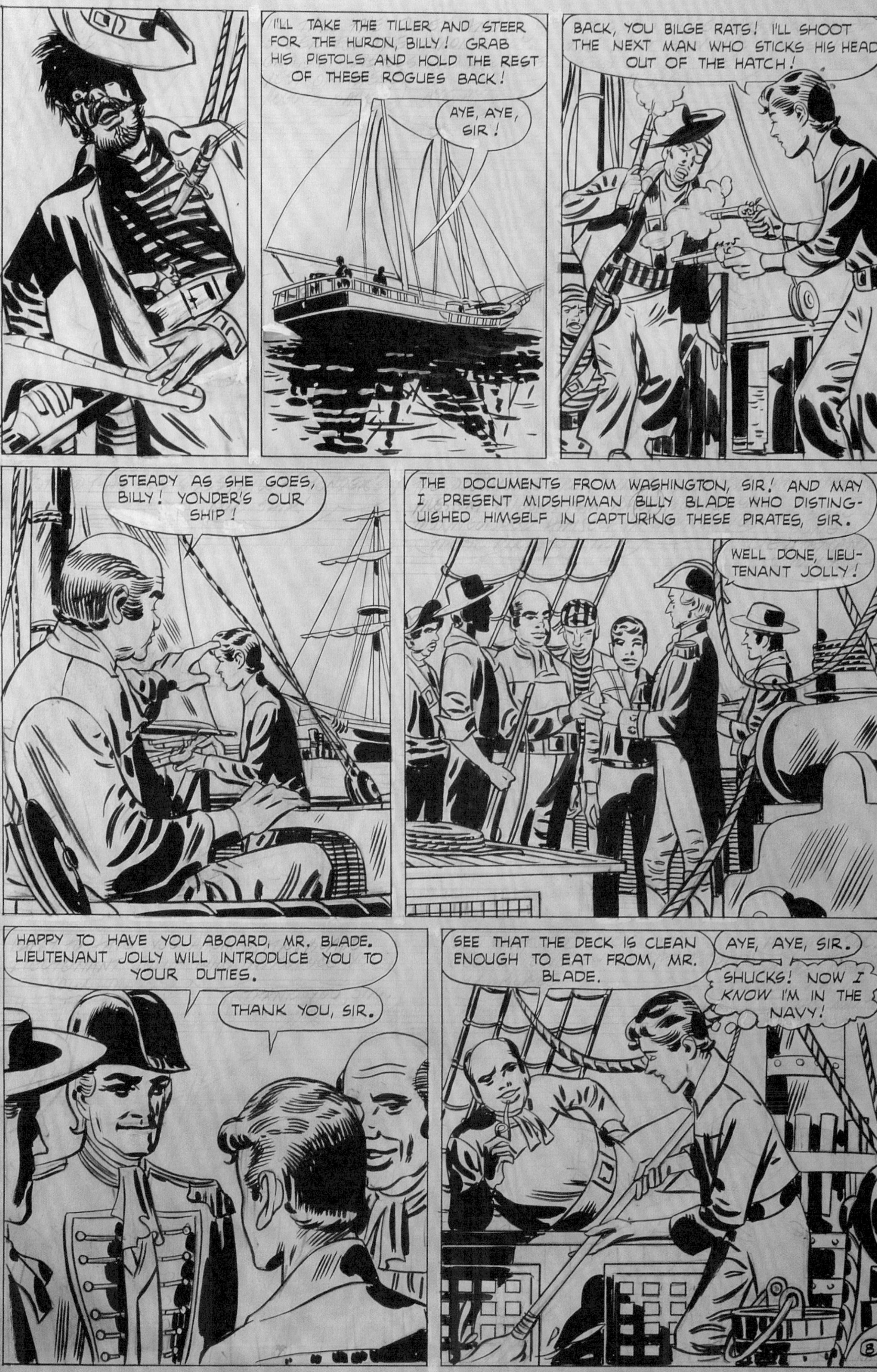
I'LL TAKE THE TILLER AND STEER FOR THE HURON, BILLY! GRAB HIS PISTOLS AND HOLD THE REST OF THESE ROGUES BACK!
AYE, AYE, SIR!
BACK, YOU BILGE RATS! I'LL SHOOT THE NEXT MAN WHO STICKS HIS HEAD OUT OF THE HATCH!
STEADY AS SHE GOES, BILLY! YONDER'S OUR SHIP!
THE DOCUMENTS FROM WASHINGTON, SIR! AND MAY I PRESENT MIDSHIPMAN BILLY BLADE WHO DISTINGUISHED HIMSELF IN CAPTURING THESE PIRATES, SIR.
WELL DONE, LIEUTENANT JOLLY!
HAPPY TO HAVE YOU ABOARD, MR. BLADE. LIEUTENANT JOLLY WILL INTRODUCE YOU TO YOUR DUTIES.
THANK YOU, SIR.
SEE THAT THE DECK IS CLEAN ENOUGH TO EAT FROM, MR. BLADE.
AYE, AYE, SIR.
SHUCKS! NOW I KNOW I'M IN THE NAVY!

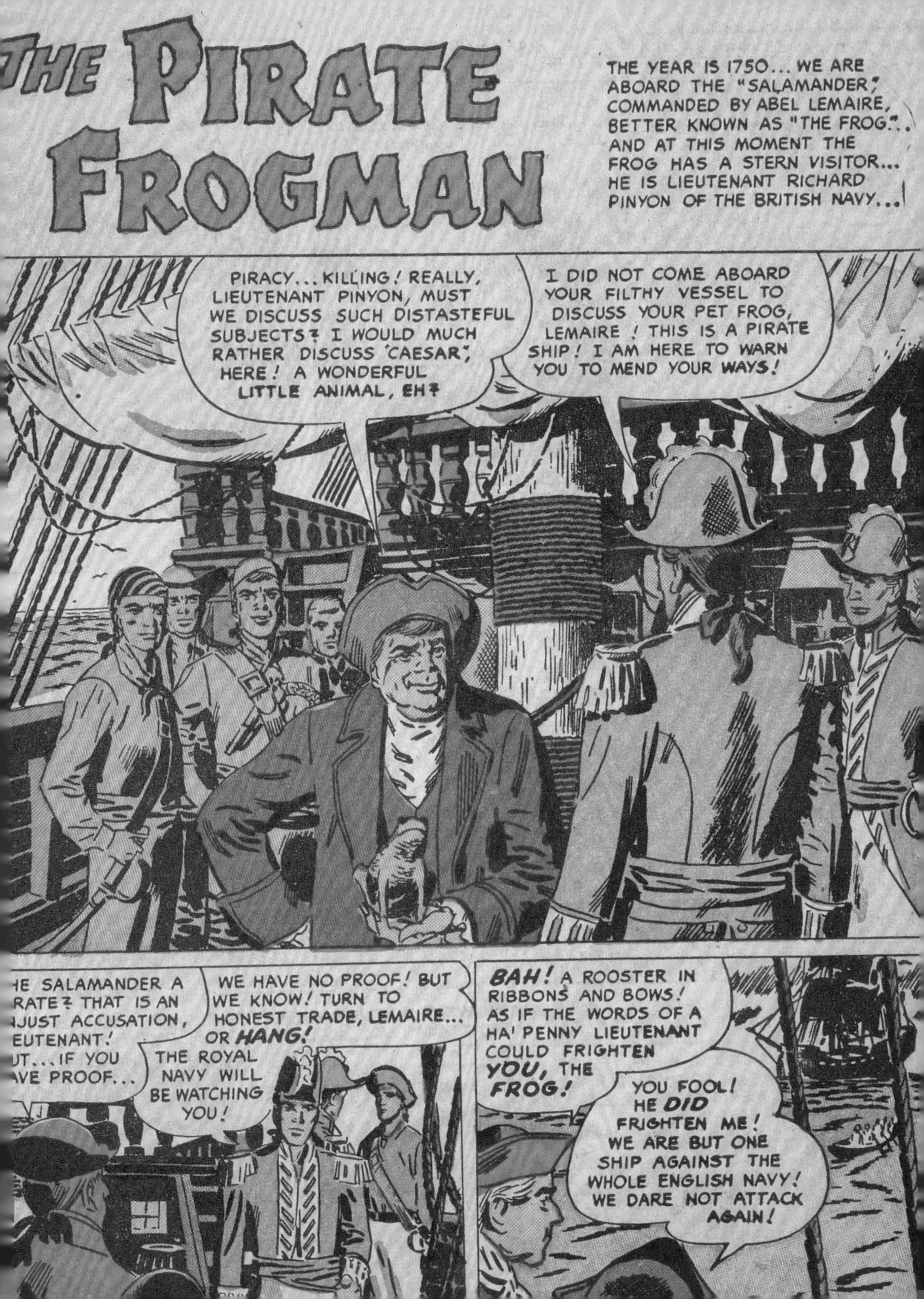
THE PIRATE FROGMAN
THE YEAR IS 1750... WE ARE ABOARD THE "SALAMANDER," COMMANDED BY ABEL LEMAIRE, BETTER KNOWN AS "THE FROG"... AND AT THIS MOMENT THE FROG HAS A STERN VISITOR... HE IS LIEUTENANT RICHARD PINYON OF THE BRITISH NAVY...!
PIRACY... KILLING! REALLY, LIEUTENANT PINYON, MUST WE DISCUSS SUCH DISTASTEFUL SUBJECTS? I WOULD MUCH RATHER DISCUSS "CAESAR", HERE! A WONDERFUL LITTLE ANIMAL, EH?
I DID NOT COME ABOARD YOUR FILTHY VESSEL TO DISCUSS YOUR PET FROG, LEMAIRE! THIS IS A PIRATE SHIP! I AM HERE TO WARN YOU TO MEND YOUR WAYS!
HE SALAMANDER A RATE? THAT IS AN NJUST ACCUSATION, EUTENANT! UT... IF YOU AVE PROOF...
WE HAVE NO PROOF! BUT WE KNOW! TURN TO HONEST TRADE, LEMAIRE... OR HANG!
THE ROYAL NAVY WILL BE WATCHING YOU!
BAH! A ROOSTER IN RIBBONS AND BOWS! AS IF THE WORDS OF A HA' PENNY LIEUTENANT COULD FRIGHTEN YOU, THE FROG!
YOU FOOL! HE DID FRIGHTEN ME! WE ARE BUT ONE SHIP AGAINST THE WHOLE ENGLISH NAVY! WE DARE NOT ATTACK AGAIN!

TRUE LIFE STORIES

Returning real-life heroes took the place of fictional ones after WWII, and television took readers away from comic book pages as well. In reaction Simon and Kirby created the romance genre, and mined the existing crime and horror ones in addition.

The latter, however, was brought to its zenith over at EC Comics, under the stewardship of William Gaines. Gaines employed some of the best artists in the business—Harvey Kurtzman, Wallace Wood, Jack Davis, Will Elder, Al Williamson—and together they explored both a new form of humor through *MAD*, and a new form of sensationalism through horror titles such as *Tales From the Crypt*. Gaines was often encouraged by his sales manager, provocateur Lyle Stuart, an occasional comic writer himself, who would make a life-long career of controversy as a writer and publisher.

Following the war there was a perceived increase in juvenile delinquency and comics were often blamed. The fact that fathers had been absent for several war years didn't seem to register with the public, and comic books, which will 'rot your brain,' were the obvious offenders.

A psychiatrist from Germany, Dr. Fredric Wertham, had a penchant for exposés, having in 1946 written a damning article on fellow countryman and psychiatrist Wilhelm Reich for *The New Republic*, which added to the chorus that helped destroy his career. Wertham turned his attention to the scourge of comic books, and published his damnation of the industry, *Seduction of the Innocent*, in 1953.

Coincidentally Meskin had read Reich and liked to discuss his teachings, along with Buddhism and politics. Reich's teachings of Orgone therapy and energy had been banned, as a large result due to Wertham, who was about to have a large affect on Meskin.

A Senate Judiciary Sub-commission on Juvenile Delinquency was formed to explore the connection between comic books and wayward youth. Led by Senators Kefauver, a Democrat from Tennessee, and Hendrickson, a Republican from New Jersey, a two-day hearing was scheduled for April 21 and 22, 1954 in the United States Courthouse in Foley Square, the seat of New York City government. The proceedings were televised live and the scheduled speakers included well-known newspaper comic strip artists Walt Kelly (*Pogo*) and Milton Caniff (*Steve Canyon* and *Terry and the Pirates*). Both were treated with the respect reflected by the popularity that comic strips were held in by the public. Gaines testified, to disastrous effect. One of Simon and Kirby studio's issues of *Black Magic*, replete with Meskin art, was used as an example of depravity.

ABOVE: Meskin
in Philadelphia.
PREVIOUS PAGE:
Page 1 from *Frogman
Comics*, Hillman, volume
1, #4, 1952.

Weighed against the McCarthy/HUAC hearings of the day, comics got off easy. The industry readily agreed to self-regulate and the Comics Code Authority was born. Still, while the field industry survived, dozens of comic books ceased publication, and hundreds of writers and artists found themselves unemployed. Joe Simon and Jack Kirby not only closed their studio, they ended their 15-year partnership, never to work together in the same capacity again. Ironically, Gaines managed to endure, thanks to the suggestion of Lyle Stuart that they "turn *MAD* into a magazine so [they] couldn't be touched by the Code."[47]

Mort Meskin suffered another nervous breakdown during this period, and signed himself into Rockland Hospital in Westchester, New York, overlooking the Hudson. Jerry Robinson visited Mort often at Rockland, and they would have long philosophical discussions while they strolled the huge grounds. When he was released, Mort went to live with Jerry and his wife Gro in their spacious West End Avenue apartment, the same one where Mort's sons, Peter and Philip, played with the Robinson's rabbit. Robinson was was by now a comic strip artist, producing *Jet Scott*, as well as comic book art and book illustration. Initially, Mort would keep the wooden doors that separated his area of the apartment drawn, but with time he would open them in the mornings and watch the activities of Robinson and his assistants, eventually engaging them in conversation. Robinson described the living environment: "It was very busy, a lot of freelance stuff, he would look in often. We were all together, I think it was a very good atmosphere for Mort, it was a creative place and he had his own compartment, he wouldn't hang out all day, you know, that was Mort."[48]

Philip Meskin: "Jerry was a strong presence in our lives. I remember being in his apartment as a child. Jerry was a good friend of my father's and stood by Dad when he was hospitalized for emotional problems in the mid-1950s. I remember Jerry had a Scandinavian wife and a daughter about my age. I used to chase that rabbit around."[49]

Peter Meskin: "One day mom announced that she and dad got divorced. We didn't really understand what it meant. Dad would visit us every week or two. And that's when we would go out and do something. He would come specially to spend time with us, bringing cardboard and tape so we could do some projects together, and mom was obviously tolerant of letting him do it."

Betty, now a single parent, also began to experience emotional difficulties, and was forced to place the boys in foster care. At first Peter and Philip were together in separate dorms organized by age at the Hartman-HomeCrest Home for Children, in Yonkers New York, but soon afterwards they were split up. The family never lived as a family unit again. Peter recalls, "We wound up in an orphanage because our parents became unable to take care of us. We lived there for about five or six years, in a variety of situations through Jewish Child Care Association of New York. They separated Philip and me in two different locations, Mt. Vernon and Queens, for four years. I never understood their reasoning, but we kept in contact as best as we could. We never really had a home again."[50]

5 PAGES FOLLOWING: Unpublished crime story which fell victim to the new Comics Code Authority. Pencils by Mort Meskin, inks by George Roussos. (Courtesy of Lars Teglbjaerg.)

Meskin needed work, and there were few options. He returned to the place of his earliest successes, DC. He was placed on their emerging mystery and fantasy anthologies, *House of Mystery*, *House of Secrets*, and *My Greatest Adventure*, and the *Mark Merlin* series, among others. His artwork had changed between his earliest DC stay and his time at S&K, and now there was a shift once again. Gone were the kinetic, compressed, claustrophobic panels filled with bold strokes and crosshatching, replaced with carefully rendered but somewhat lifeless outlines and subdued shadows, the result of attempting to conform to the DC house style, what cartoonist Jules Feiffer referred to as "looking like it was drawn in a bank." Replacing the kinetic, overwrought, emotionally compressed panels of most of his S&K work was art that appeared more carefully rendered, but lacked the energy of what he had done prior. There was less dramatic use of shadow, although what many feel replaced it was an elevated gift of storytelling. Still, as Dan Barry remembered, "[His] stuff was lost on the public. He worked in great big compositions and it lacked detail, but the readers see detail, they like that."[51]

Upon closer examination, what one sees is a removal of all artifice in favor of concise storytelling. This, however, was apparently lost on the powers-that-be at DC, in particular on editors Mort Weisinger and Robert Kanigher, who at best treated Meskin with indifference, and at worst, with sadistic scorn.

[TEXT CONTINUES ON PAGE 156]

ONCE AGAIN, THE BOOK OF THE MONTH TAKES YOU TO A CLASSIC. THIS TIME IT'S A LITTLE DITTY WE CALL THE TRAGEDY OF...

MAC BETH

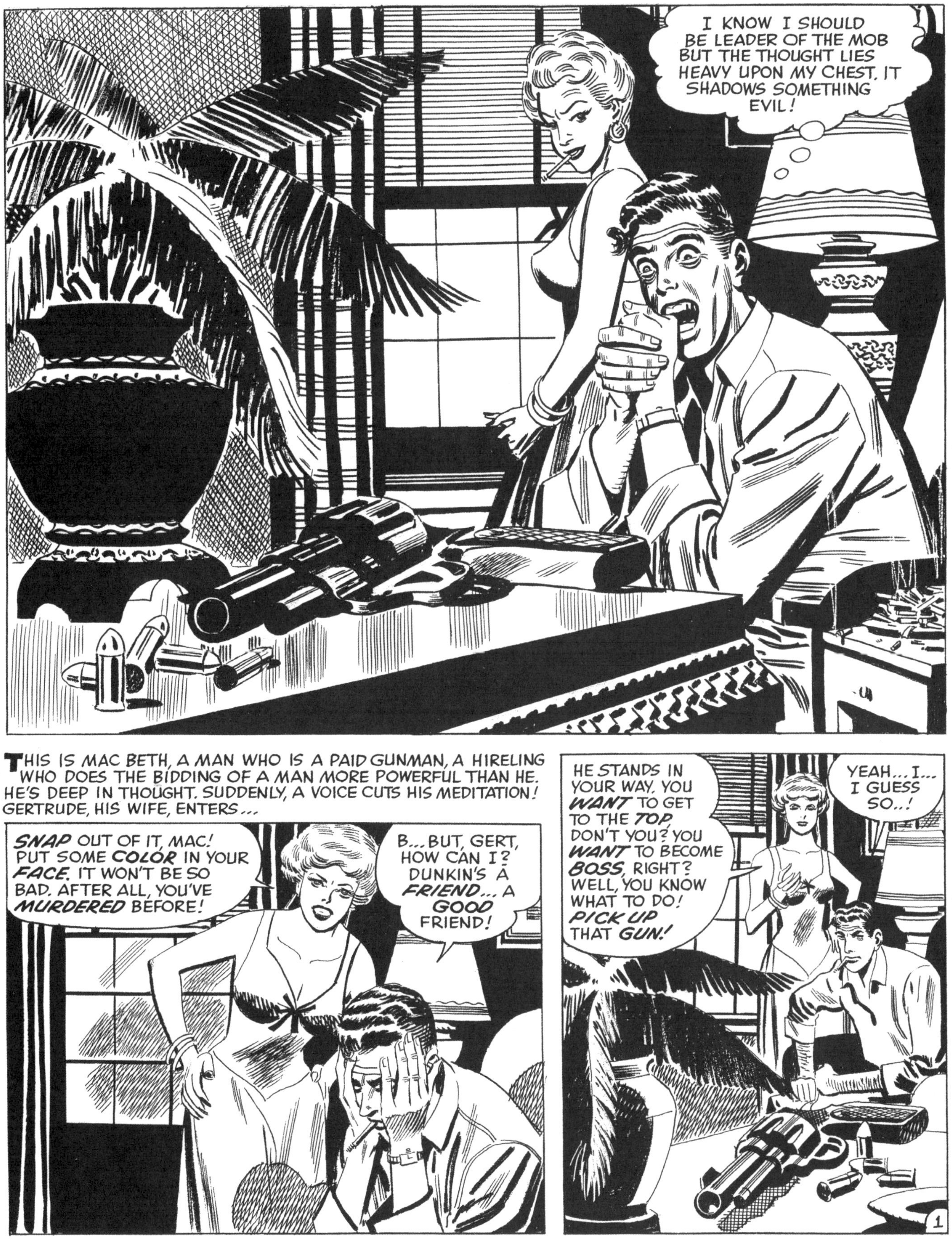

I KNOW I SHOULD BE LEADER OF THE MOB BUT THE THOUGHT LIES HEAVY UPON MY CHEST. IT SHADOWS SOMETHING EVIL!
THIS IS MAC BETH, A MAN WHO IS A PAID GUNMAN, A HIRELING WHO DOES THE BIDDING OF A MAN MORE POWERFUL THAN HE. HE'S DEEP IN THOUGHT. SUDDENLY, A VOICE CUTS HIS MEDITATION! GERTRUDE, HIS WIFE, ENTERS...
SNAP OUT OF IT, MAC! PUT SOME COLOR IN YOUR FACE. IT WON'T BE SO BAD. AFTER ALL, YOU'VE MURDERED BEFORE!
B... BUT, GERT, HOW CAN I? DUNKIN'S A FRIEND... A GOOD FRIEND!
HE STANDS IN YOUR WAY. YOU WANT TO GET TO THE TOP, DON'T YOU? YOU WANT TO BECOME BOSS, RIGHT? WELL, YOU KNOW WHAT TO DO! PICK UP THAT GUN!
YEAH... I... I GUESS SO...!
1

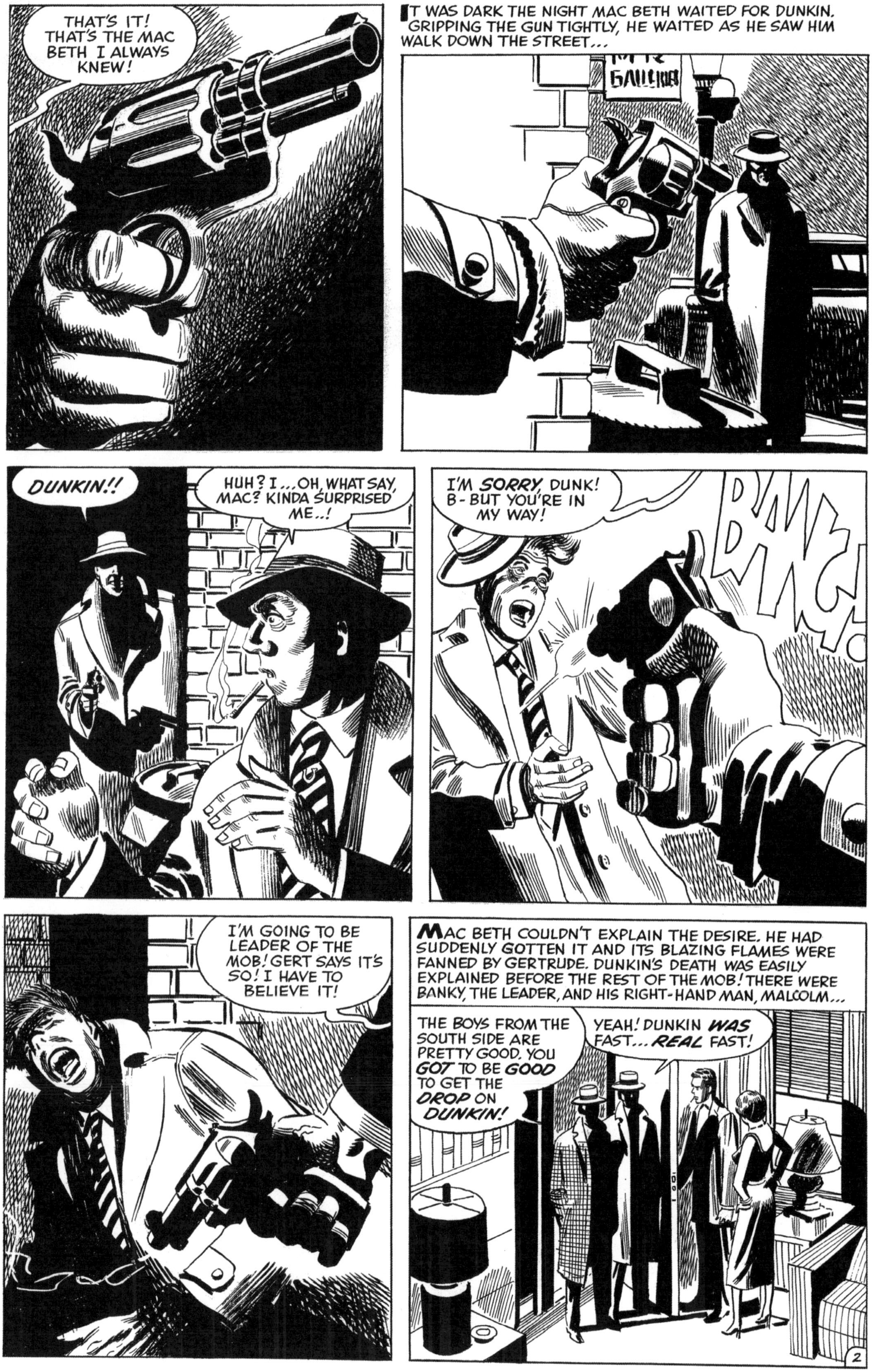
THAT'S IT! THAT'S THE MAC BETH I ALWAYS KNEW!
IT WAS DARK THE NIGHT MAC BETH WAITED FOR DUNKIN. GRIPPING THE GUN TIGHTLY, HE WAITED AS HE SAW HIM WALK DOWN THE STREET...
DUNKIN!!
HUH? I...OH, WHAT SAY, MAC? KINDA SURPRISED ME..!
I'M SORRY, DUNK! B-BUT YOU'RE IN MY WAY!
BANG!
I'M GOING TO BE LEADER OF THE MOB! GERT SAYS IT'S SO! I HAVE TO BELIEVE IT!
MAC BETH COULDN'T EXPLAIN THE DESIRE. HE HAD SUDDENLY GOTTEN IT AND ITS BLAZING FLAMES WERE FANNED BY GERTRUDE. DUNKIN'S DEATH WAS EASILY EXPLAINED BEFORE THE REST OF THE MOB! THERE WERE BANKY, THE LEADER, AND HIS RIGHT-HAND MAN, MALCOLM...
THE BOYS FROM THE SOUTH SIDE ARE PRETTY GOOD. YOU GOT TO BE GOOD TO GET THE DROP ON DUNKIN!
YEAH! DUNKIN WAS FAST... REAL FAST!
2

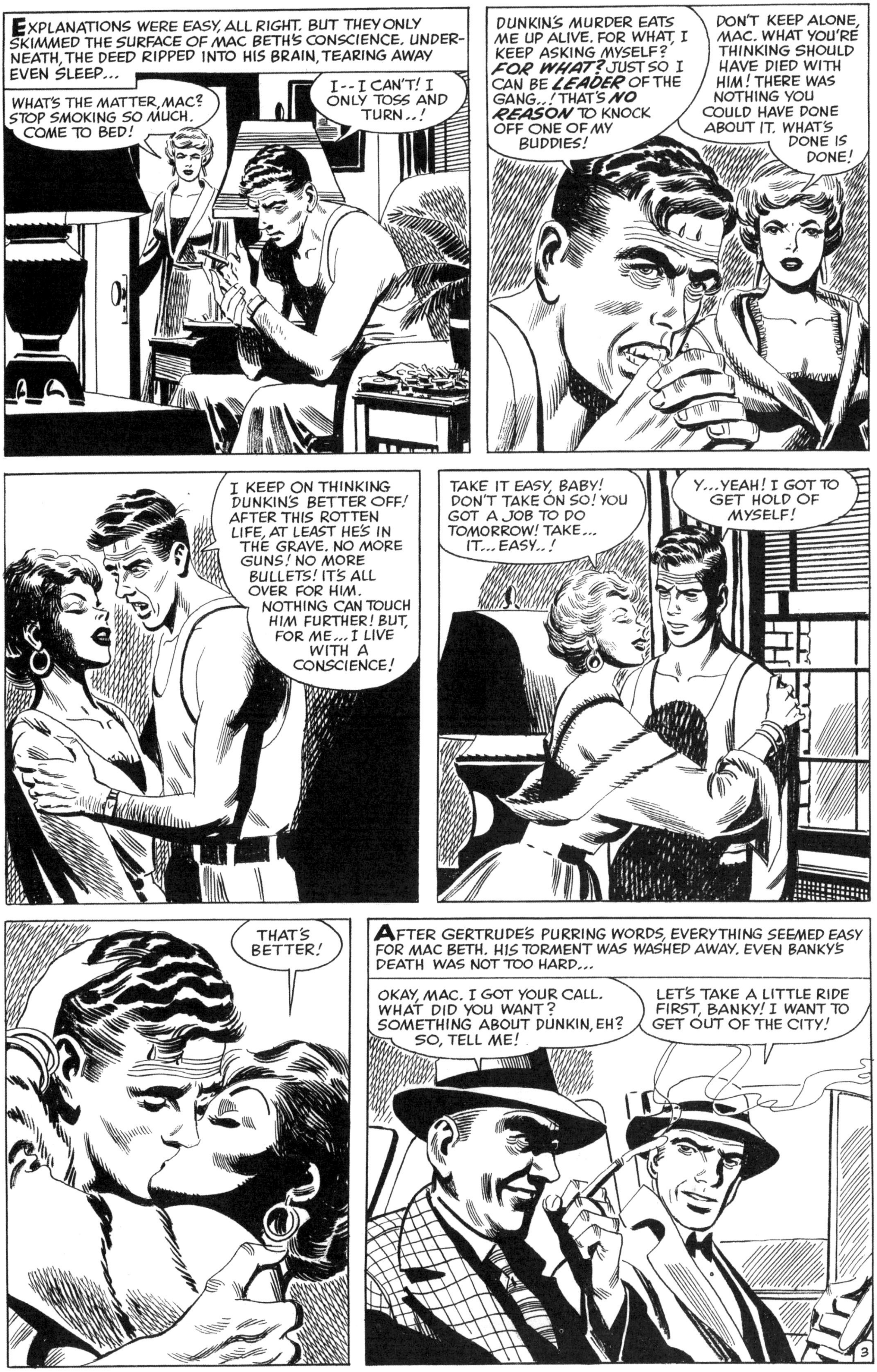
EXPLANATIONS WERE EASY, ALL RIGHT. BUT THEY ONLY SKIMMED THE SURFACE OF MAC BETH'S CONSCIENCE. UNDERNEATH, THE DEED RIPPED INTO HIS BRAIN, TEARING AWAY EVEN SLEEP...
WHAT'S THE MATTER, MAC? STOP SMOKING SO MUCH. COME TO BED!
I--I CAN'T! I ONLY TOSS AND TURN..!
DUNKIN'S MURDER EATS ME UP ALIVE. FOR WHAT, I KEEP ASKING MYSELF? FOR WHAT? JUST SO I CAN BE LEADER OF THE GANG..! THAT'S NO REASON TO KNOCK OFF ONE OF MY BUDDIES!
DON'T KEEP ALONE, MAC. WHAT YOU'RE THINKING SHOULD HAVE DIED WITH HIM! THERE WAS NOTHING YOU COULD HAVE DONE ABOUT IT. WHAT'S DONE IS DONE!
I KEEP ON THINKING DUNKIN'S BETTER OFF! AFTER THIS ROTTEN LIFE, AT LEAST HE'S IN THE GRAVE. NO MORE GUNS! NO MORE BULLETS! IT'S ALL OVER FOR HIM. NOTHING CAN TOUCH HIM FURTHER! BUT, FOR ME... I LIVE WITH A CONSCIENCE!
TAKE IT EASY, BABY! DON'T TAKE ON SO! YOU GOT A JOB TO DO TOMORROW! TAKE... IT... EASY..!
Y...YEAH! I GOT TO GET HOLD OF MYSELF!
THAT'S BETTER!
AFTER GERTRUDE'S PURRING WORDS, EVERYTHING SEEMED EASY FOR MAC BETH. HIS TORMENT WAS WASHED AWAY. EVEN BANKY'S DEATH WAS NOT TOO HARD...
OKAY, MAC. I GOT YOUR CALL. WHAT DID YOU WANT? SOMETHING ABOUT DUNKIN, EH? SO, TELL ME!
LET'S TAKE A LITTLE RIDE FIRST, BANKY! I WANT TO GET OUT OF THE CITY!
3

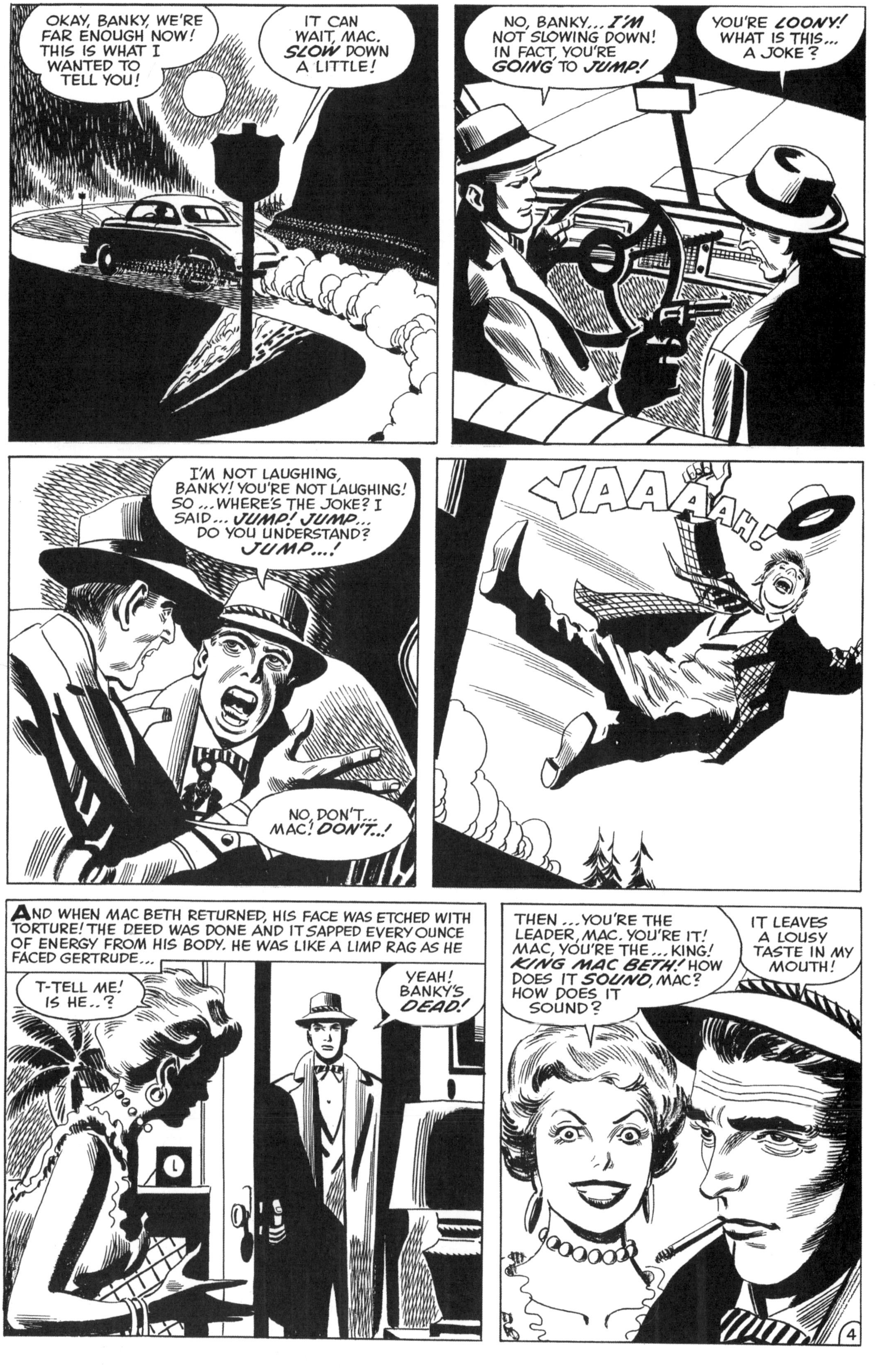
OKAY, BANKY, WE'RE FAR ENOUGH NOW! THIS IS WHAT I WANTED TO TELL YOU!
IT CAN WAIT, MAC. SLOW DOWN A LITTLE!
NO, BANKY... I'M NOT SLOWING DOWN! IN FACT, YOU'RE GOING TO JUMP!
YOU'RE LOONY! WHAT IS THIS... A JOKE?
I'M NOT LAUGHING, BANKY! YOU'RE NOT LAUGHING! SO ... WHERE'S THE JOKE? I SAID... JUMP! JUMP... DO YOU UNDERSTAND? JUMP...!
NO, DON'T... MAC! DON'T..!
YAAAAAH!
AND WHEN MAC BETH RETURNED, HIS FACE WAS ETCHED WITH TORTURE! THE DEED WAS DONE AND IT SAPPED EVERY OUNCE OF ENERGY FROM HIS BODY. HE WAS LIKE A LIMP RAG AS HE FACED GERTRUDE...
T-TELL ME! IS HE..?
YEAH! BANKY'S DEAD!
THEN ... YOU'RE THE LEADER, MAC. YOU'RE IT! MAC, YOU'RE THE ... KING! KING MAC BETH! HOW DOES IT SOUND, MAC? HOW DOES IT SOUND?
IT LEAVES A LOUSY TASTE IN MY MOUTH!
4

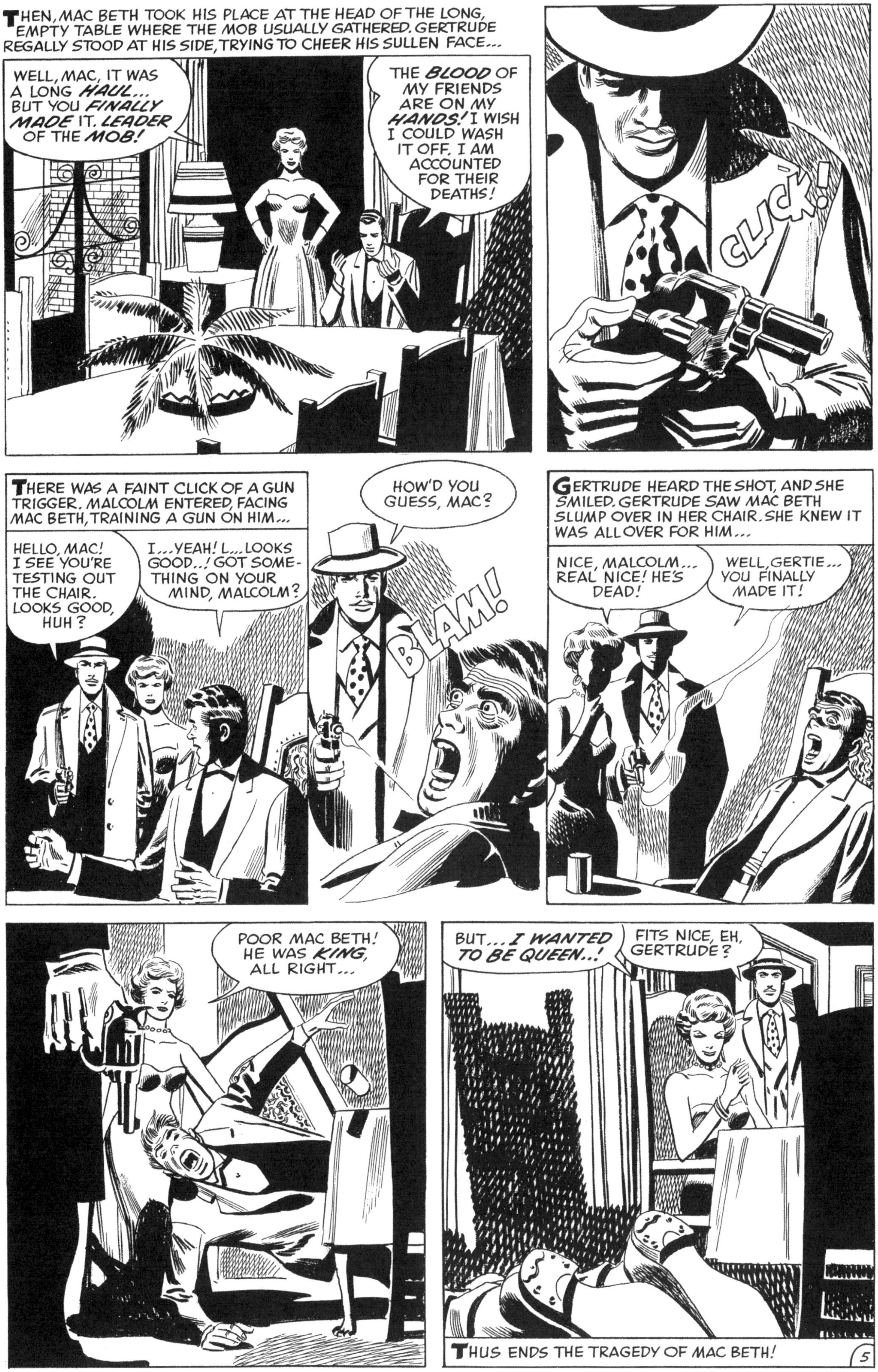
THEN, MAC BETH TOOK HIS PLACE AT THE HEAD OF THE LONG, EMPTY TABLE WHERE THE MOB USUALLY GATHERED. GERTRUDE REGALLY STOOD AT HIS SIDE, TRYING TO CHEER HIS SULLEN FACE...
WELL, MAC, IT WAS A LONG HAUL... BUT YOU FINALLY MADE IT. LEADER OF THE MOB!
THE BLOOD OF MY FRIENDS ARE ON MY HANDS! I WISH I COULD WASH IT OFF. I AM ACCOUNTED FOR THEIR DEATHS!
CLICK!
THERE WAS A FAINT CLICK OF A GUN TRIGGER. MALCOLM ENTERED, FACING MAC BETH, TRAINING A GUN ON HIM...
HELLO, MAC! I SEE YOU'RE TESTING OUT THE CHAIR. LOOKS GOOD, HUH?
I... YEAH! L... LOOKS GOOD..! GOT SOMETHING ON YOUR MIND, MALCOLM?
HOW'D YOU GUESS, MAC?
BLAM!
GERTRUDE HEARD THE SHOT, AND SHE SMILED. GERTRUDE SAW MAC BETH SLUMP OVER IN HER CHAIR. SHE KNEW IT WAS ALL OVER FOR HIM...
NICE, MALCOLM... REAL NICE! HE'S DEAD!
WELL, GERTIE... YOU FINALLY MADE IT!
POOR MAC BETH! HE WAS KING, ALL RIGHT...
BUT... I WANTED TO BE QUEEN..!
FITS NICE, EH, GERTRUDE?
THUS ENDS THE TRAGEDY OF MAC BETH!

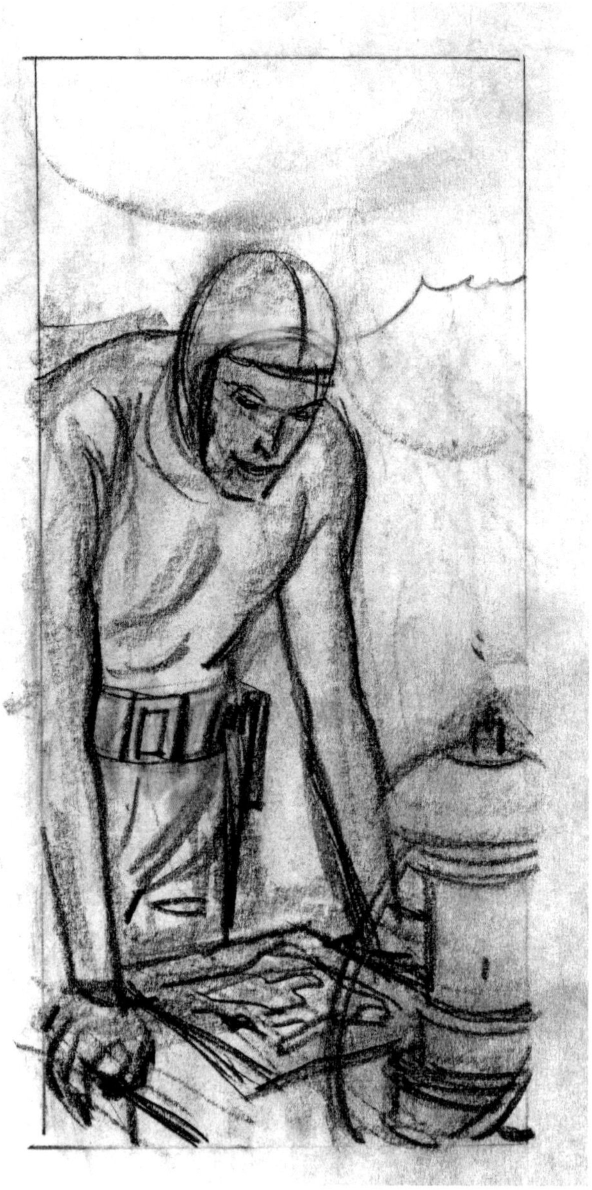

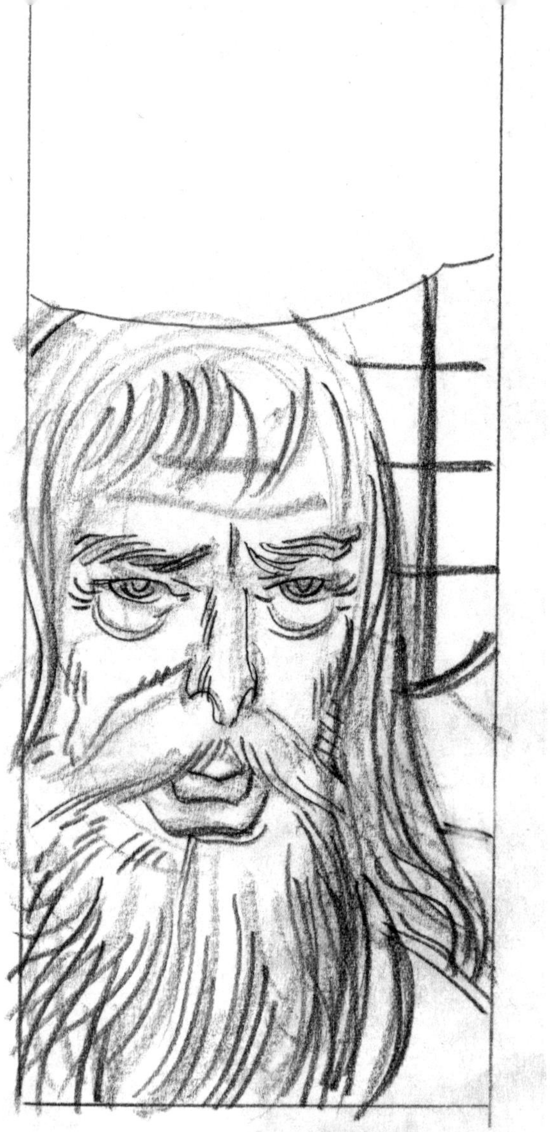

Pencil sketches for an unknown comic story. Meskin liked to work large, and many of these panels are as wide as 9 inches.

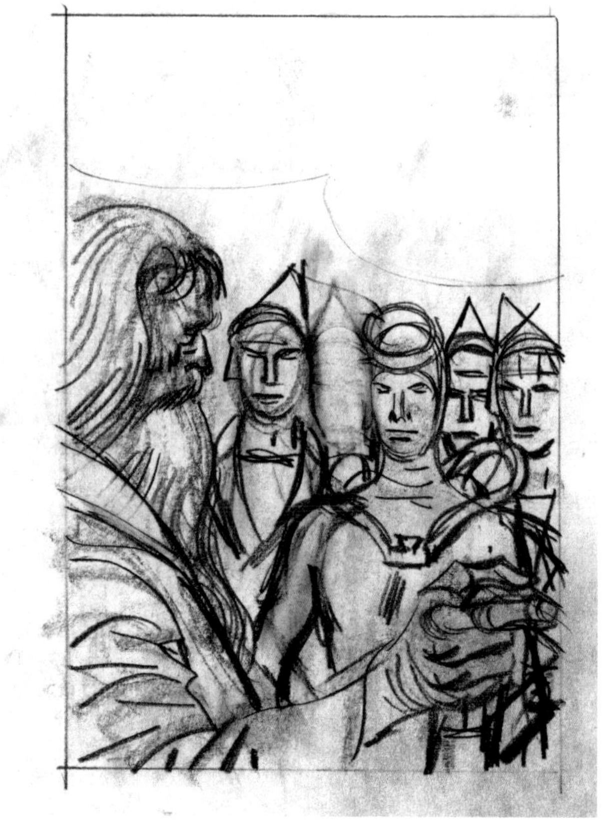

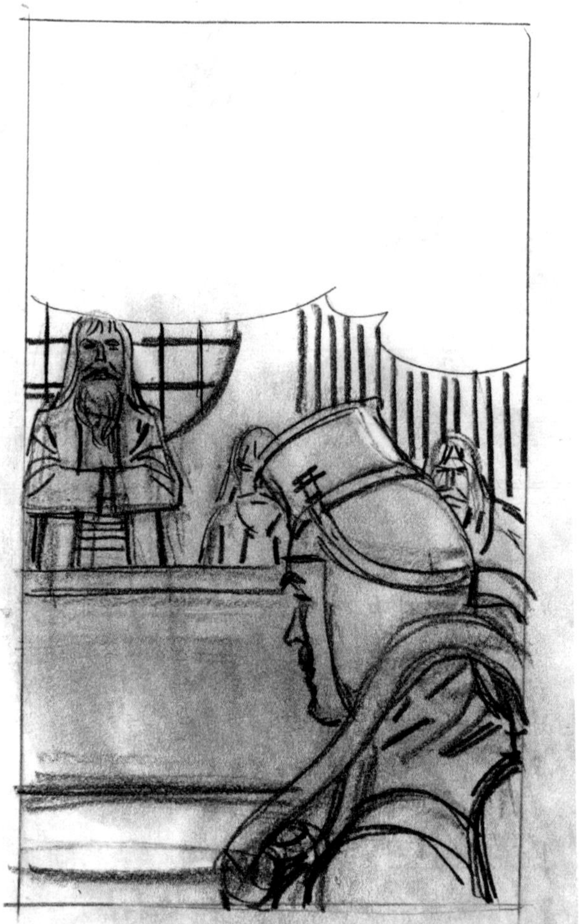

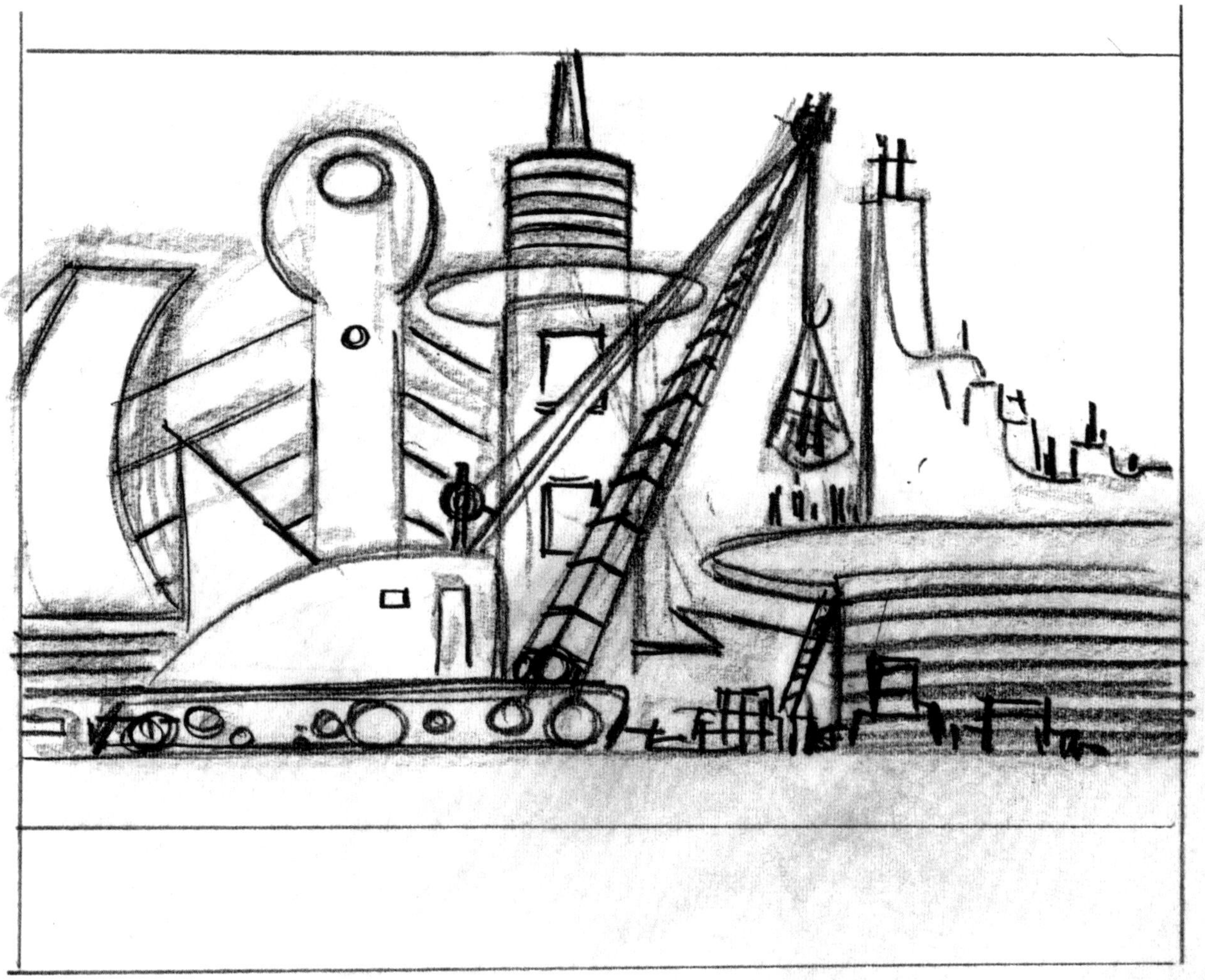

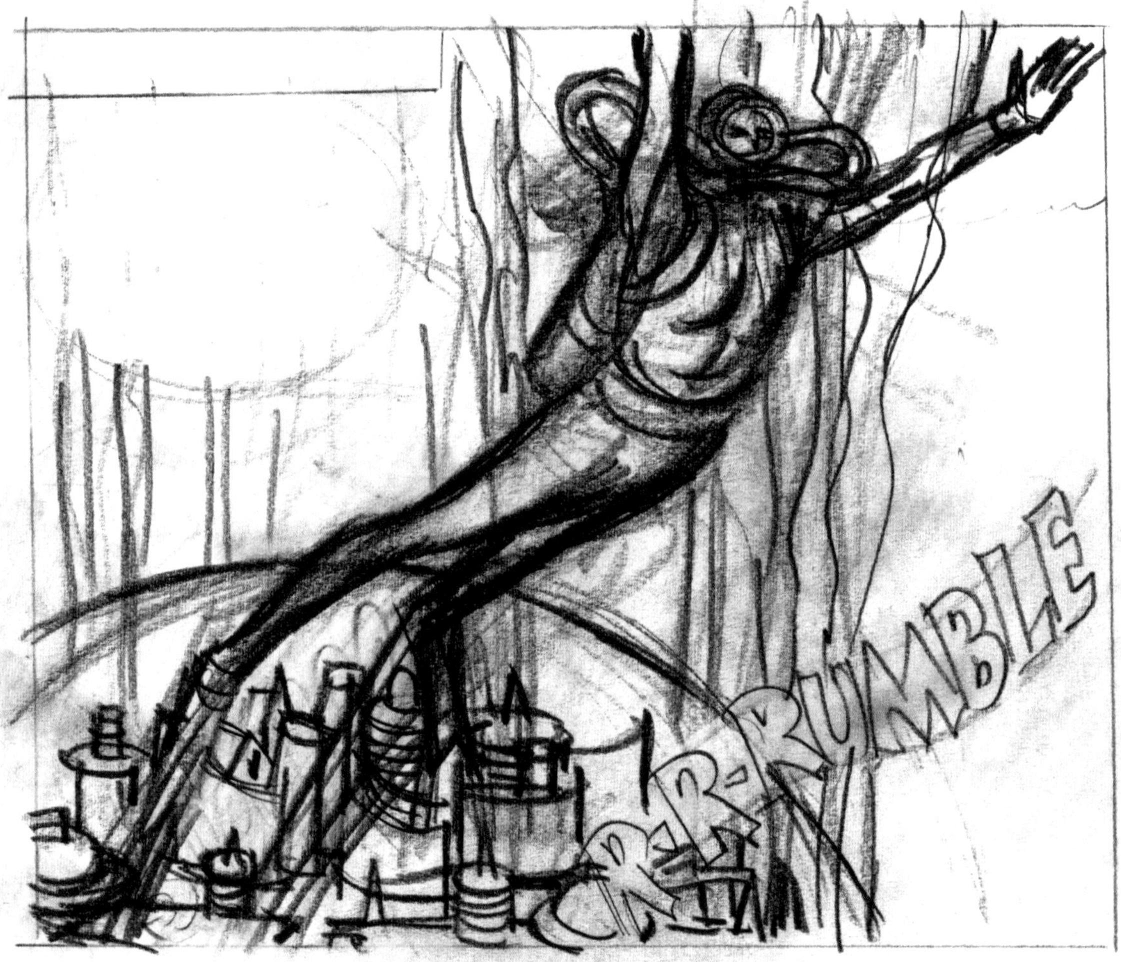
CR-R-RUMBLE

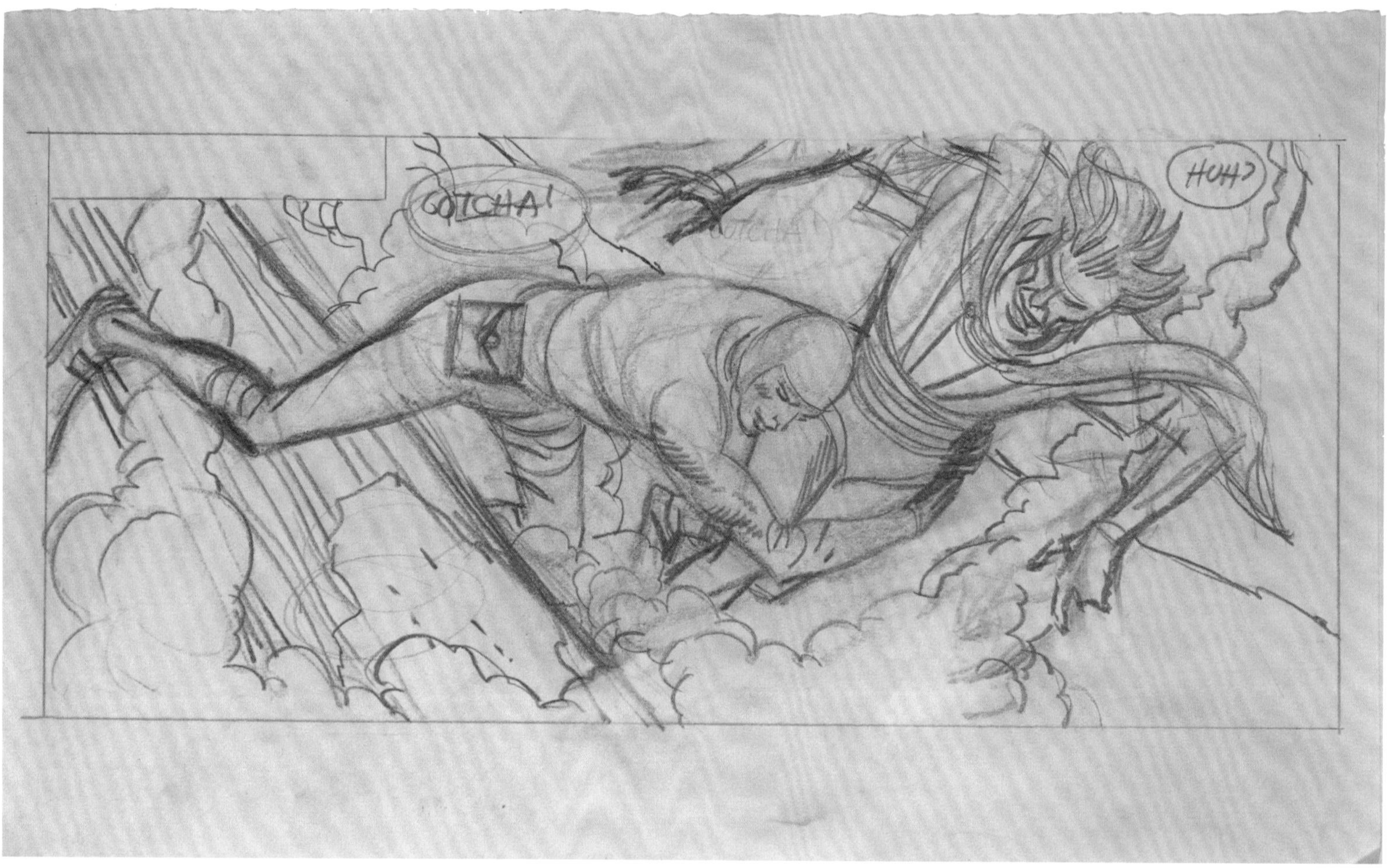
GOTCHA!
HUH?

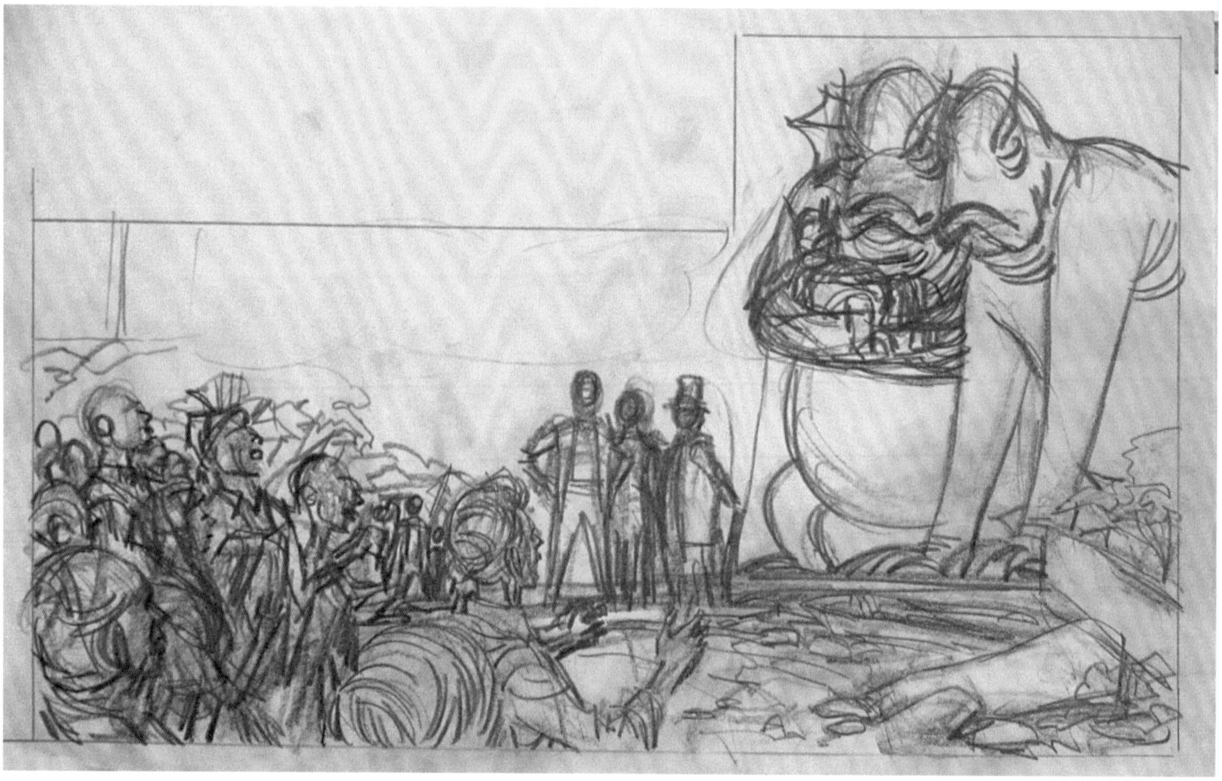

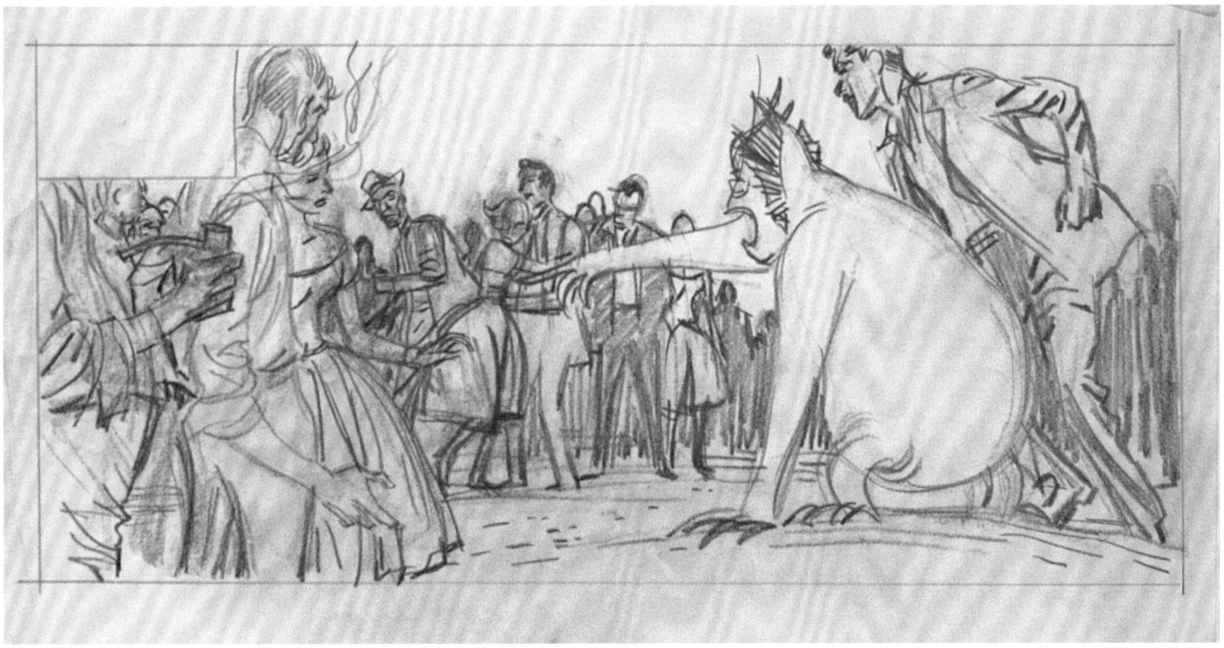

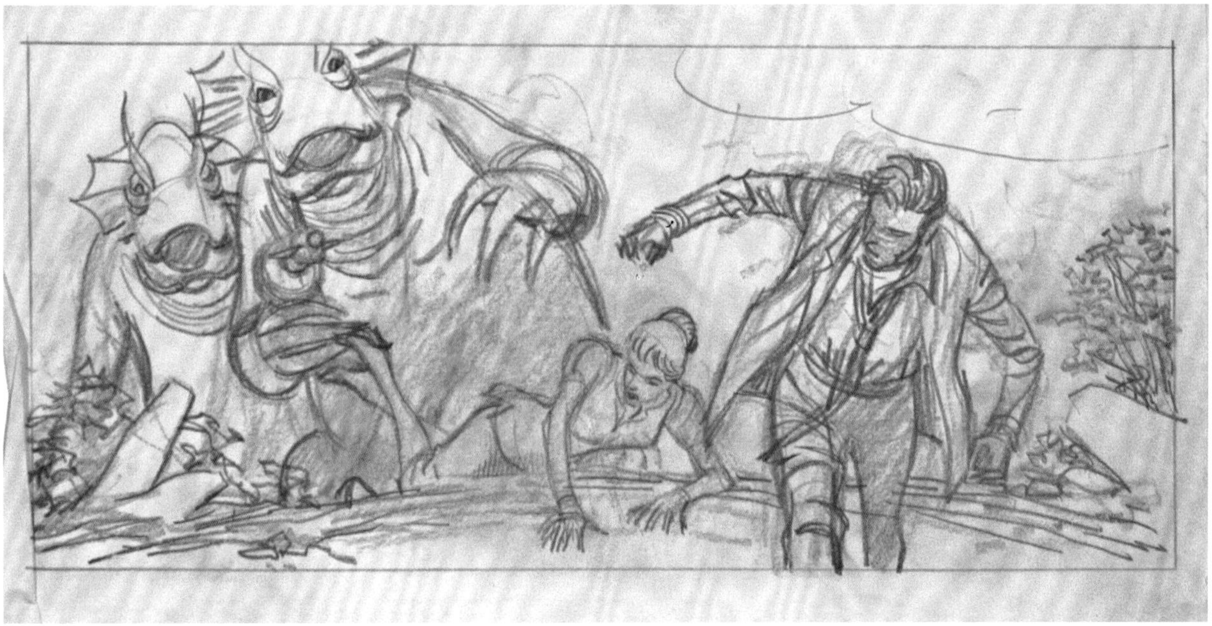

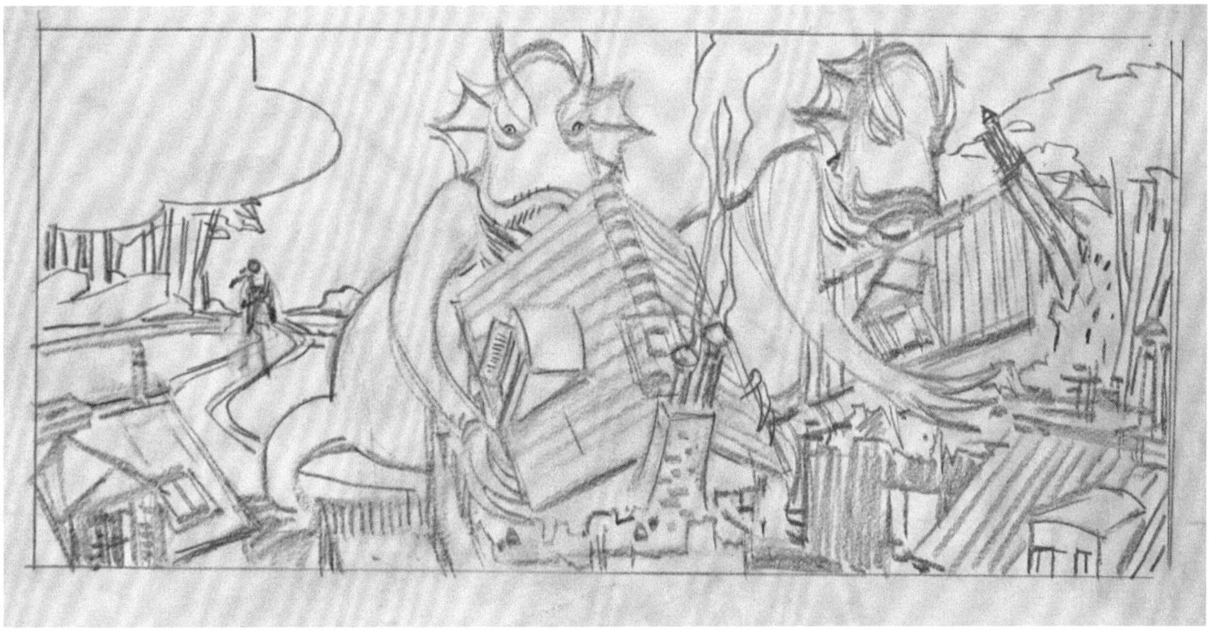

The story is told that Kanigher, upon reviewing a war story that Meskin illustrated, demanded that he crawl across the floor to prove he knew what a soldier would look like crawling beneath barbed wire carrying a rifle. What is clear is that the editorial staff had no idea of the great artistic talent they had working for them, viewing Meskin and all artists as a means to an end—product.

Joe Kubert: " [Mort] was such a laid-back guy. I never saw him angry, I'd never seen him upset, but that might not be too unusual because I never socialized with him, I never had that much to do with him on a personal or social basis, we would get together only when we were doing the work. The sad part of what was happening with Mort, he might have been put upon by others, not abused, but just not treated for the person that he was, because he was so shy or reticent. A lot of artists are like that, a lot of guys that do the stuff that we do, have a tendency to be most happy when they're left alone, and not socialize. That stutter would become a little more obvious when there was any sign of pressure, I may have been present when he was with an editor and the editor was suggesting something to him and Mort was uptight, he worked for several guys besides myself, and if Mort became a little too uptight the stutter was more obvious."[52]

Even though Meskin inked much of his own work during this return to DC, the assembly-line mentality had become standard practice in the industry, and artists were considered cogs in the machine. The collaborative nature of the business removed it in the public's eye as anything other than disposable junk, and indeed those employed in the industry, embarrassed by the profession, would prefer misconceptions about their line of work to being identified as working in comic books.

Meskin went to live in a carriage house on Commerce Street in Greenwich Village, in the same building as friend and inker George Roussos. He lived alone in a one-room studio apartment barely large enough to contain his bed and drawing board, with high ceilings and shelves covered with books, and a shared bathroom down the hall. With the restrictions placed on him at DC, he began to create personal art, paintings, drawings, collages, by the dozens, sketching outdoors, cutting and pasting bits of art, painting on glass, experimenting in varied media. The two friends would walk the streets of the village late into the night, talking. "He was a very learned guy, extremely intelligent guy. In the mornings he would go out and paint boats. He went down to the pier painting boats, he went out and illustrated street scenes, with cars and lampposts, they were beautiful, black and white, with wash," recalls Roussos. [53]

16 Commerce Street, Greenwich Village, NY, where Meskin and George Roussos resided. RIGHT: Original art from *House of Secrets* #58, 1963. Pencils by Mort Meskin, inks by George Roussos. (© DC Comics. All Rights Reserved. Used with Permission.)

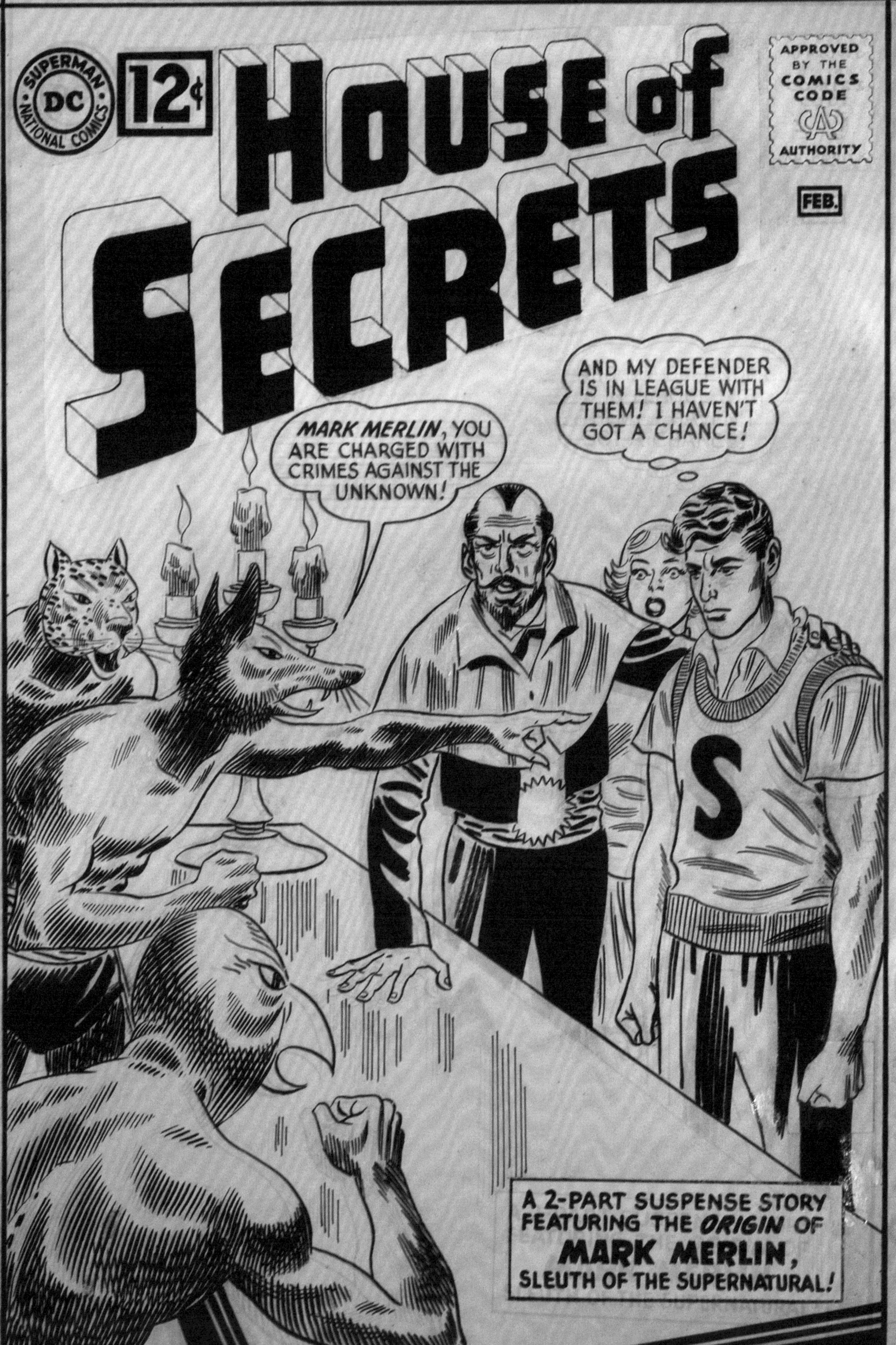
SUPERMAN DC NATIONAL COMICS
12¢
HOUSE of SECRETS
APPROVED BY THE COMICS CODE AUTHORITY
FEB.
MARK MERLIN, YOU ARE CHARGED WITH CRIMES AGAINST THE UNKNOWN!
AND MY DEFENDER IS IN LEAGUE WITH THEM! I HAVEN'T GOT A CHANCE!
S
A 2-PART SUSPENSE STORY FEATURING THE ORIGIN OF
MARK MERLIN,
SLEUTH OF THE SUPERNATURAL!

At first, a still-shaken Meskin leaned on his friend Roussos to provide layouts for his DC work. "Mort didn't want to do too much work, his basic principle: 'You could only live so much.' Otherwise it became overwhelming. Most artists are like hungry wolves, they grab this job and they could handle it. He could only do so much." [67] Thanks to Roussos, this practice was short-lived. "I assured him that he was one of the best. After a year of doing his layouts I said 'Mort, you are doing very well on your own, you don't need me, you can do stuff much better than I can.'"[54]

Leonard Starr: "I was sharing a studio in New York with Johnny Prentice when we got a call from Mort asking if maybe we had an empty drawing board where he could work for a bit. Johnny thought as highly of Mort as I did so sure, we'd clear a board and he could use it as long as he liked. Mort settled in very tentatively, he'd been given a script and was very nervous about it. 'It'll be great, Mort, you'll see!' We were hopeful, why couldn't it happen? But watching him was very painful. For some reason he wouldn't use a pencil. He would lay out the page with charcoal, erase it, do it again. He'd then try laying it out with a blue wash so that once he'd inked the page there'd be nothing to erase. Nothing worked. It was upsetting, feeling helpless watching him struggle, the memory of all those figures swarming with life on his drawing board back then still fresh. After a couple of weeks he finally he gave up, thanked us for the use of the studio, returned the key. Will you be okay, Mort? 'Oh, sure.' Anything we can do? 'No, no. I'll be fine.' It was the last time we ever saw him and we never heard of what became of him, but whatever it might have been, we could only hope that it wouldn't be too hard for him to bear."[55]

Eventually gaining confidence, Meskin suggested to Roussos that they open an art school. They rented a room for a small fee, and set it up with easels

Meskin and Roussos's carriage house apartments were next to the Cherry Lane Theater, as indicated by the arrow on the sign in Meskin's panoramic pen-and-ink drawing on colored paper.

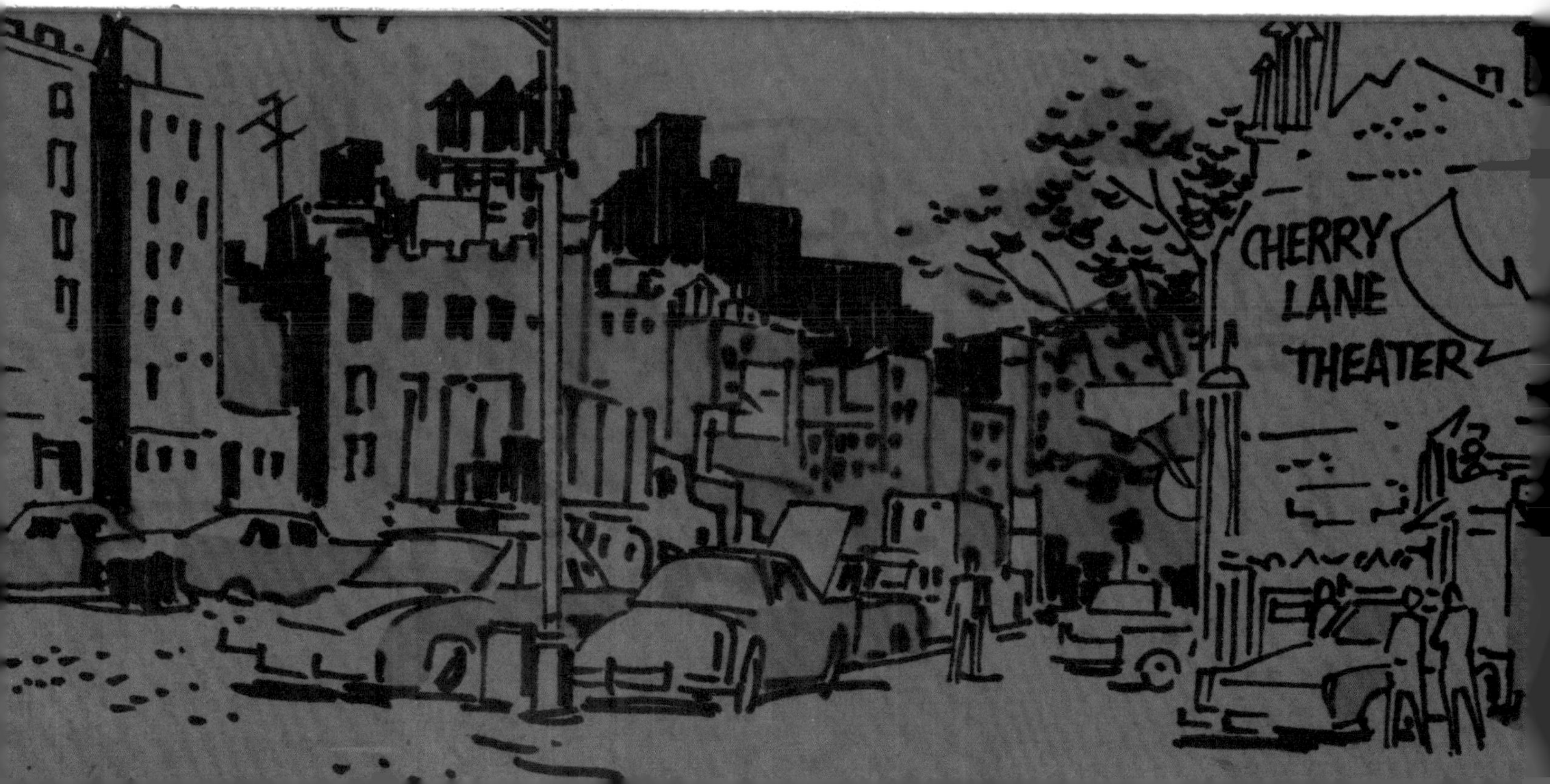
CHERRY
LANE
THEATER

and chairs. Mort adorned the walls with his paintings. Soon they were off and running. "We had about 10 or 15 students at one time. We had quite a number of people, a couple of the (comic book) artists came down, we had a lot of classes. Mort was sort of shy. He should have helped the people, he did to some extent, but not as much as he should. We only charged a buck a night and we bought oranges and tea and coffee so the profit went out the window." [56]

Undeterred, Meskin had a show of his paintings at the Emar Gallery. Shortly thereafter he decided to open a store in the village, with Roussos, to sell his voluminous artwork and penned his own press release, anonymously:

Meskin stands in the doorway of the store front where he sold his artwork.

About the artist:

Long one of New York's top commercial artists, Mort Meskin has now turned his talent to his first love — watercolors. In the main he seeks to capture the color pattern and sweep of battered boats in drydock, perhaps an unconscious expression of his frustrated love for the sea. A native New Yorker, Mr. Meskin thus far has to settle for the Staten Island Ferry, but he is predominately an outdoor man, having sketched and painted on numerous camping trips throughout the United States. His one man show at the Emar Gallery, Greenwich Village, has met with much critical acclaim by both artists and public. Mr. Meskin's paintings are always charming and unfailingly in good taste.

Mr. Meskin studied under two of the country's foremost color authorities at Pratt Institute and the Art Students League. In the commercial black and white field he rapidly won recognition and for a time taught at the Cartoonists and Illustrators Institute in New York, but he chafes easily under the commercial grind and finds refuge and contentment in his favorite combination — watercolors and the Waterfront.

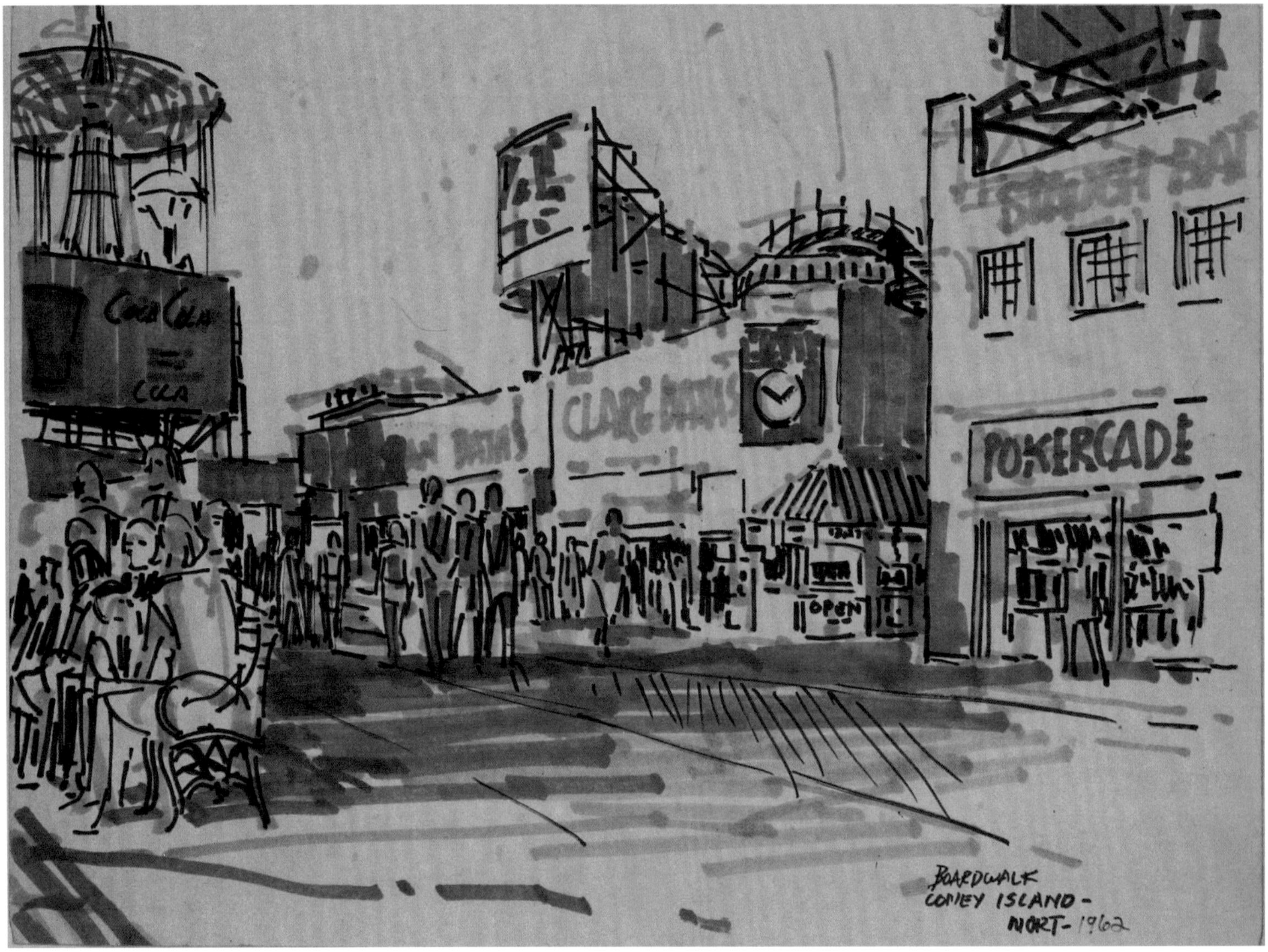
COCA COLA
COCA
CLARE BATHS
POKERCADE
OPEN
BOARDWALK
CONEY ISLAND-
NORT- 1962

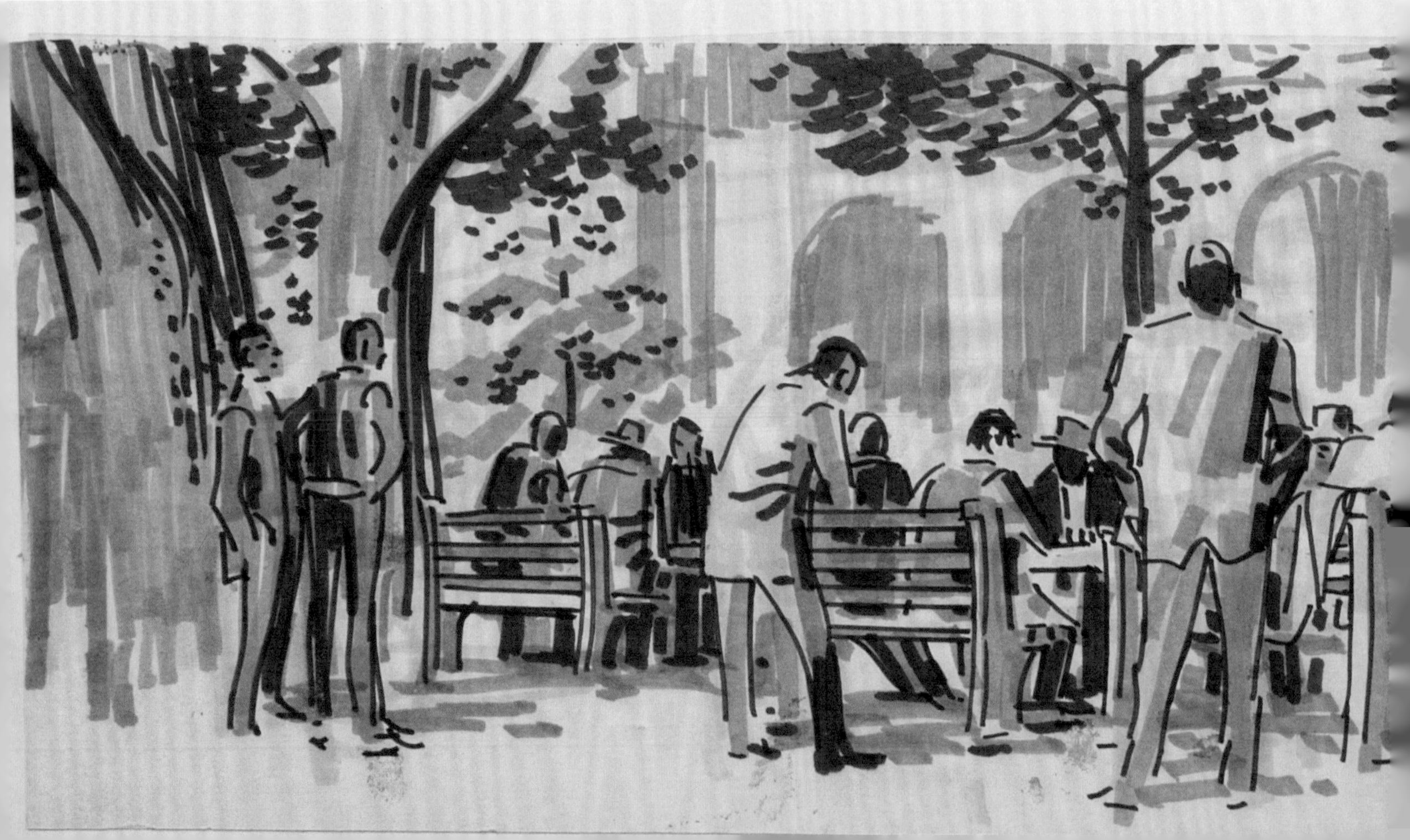

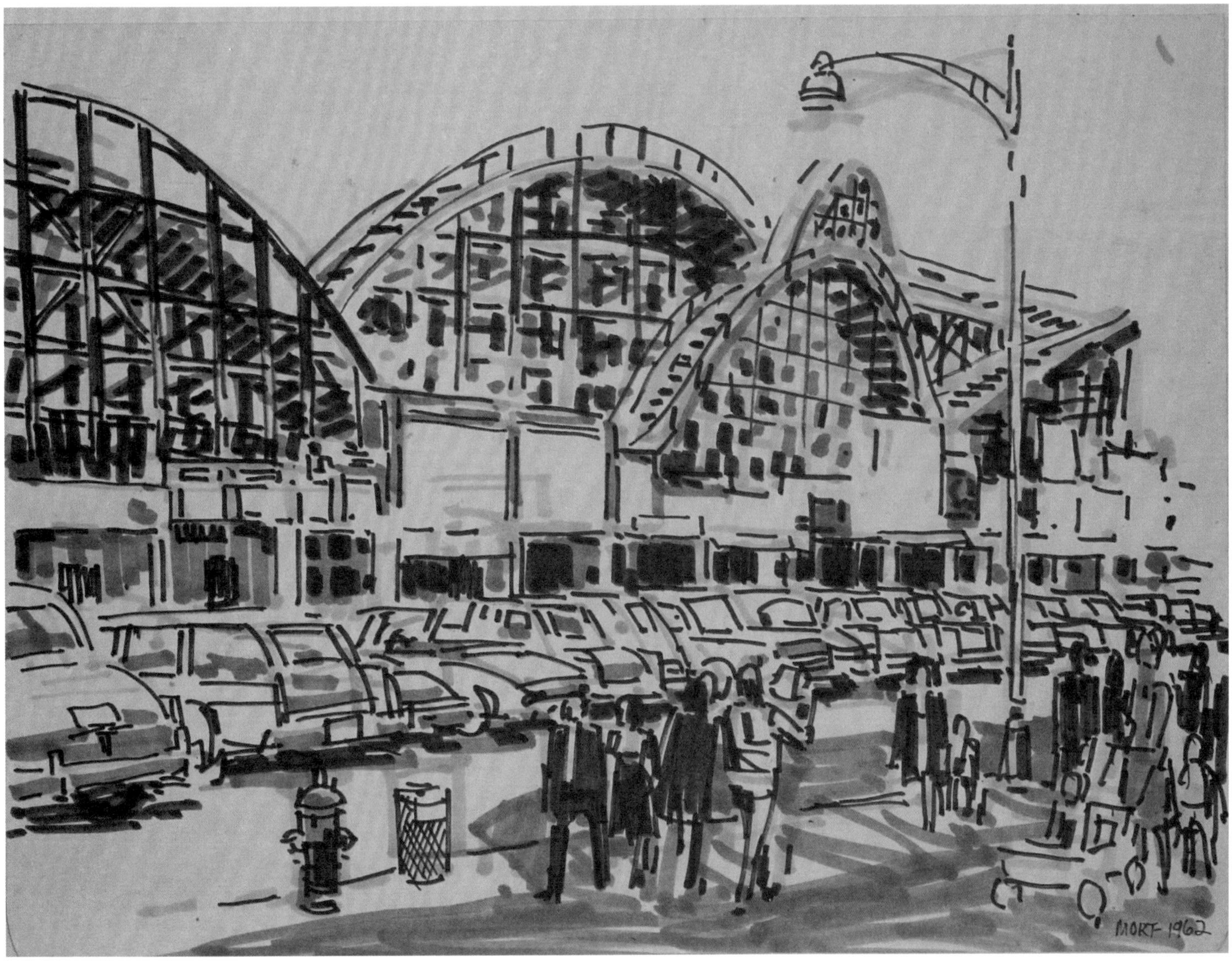
MORT 1962

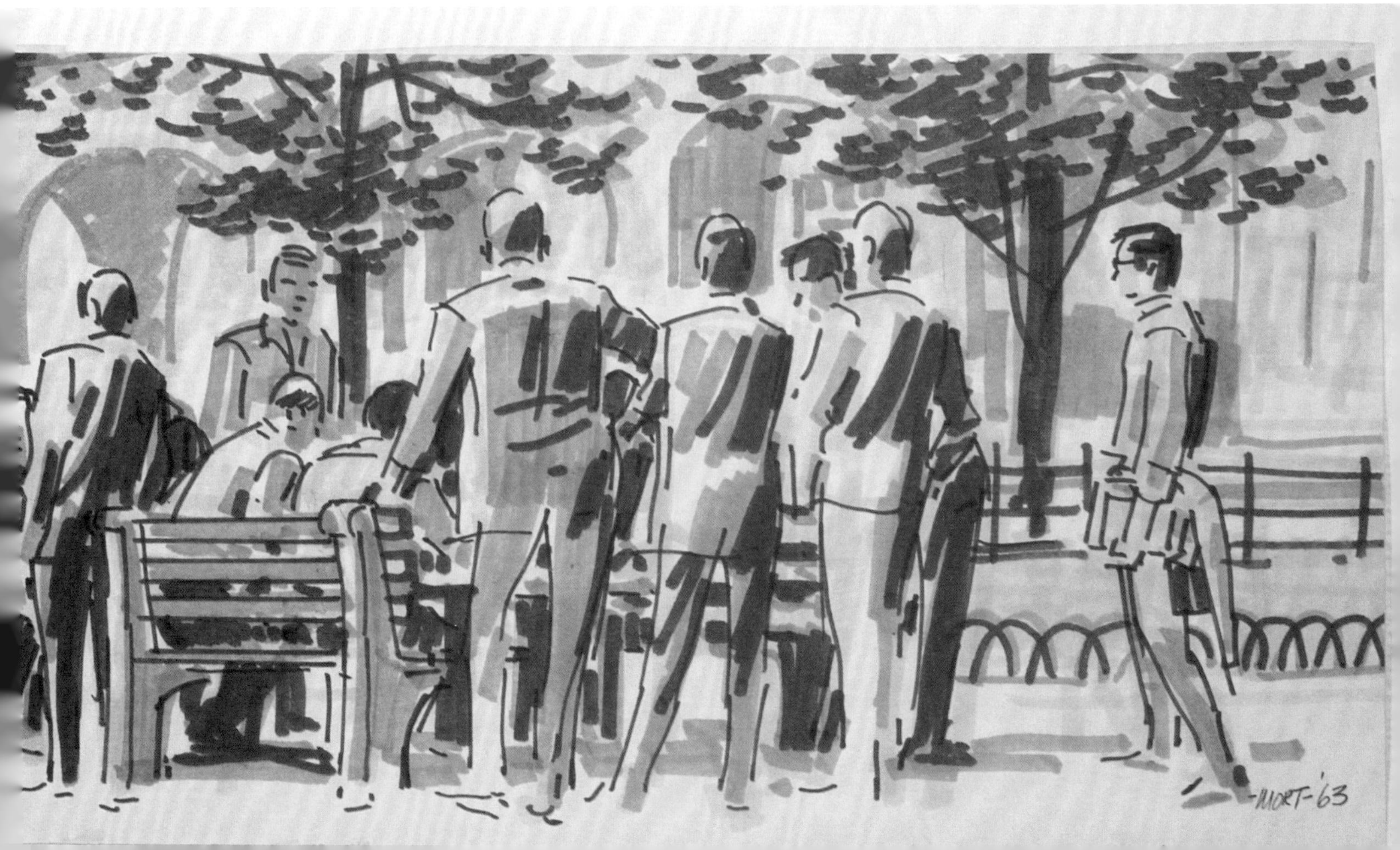
MORT-'63

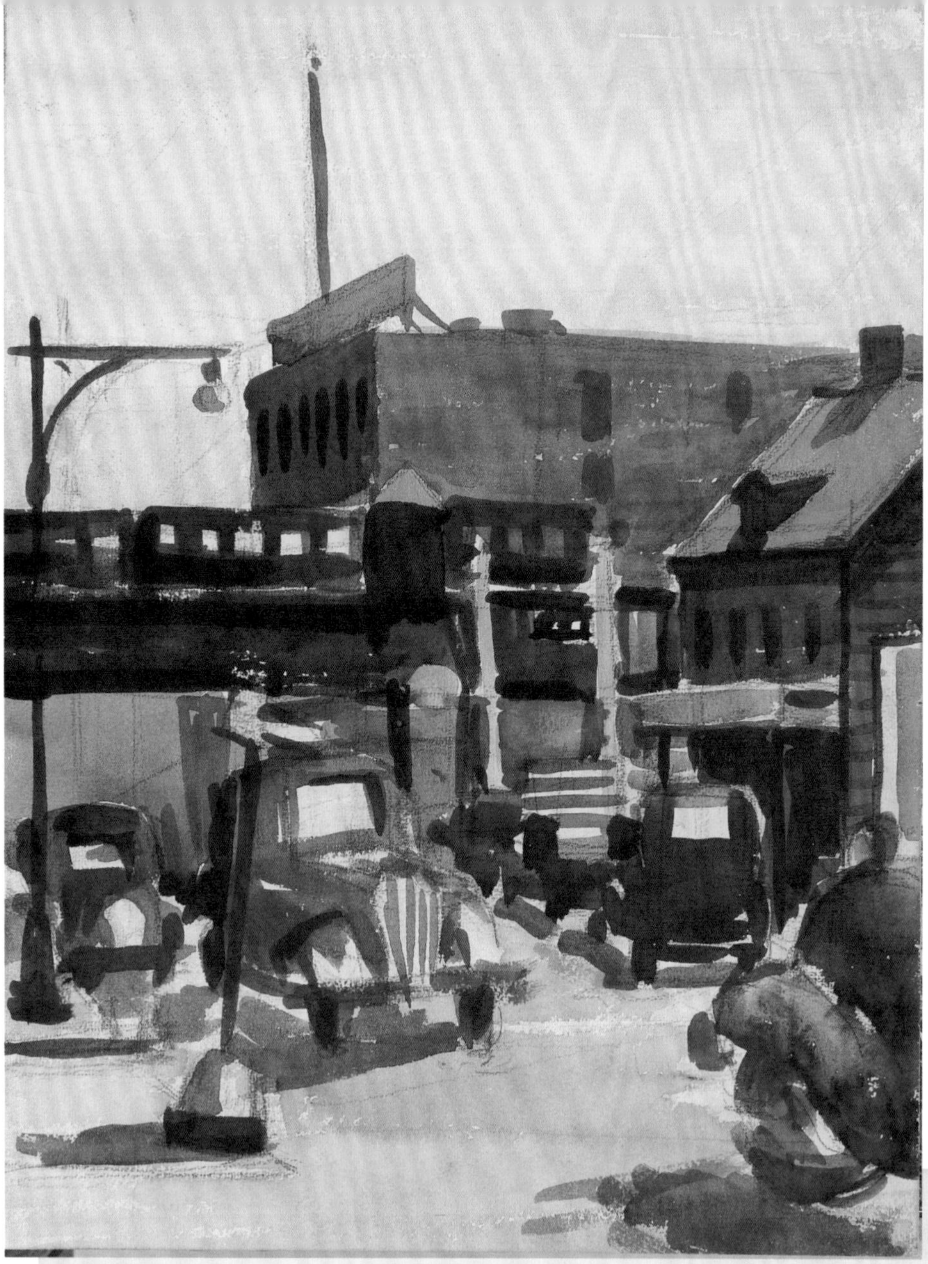

Greenwich Village street scenes and the nearby shipyards on the Hudson were favorite subjects of Meskin.

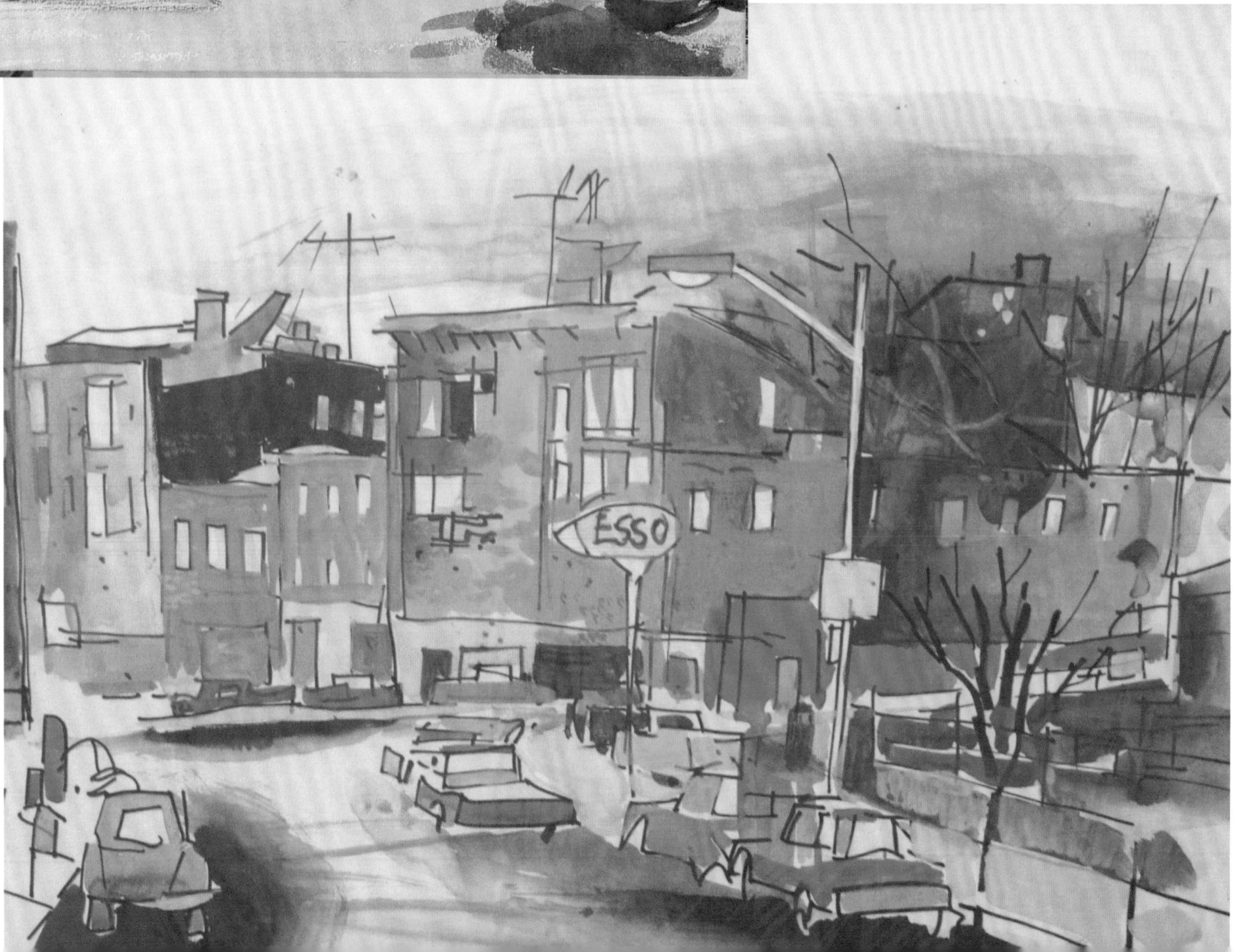
ESSO

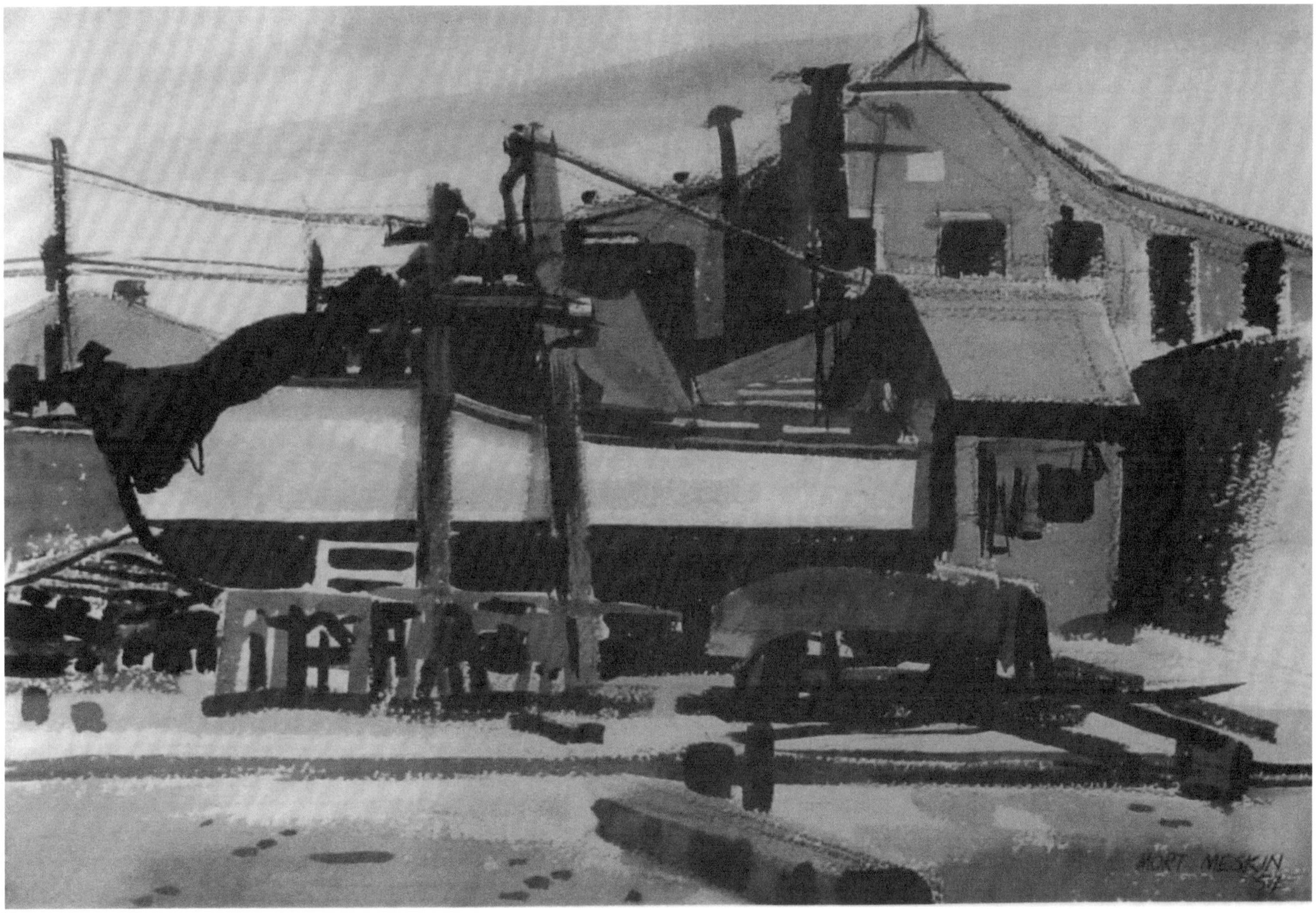
MORT MESKIN

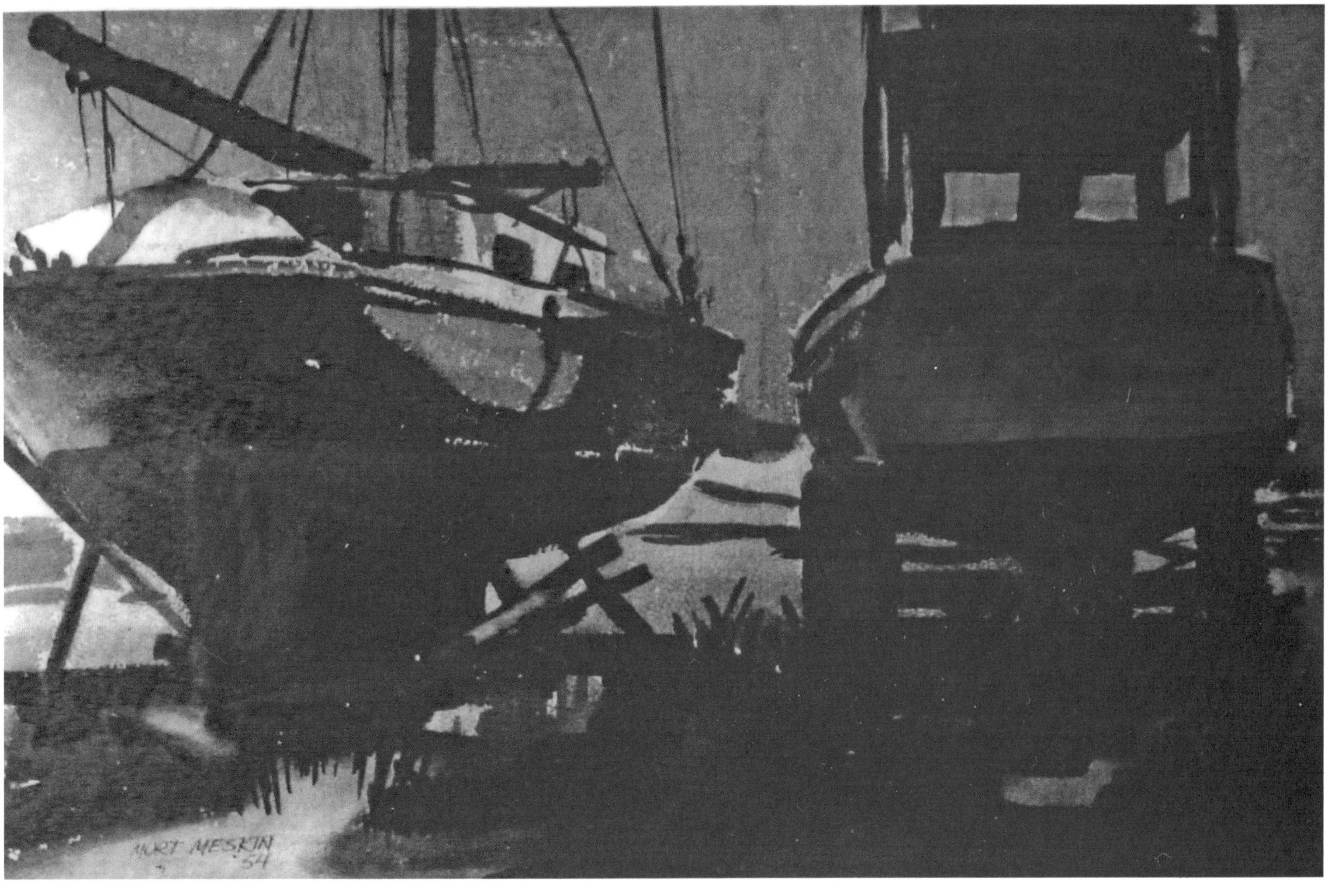
MORT MESKIN
'54

This endeavor too was short-lived.

Although the family unit was no longer together, Mort did the best he could for his sons. He would pick the boys up from their respective foster homes and take them on outings to Prospect Park and Coney Island.

"Philip and I were walking with Dad through, I think it was Prospect Park or the Brooklyn Botanical Gardens, and there was a swing set, just the vertical and horizontal support bars and my dad said, 'Oh, I used to do the high bar,' and we said, 'We know that, Dad, when you were young,' and he said, 'I could still do that!' and we snickered, 'Oh no, Dad! Don't hurt yourself!' and that's when he got annoyed with us and shimmied right up onto the high bar and he began to swing around, forgetting that he hadn't emptied his pockets and his keys and his change and his comb and his wallet and God knows what everything falling out of his pockets and it falls all over the place, but he does it! He swings on the high bar like an Olympic champion and he does a flip, somersaulting in mid-air and he lands on his feet with a flourish: Ta-dah!! His status, in our eyes as young children, rose 120%. All of a sudden he was one of the super characters in his comic books. We were very proud."

"One of the highlights of my life, was going to a father and son dinner with my dad. I have very few memories of us doing things like that together. Another time that was a very wonderful memory was of him taking me to Philadelphia, to the Benjamin Franklin Memorial Institute. In addition to art, we were both fascinated by science."[57]

As time went on both sons would go visit their father at his apartment in Greenwich Village near the Cherry Lane Theater. He would take them over to a pier on the Hudson. Philip Meskin: "I used to go down and visit him, he'd be at his drawing board and then we'd go down and have sandwiches, I'd go by the fire escape and whistle, he'd come on down, we'd go down to the docks in the West Village, he'd go back to work, I'd hang out in Washington Square reading the *Village Voice* and smoking Gauloises."

Peter Meskin: "That was a very emotional period, it was an important period, because it was the first and only time I saw Dad cry, there in the apartment. He said, 'My boys, my boys, what will become of my boys?' and it made me realize that we were still loved and that he really cared about us. Later he would have Philip live with him for a while but he was never able to make a home for the three of us together."[58]

Although now somewhat distant, Mort remained a loving father. Peter recalls, "Dad was encouraging about everything I did. I must tell you, anything I ever attempted in my life was fully supported and encouraged by my dad. Dad would design birthday cards and other kinds of cards for me over the years.

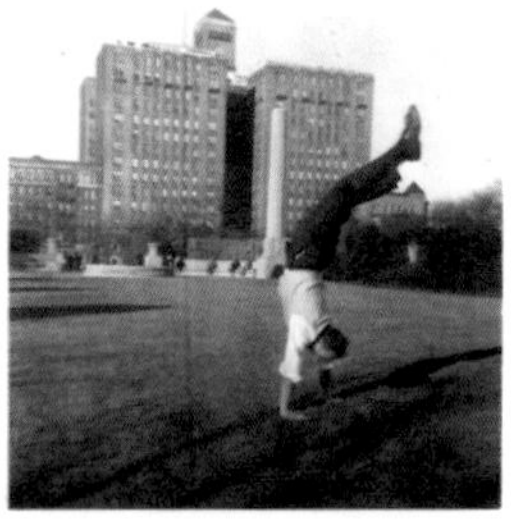

ABOVE: Meskin does a handstand in Prospect Park, Brooklyn. RIGHT AND PAGES FOLLOWING: Meskin's art for the various DC anthology titles, 1956-1965. (© DC Comics. All Rights Reserved. Used with Permission.)

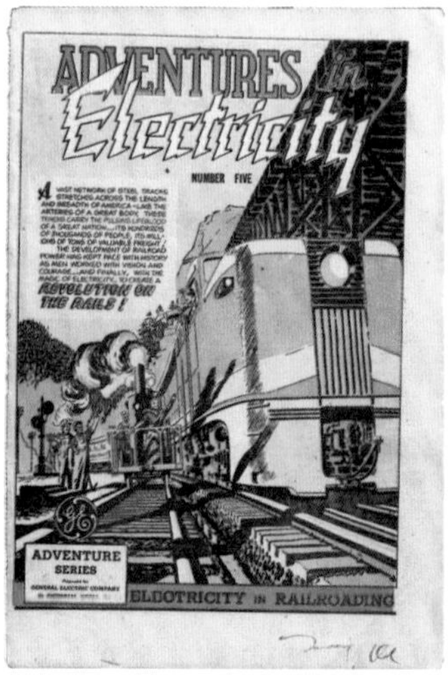
ADVENTURES
Electricity
NUMBER FIVE
ADVENTURE SERIES

Adventures in Electricty was a coverless comic produced by George Roussos for General Electric. Roussos would frequently ask Meskin to contribute to his projects, as he did on this issue.

SPARTA HOUSE OF SECRETS 59

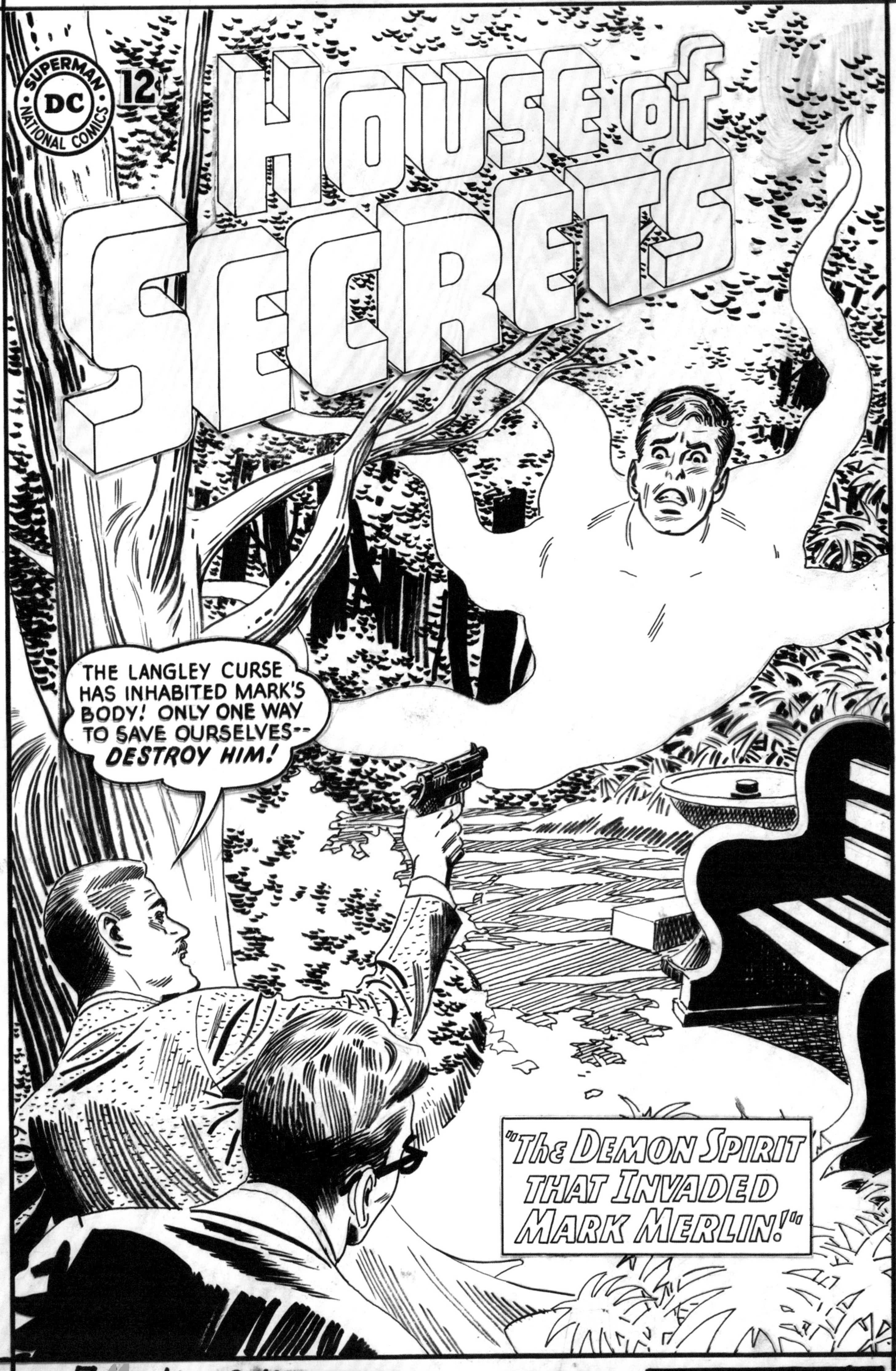

YELLOW TS
RED TS
BLACK TS
BLUE TS

Anything I happened to be doing at that time, he'd draw me a picture of it as if he were celebrating my life. He loved it when I became a charter boat captain. It absolutely thrilled him. I haven't really followed in his footsteps, but everything I've done, he either wished he had done or he dreamed of doing."

Mort's philosophical yearnings and erudition continued during these years. Peter Meskin: "I remember him reading a lot of art books, and he loved to read children's books. He loved the artwork in them and loved any kind of children's books that explained something. He thought that many of the people who wrote children's books taught things better to the children than adults did and that they made it more interesting. To this day, I read and enjoy all sorts of children's books. He loved to read about artists. He loved Vermeer, Degas, Monet, Renoir, people like that."[59]

[TEXT CONTINUES ON PAGE 172]

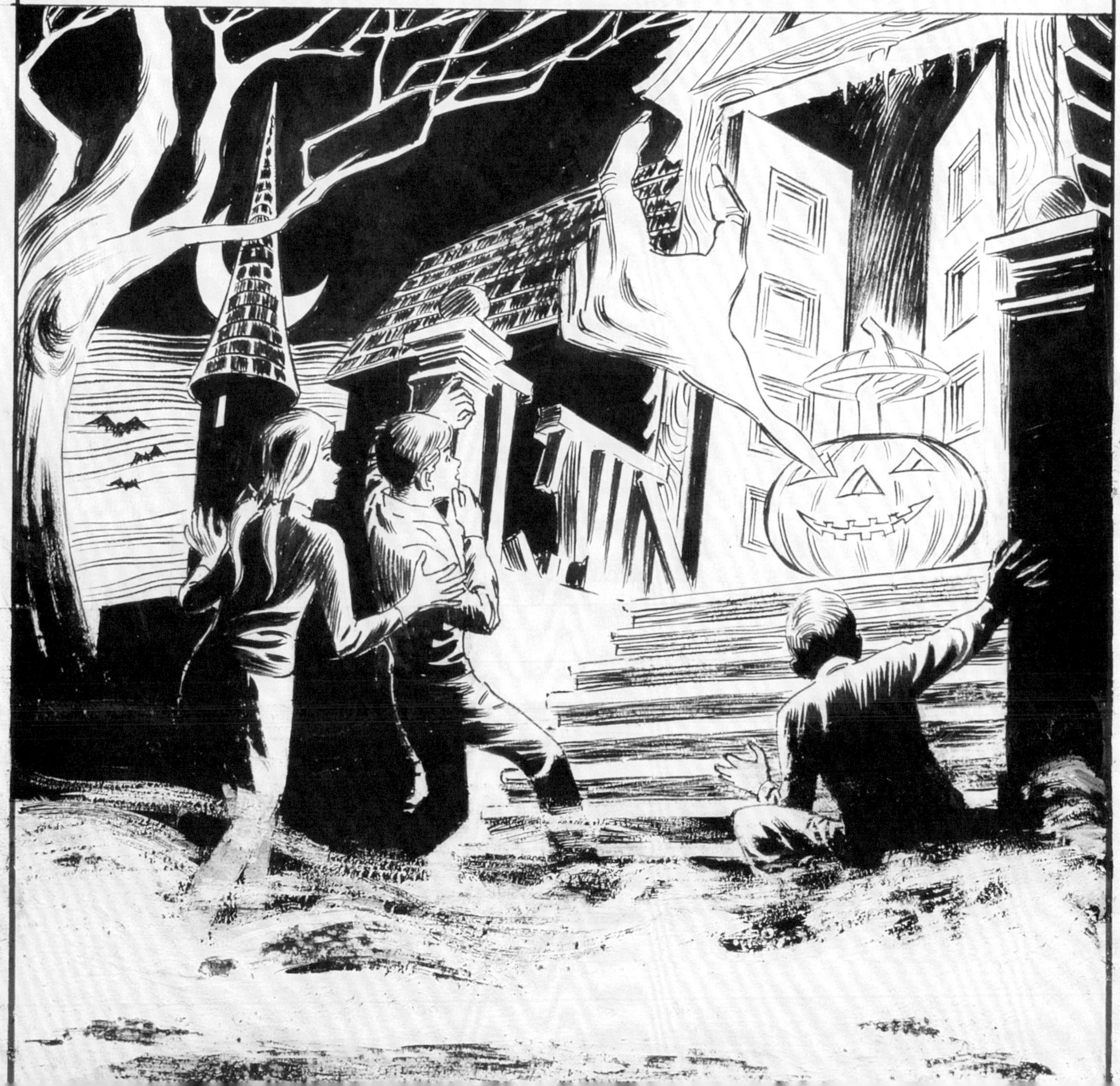

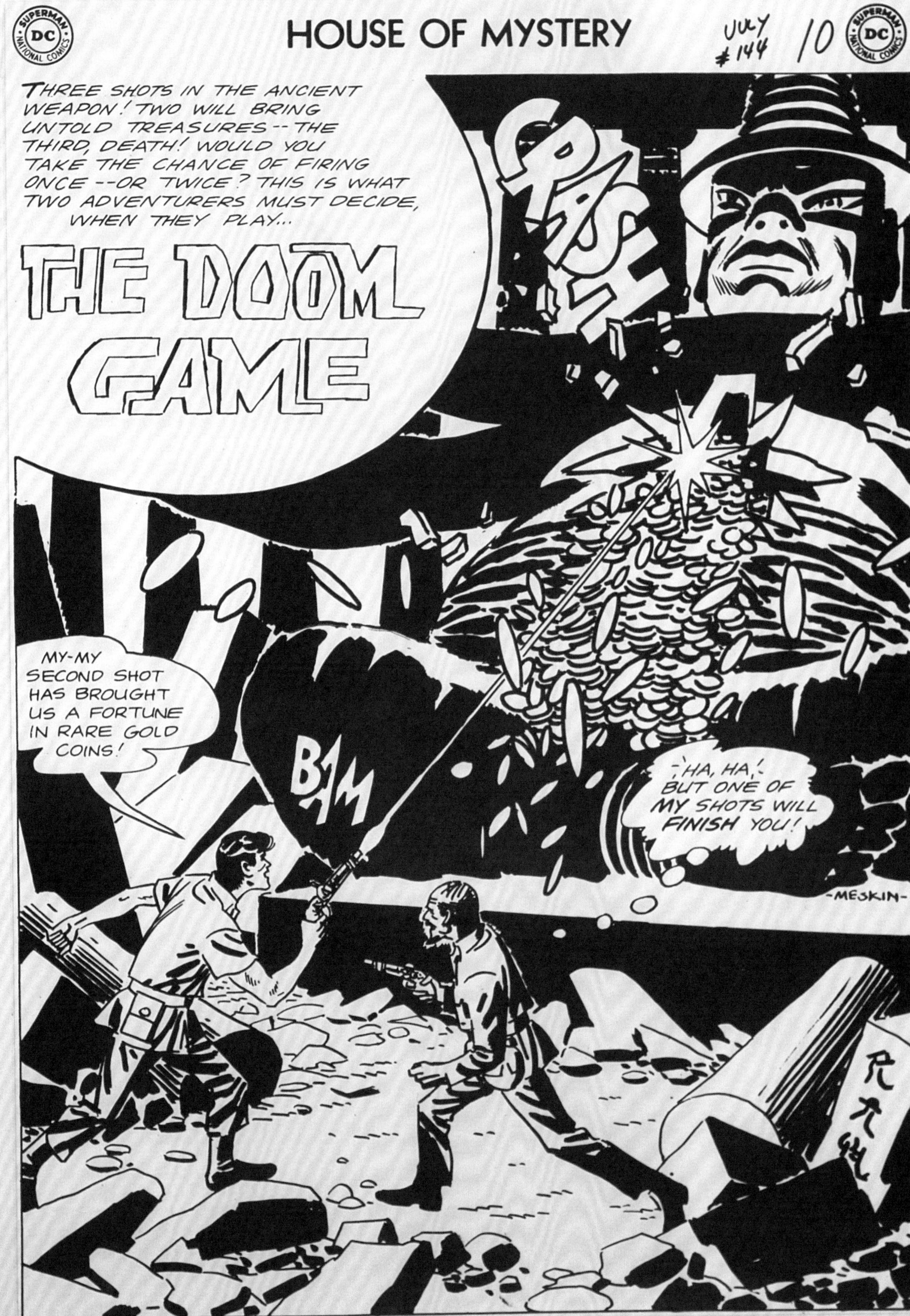

HOUSE OF MYSTERY
JULY #144
10
THREE SHOTS IN THE ANCIENT WEAPON! TWO WILL BRING UNTOLD TREASURES--THE THIRD, DEATH! WOULD YOU TAKE THE CHANCE OF FIRING ONCE--OR TWICE? THIS IS WHAT TWO ADVENTURERS MUST DECIDE, WHEN THEY PLAY...
THE DOOM GAME
CRASH
MY-MY SECOND SHOT HAS BROUGHT US A FORTUNE IN RARE GOLD COINS!
BAM
HA, HA! BUT ONE OF MY SHOTS WILL FINISH YOU!
-MESKIN-

LEFT: Unpublished cover artwork from *House of Mystery*.

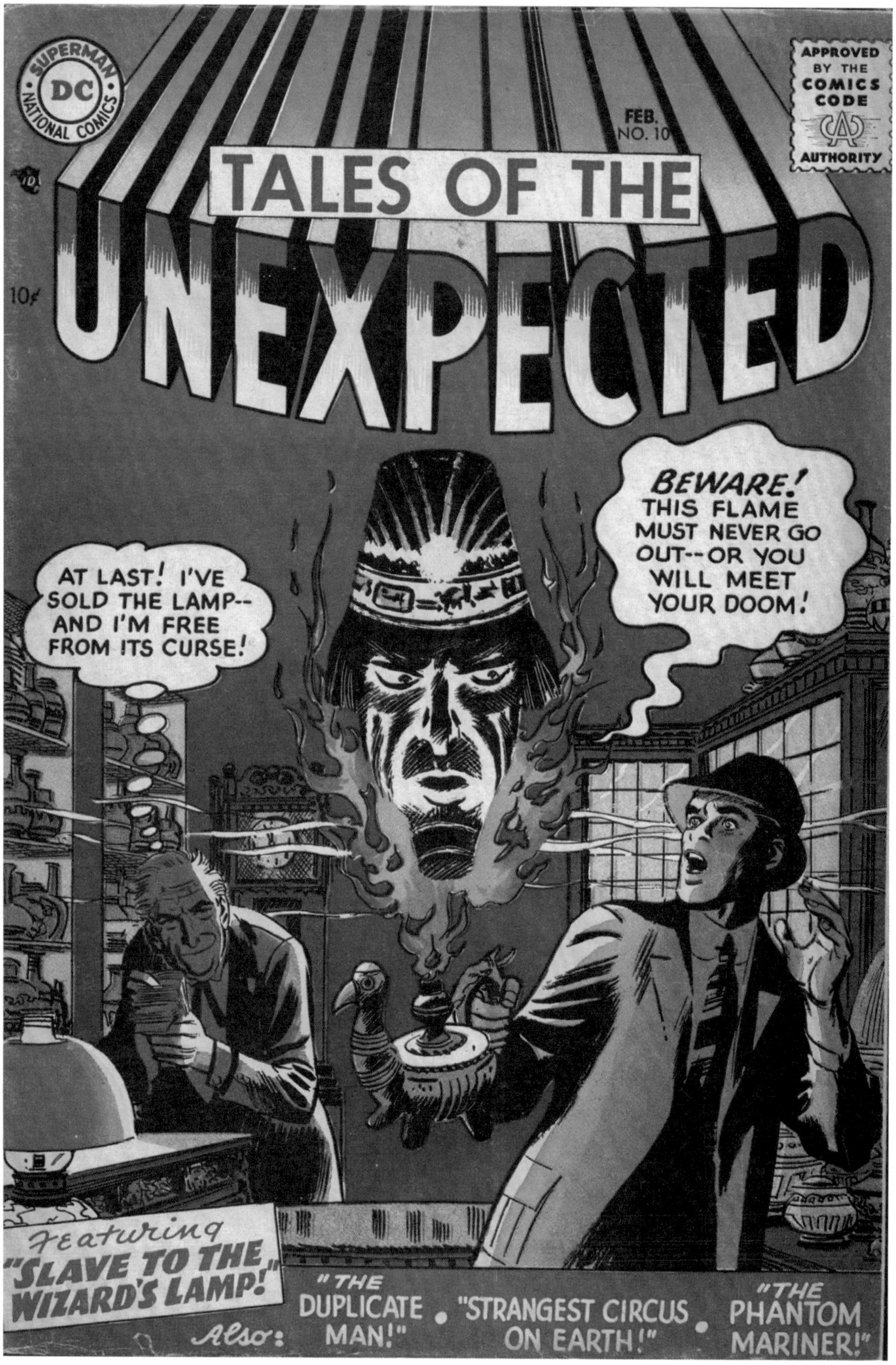
SUPERMAN DC NATIONAL COMICS
APPROVED BY THE COMICS CODE AUTHORITY
FEB. NO. 10
TALES OF THE UNEXPECTED
10¢
AT LAST! I'VE SOLD THE LAMP-- AND I'M FREE FROM ITS CURSE!
BEWARE! THIS FLAME MUST NEVER GO OUT--OR YOU WILL MEET YOUR DOOM!
Featuring "SLAVE TO THE WIZARD'S LAMP!"
Also: "THE DUPLICATE MAN!" • "STRANGEST CIRCUS ON EARTH!" • "THE PHANTOM MARINER!"

Printed cover and original artwork for *Tales of the Unexpected* #10, 1957.

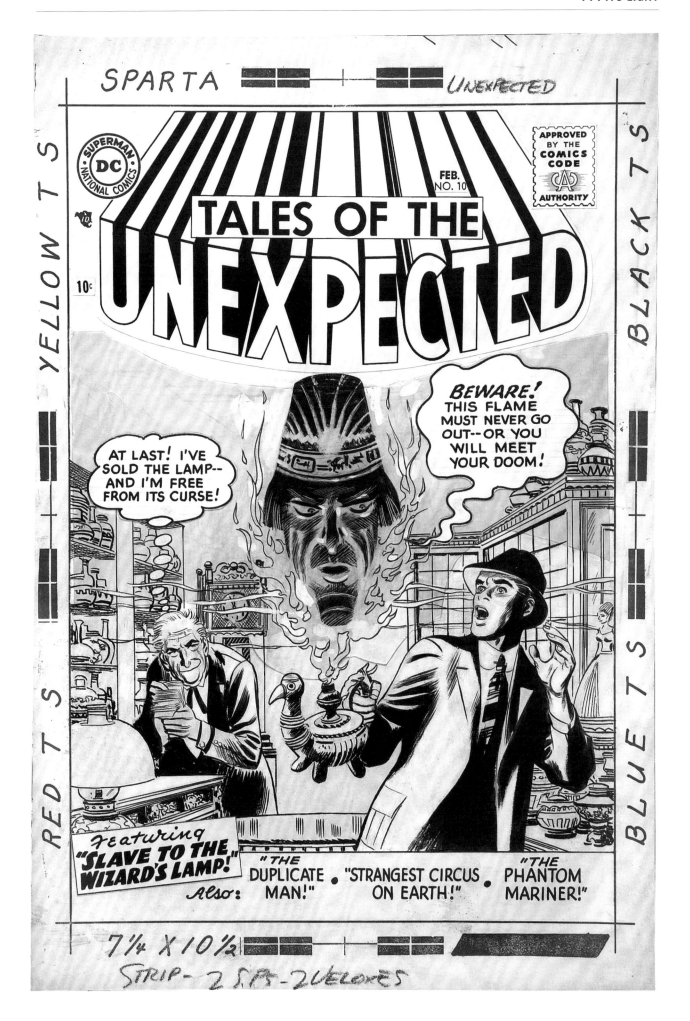

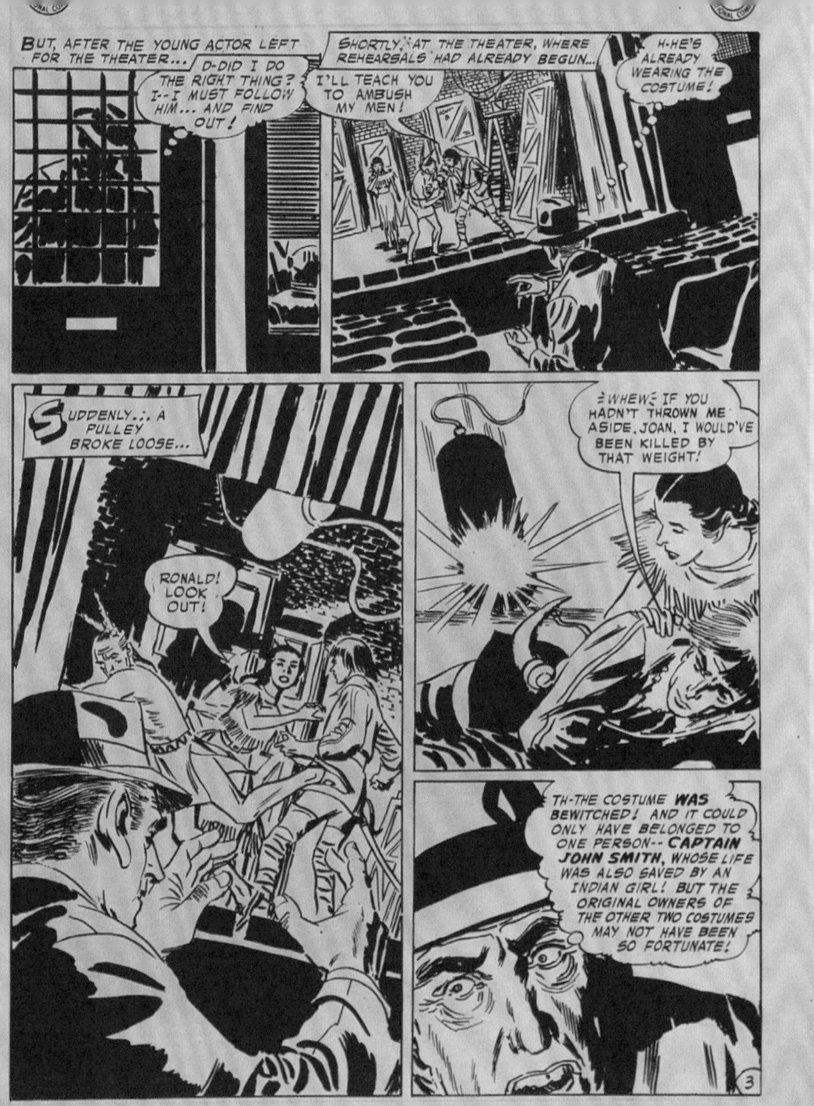
BUT, AFTER THE YOUNG ACTOR LEFT FOR THE THEATER...
D-DID I DO THE RIGHT THING? I--I MUST FOLLOW HIM... AND FIND OUT!
SHORTLY, AT THE THEATER, WHERE REHEARSALS HAD ALREADY BEGUN...
I'LL TEACH YOU TO AMBUSH MY MEN!
H-HE'S ALREADY WEARING THE COSTUME!
SUDDENLY... A PULLEY BROKE LOOSE...
RONALD! LOOK OUT!
WHEW! IF YOU HADN'T THROWN ME ASIDE, JOAN, I WOULD'VE BEEN KILLED BY THAT WEIGHT!
TH-THE COSTUME WAS BEWITCHED! AND IT COULD ONLY HAVE BELONGED TO ONE PERSON--CAPTAIN JOHN SMITH, WHOSE LIFE WAS ALSO SAVED BY AN INDIAN GIRL! BUT THE ORIGINAL OWNERS OF THE OTHER TWO COSTUMES MAY NOT HAVE BEEN SO FORTUNATE!
3

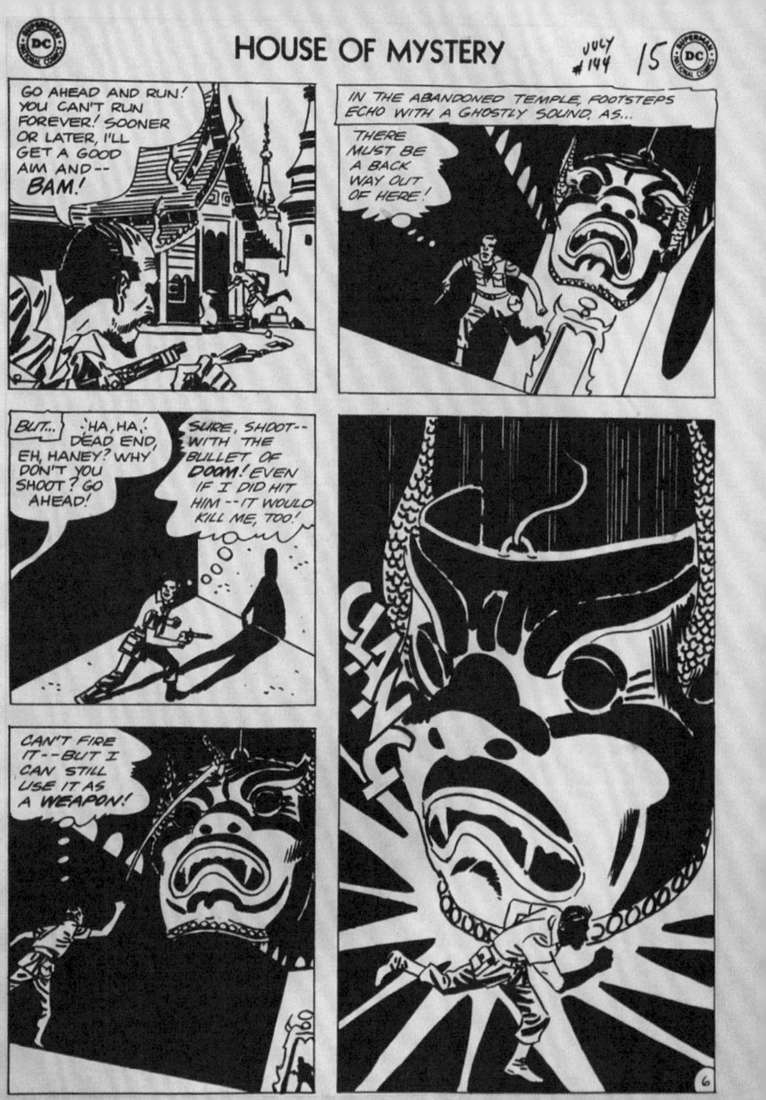
HOUSE OF MYSTERY
JULY #144
15
GO AHEAD AND RUN! YOU CAN'T RUN FOREVER! SOONER OR LATER, I'LL GET A GOOD AIM AND--BAM!
IN THE ABANDONED TEMPLE, FOOTSTEPS ECHO WITH A GHOSTLY SOUND, AS...
THERE MUST BE A BACK WAY OUT OF HERE!
BUT...
HA, HA! DEAD END, EH, HANEY? WHY DON'T YOU SHOOT? GO AHEAD!
SURE, SHOOT--WITH THE BULLET OF DOOM! EVEN IF I DID HIT HIM--IT WOULD KILL ME, TOO!
CAN'T FIRE IT--BUT I CAN STILL USE IT AS A WEAPON!
CLANG
6

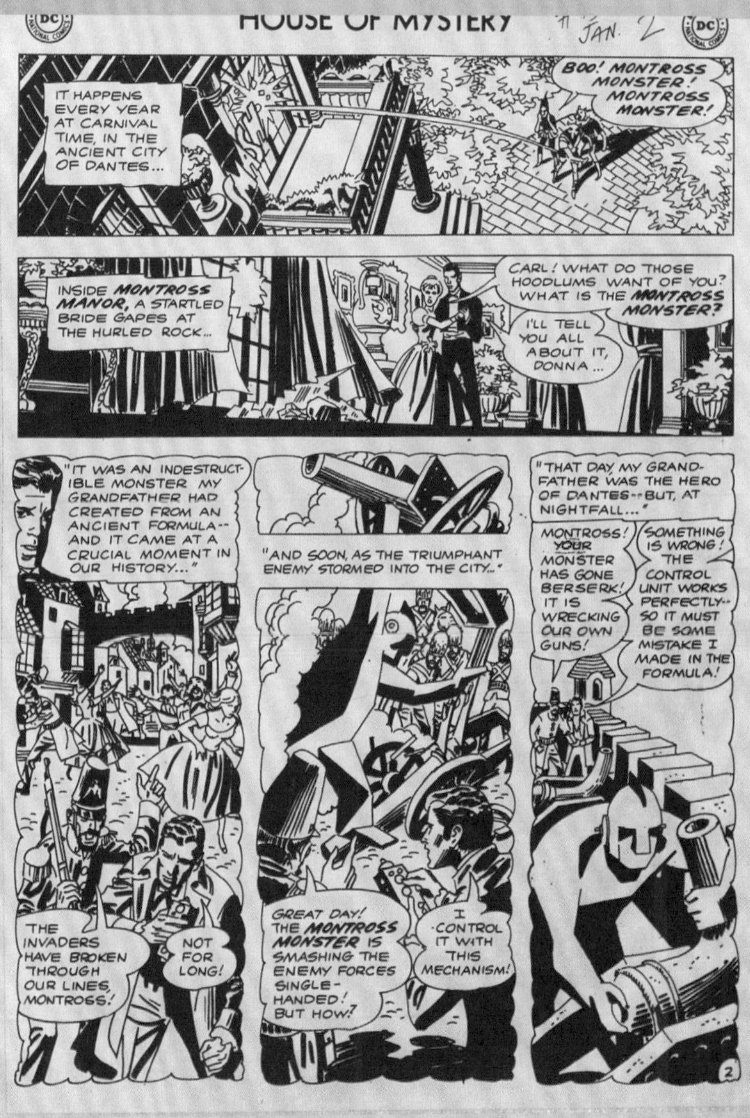
HOUSE OF MYSTERY
JAN. 2
IT HAPPENS EVERY YEAR AT CARNIVAL TIME, IN THE ANCIENT CITY OF DANTES...
BOO! MONTROSS MONSTER! MONTROSS MONSTER!
INSIDE MONTROSS MANOR, A STARTLED BRIDE GAPES AT THE HURLED ROCK...
CARL! WHAT DO THOSE HOODLUMS WANT OF YOU? WHAT IS THE MONTROSS MONSTER?
I'LL TELL YOU ALL ABOUT IT, DONNA...
"IT WAS AN INDESTRUCTIBLE MONSTER MY GRANDFATHER HAD CREATED FROM AN ANCIENT FORMULA--AND IT CAME AT A CRUCIAL MOMENT IN OUR HISTORY..."
THE INVADERS HAVE BROKEN THROUGH OUR LINES, MONTROSS!
NOT FOR LONG!
"AND SOON, AS THE TRIUMPHANT ENEMY STORMED INTO THE CITY..."
GREAT DAY! THE MONTROSS MONSTER IS SMASHING THE ENEMY FORCES SINGLE-HANDED! BUT HOW?
I CONTROL IT WITH THIS MECHANISM!
"THAT DAY MY GRANDFATHER WAS THE HERO OF DANTES--BUT, AT NIGHTFALL..."
MONTROSS! YOUR MONSTER HAS GONE BERSERK! IT IS WRECKING OUR OWN GUNS!
SOMETHING IS WRONG! THE CONTROL UNIT WORKS PERFECTLY--SO IT MUST BE SOME MISTAKE I MADE IN THE FORMULA!
2

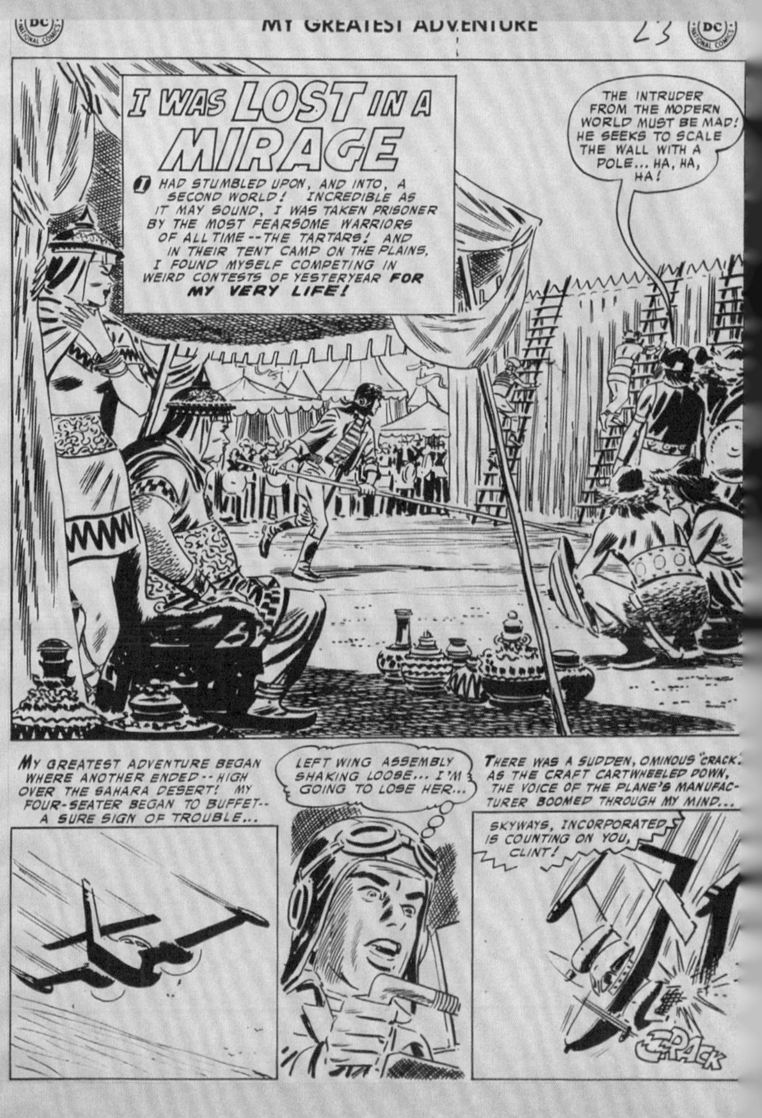
MY GREATEST ADVENTURE
23
I WAS LOST IN A MIRAGE
I HAD STUMBLED UPON, AND INTO, A SECOND WORLD! INCREDIBLE AS IT MAY SOUND, I WAS TAKEN PRISONER BY THE MOST FEARSOME WARRIORS OF ALL TIME--THE TARTARS! AND IN THEIR TENT CAMP ON THE PLAINS, I FOUND MYSELF COMPETING IN WEIRD CONTESTS OF YESTERYEAR FOR MY VERY LIFE!
THE INTRUDER FROM THE MODERN WORLD MUST BE MAD! HE SEEKS TO SCALE THE WALL WITH A POLE... HA, HA, HA!
MY GREATEST ADVENTURE BEGAN WHERE ANOTHER ENDED--HIGH OVER THE SAHARA DESERT! MY FOUR-SEATER BEGAN TO BUFFET--A SURE SIGN OF TROUBLE...
LEFT WING ASSEMBLY SHAKING LOOSE... I'M GOING TO LOSE HER...
THERE WAS A SUDDEN, OMINOUS "CRACK" AS THE CRAFT CARTWHEELED DOWN, THE VOICE OF THE PLANE'S MANUFACTURER BOOMED THROUGH MY MIND...
SKYWAYS, INCORPORATED IS COUNTING ON YOU, CLINT!
CRACK

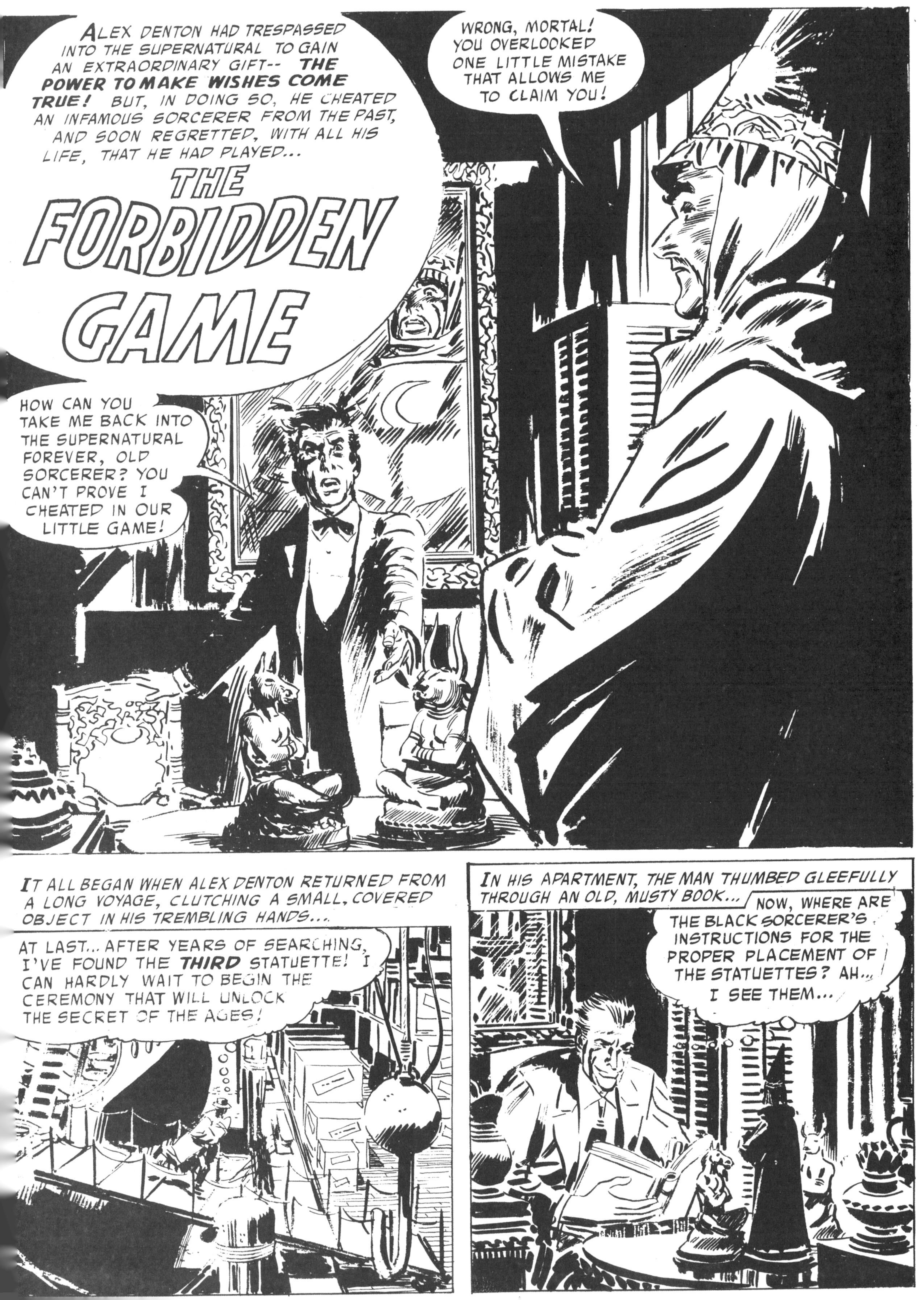
ALEX DENTON HAD TRESPASSED INTO THE SUPERNATURAL TO GAIN AN EXTRAORDINARY GIFT-- THE POWER TO MAKE WISHES COME TRUE! BUT, IN DOING SO, HE CHEATED AN INFAMOUS SORCERER FROM THE PAST, AND SOON REGRETTED, WITH ALL HIS LIFE, THAT HE HAD PLAYED...
THE FORBIDDEN GAME
WRONG, MORTAL! YOU OVERLOOKED ONE LITTLE MISTAKE THAT ALLOWS ME TO CLAIM YOU!
HOW CAN YOU TAKE ME BACK INTO THE SUPERNATURAL FOREVER, OLD SORCERER? YOU CAN'T PROVE I CHEATED IN OUR LITTLE GAME!
IT ALL BEGAN WHEN ALEX DENTON RETURNED FROM A LONG VOYAGE, CLUTCHING A SMALL, COVERED OBJECT IN HIS TREMBLING HANDS...
AT LAST... AFTER YEARS OF SEARCHING, I'VE FOUND THE THIRD STATUETTE! I CAN HARDLY WAIT TO BEGIN THE CEREMONY THAT WILL UNLOCK THE SECRET OF THE AGES!
IN HIS APARTMENT, THE MAN THUMBED GLEEFULLY THROUGH AN OLD, MUSTY BOOK...
NOW, WHERE ARE THE BLACK SORCERER'S INSTRUCTIONS FOR THE PROPER PLACEMENT OF THE STATUETTES? AH... I SEE THEM...

During those days, however, he would devote less time to discussing politics than he did in his youth, preferring to spend his little spare time creating art. He drew constantly and experimented with materials and painting technique.

Peter Meskin: "Sometimes, he would say that he wasn't an artist, just an experimenter. He was always experimenting; everything was an experiment. One of his joys was to give me his artwork because I appreciated it so much, and not just to to me, but to other members of the family, too. Dad would often tell me that it was very important to him to give me his artwork and I'd proudly hang his gifts in my home. He loved coming by and looking at them as if he were in an art gallery. He wasn't very political and didn't focus on a lot of that. He spent more time drawing. He drew constantly. He was very prolific. Dad drew and painted tons of things. He would experiment with painting materials and painting techniques and work on that. ...He called it 'love on paper'...

"During my college days when I was having my existential crises, I went to see him and Dad validated that the way I perceived the world was correct and real and was to be trusted. What he was saying to me was, 'Peter, you can philosophize about what is "real" and what isn't real, but reality is right in front of you.' He banged his fist on the table and said, 'This is real.' That's about all he said, and that was enough. It's what you feel and what you touch and experience. Trust yourself and believe in the truth of your senses and don't doubt yourself. Just because someone might have some lengthy philosophical approach to it with other confusing interpretations of reality doesn't mean that life isn't as you perceive it to be. You can read all of the existentialists like Sartre and Camus, and then you can forget about them and get on with your life. He was an interesting mix of a man. Pretty philosophical and very basic."[60]

ABOVE: Mort with Philip (top) and Peter, Cape Cod. BELOW: Meskin sketching at the Brooklyn Botanical Gardens, 1950s.

Philip Meskin: He was the one who got me into philosophy. He was an intellectual thinker who never committed. He would read voluminously: anthropology and sociology, for example. He read lots of Freud, Piaget, and others. He was heavy into Wilhelm Reich. And then, the psychology moved into Buddhism. He was very enamored by it and read extensively about it, but he never attempted to find out if it was real.[61]

Peter Meskin: He'd say that religion brought families together, that it brought cohesiveness. It was important for humans to have religion and believe in it. How strong a believer he was I really don't know. I know he believed in God but he was more of a humanist. He cared about people and thought that people did good and that they did evil but people had to be responsible for what they did."[62]

Philip agrees: "[Dad was] not a philosophical humanist; he wasn't dogmatically anything. He was just a natural humanist and gentle man. He wasn't out to hurt anyone, and to me, that's my ideal, even to this day. That's the kind of person I want to be, and I strive to interact that way with the world. Dad didn't verbalize his feelings a lot. Dad was closed to discussing certain historical details of our lives. He didn't like to talk about the robbers of the past."[63]

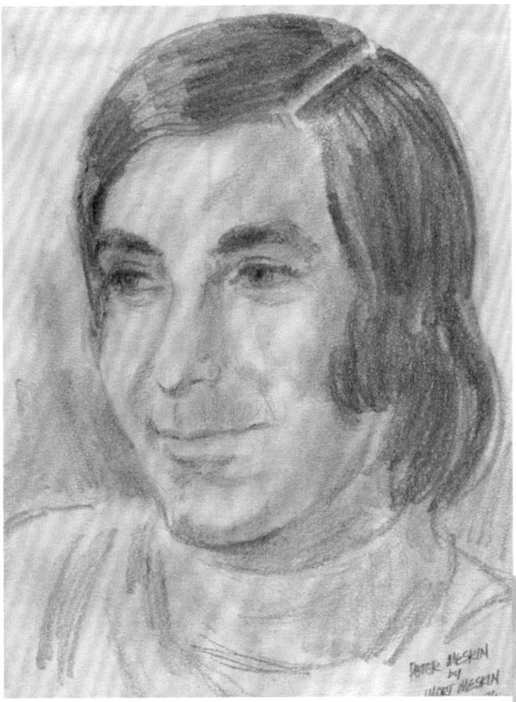
PETER MESKIN
by
MORT MESKIN

Portraits of Peter, top, and Philip, below, by Mort Meskin.

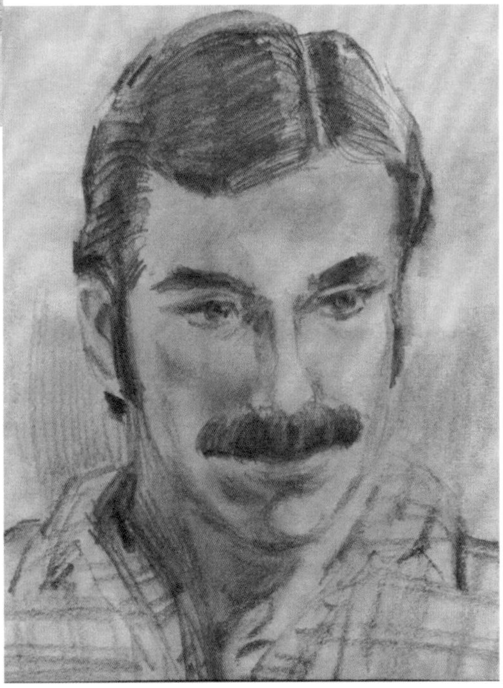

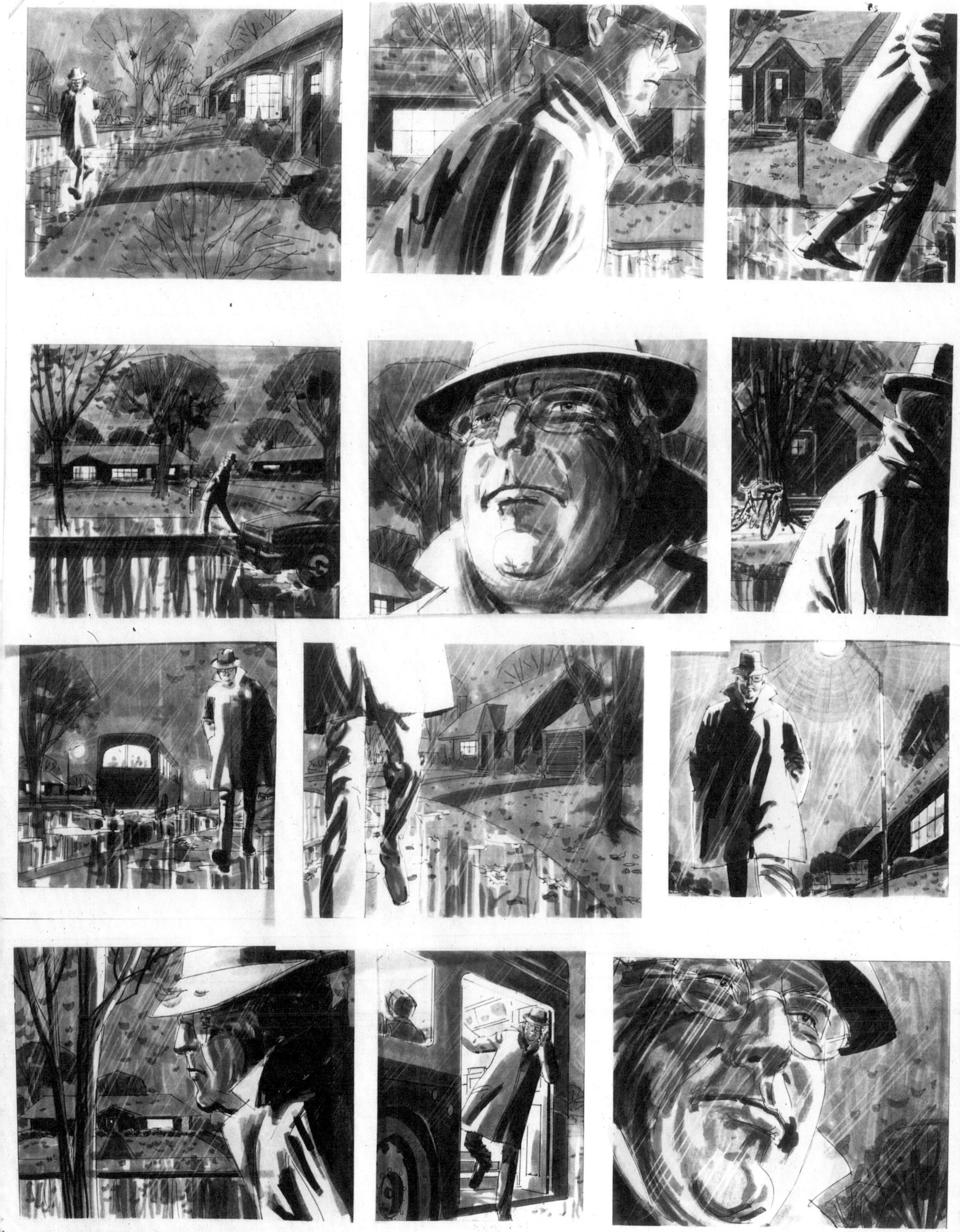

INTO THE LIGHT

In the early 1960s Meskin took up ballroom dancing. At one such dance, he was approached by Molly Saffran, who asked him to dance. At first he was reluctant, mistakenly believing her to be a "10 cents a dance" employee of the hall. But the outgoing and assertive Molly wouldn't take no for an answer. This was the first of many dances over the course of the next 30-plus years.

Molly had three children, Betty, Richard, and Helen, from her previous marriage. She was a strong, matriarchal woman and very protective of the more passive Mort. Molly helped him get off medication, and according to Peter, "He became much more alive and self-assured with Molly. It worked for him."

Philip Meskin: "It was Molly who had a major impact on his life. He went from living in an apartment by himself in Greenwich Village, which to me had some charm. But getting together with Molly was a life-enhancing thing for him. He and Molly had a mutually beneficial relationship. They were in love."[64] Eventually he even lost his stutter.

Peter Meskin: "I can see in some of Dad's work when he was trying to solve emotional problems. I have a lot of paintings of faces, faces within faces... trying to discover who he was and how he was feeling. He was working his way back from not having been well to getting his balance in the world again. From there, he gradually got better and better. He met his second wife, Molly, and had a very good relationship with her. She helped him to get better and to recover. Molly was really the best thing that happened to my father in the second part of his life."[65] Philip Meskin: "He always had a drawing pad with him and made thousands of little drawings."[66]

Peter Meskin: "He'd go through phases. He'd get into what I call his Haikus, very Japanese-inspired art. He'd do it with markers and did hundreds of them, lovely, charming little things. He experimented so much that he'd mix things out of the medicine cabinet and the kitchen. Molly's son Richard is a doctor, and he once went to an Army-Navy store and bought Dad a gas mask because some of the things he was mixing were poisonous. As a joke, Richard came in wearing a gas mask and gave it to my dad."[67]

Peter Meskin: "He needed the right mate and unfortunately, my real mother wasn't that for him in the long run and Molly was. He needed a strong woman to help him make decisions and to help guide him through life. Molly was able to do that for him. She was a strong woman and they were very much in love. Sometimes the chemistry just doesn't work, although I must tell you that in my early years, my parents were very loving towards us and

ABOVE: Mort and Molly. LEFT: Storyboard art for DDBO. Using a system called Animatics, the storyboards would then be crudely animated in order to sell the clients on the concepts for television commercials.

each other and everything seemed hunky-dory, as my mother would say, to me."[68]

Meskin remained at DC for ten years. This later period saw the superhero revival brought about in part by the 1950s revamp of *The Flash*, whose co-creator Carmine Infantino credits Mort with influencing his approach. Shortly afterward the superhero "Silver Age" would be in full swing: *Justice League of America*, *Green Lantern*, and *The Atom* at DC; *Fantastic Four*, *The Hulk*, *The Avengers*, and *The X-Men* at the newly reconstituted Marvel, thanks to co-creators Jack Kirby and Stan Lee. Marvel's biggest success would soon become *Spider-Man*, with a decidedly Meskin feel, thanks to former S&K studio mate and former Robinson student Steve Ditko. One would think Meskin would have been a natural to participate in the genre he had helped found, but instead he was kept on anthology books by editors who were either blind to, or jealous of, his talent.

By 1965 Meskin had enough. Marvin Stein, a fellow artist from his Simon & Kirby days, had left comics in 1958 for the more lucrative field of advertising and in 1961 he landed at the advertising agency Batten, Barton, Durstine & Osborn as a storyboard artist and illustrator. Stein recalled, "The industry realized the value of ex-comic book artists when it came to storyboarding, because all the commercials are pre-sketched." By 1965 Stein was ready to head into animation (he was also illustrating the comic strip *McGurk's Mog* with Bud Wexler for *New York Newsday*) and told Meskin about the open position. Meskin was immediately hired, and was soon working on national campaigns for such clients as Pepsi, Schaeffer Beer, General Electric, and a roster of blue chip companies.

RIGHT: Storyboard art for Pepsi. Meskin worked with markers during this period, although he continued to experiment with other media as well.

According to George Roussos, Meskin "moves things around, almost like in movie pictures. That's what they liked about him at the agency; they asked him to do that Johnny Quick type of action when they needed to show a product and the movement it was taking.

"He thought there was a future here. He wanted a steady job, he felt he could make an income, and then social security and retirement. They liked him and respected him, he was a damn good artist and he fit into that business beautifully. They recognized a good artist. The agency used to pay good money, they were dealing with national accounts and they wanted the best artwork possible."[69] Stein concurs: "The talent that came into the agencies was fantastic." [70] Charles Biro, Noel Sickles, George Olesen, Martin Nodell, Art Saaf, and Joe Simon were among the many who migrated over from comics.

Alphonse Normandia, BBD&O Chief: "I used to like hiring guys from comics because they were so used to working long hours for no money. There was no money on those [comics]—what was it, 10 bucks a page? Mort thought he died and went to heaven. He'd be here 2 in the morning, 3 in the morning, 'Oh, what a

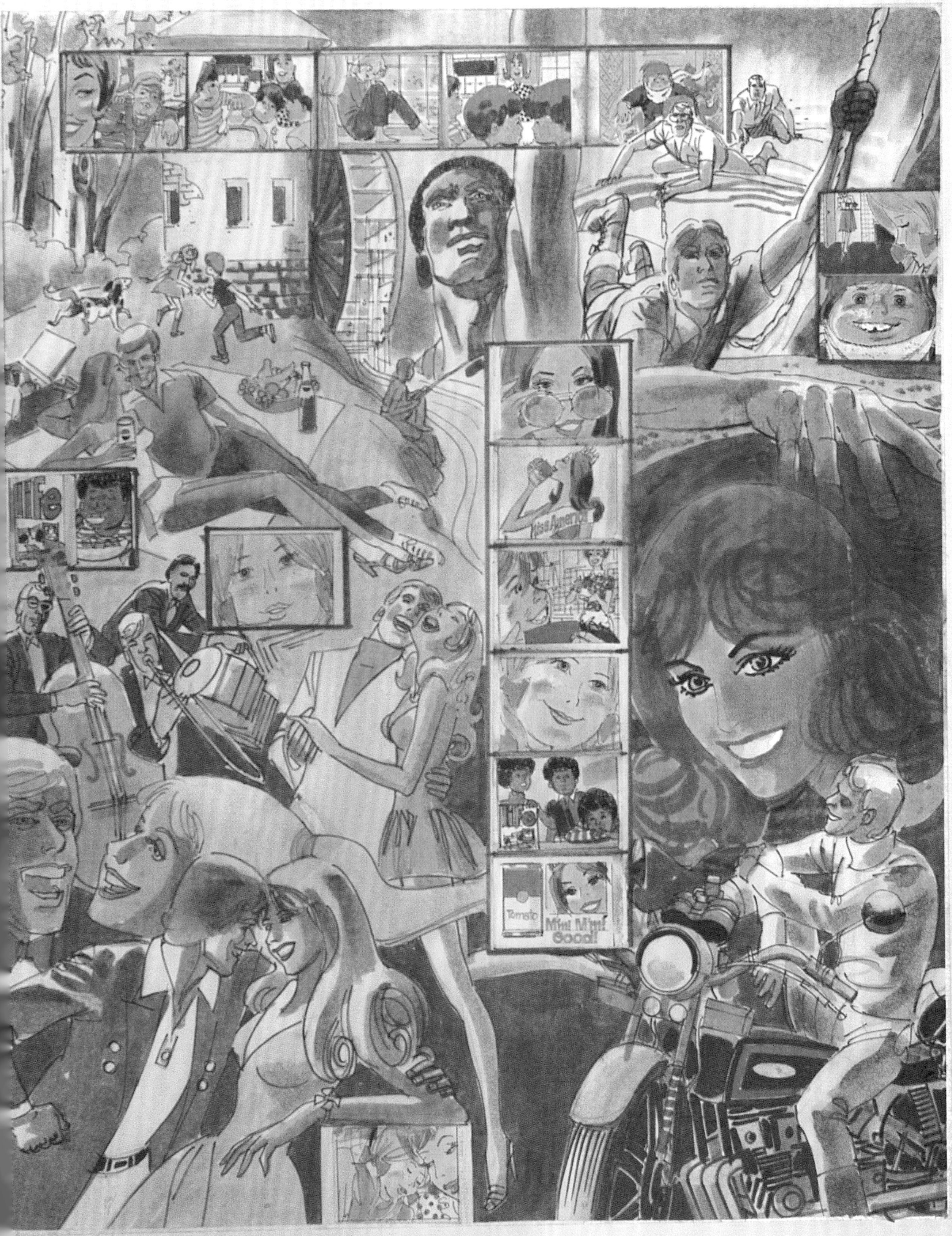
Tomato
M'm! M'm!
Good!

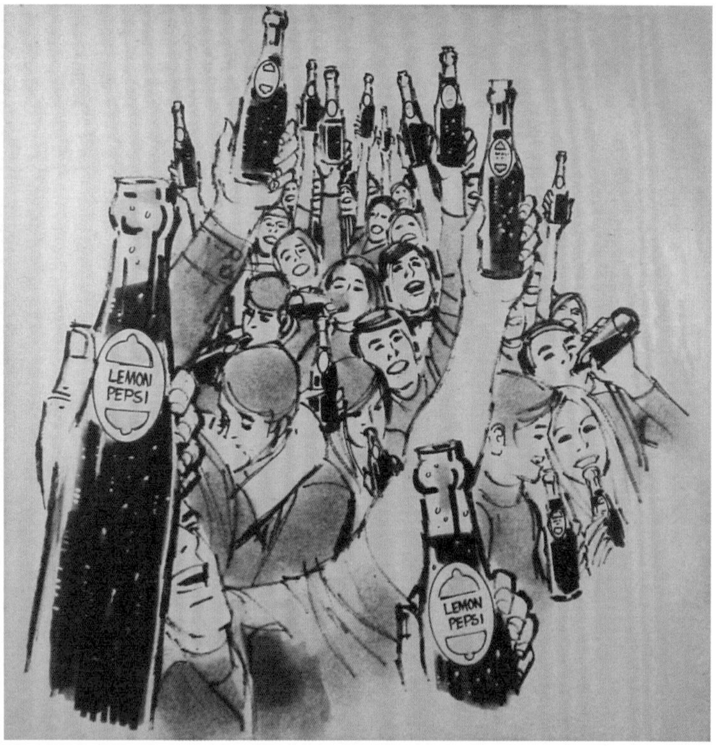
LEMON PEPSI
LEMON PEPSI

THIS SPREAD AND NEXT: Meskin worked on print ads as well, here again for Pepsi. His marker comps (short for "comprehesive layouts") would be used to sell the client on the concept and design of the ad, for photographers and designers to follow.

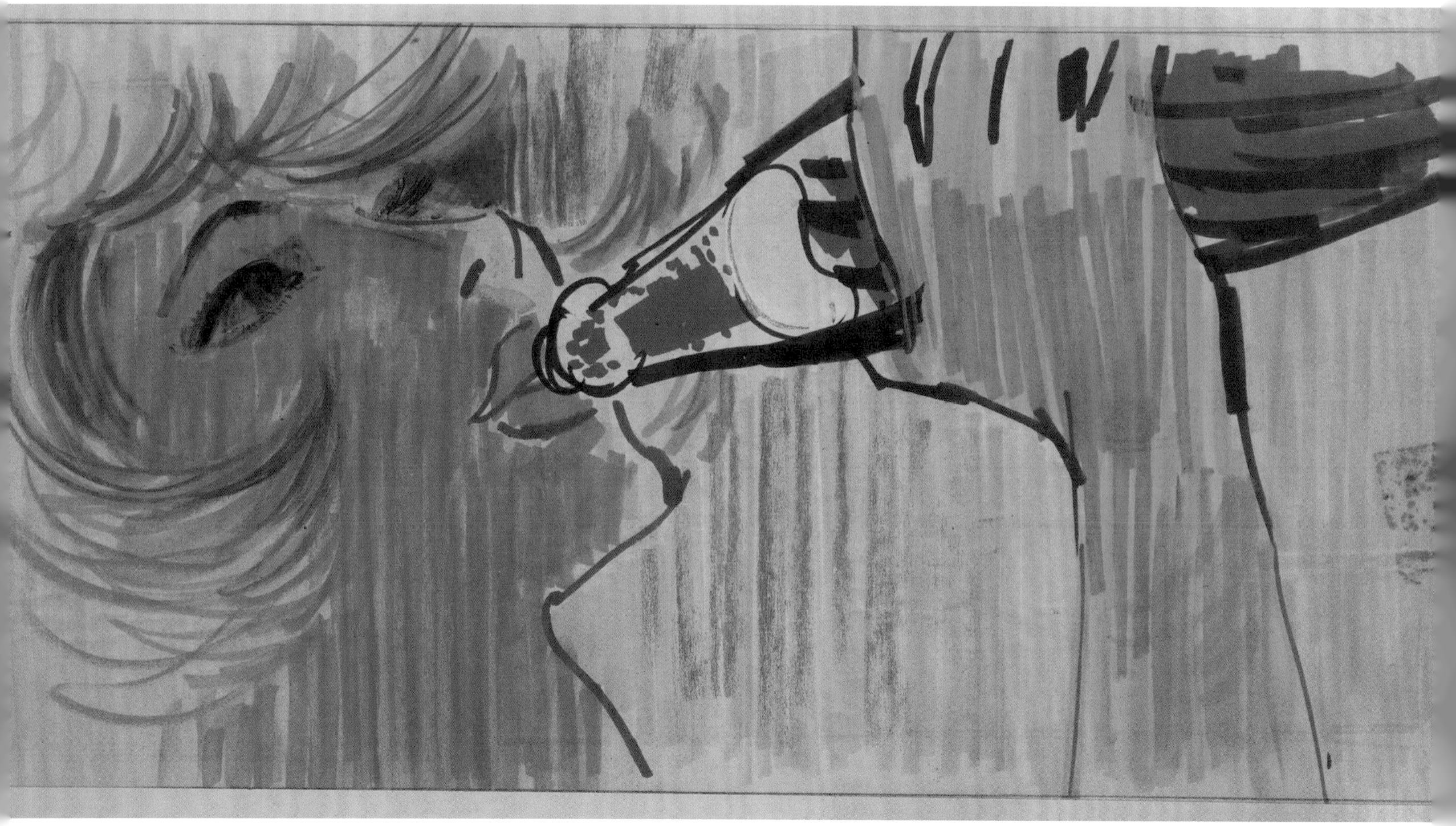

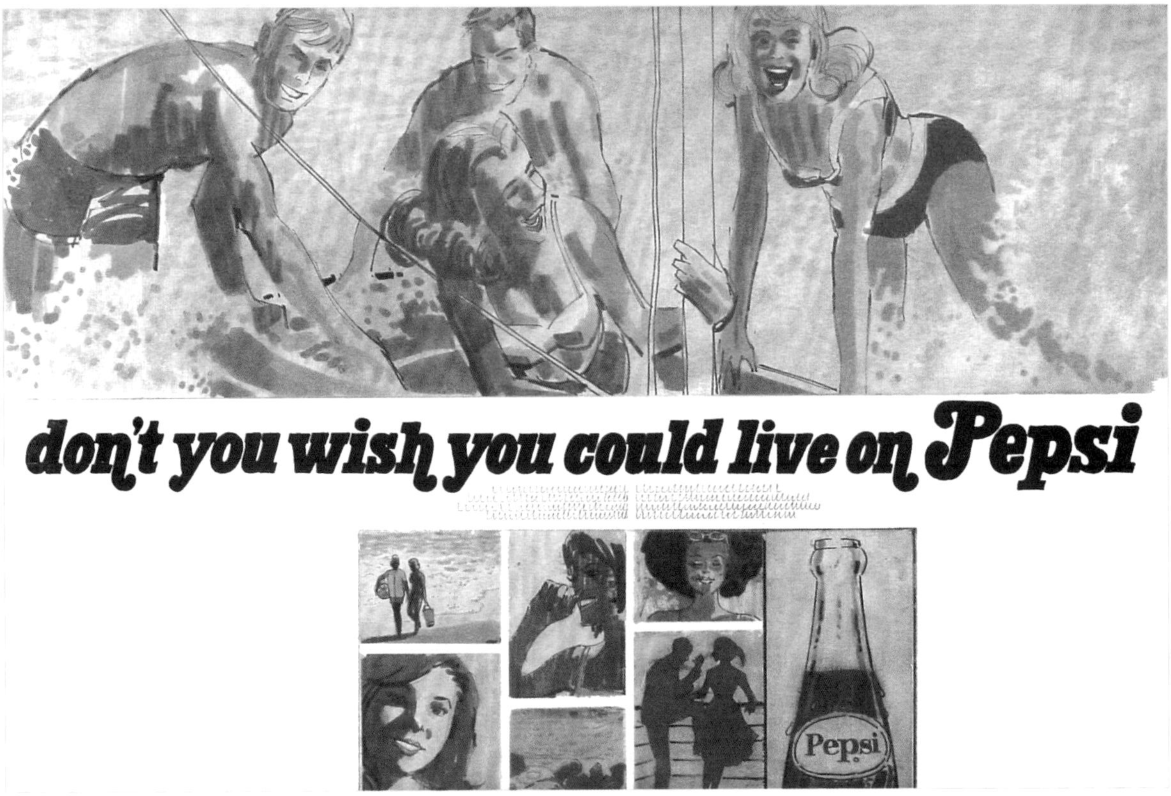
don't you wish you could live on Pepsi
Pepsi

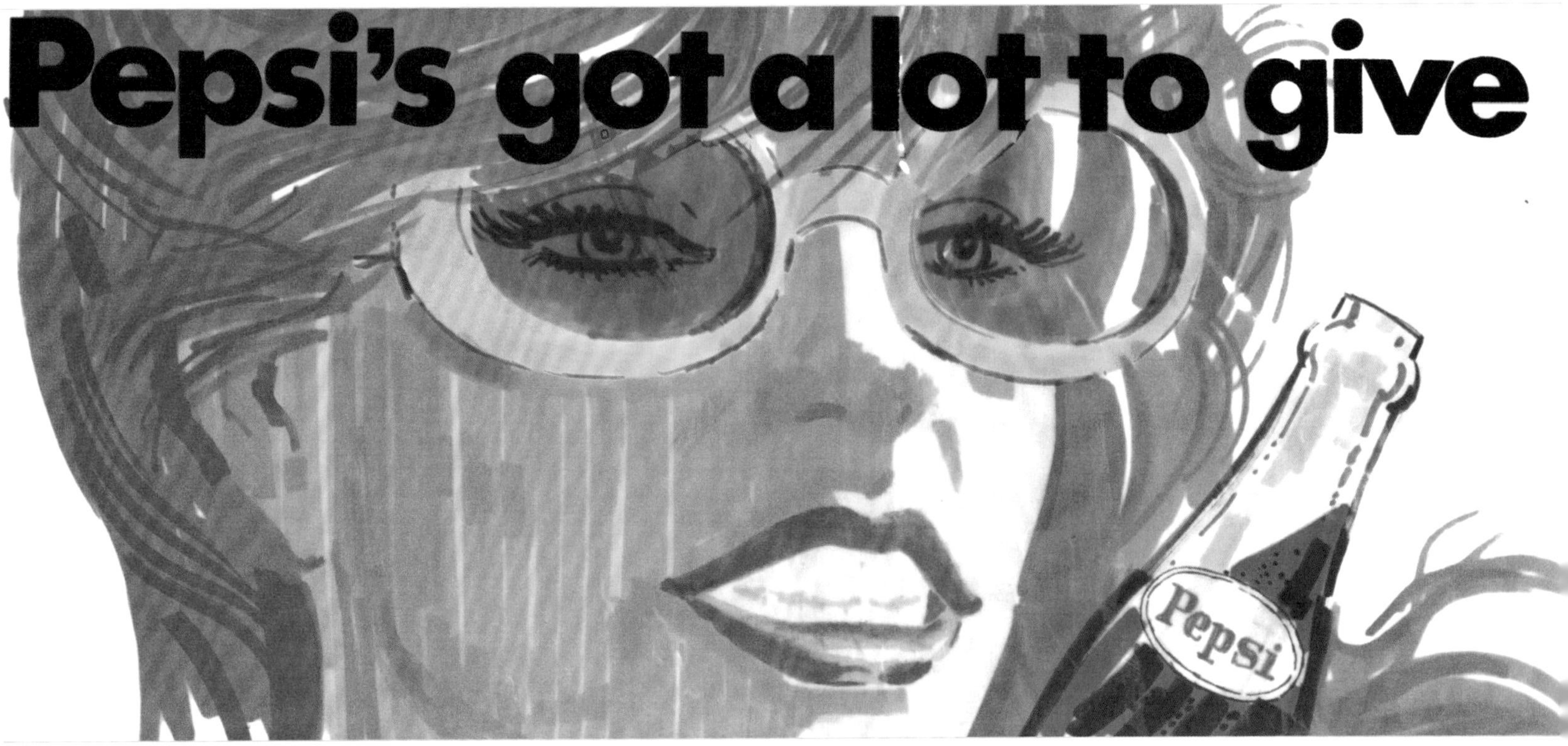
Pepsi's got a lot to give
Pepsi

DIET PEPS[I]
someone will be
watching...

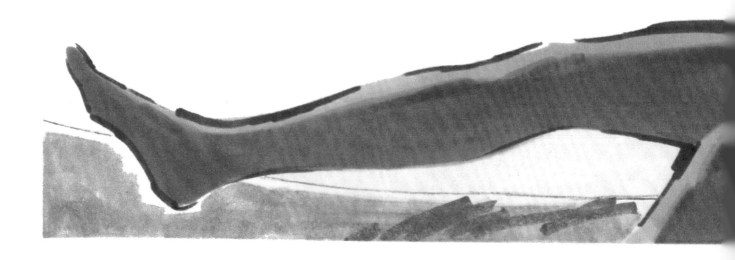

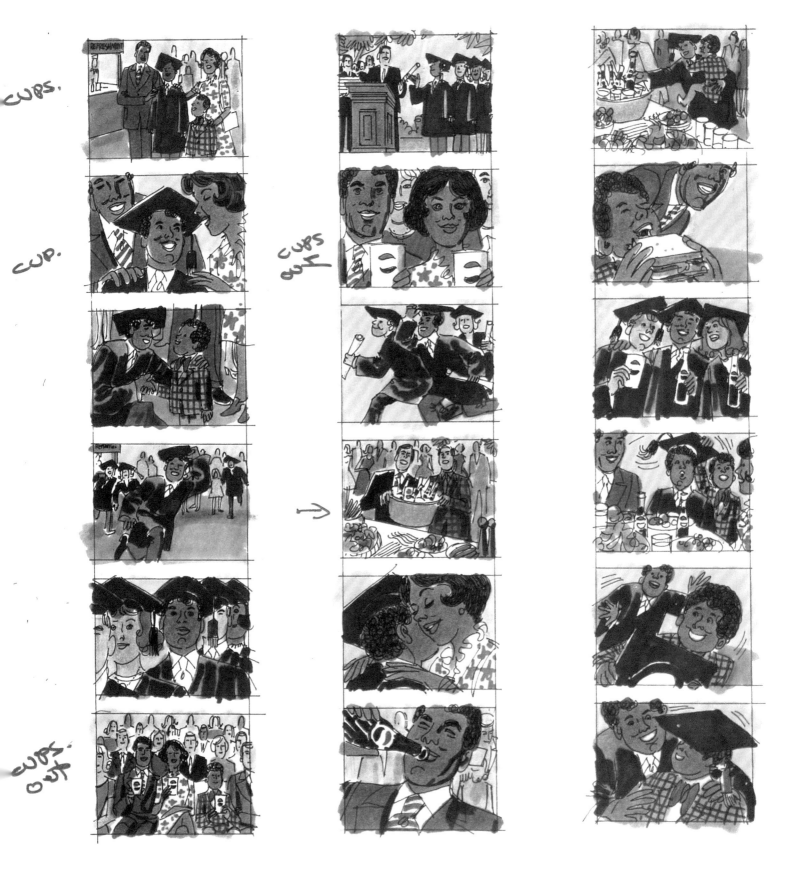

CUPS.

CUP.

CUPS OUT.

CUPS OUT

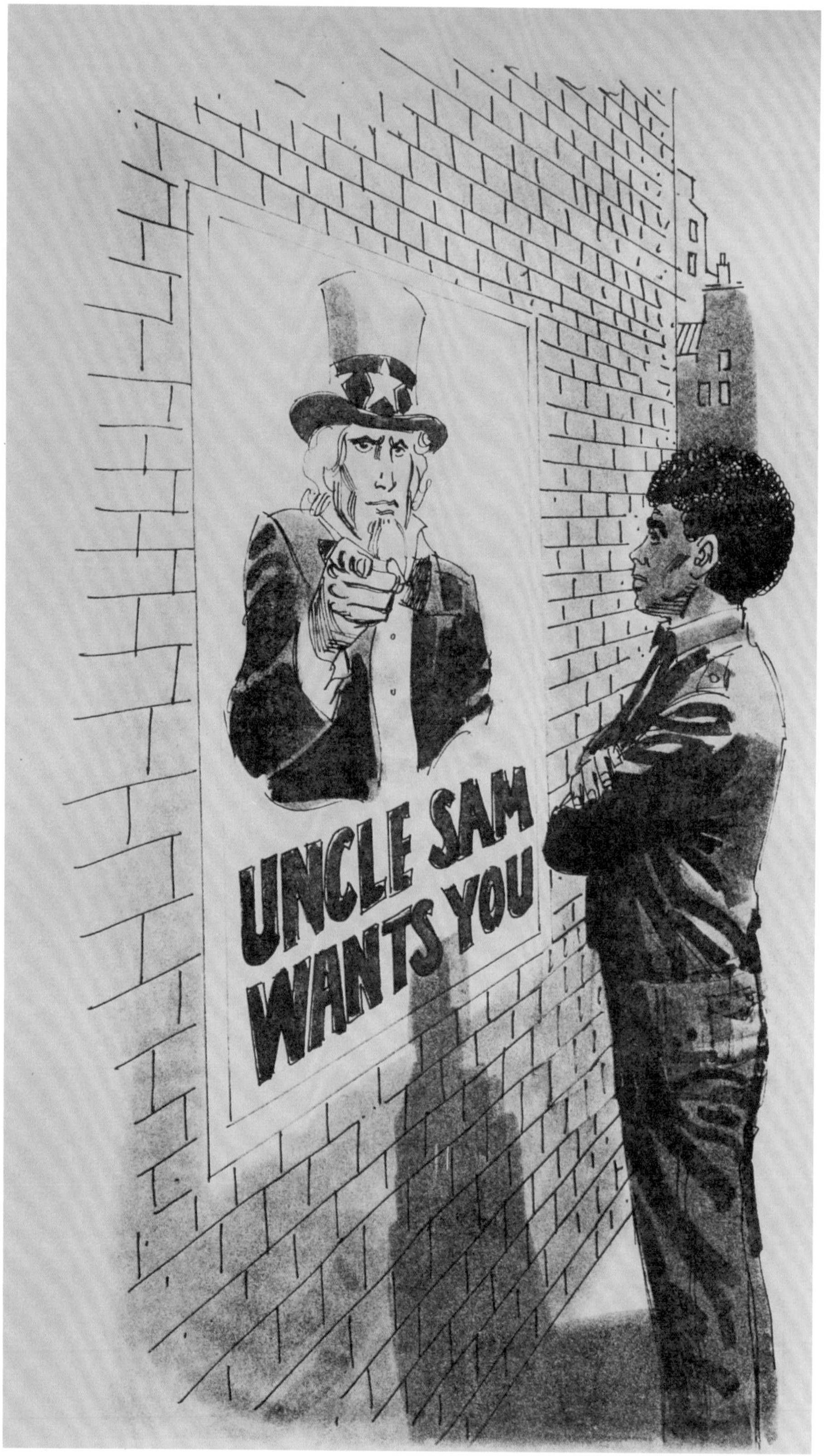
UNCLE SAM
WANTS YOU

NEW YORK: HELP WANTED
FIRST NATIONAL CITY

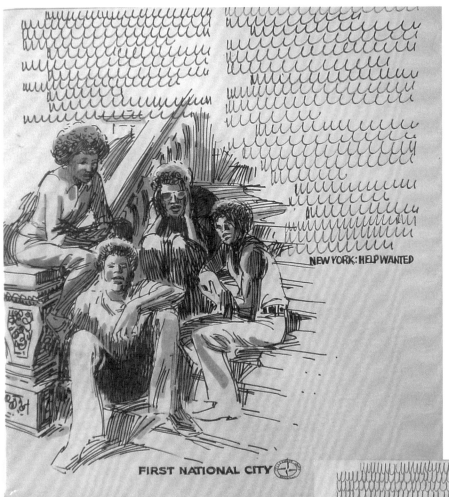

For black-and-white newspaper ads Meskin worked in pen and ink and wash.

NEW YORK: HELP WANTED
FIRST NATIONAL CITY

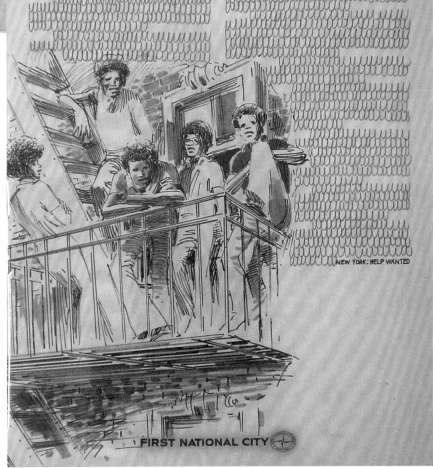

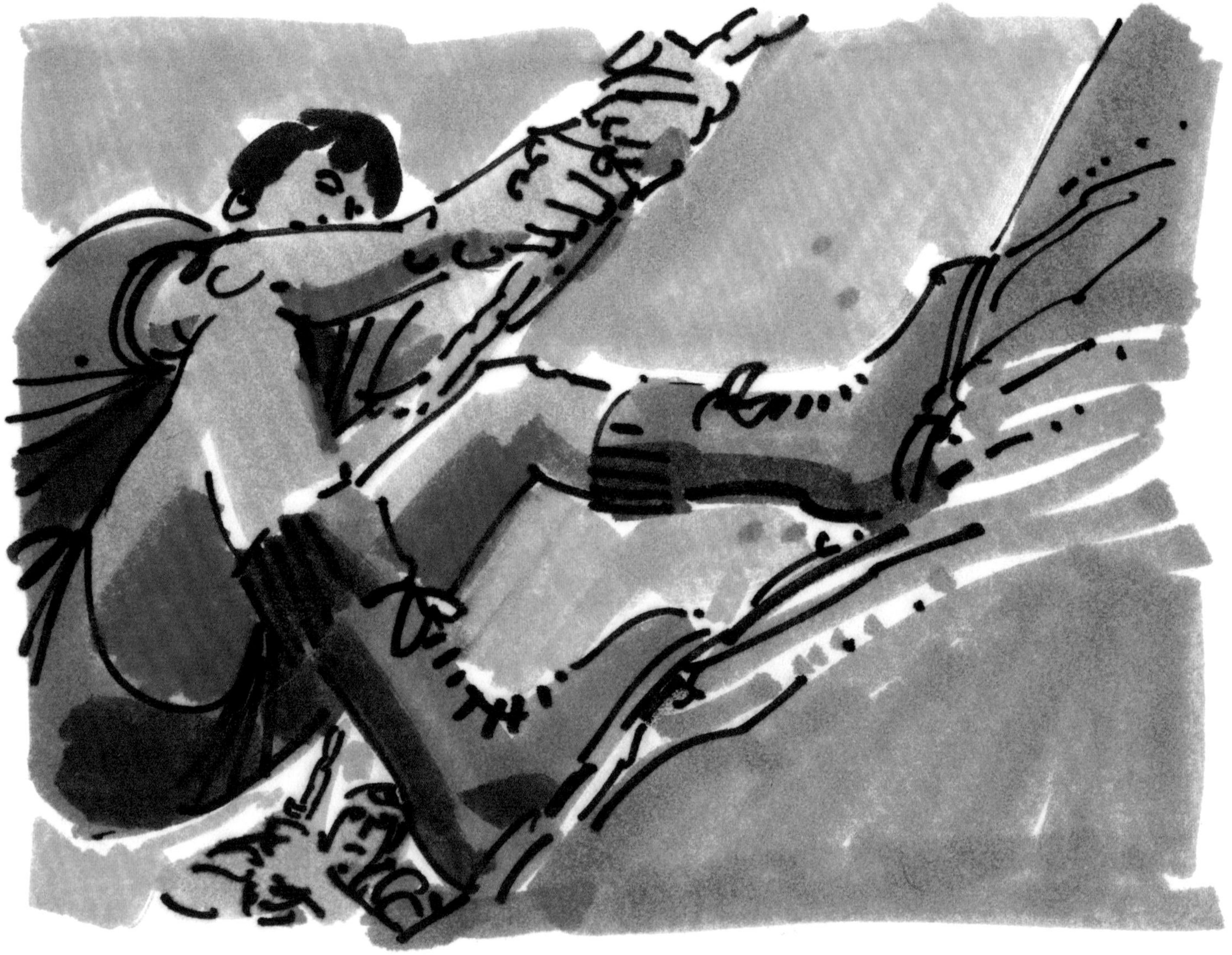

As evidenced by these storyboard details, Meskin had not lost his flair for action.

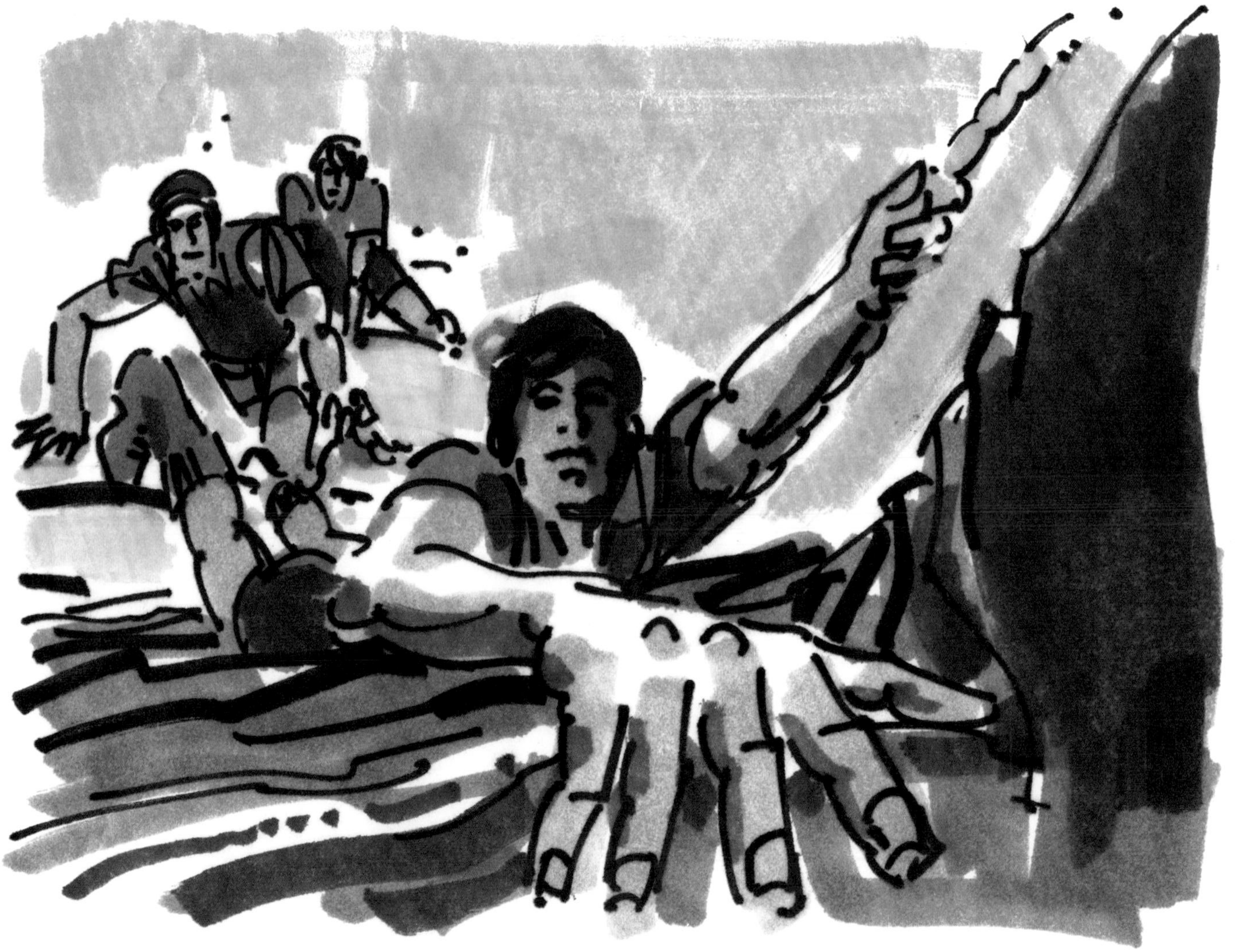

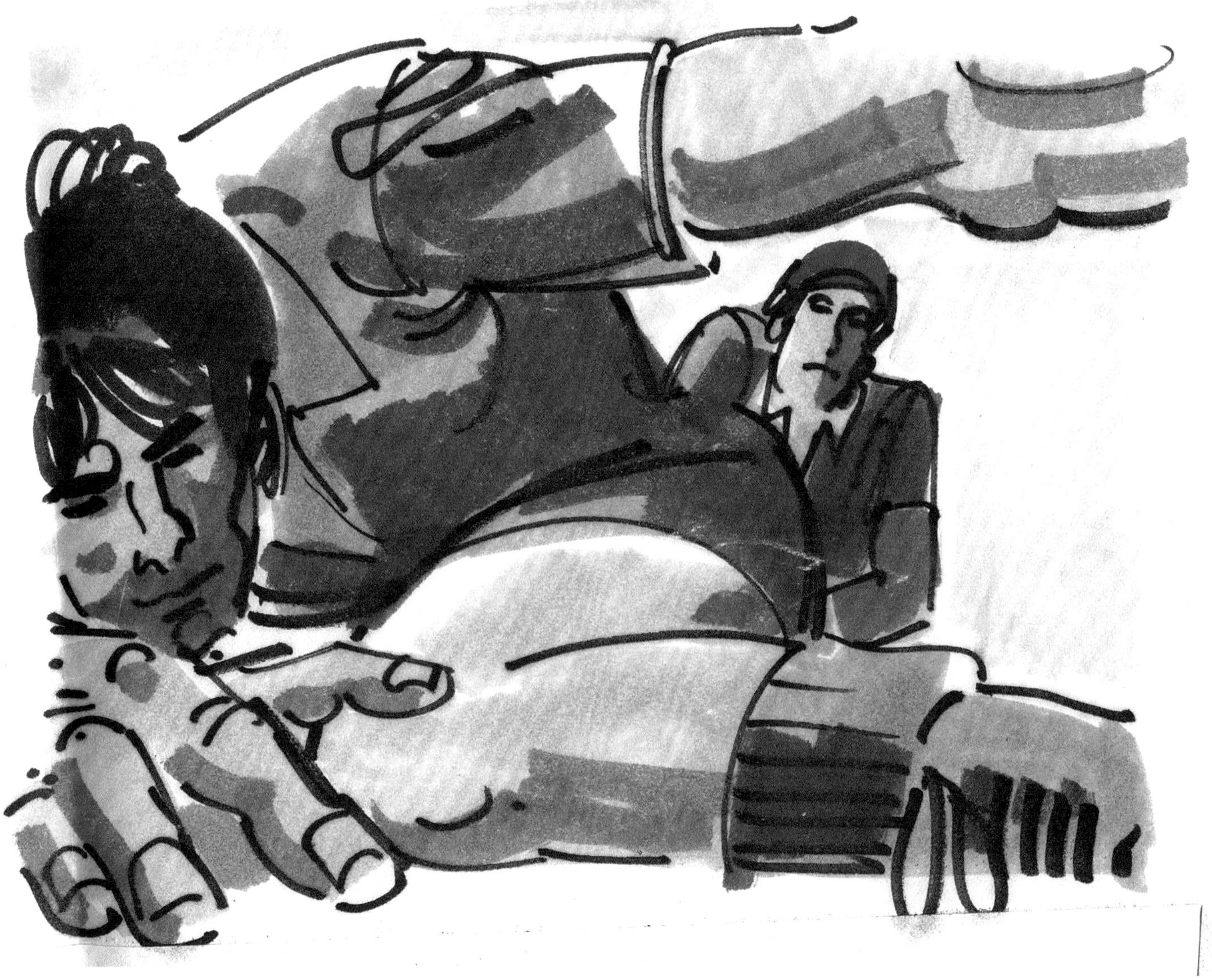

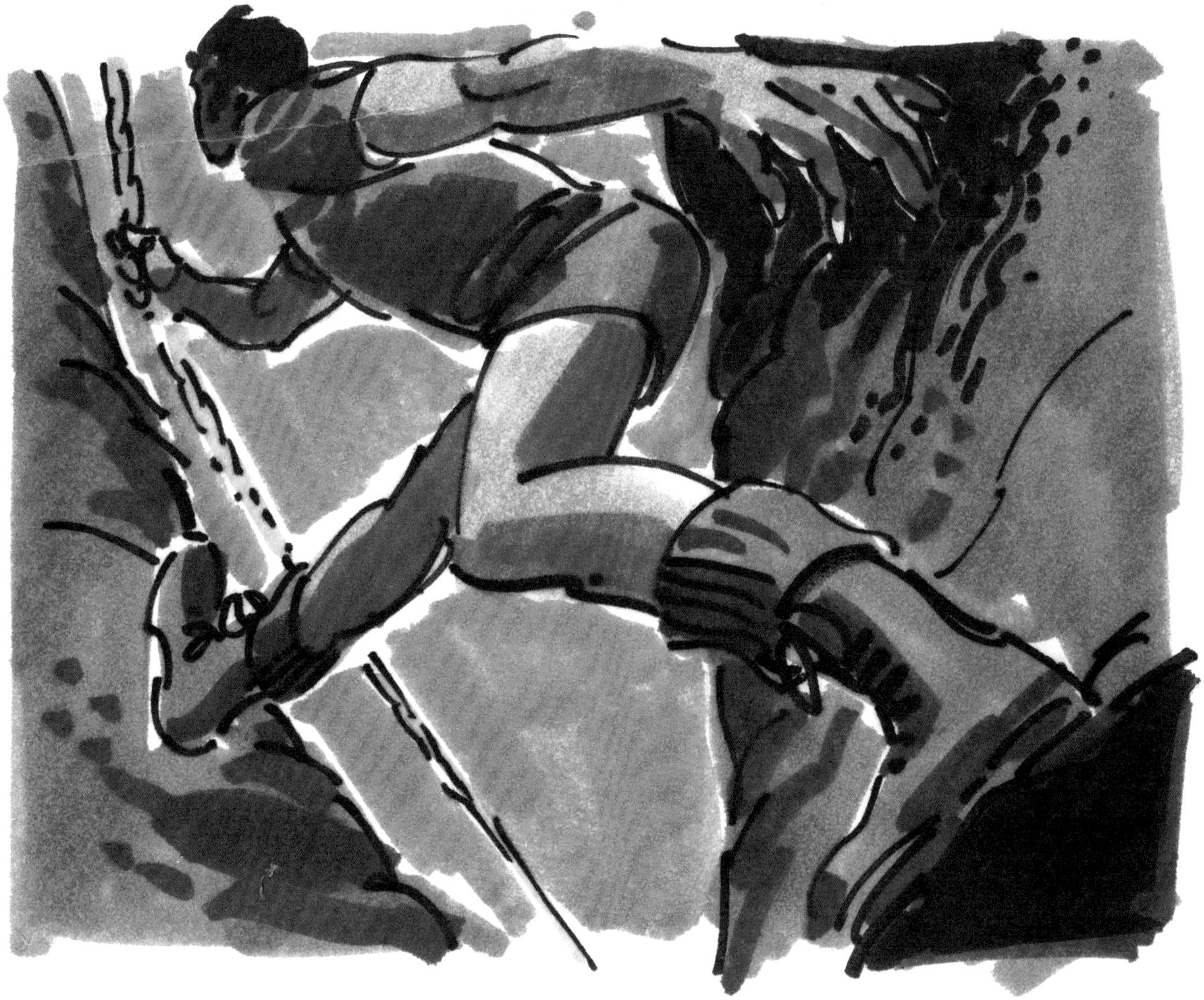

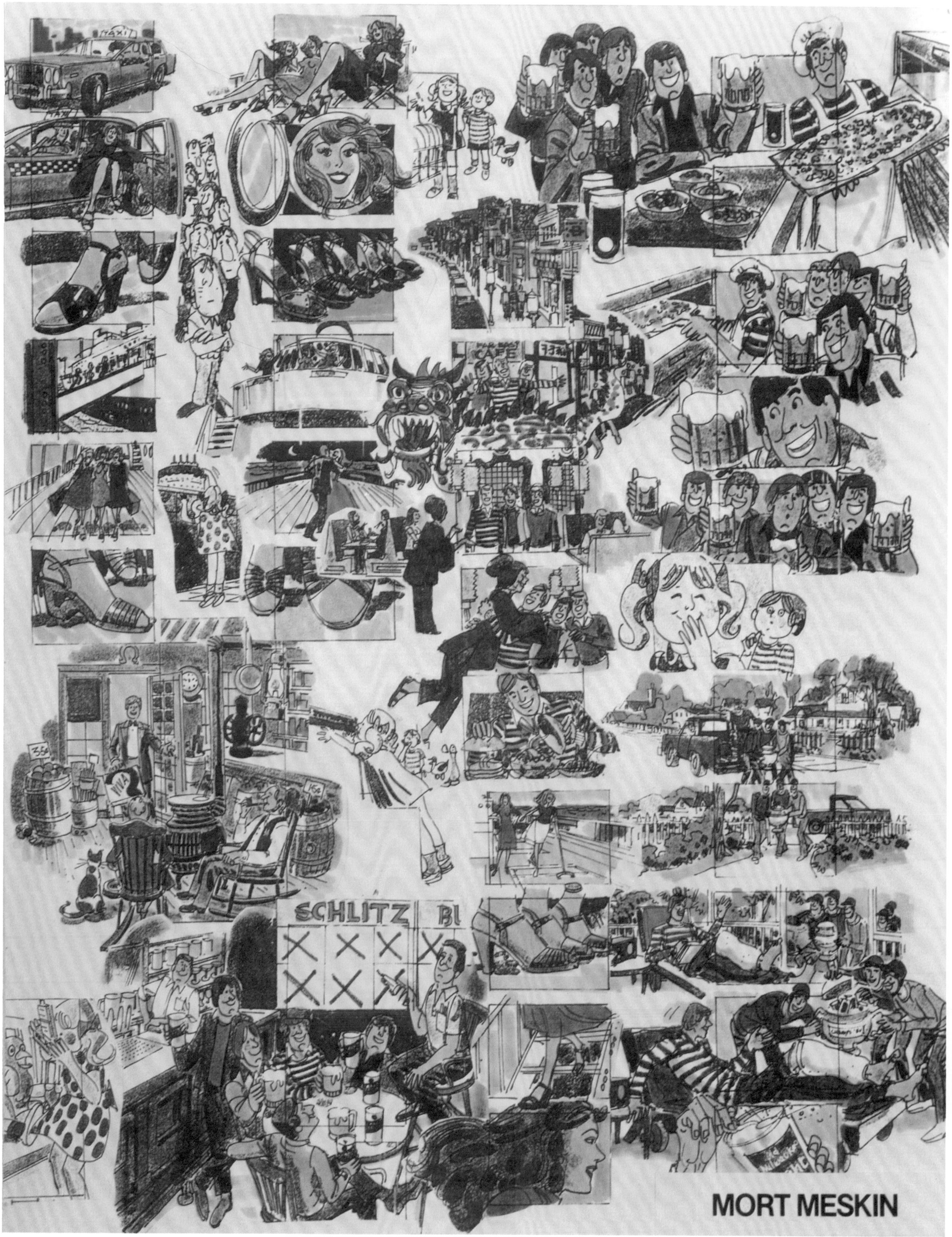
TAXI
CAFE
SCHLITZ
MORT MESKIN

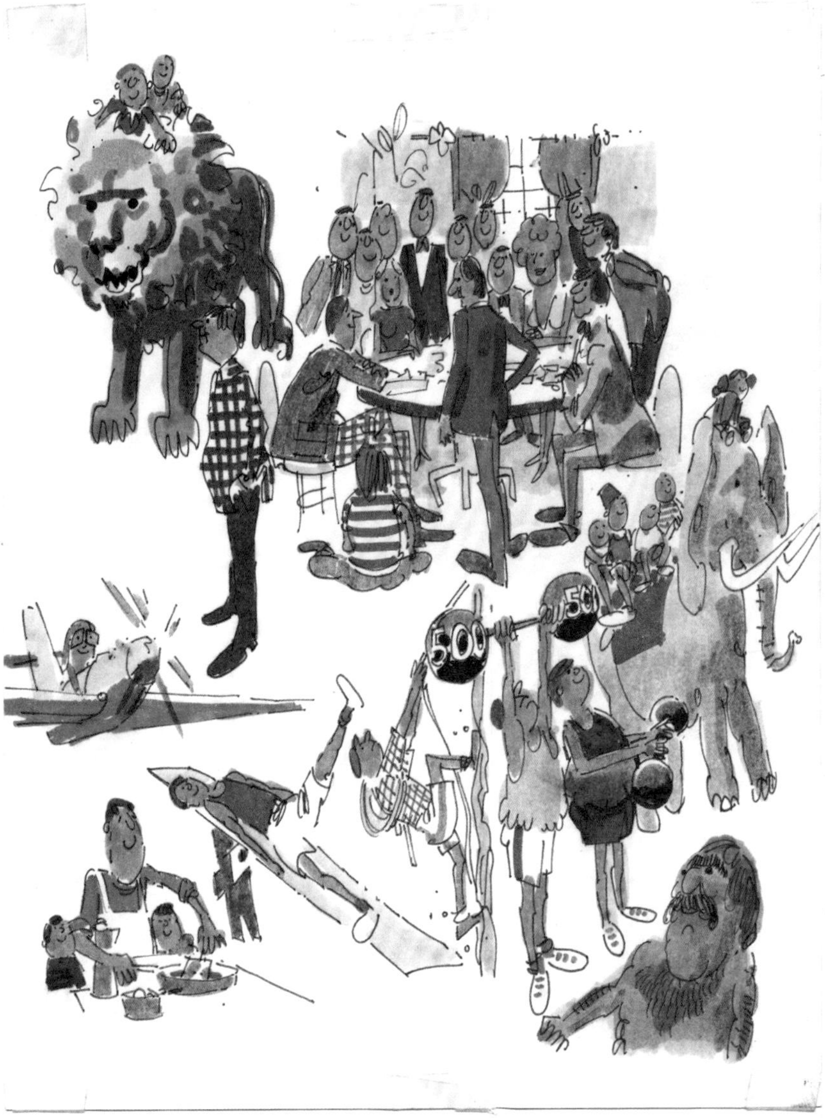
500
50

Meskin was so comfortable working in a cartoon style during his advertising years, one wonders why he didn't do more humor comic books.

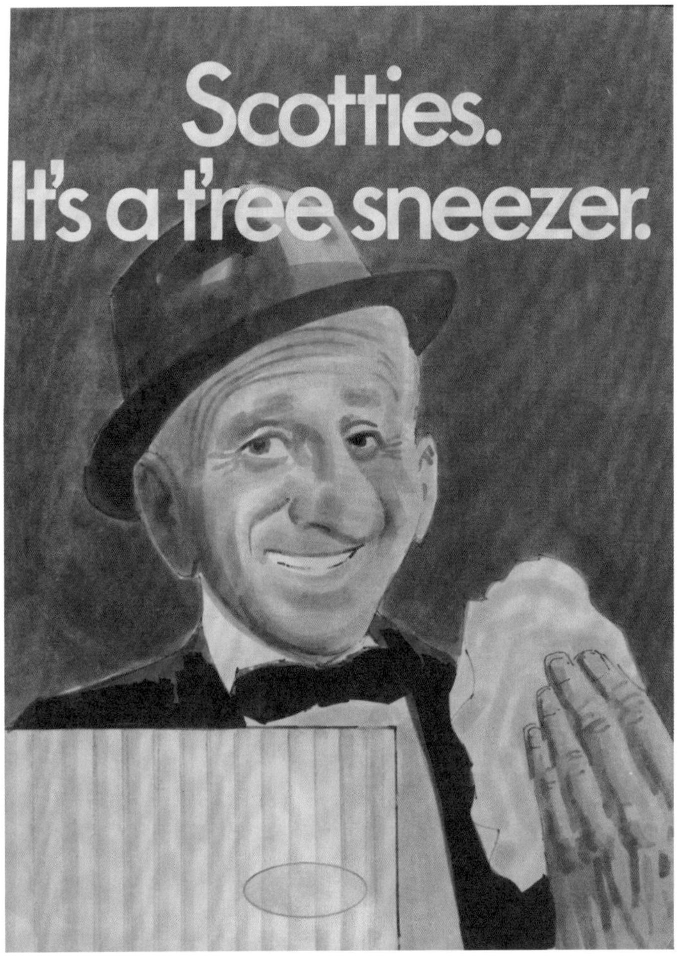
Scotties.
It's a t'ree sneezer.

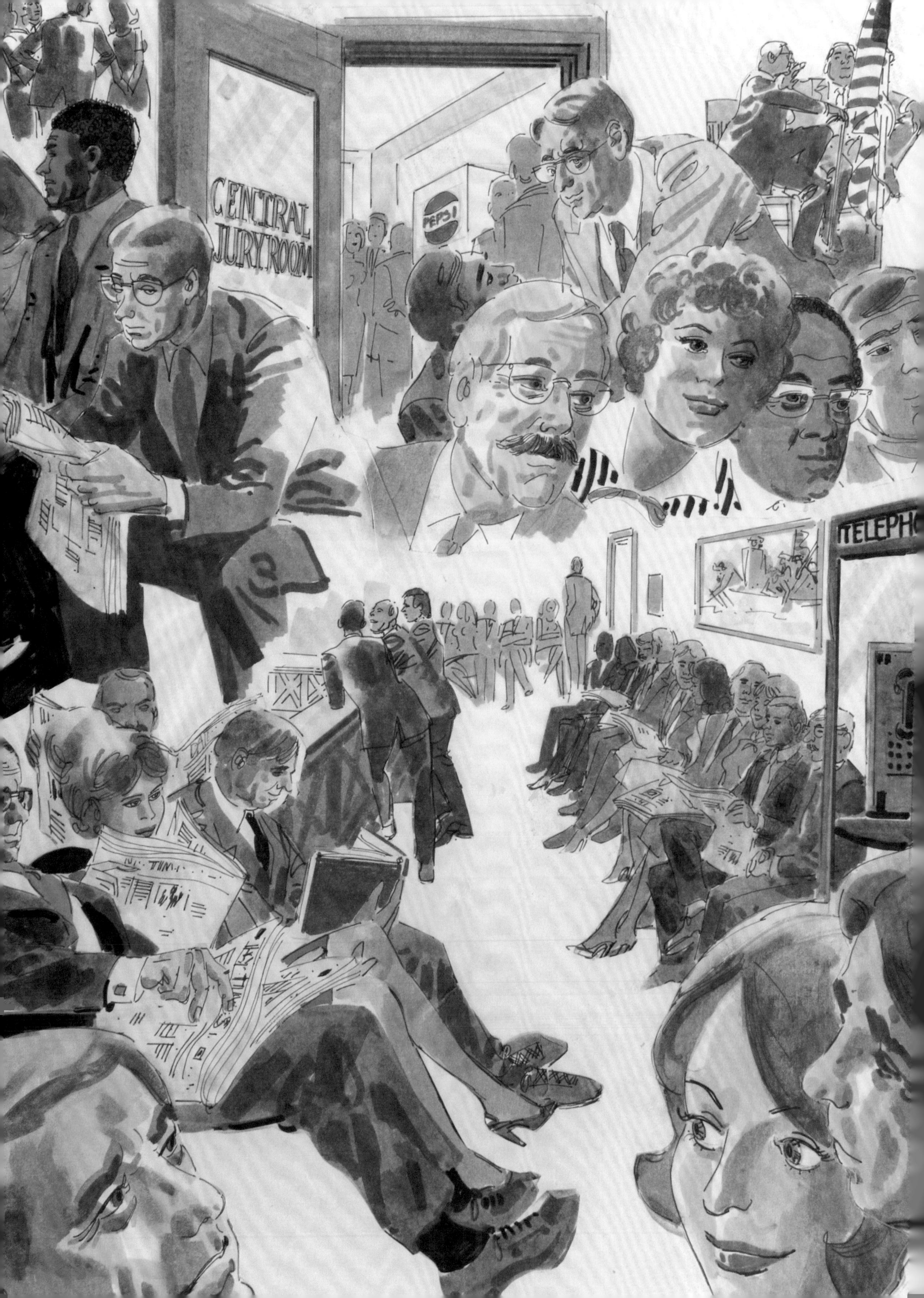
CENTRAL JURY ROOM
PEPSI
TELEPHO

great job this is.' He really thought he had the world conned."

Art Director Leslie Avery Gould: "He was very fast. And he also was more willing to get it out when you needed it. For some people that was too much pressure. Maybe it was a challenge for him. I don't know what would make somebody do that, it may have been the person asking, knowing that somebody respected his work."[71]

Jerry Robinson: "[Mort] could steel himself, just like when he was turning out all those [comic] pages, had this real ability to focus, and concentrate."[72]

The artists worked on the eighth floor, an open space filled with cubicles. Fellow comics émigré George Olesen, best known for his work on the *Phantom* newspaper strip (who had also been brought over by Marvin Stein), recalls, "We didn't have a door to block entry for anyone who wanted to drop off a bulletin, or a notice, or to let one of the 'wheels' come in, so they could drop in and drop out very easily, without knocking doors. I was right across from Mort, we saw each other every day. My 'door' lined up with his 'door.' Mort was usually working; he liked work as much as anybody I know. I would go there when things were dull to see if I could key up some of his stories. He was a storyteller for me."[73]

LEFT: Meskin skecthes his surroundings while on jury duty. He couldn't resist a subtle nod to one of DDBO's main clients. He created dozens of such drawings to pass the time.

Still, according to Joe Kubert, it was not an easy field. "When [comic book artists] switched over to doing some advertising, the pressures in advertising are a hell of a lot more than comic books. I've done a little bit in that area, I know what that means, working under the thumb of a lot more people, but there was a lot more dough for cartoon illustrations for advertising, there was a lot more money floating around, you got paid a lot more, a lot of people on top of you, and in order for them to justify what they were going home with, their salary, they had to pitch in and say something, whether what they were saying made any sense or not. And those kinds of pressures have a tendency to push an artist to take a fatal way of doing stuff than what they would do otherwise. That is in order to be able to satisfy what a whole group of people that you're showing your stuff to, while you are working, you are thinking, whether consciously or subconsciously, how to make sure that this is going to be accepted. I've got to satisfy this guy, and this guy and this guy. And invariably that waters the work down terribly."[74]

Typically, Meskin experimented with new means to produce his art. Alphonse recalls, "He would always be doing stuff on his own time. He was always fooling around with new techniques. He was always experimenting with mediums. Paper towels, anything, blotting paper."[75]

After two and a half decades of toiling in the industry he helped create, Meskin was finally afforded the respect and compensation he so deserved.

"He was well thought of," Normandia continued. "And kids would come up looking for jobs. 'You got Mort Meskin working here?' None of us really knew the good reputation that he had." One such fan and comic art-collector, Ethan Roberts, made the pilgrimage to the BBD&O offices to meet Meskin and to give him the article he penned on *The Vigilante* for the fanzine *Comic World*.

"I heard that he was working at one of New York's largest agencies, BBD&O. So I looked up the address and went down to their offices. I was dressed very casually, jeans and a sweatshirt, and had not shaved that day. The receptionist agreed to tell Mort Meskin that I was there to see him and had something to give him. When Meskin came out, he stood as far away from me as possible and asked me to give the receptionist the package. She then gave it to him and he disappeared back into the offices. I never heard his opinion of the article. It's my regret that I didn't capitalize on the opportunity to actually speak to one of my heroes."[76]

Peter Meskin: "At BBD&O, Dad made a lot more money than he did in comic books. My dad had remarried and it was a good marriage. I think it gave him more confidence. He was more settled and finally came into his own."[77]

Jerry Robinson: "He just amazed everybody because of the way he could visually tell a story. Few in TV were as well trained in those days to do storyboards. He knocked them cold, because they didn't have anybody who had that kind of ability, who could visualize and tell a story in sequence, and from their imagination, without references, as Mort could."[78]

Back at DC he was barely missed. When a fellow artist asked editorial director [and son of founder Harry] Irwin Donenfeld where Meskin was, Donenfeld replied, "We had to let Mort Meskin go. Mort quit drawing fingernails."[79]

Meskin remained with BBD&O for 17 years. Towards the end of his tenure the art department was sold off to a private owner, and all the artists were no longer employees but freelance, sans benefits. They were given the option to work at home, but Molly insisted Mort continue to work in the office, so that he wouldn't become isolated. With much free time until his services were required, he produced hundreds of pieces of art, constantly experimenting. Many were on paper towels, some gems no larger than 3" x 5".

One day Carmine Infantino, now an editor at DC, received an unexpected call at his home. It was Meskin, currently employed at BBD&O, saying he was in the neighborhood. They met and Infantino took him to lunch. "Mort seemed sad and wasn't happy in advertising, feeling bored and that it didn't utilize his talents." Infantino asked him about his emotional problems and Meskin replied,

"That is a sewer you don't want to go down." Infantino asked Meskin to return to comics, but he said he "never would."[80]

"I don't know if he was that happy doing it, at the time. There were certain advantages that I think were good for him, having a more regular life, going to regular work, creatively he had a hard time, and he did a lot of other things, painting, sketching," Robinson recalls.[81]

Peter Meskin: "When he was at BBD&O, he got bored at times because he knocked out the work they wanted him to do very quickly and he was faster than anybody there. But then he didn't know what to do with himself because he'd have nothing to do. He'd literally go into the bathroom and climb the walls. He'd take all the paper towels and go to his cubicle and practice sketching on those towels. He had hundreds, maybe thousands of them, and was going to throw them all away, and I told him, 'Don't throw them away, Pop. I love your work. Give them to me.' And I have piles of those paper towels to this day...nudes, horses, people in all kinds of positions. Some drawings were only roughs, and some were very detailed. He'd practice layouts and storyboards. Whatever came to mind."[82]

In 1964 Meskin once again provided shelter for his high school aged son. Philip described the arrangement: "Pop and I got an apartment in Yonkers. This way I could go off on the weekend and pop could spend time with Molly. That's how we got to Yonkers. I was still going to the Bronx High School of Science. During those years we lived together, he went through all the 'ologies,' he was a voluminous reader of anthropology, sociology, and then he got into psychology, and with psychology he got into Reich, and all of Freud, and from there, which is what warms my heart the most, he got into Buddhism, and that was a level of interaction that we had between us, too. I sort of warmed to my father. Pop's involvement with Buddhism was more than intellectual, but he never participated in any Buddhist organizations, any meditation that I am aware of, although I think when he was 21 he lived on grapes for three months, trying to find the meaning of life."[83]

Peter Meskin: "He was an experimentalist with art until the day he died, he was always experimenting, always looking for a new angle. When I asked him why he did that he said, 'It's fun.' He was very modest. Very shy. Didn't give interviews because at that point he didn't want anything more to do with the comics, he just wanted to have his family life. He didn't want fame. He didn't want the limelight aimed at him."[84]

Philip Meskin: "He was a gentle, non-aggressive person who was living his life. In his way he was loving, he was gentle, he was a good

Meskin was able to work so quickly that he had much free time between assignments. He created art on paper towels from the bathroom (left) and anything he had on hand.

man, he's someone I will have and will continue to use as a role model, to be a good person. He also was shy and he also had a bad stutter which didn't make him a social butterfly, he was a shy man, but he was good. I remember fighting with my pop, but most of the time we weren't with him, I grew up without him. In later years, my business was in Yonkers and he lived in Yonkers, he would come by for lunch, it was the something that Molly helped facilitate, because Molly controlled Pop, which I don't think was all bad, I think her controlling of him let him have a better life then had he stayed alone. Good and bad. But he had a happy life with Molly."[85]

In the mid-1970s, after a decade and a half of courtship, Molly and Mort married. They resided on 2 Sunnyside Drive, in Yonkers. In the evenings they would continue to go ballroom dancing, often at the famed Roseland Ballroom in Manhattan. According to Alphonse, "He and his wife loved it, going to Roseland regularly, once or twice a week they would go."

Pete Meskin: "He had completely stopped stuttering, and became a raconteur, and a philosopher: Dad could talk a blue streak. He had a very good second marriage. Molly was very, very good to him and really gave him a strong sense of self and empathy. I think his relationship with her and her family really strengthened him."[86]

In 1978, they traveled to Israel to attend the wedding of Philip, who had emigrated years earlier. "I was very happy they came, it was very emotional. I hadn't seen them in a bunch of years."[87]

ABOVE: Peter, Mort and Philip, 1992. RIGHT: "Holy Man," crayon pastels and scratchboard technique, date unknown.

KEEP UP THE GOOD WORK

By 1982, age 66, Meskin was ready to retire.

Peter Meskin: "When he retired in the mid-'80s, I asked him how it felt. He said, 'You know how it feels when you used to have a toothache and you don't have it any more? You don't think about it.'"[88] Still, he kept drawing and painting. He produced art just about every day of his life.

Retirement for Meskin turned out to be as active as his art career. He joined Molly, who had began volunteer work years earlier in the nursing home wing of St. Josephs Hospital in Yonkers, New York, not far from their apartment. They came regularly, 50 to 60 hours a month, as much as fifteen hours a week, and volunteered in the activities department, which was very much needed, according to director Connie Kaufman: "Not only did he do drawings, he was a nice person to have around; for people in the nursing home just somebody saying hello to them makes a difference."

Meskin worked in myriad styles. The above is reminiscent of a *New Yorker* illustration from the 1940s. BELOW RIGHT: A cartoon based on Peter and Diane's wedding.

He would arrive with Molly, usually wearing a slouch hat. He would greet his fellow volunteers and nursing home residents with a sing-song "Good-morn-ing, Lay-deez!" He decorated the halls with his artwork during the holidays, made cards for the residents, and joined in the sing-alongs led by Molly, who played piano with one hand. She would also give dance lessons. Fellow long time volunteer Lena Trippardella remembered fondly: "They used to come early, him and his wife, they used to do arts and crafts, they used to do transporting. He came a lot, they came almost every day. They were very good people. He made a lot of nice things. He was a sweetheart, I loved him. Very soft-spoken, very gentle. When you wanted to have something done, like arts and crafts, he would do it for you. No matter what you asked for, if you wanted a bunny, sometimes you have to decorate the place to make people cheerful. And he would come up and do anything, and talk to the people. He was great. I remember all the nice things he did for me. He used to say 'Lena, you better keep up, keep up the good work.'

"Molly, she was a nice person, just as nice as him. She would do the transporting, she would do everything, she would write some things out too, if they needed help in the office, help with the piano, keep the party going. Keep everybody going. Very nice. He was a very nice young man. You know what I liked about him with the people there, they would play cards, or they would have them talking, or they would play music there. He did great work. He was funny. Now this is all volunteer. I love to sit with the people, like Mort used to do. He'd play cards, he'd play Bingo, and he'd be there and we'd be with them. He was a great man, and she was great, a good entertainer, and everything was fine. 'You Are My Sunshine,' that was her favorite. He would say jokes now and then. They were good leaders, we followed them, we did what they wanted."[89]

Meskin created light-hearted greeting cards for every occasion—birthdays, weddings, religious holidays, Bar Mitzvahs.

Peter Meskin: "He got enormous pleasure from doing volunteer work and from giving his paintings away. I went to visit him a couple of times there, and you'd see these ladies in wheelchairs, almost catatonic. Dad would come by and they would perk up, roses in their cheeks. He would flirt with them and they would just about start hopping out of their wheelchairs."[90]

Fellow Volunteer Mary Gomez: "He was a great artist, his wife was a great person. She used to play the piano, in the dining room, she used to come in early and sing with them, she used to play cards, whatever they wanted, she did everything... anything you wanted he'd make. But then he got sick. He was the nicest man, he got sick. I knew him when I came here. I met his wife, she was a lovely person. And he was a very good-looking man. He smoked, too."[107]

Meskin's long addiction to cigarettes eventually took its toll. He developed cancer of the esophagus, and also lung cancer in the early '90s. Still, according to Peter, he never lost his sense of humor or perseverance.

Peter Meskin: "He did stop [smoking], but too late. That's why he had an operation on his throat and had his larynx removed. And he spoke with one of those devices that you hold to you neck, where you sound like a robot. But he was very good about it, he was very positive and kept up his spirits and somehow found the strength to be very funny while he was suffering. I mean, Dad stuttered when I was young but that didn't keep him from reading books to us. He never let his illness get him down at all. Not until the very end. As long as he wasn't in physical pain, it didn't bother him. At least I never saw it bother him. I don't think it really did, and the fact that Molly had a positive attitude helped him, too. As long as he was with Molly, he was A-OK.They just kept moving on. One of the things he and Molly would say was, 'With the hour comes the power.' They would say that for all kinds of situations. There was a lot of love between them. I loved Molly for loving my dad so much and for giving him a second chance at life.[91]

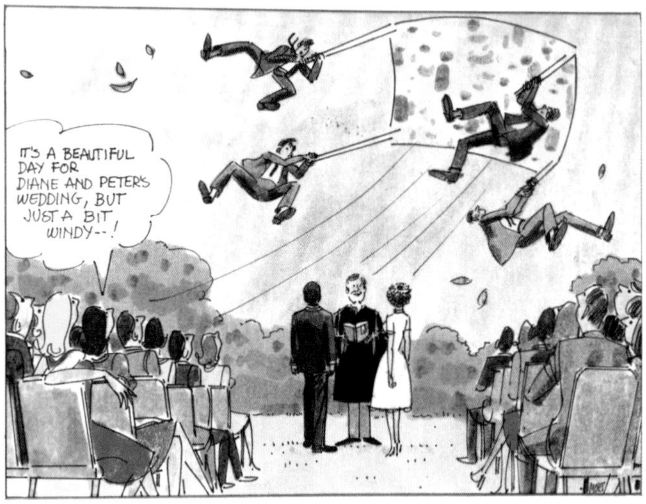
IT'S A BEAUTIFUL DAY FOR DIANE AND PETER'S WEDDING, BUT JUST A BIT WINDY--!

"He was very brave and he would tell jokes and make the nurses laugh like you wouldn't believe; even with [the device] he kept up his sense of humor, he would have people cracking up all over the place, he could carry on lengthy conversations, he got very good with it. And he took it in stride. He really was a model to all of us. I hope I go out with as much dignity as my dad did. He really had a lot of strength of character at the end."[92]

Jerry Robinson: "I remember the last time I spoke to him, I heard that he had been ill, and then I found out that he had his voice box removed. It was very eerie for me to all of a sudden to hear this disassociated voice, this mechanical voice, he would say things, I knew it was Mort, but in a voice that was without any emotion or personality and I was just shaken after hearing him. But even then he was very pleased to talk, I did want so to see him. He said, 'Please come to see me, drop by, it's so good to hear from you.' I was going to drive up to see him, but something interfered. It usually does. I'm really disappointed I didn't get to see him in his later years. In life you should do these things right away."[93]

ABOVE:
An example of a
Meskin "haiku."

Philip Meskin: "The irony was that, in order for the doctors to operate on his throat, they had to first give him a bypass operation to strengthen his heart. They gave him the surgery and it was totally successful. In the end, as he was dying of cancer, his heart was in better shape than it ever had been. Whatever he was getting out of all this, philosophy helped him. The cancer and the hospital stays didn't faze him. He handled everything with great dignity."[94]

Peter Meskin: "My favorite memory near the end of Dad's life was when we took a walk together in Manor Park in Larchmont. The park was on the water, on Long Island Sound in a beautiful neighborhood with sailboats floating on their moorings. We talked about life and art and just really enjoyed being together for that hour and a half. We were looking at the boats on the water; it's not very far from where I taught sailing on City Island. We walked arm in arm. We always loved being near the water together. That was a special time. Right after that he became incapacitated and wasn't able to take that walk again."[95]

Lena: "We didn't want to lose him. He was great. He was nice. Then when he was home, she [Molly] stayed home and watched him. He came once more and said goodbye, and that was goodbye forever."

Mort Meskin died in April of 1995, a month shy of his 79th birthday. Although his passing was duly noted in the comics press, none of the major newspapers ran an obituary.

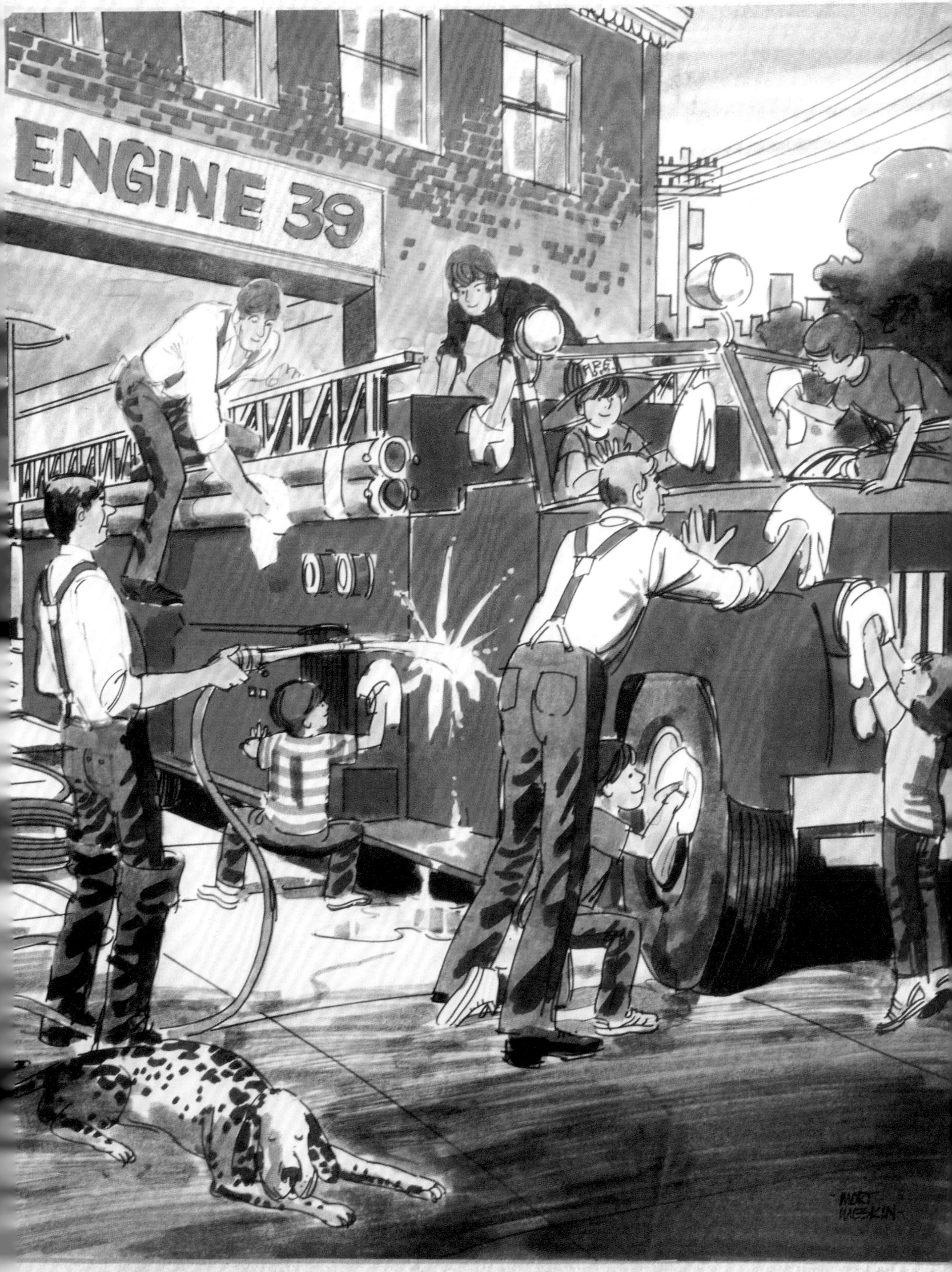
ENGINE 39
MORT MESKIN

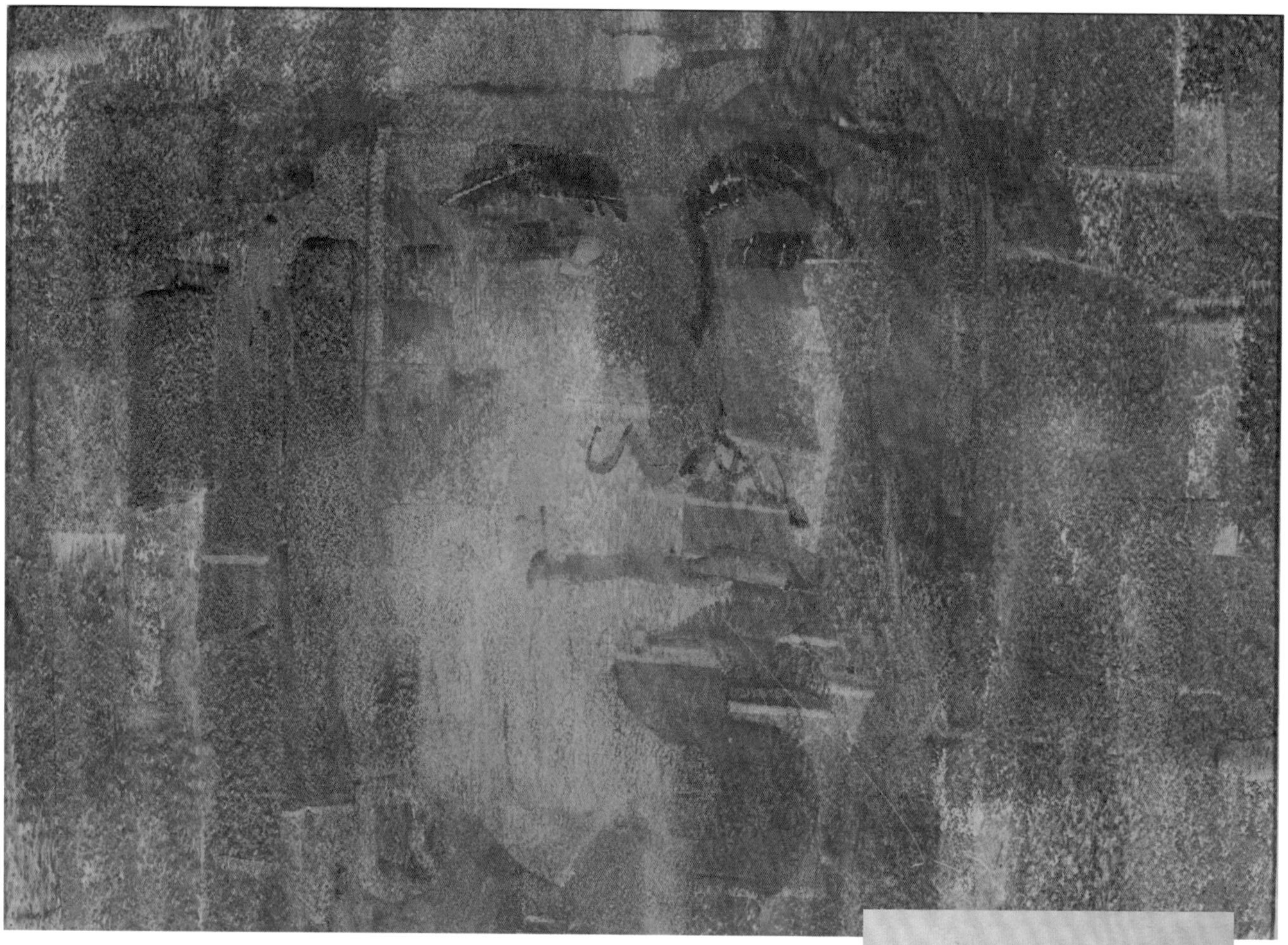

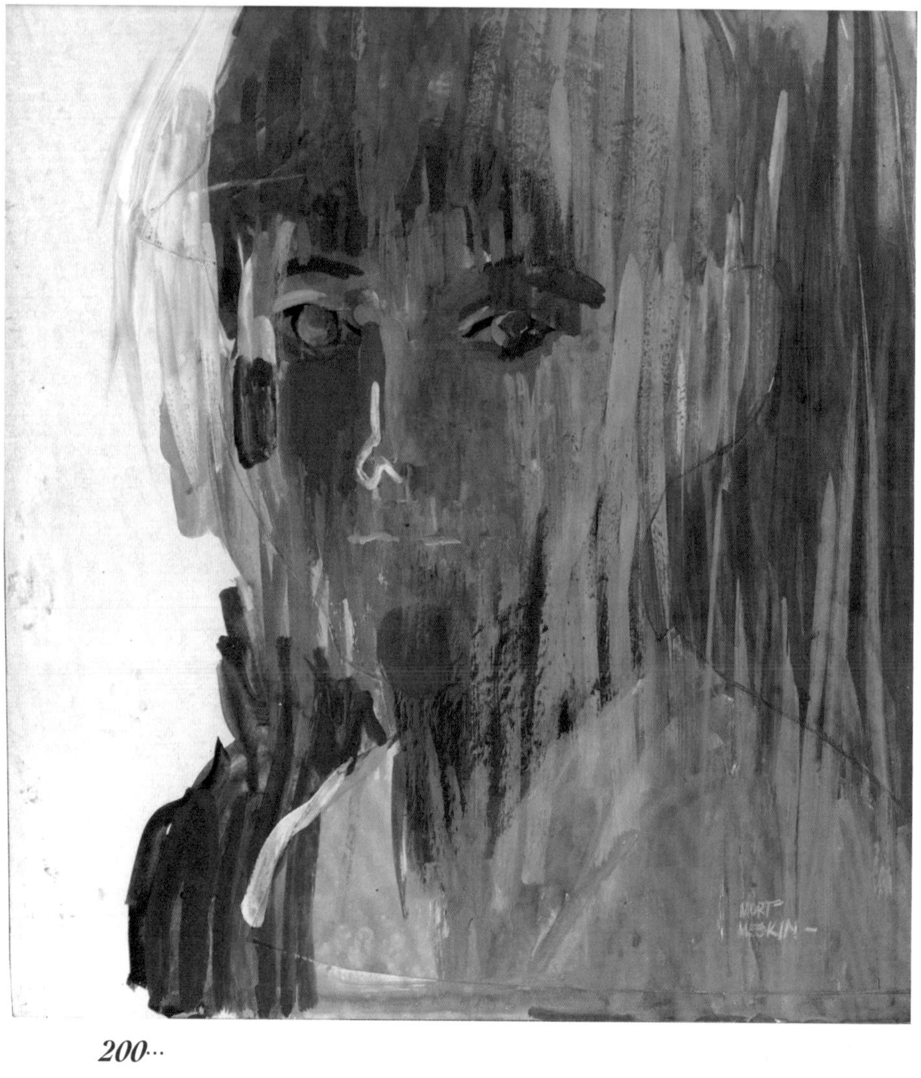

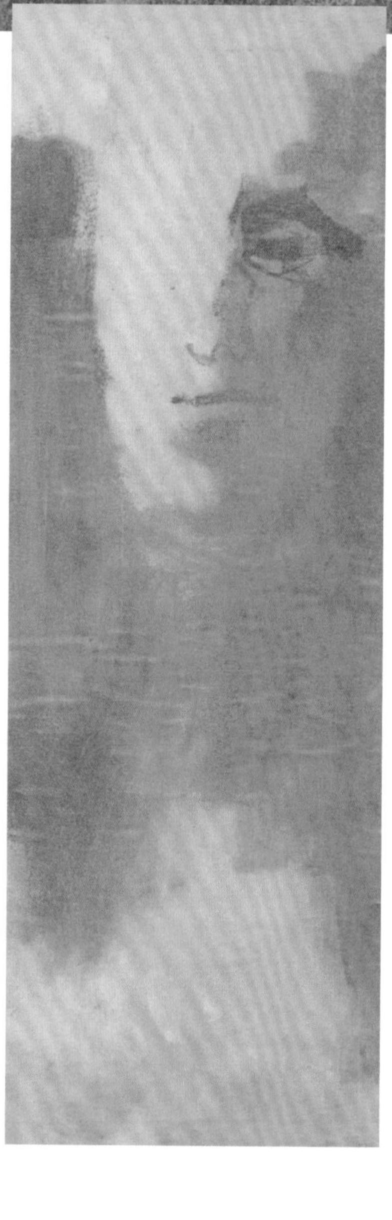

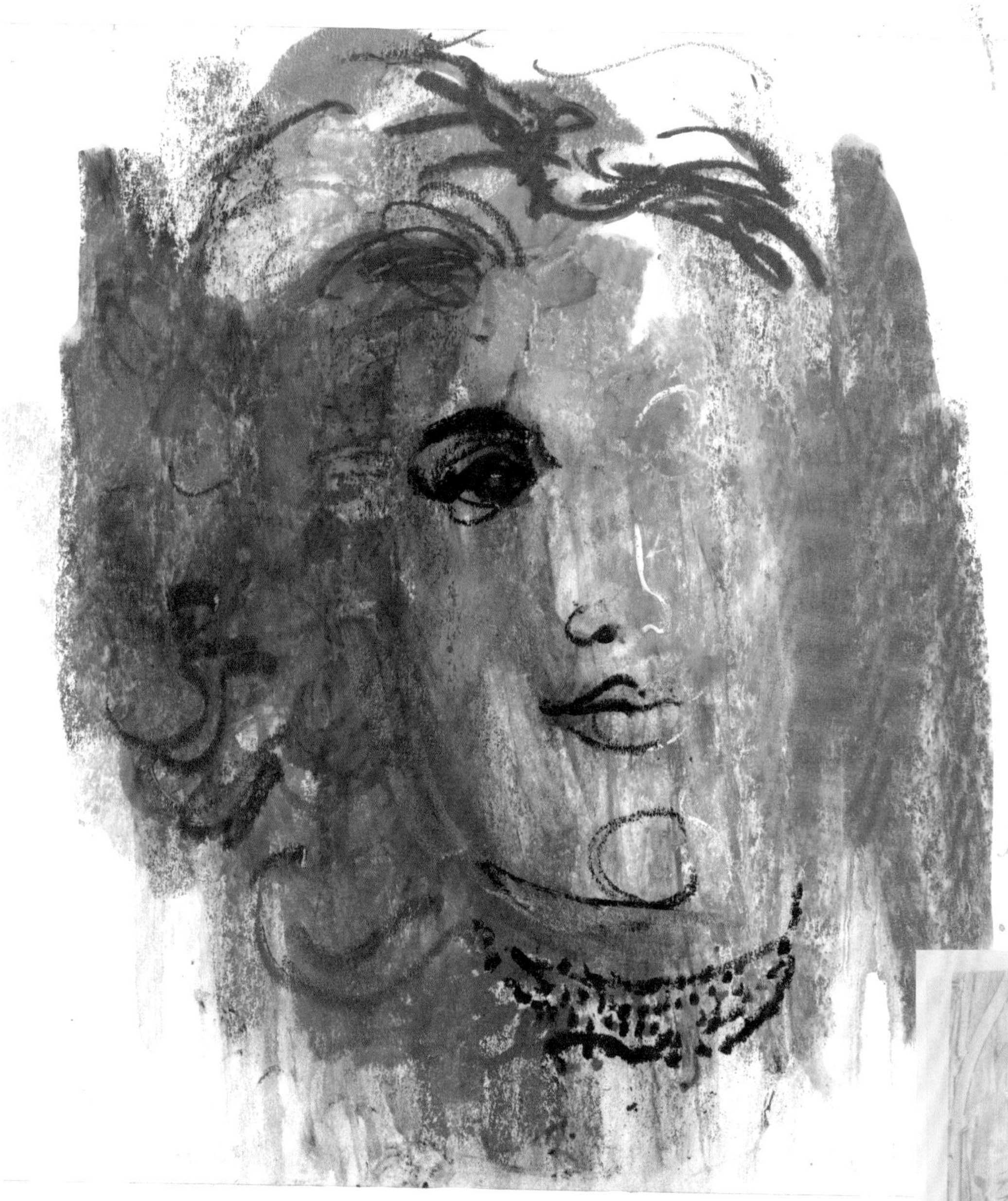

According to George Roussos, Meskin felt he struggled with rendering faces. In his personal work he drew them by the dozens.

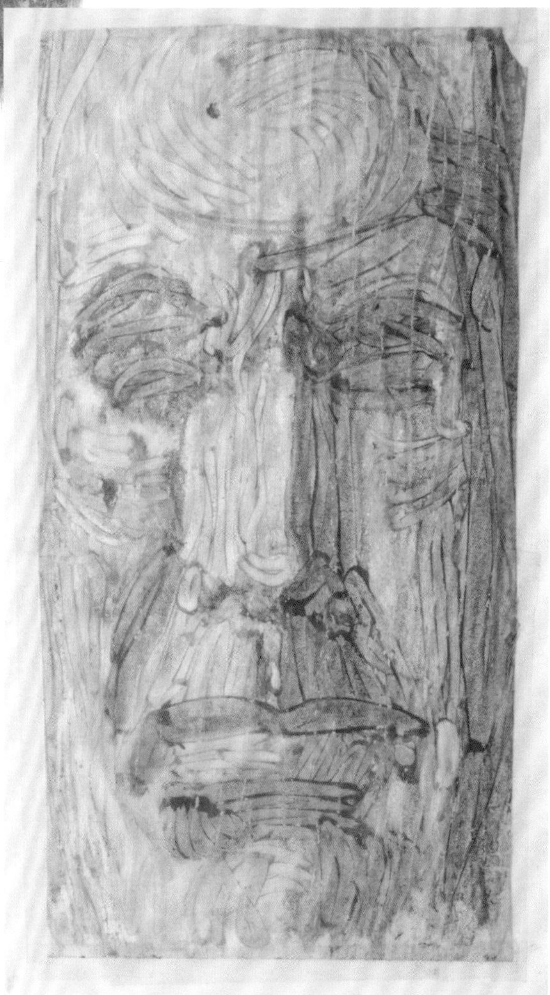

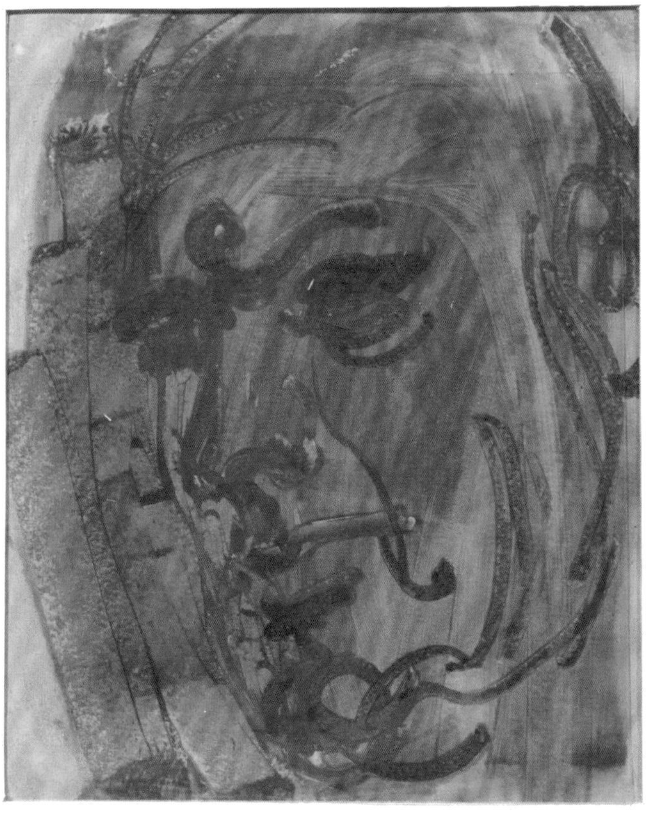

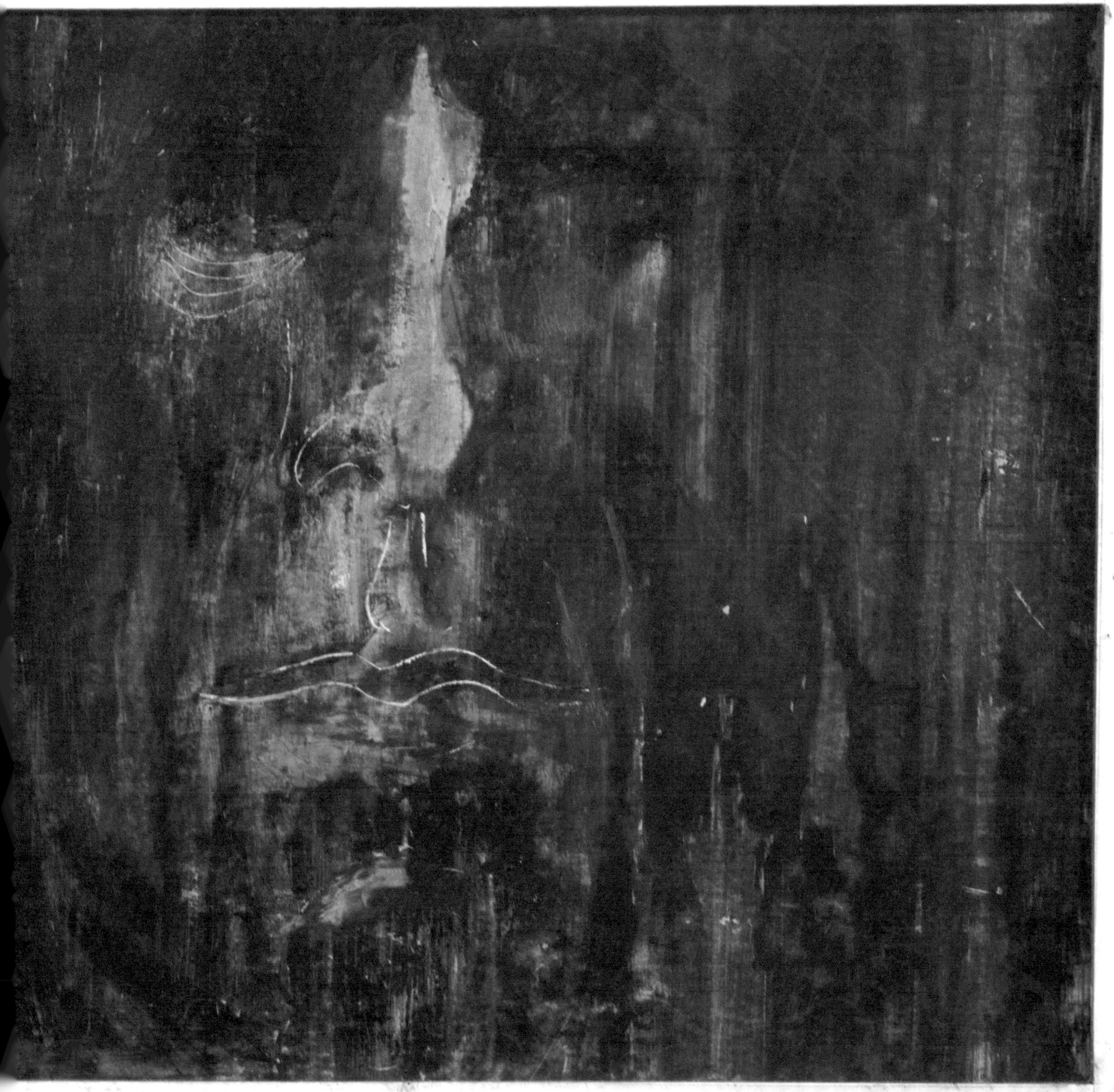

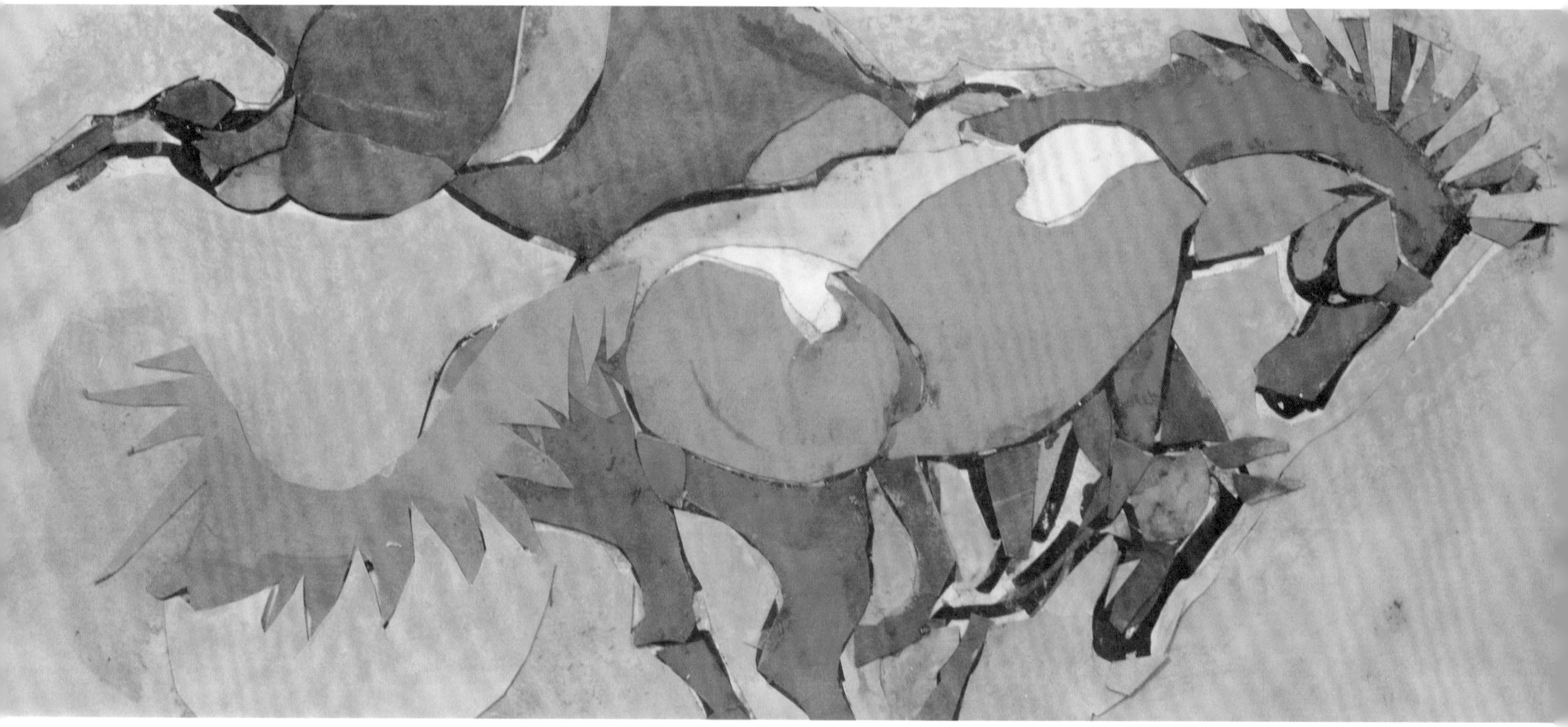

An indefatigable experimenter, Meskin continued to explore all media: cut paper, combined with painting, pen and ink on colored paper and many others.

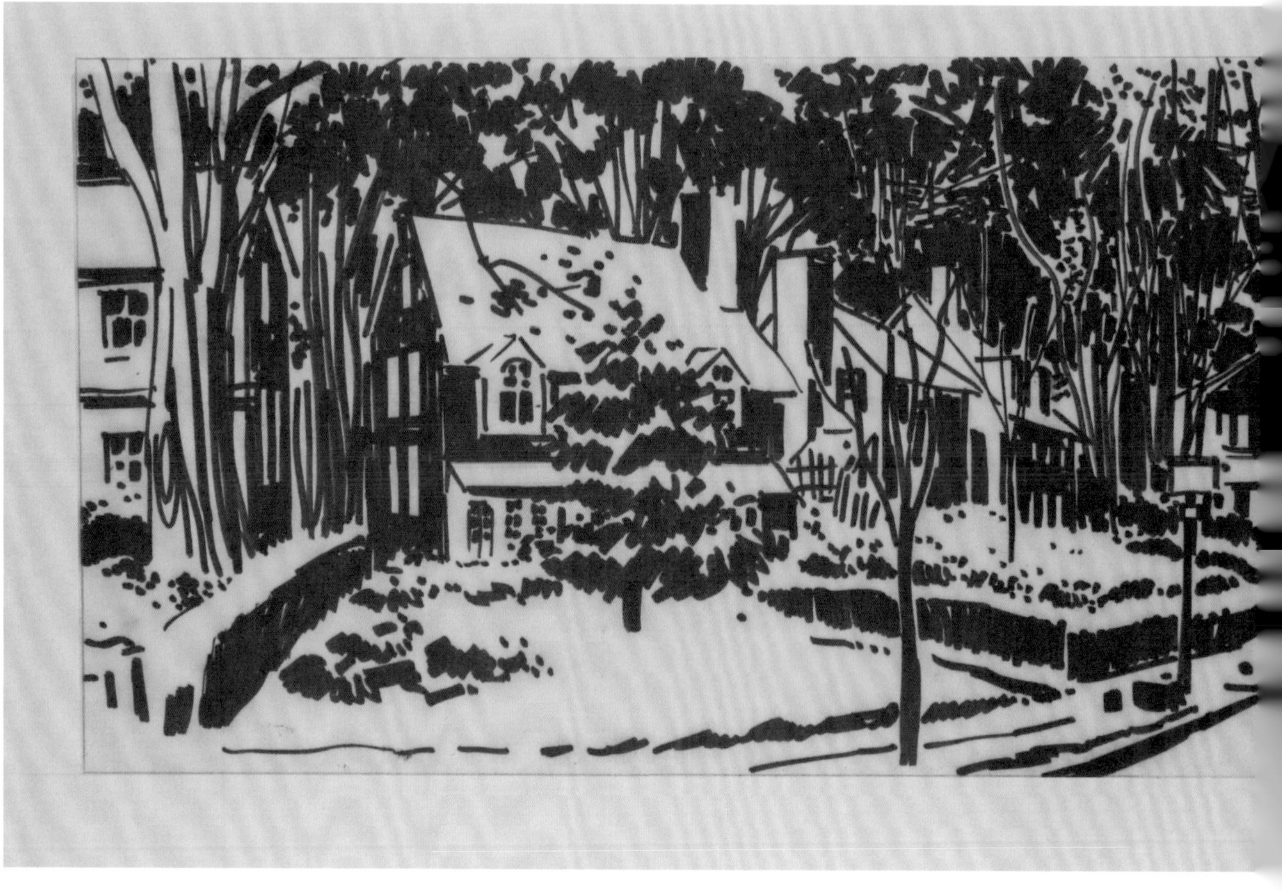

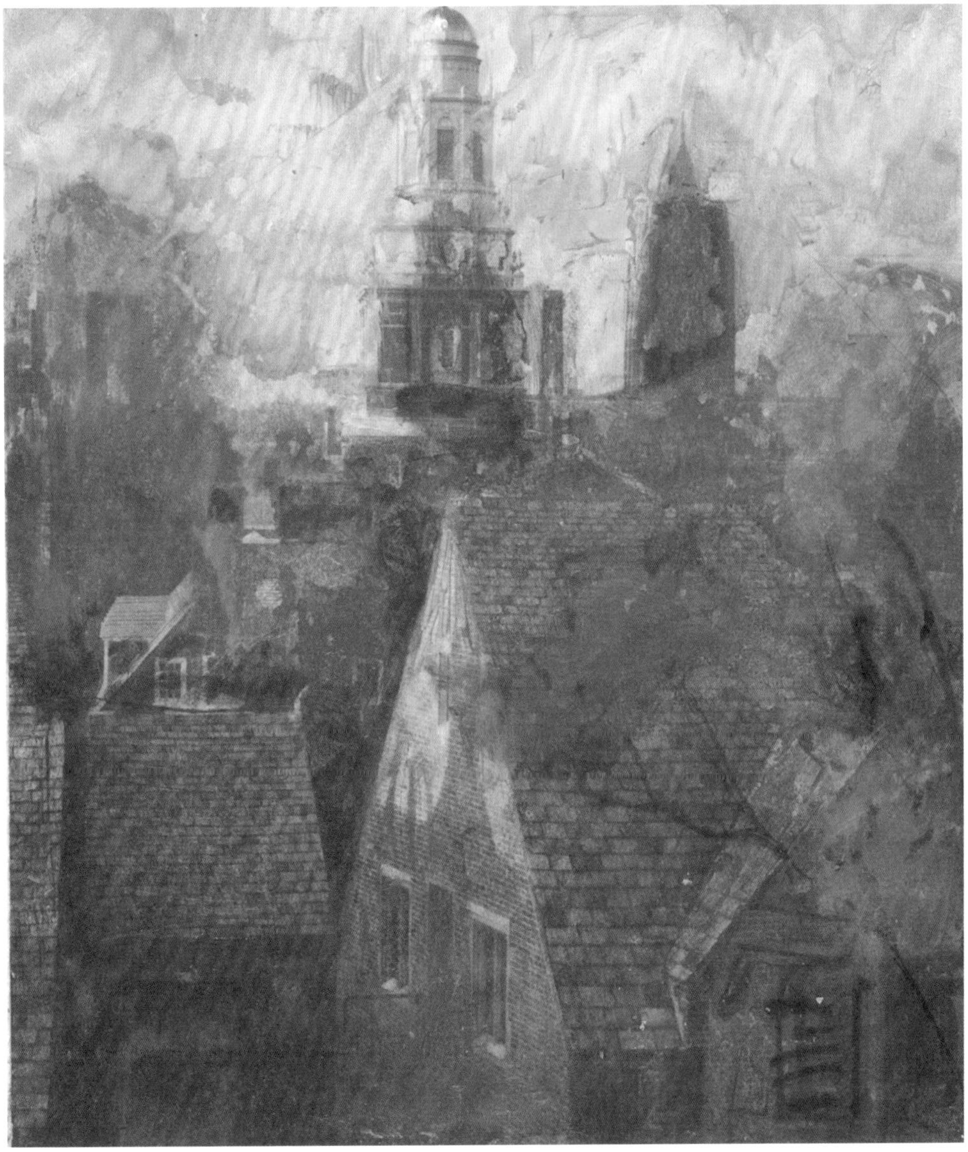

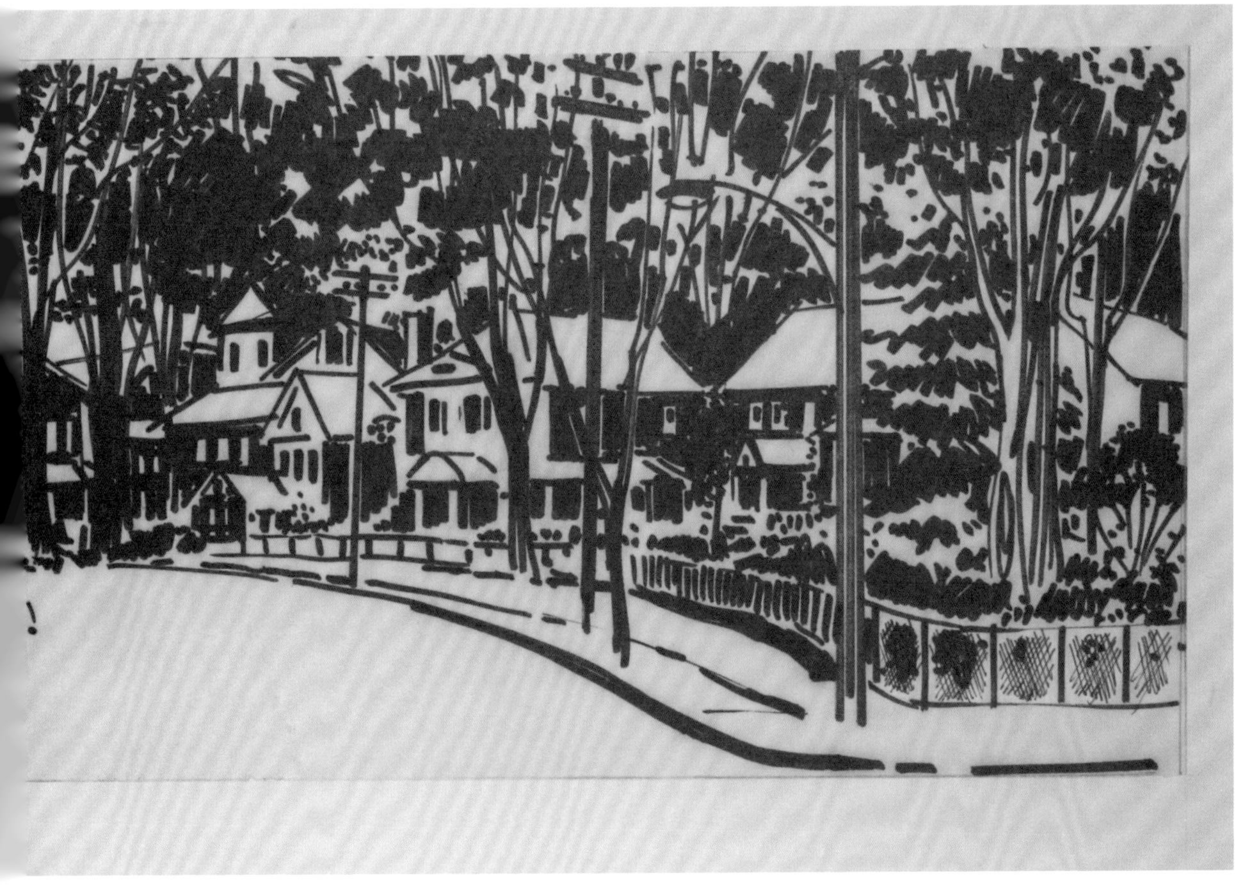

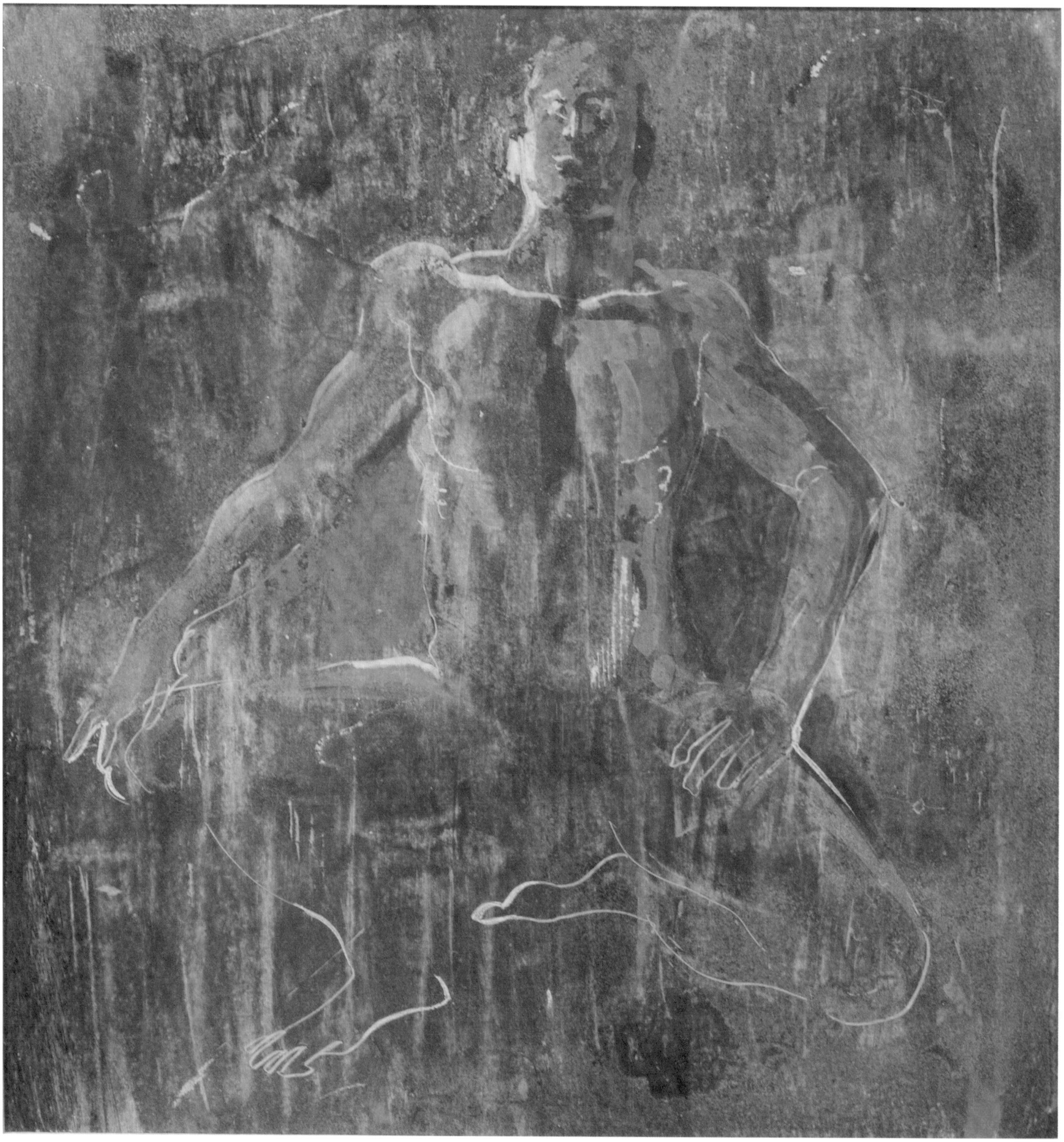

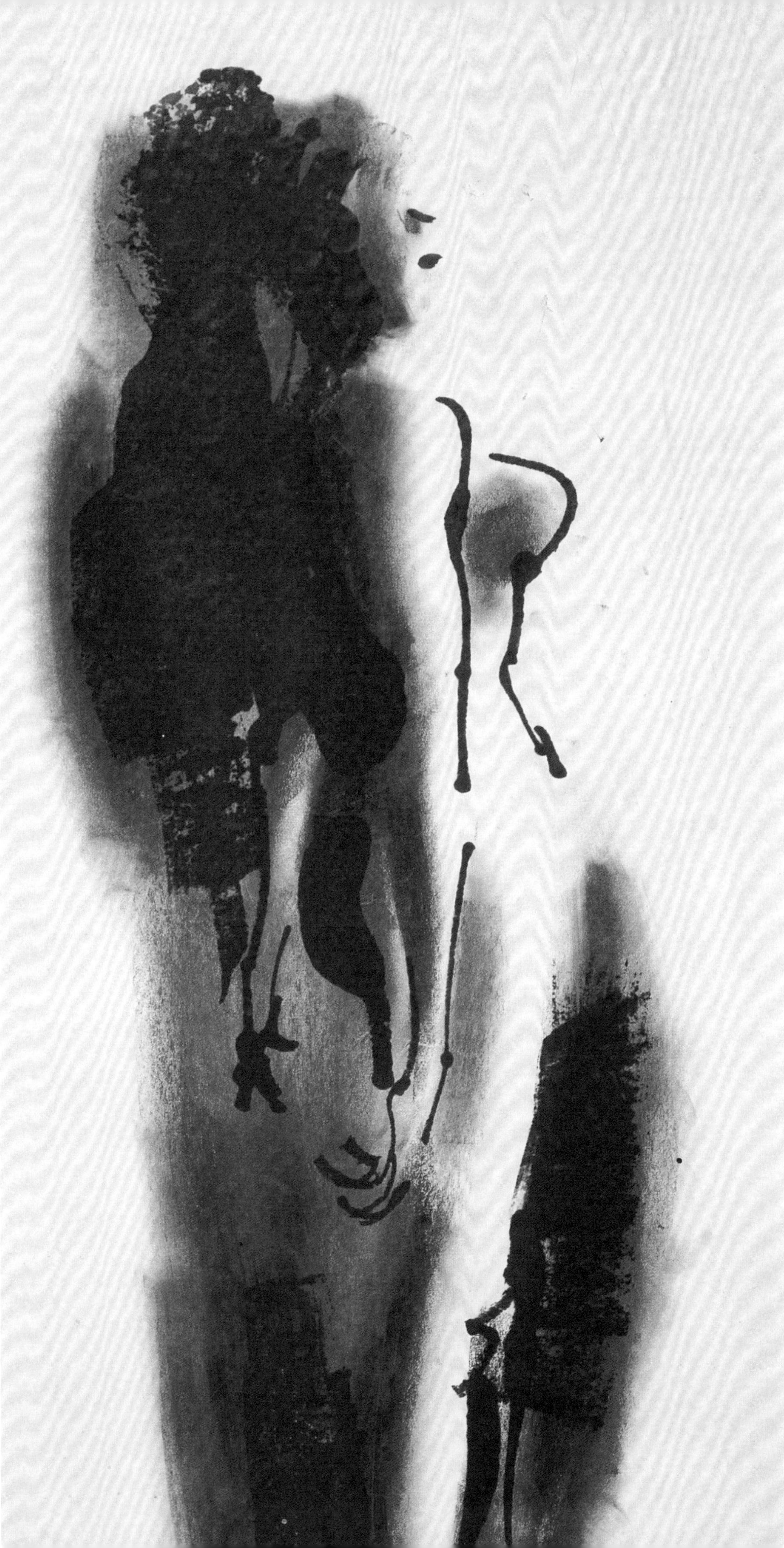

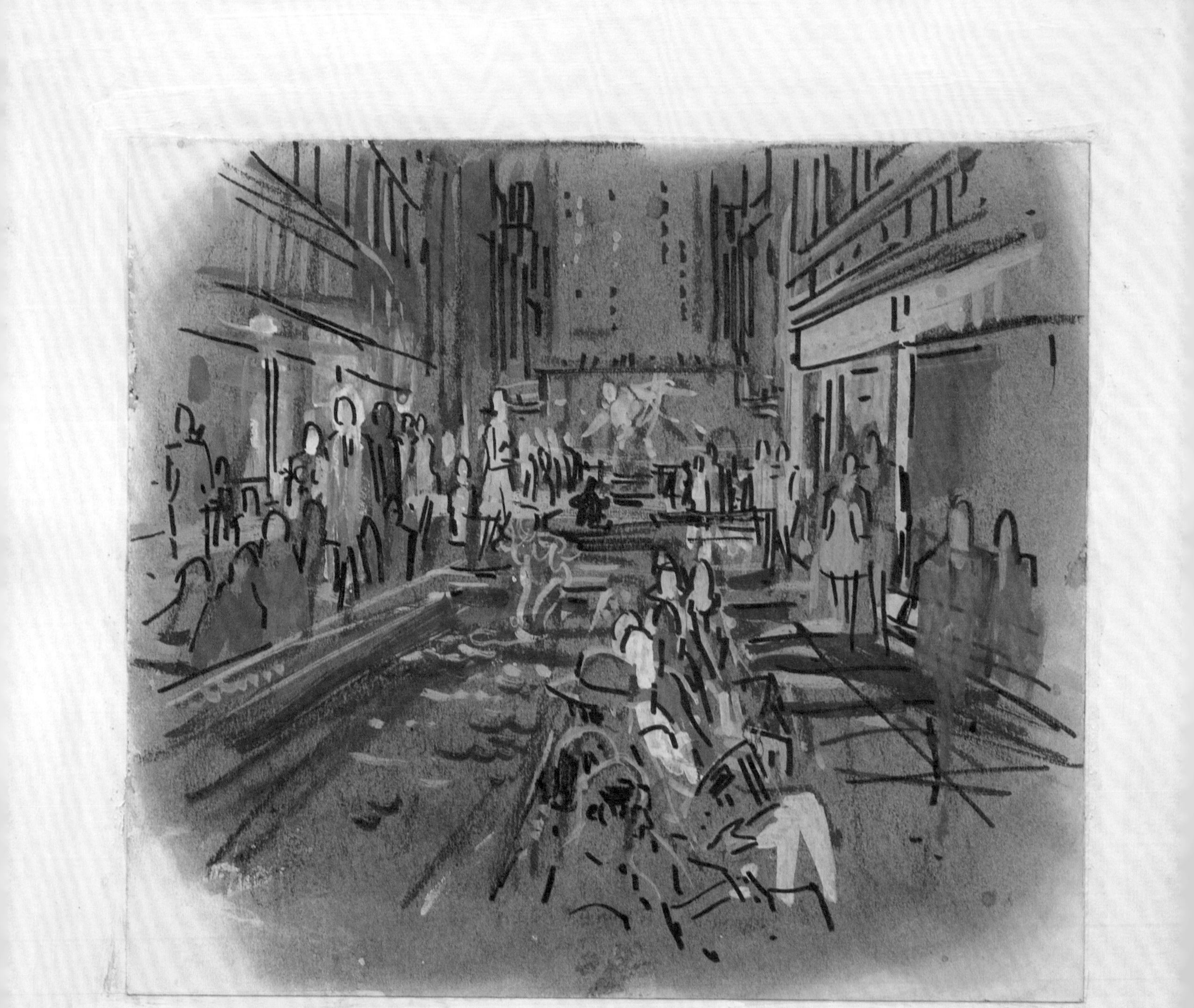

ABOVE: Rockefeller Center, NY. TOP RIGHT: "Goddess." BOTTOM RIGHT: Meskin revives a theme in his personal art that appeared earlier in a *Johnny Quick* panel (see page 39).

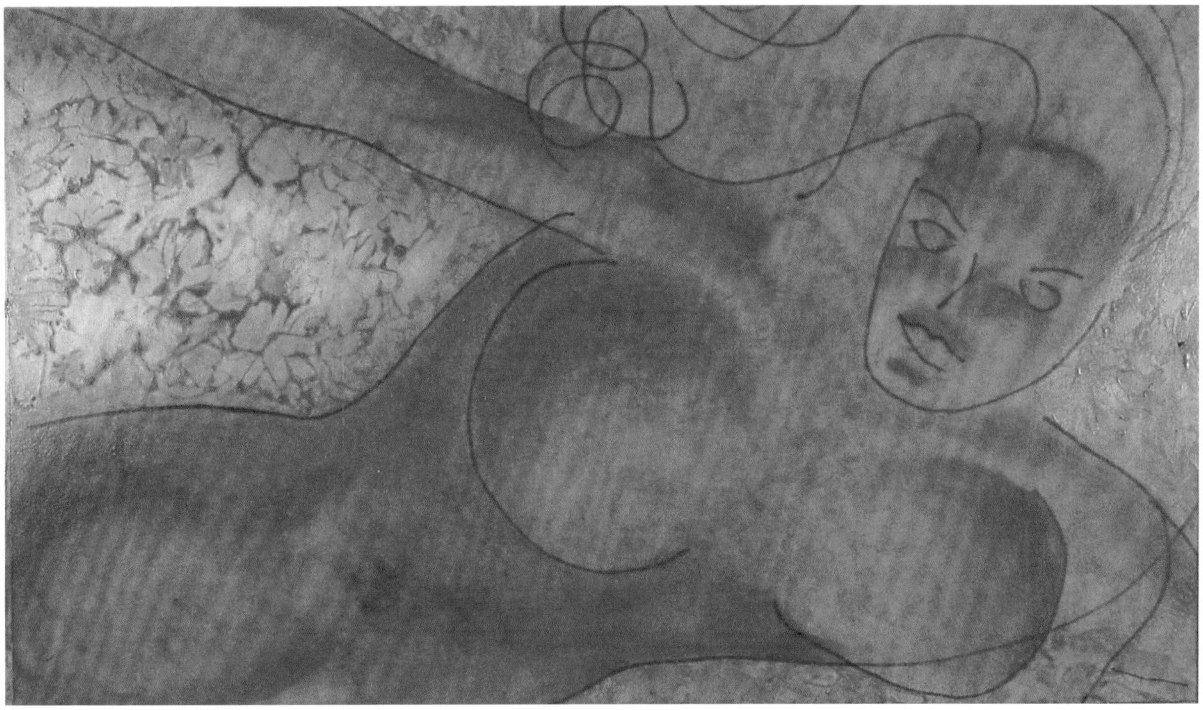

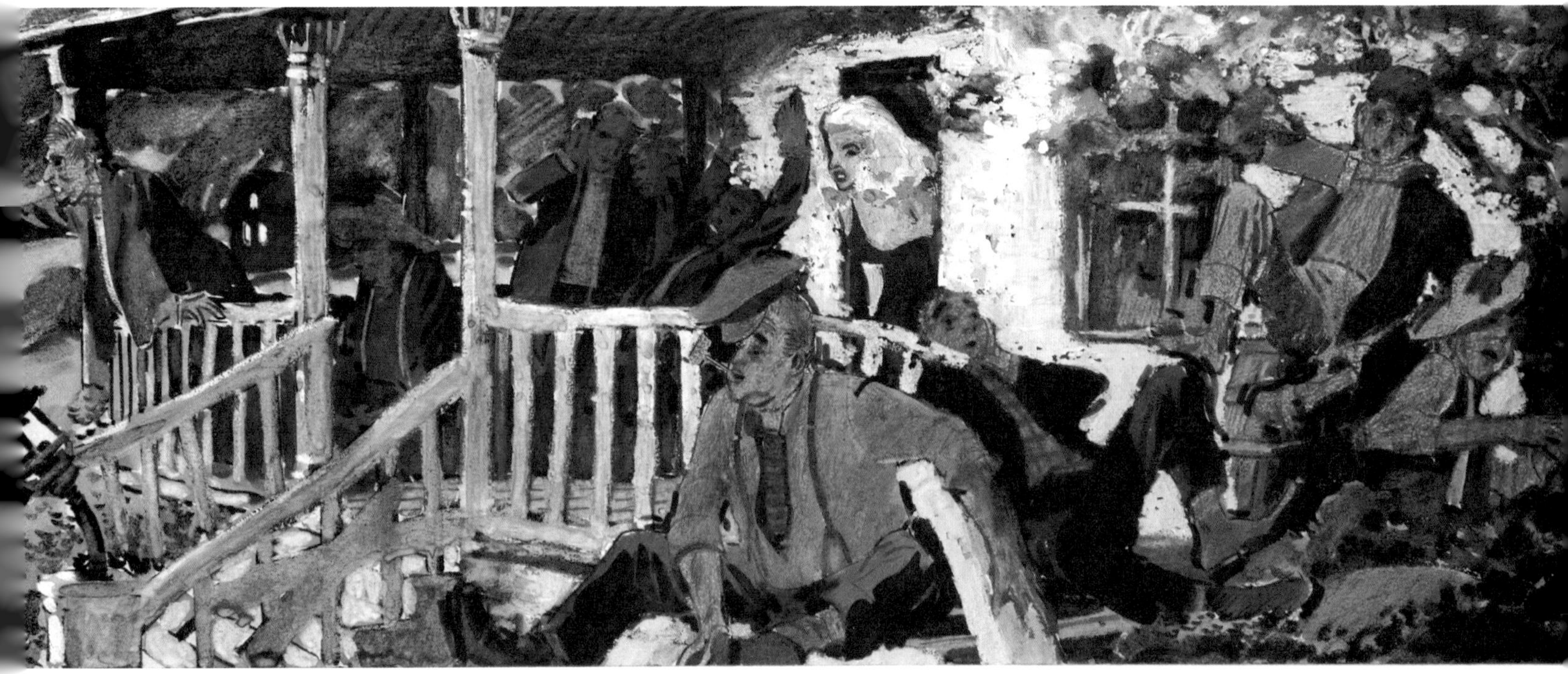

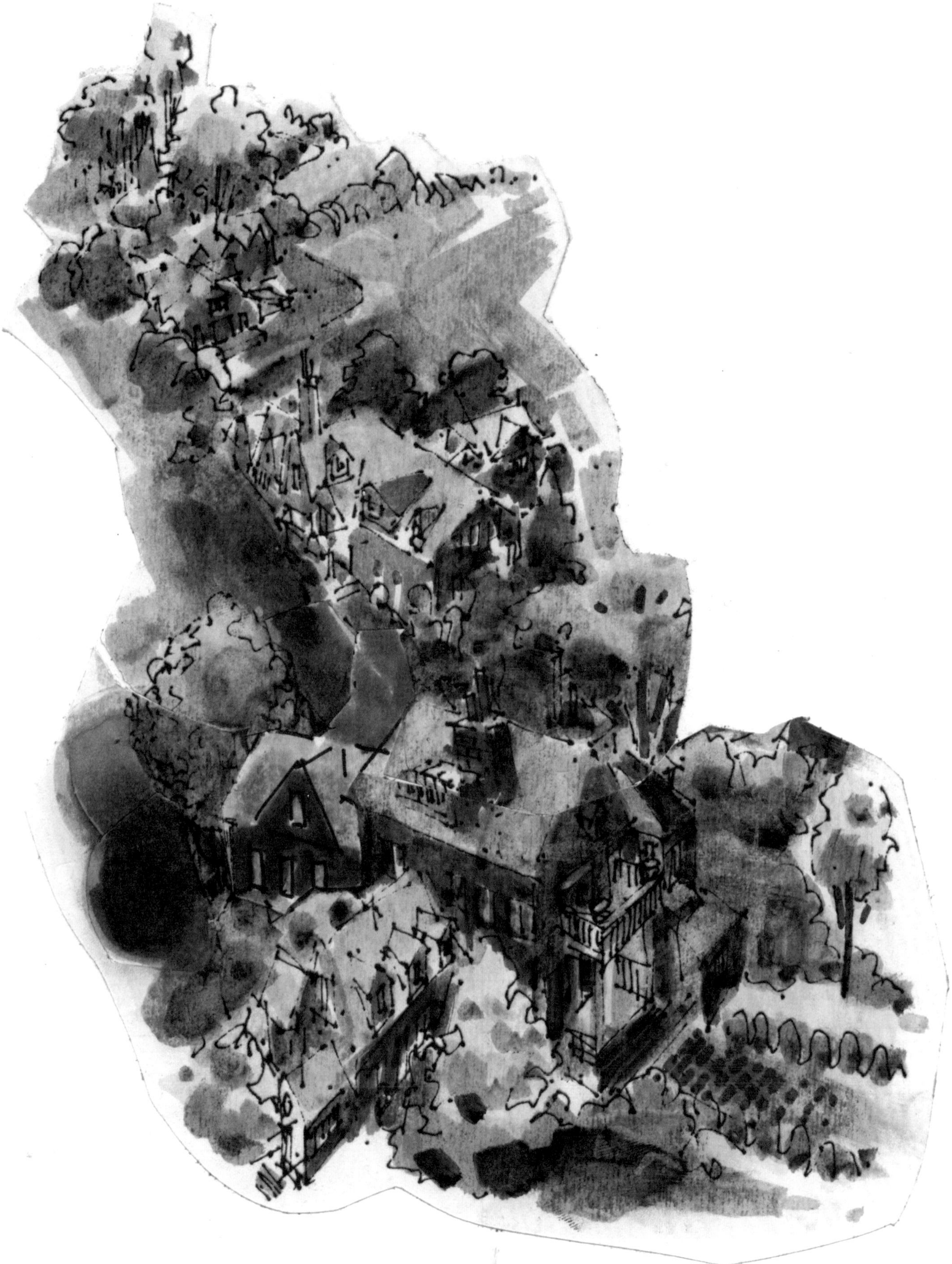

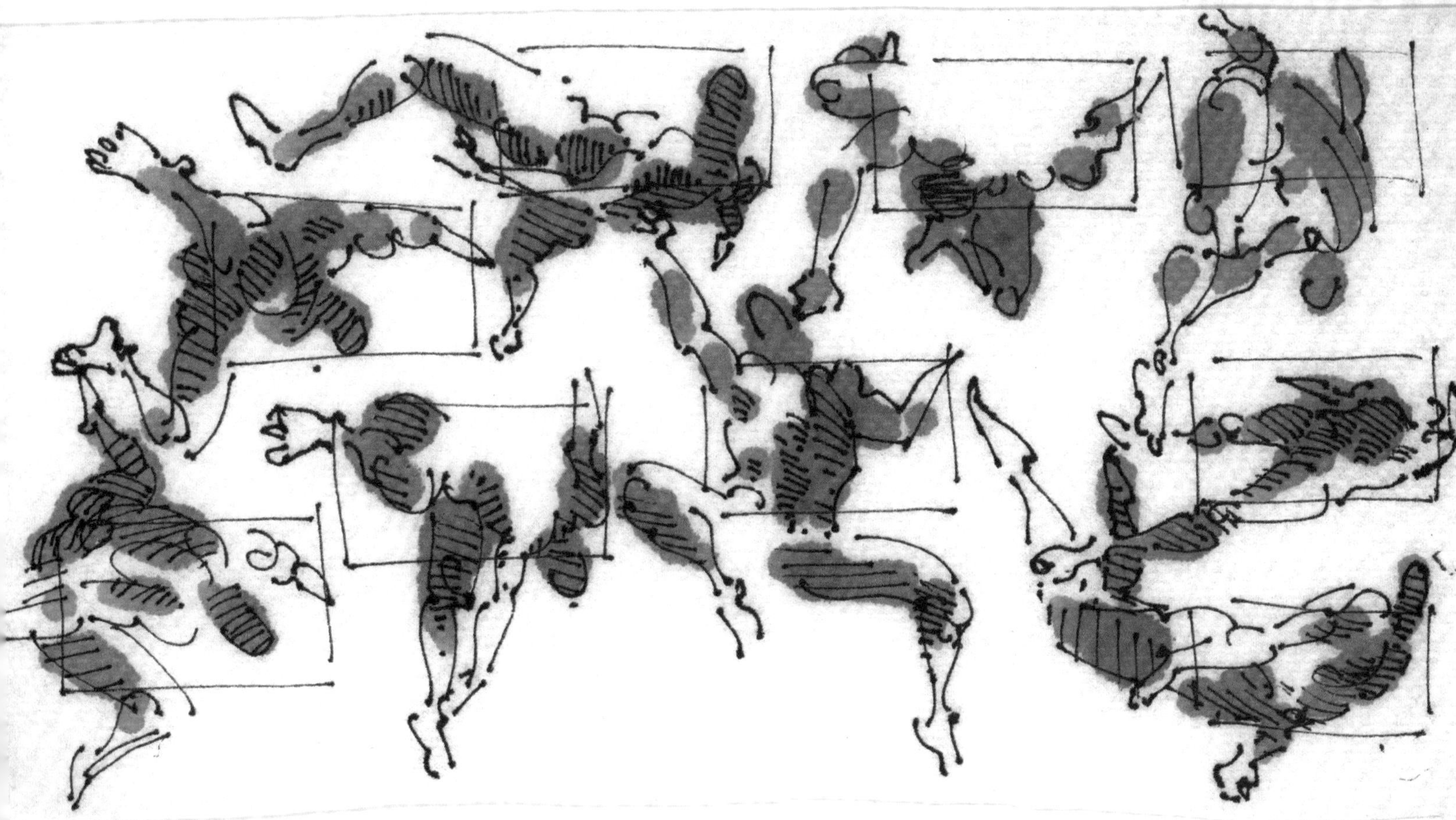

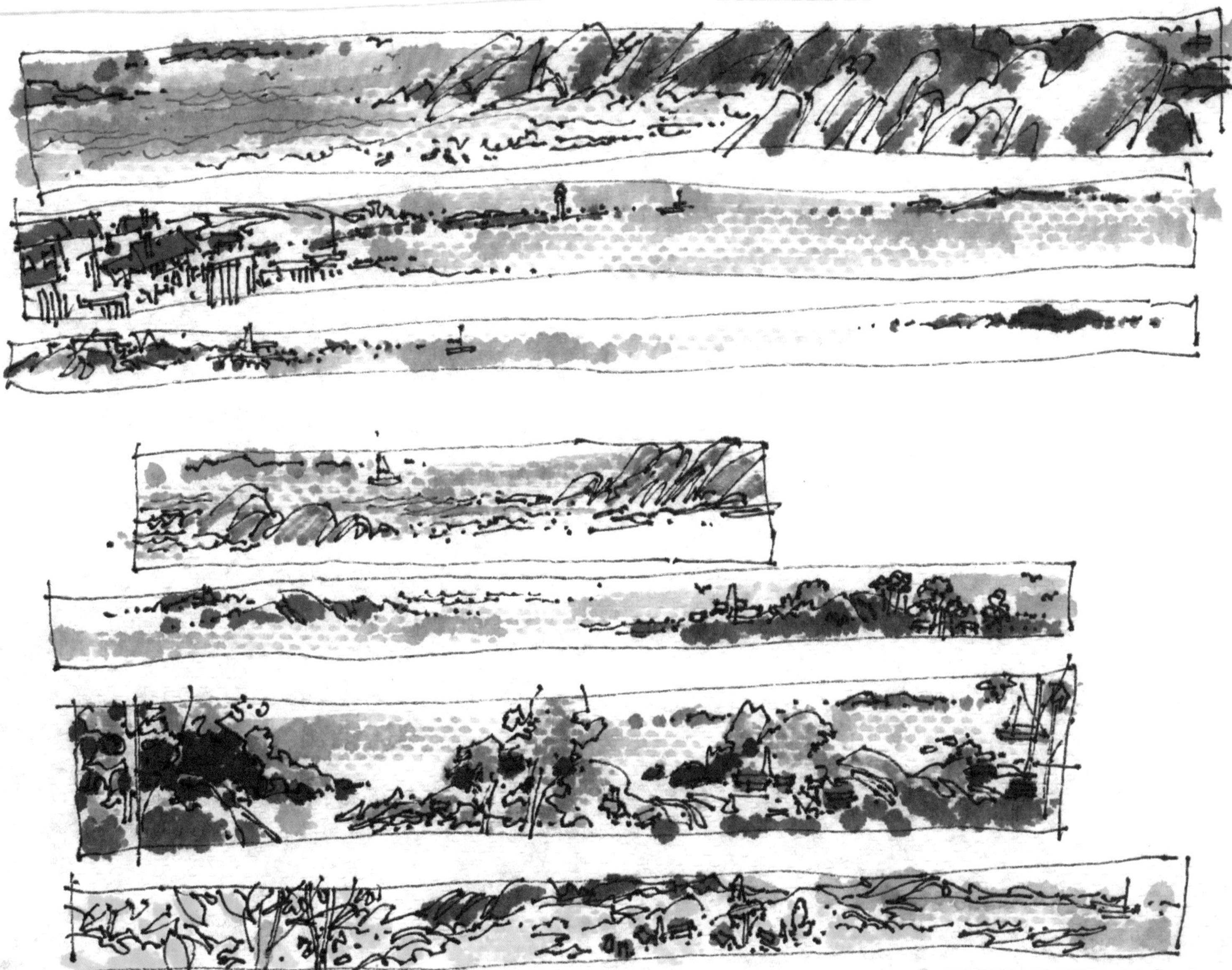

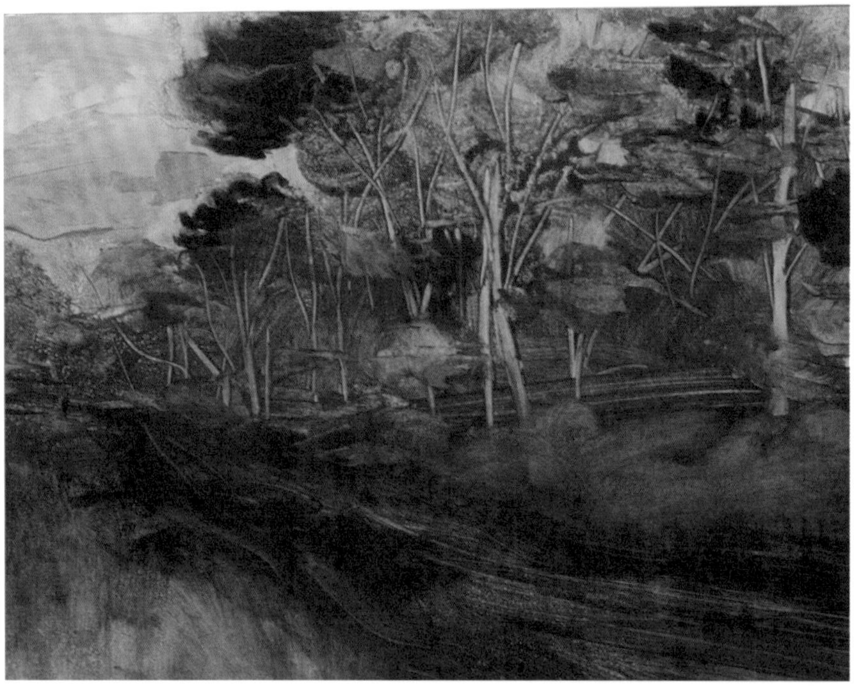

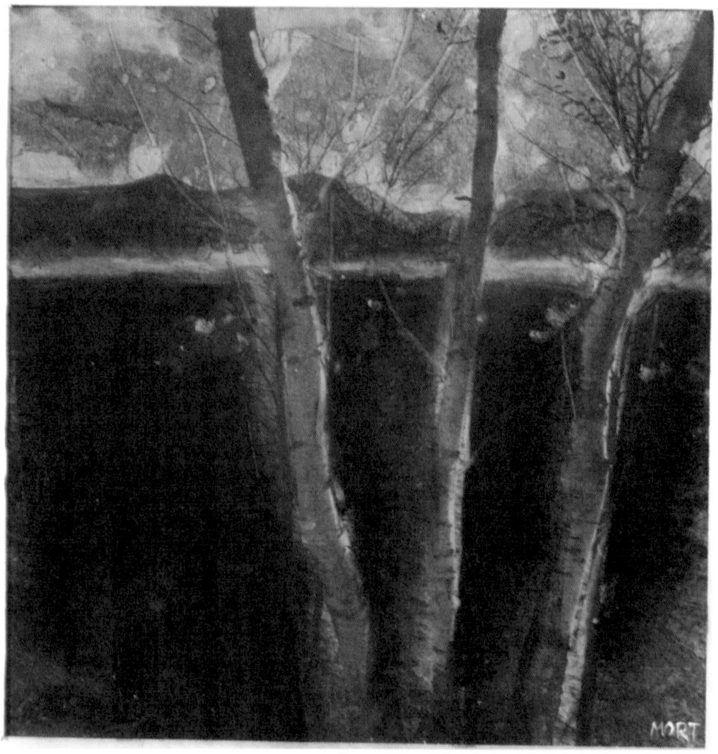
MORT

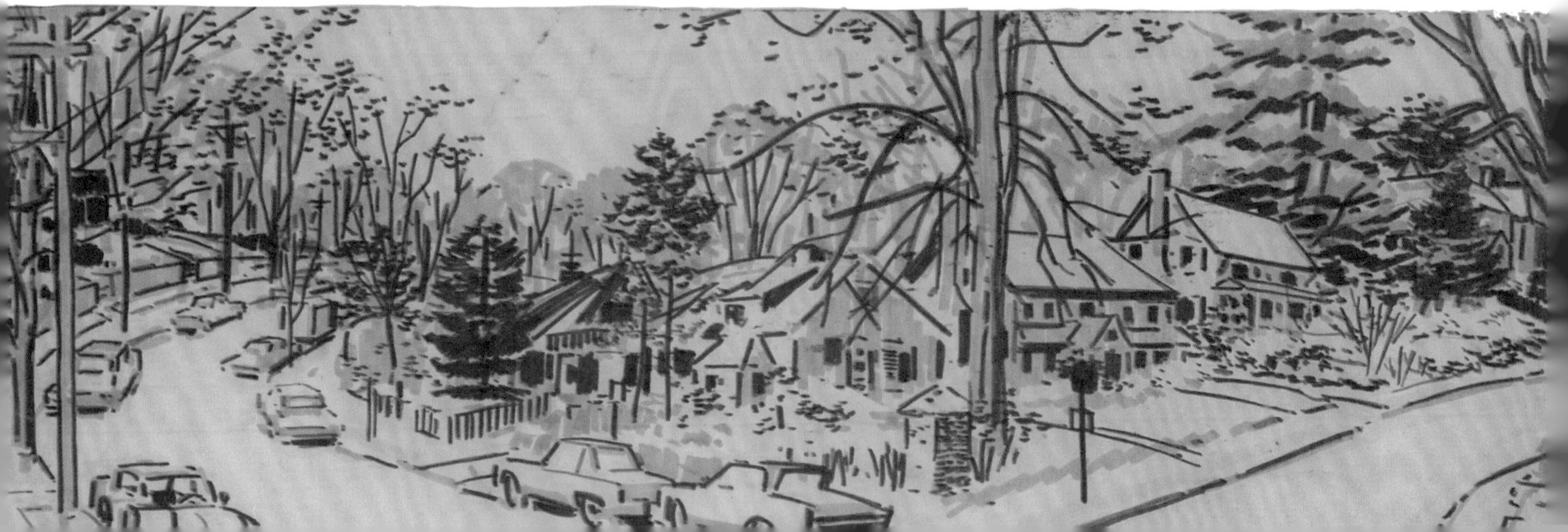

CODA

It is only in the 21st century that the value of the American art form known as "comics" has begun to be recognized. Yet even as many embrace the more rarefied-sounding "graphic novel," others dismiss the comic book, seeing it as simply an assembly-line product keeps many from viewing it as anything more than a commercial endeavor. Yet if one compares it to jazz, or another American creation, rock 'n' roll, those are group efforts as well. Jazz in the beginning was as much a commercial effort as any other, albeit one that transformed the musical landscape of our culture. Louis Armstrong, Ella Fitzgerald, Billie Holiday, Count Basie, Duke Ellington all were commercial artists who had top ten hits throughout their careers. Does this make any one of them less of an artist? In the earliest days of jazz, Armstrong wasn't considering that he was helping to develop an art form, he was following his muse, supporting himself with his talent and digging his way out of poverty. As were these young men from the Bronx, Manhattan, Brooklyn: Kane, Finger, Eisner, Kirby, Robinson, Roussos, Stein, and Meskin, to name a few. They would riff together as artists—pencils eradicated, replaced by inks, words and color added, to create, despite the poor newsprint reproduction, at its best a cohesive work of art, and at the very least enduring entertainment.

It is a great time for comics. Publishers have realized their worth and continue to archive and preserve these treasures for future generations. Their influence has spilled not only onto the movie screen but also into the very fabric of our culture. All indications are that this will continue for generations to come.

And at the very beginning there was this shy kid from Brooklyn named Mort.

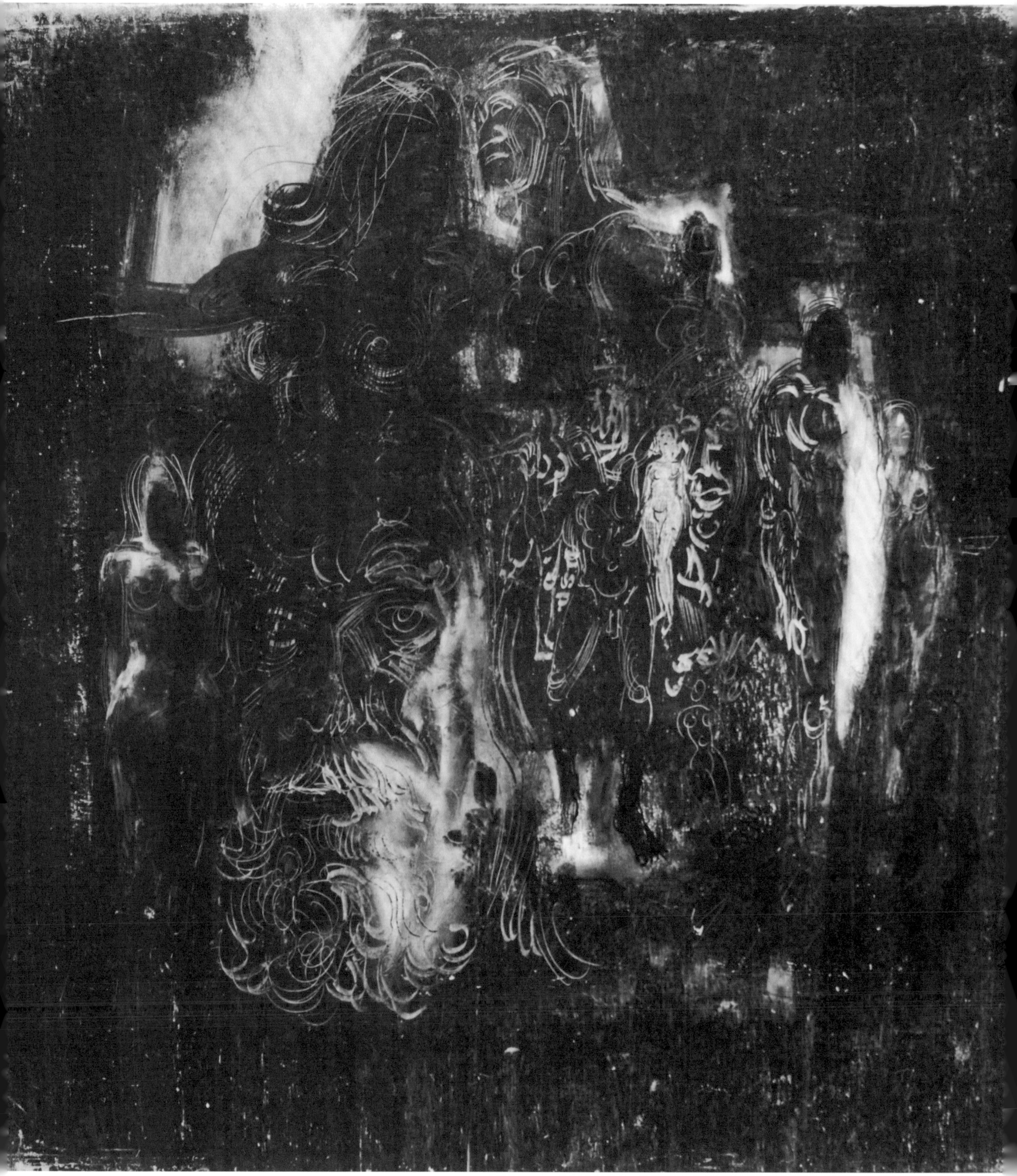

Endnotes

1. Interview with Jerry Iger, the *Cubic Zirconia Reader*, 1985.

2. Author's interview with Joe Kubert, October 14, 2008.

3. Author's interview with Jerry Robinson, September 8, 2008.

4. Composite of interviews with Jerry Robinson by the author on September 8, 2008 and by Dylan Williams on March 12, 2000.

5. Composite of interviews with Jerry Robinson by the author and Dylan Williams.

6. Author's interview with Jerry Robinson, conducted September 8, 2008.

7. Author's interview with Jerry Robinson.

8. *The History of DC Comics*, Ron Goulart, editor, New Media, 1989.

9. Author's interview with Jerry Robinson.

10. *The Comics Journal*, Gil Kane interview by Gary Groth, April 1996, #186.

11. Composite of interviews with Jerry Robinson by the author and Dylan Williams.

12. *Comic and Fantasy Art* #29, Amateur Press Association, 1979.

13. Interview with George Roussos by Dylan Williams, March 12, 2000.

14. Author's interview with Jerry Robinson.

15. *This is Orson Welles*, Orson Welles, Peter Bogdanovich, Jonathan Rosenbaum, Da Capo Press, New York, 1998.

16. *This is Orson Welles*.

17. *The Great Comic Book Heroes*, Jules Feiffer, The Dial Press, New York, 1965.

18. Author's interview with Jerry Robinson.

19. Author's interview with Joe Kubert.

20. *The Comics Journal*, #172, November 1994, interview with Joe Kubert by Gary Groth.

21. Interview with George Roussos by Dylan Williams, March 12, 2000.

22. Author's interview with Joe Kubert, conducted October 14, 2008.

23. *The Steranko History of the Comics*, vol. 1, James Steranko, Supergraphics, Reading, PA, 1970. According to Steranko, he attempted to interview Meskin for this volume, but "Mort stuttered so badly that it was almost impossible—and I did not want to make him any more uncomfortable than he may have already been. He was eager to have an intelligent, comprehensive conversation about his work, but his impediment—the worst I ever encountered—prevented it."

24. Author's interview with Peter Meskin, November 21, 2008.

25. *AlterEgo* vol. 3, #24, May 2003, TwoMorrows, Raleigh, NC. Interviews with Peter and Philip Meskin by Jim Amash.

26. Author's interview with Peter Meskin.

27. *AlterEgo* vol. 3, #24.

28. Author's interview with Peter Meskin.

29. *AlterEgo* vol. 3, #24.

30. *Robin Snyder's History of Comics*, April 1992, vol. 3, #4.

31. Composite of interviews with Jerry Robinson by the author and Dylan Williams.

32. *Comic Book Marketplace* #70, interview with Jerry Robinson by Will Murray, August 1999.

33. Interview with Jerry Robinson by Dylan Williams, March 12, 2000.

34. Interview with Marvin Stein by Dylan Williams, 2000.

35. *The Jack Kirby Collector* #25, 1999.

36. *Jack Magic*, Greg Theakston, yet to be published, used with permission.

37. *The Comic Book Makers*, Joe and Jim Simon, Vanguard Productions, NJ, 2003.

38. Author's interview with Joe Simon, March 11, 2008.

39. *The Jack Kirby Collector*.

40. Dan Barry interview by Dylan Williams.

41. Author's interview with Joe Simon, March 11, 2008.

42. *The Steranko History of the Comics*, vol. 1.

43. Composite of interviews with the author by Dylan Williams.

44. Interview with George Roussos by Dylan Williams.

45. Interview with Al Williamson, *The Jack Kirby Collector* #15, 1994.

46. Interview with George Roussos by Jon B. Cooke, May 27 and November 26, 1997, *The Jack Kirby Collector*.

47. Author's discussions with Lyle Stuart, 1987.

48. Author's interview with Jerry Robinson.

49. *AlterEgo* vol. 3, #24.

50. Author's interview with Peter Meskin.

51. Dan Barry interview with Dylan Williams.

52. Author's interview with Jerry Robinson.

53. Interview with George Roussos by Dylan Williams.

54. Interview with George Roussos by Dylan Williams, December 9, 1999.

55. Author's interview with Leonard Starr, December 2, 2009.

56. Interview with George Roussos by Dylan Williams, December 9, 1999.

57. Author's interview with Peter Meskin.

58. Author's interview with Philip Meskin, November 2008.

59. Author's interview with Peter Meskin.

60. *AlterEgo* vol. 3, #24.

61. Author's interview with Peter Meskin.

62. Author's interview with Philip Meskin.

63. Author's interview with Peter Meskin.

64. *AlterEgo* vol. 3, #24.

65. Interview with Peter Meskin by Dylan Williams, September, 1 2002.

66. Author's interview with Philip Meskin.

67. Author's interview with Peter Meskin.

68. Author's interview with Peter Meskin.

69. Interview with George Roussos by Dylan Williams, 2000.

70. Interview with Marvin Stein by Dylan Williams, 2000.

71. Dylan Williams interview at the DDBO office with Alphonse Normandia and Leslie Avery Gould, 2000.

72. Interview with Jerry Robinson by Dylan Williams, March 12, 2000.

73. Author's interview with George Olesen, November 29 and 30, 2009.

74. Author's interview with Joe Kubert.

75. Dylan Williams interview at DDBO.

76. Composite of conversation with Ethan Roberts and the author, July 2009, and *Comic and Fantasy Art* #29.

77. *AlterEgo* vol. 3, #24.

78. *Comic and Fantasy Art* #29.

79. *AlterEgo* vol. 3, #24.

80. Author's interview with Carmine Infantino, July 22, 2009.

81. Author's interview with Jerry Robinson.

82. *AlterEgo* vol. 3, #24.

83. Dylan Williams interview with Philip Meskin.

84. Dylan Williams interview with Peter Meskin.

85. Author's interview with Philip Meskin.

86. Dylan Williams interview with Peter Meskin.

87. Author's interview with Philip Meskin.

88. Author's interview with Peter Meskin.

89. Dylan Williams interviews at St. Joseph's nursing home with Connie Kaufman, Lena Trippardella and Mary Gomez, conducted on November 16, 2000.

90. Dylan Williams interview with Peter Meskin.

91. Composite of interviews with Peter Meskin with the author and Jim Amash in *AlterEgo* #24.

92. Interview with Peter Meskin by Dylan Williams, February 16, 2000.

93. Composite of interviews with Jerry Robinson by Dylan Williams, February 29, 2000 and March 12, 2000.

94. *AlterEgo* vol. 3, #24.

95. *AlterEgo* vol. 3, #24.

Acknowledgments

There are some without whom this book would not exist. I want to thank Jerry Robinson for his willingness to share his memories and the work of his old friend Mort, and for his encouragement and support. Peter Meskin for continually opening his home and his heart, likewise his lovely wife Diane and brother Philip. Paul Greene for sharing the work and memories of his father. And Dylan Williams, who unselfishly shared his own considerable research, knowledge and love of both Mort and this art form without hesitation. Words simply can't express my debt to them all. Thank you to my agent Sandy Choron who understands a work of love sometimes trumps the bottom line. And much appreciation to my publisher Gary Groth, not only for agreeing to publish this book but also for his many years of service elevating comics from the dustbins to the bookshelf. I also am indebted to Greg Theakston and Harry Mendryk for their insight and willingness to share their knowledge and collections, likewise Ger Apeldoorn, Ethan Roberts, and Lars Teglbjaerg. Thank you to Kevin Miller, Jerry's assistant and my former student. A special thanks to those talented men who were willing to spend time discussing Mort with me: Joe Simon, Jim Steranko, Leonard Starr, Joe Kubert, George Olesen, Carmine Infantino, and Irwin Hasen. The online comics community is singular in its incredible willingness to share their collections and love, and I wish to thank Dr. Michael Vassallo, Nick Caputo, Paul Handler, Jeff Singh, Mykal Banta, Charles Pelto, Paolo Giovenale, George Hagenauer, David Armstrong, Gregory Huneryager, Ben Saunders and Gretchen Ranger of the Jordan Schnitzer Museum of Art at the University of Oregon, Carolyn Rice Dean, Keif Simon, Rob Imes, David Pepper. Thank you to my Kirby-list cohorts and upstarts James Romberger, Stanly Taylor, Kris Brownlow, Allen Smith, Glen Story, Kenn Thomas and Rand Hoppe for their enthusiasm and support and to all those on the Yahoo Meskin-list as well. A special thank you to my friends Steve Cohen and Jim Simon for all their help, and my lifelong buddy Norris Burroughs: is it time to resurrect Cosmic Comics? Thank you to my mom who long ago was willing to give me that extra dime and appreciated that comics were improving my vocabulary. To my wife Kati, willing to put up with all those white boxes. A big thanks to my daughter Janna, for her production help and expertise, and the comfort in the knowledge that with her talent and enthusiasm this wonderful art form has a future. Lastly, to all those folks who worked tirelessly creating the books that have provided so many with so much pleasure.

Fantagraphics Books
7563 Lake City Way NE
Seattle, Washington 98115

Editor: Gary Groth
Designer: Steven Brower
Production: Janna Brower
Associate Publisher: Eric Reynolds
Publishers: Gary Groth and Kim Thompson

To receive a free full-color catalog of comics, graphic novels, prose novels, artist monographs, and other fine works of artistry, call 1-800-657-1100, or visit www.fantagraphics.com. You may order books at our website or by phone.

Distributed in the U.S. by W.W. Norton and Company, Inc. (212-354-5500)

Distributed in Canada by the Canadian Manda Group (416-516-0911)

Distributed in the United Kingdom by Turnaround Distribution (108-829-3009)

ISBN: 978-1-60699-358-3

First Fantagraphics Books printing: July, 2010

Printed in China

INDEX

INDEX

INDEX